Universal
Higher
Education

UNIVERSAL HIGHER EDUCATION

COSTS, BENEFITS, OPTIONS

Edited by LOGAN WILSON
with OLIVE MILLS

AMERICAN COUNCIL ON EDUCATION • *Washington, D.C.*

© 1972 by American Council on Education
One Dupont Circle
Washington, D.C. 20036

Library of Congress Catalog Card No. 72–79161

ISBN 0–8268–1405–0

Printed in the United States of America

Contributors

WALTER ADAMS
Senior Research Associate, Bureau of Applied Social Research, Columbia
University

FREDERICK E. BALDERSTON
Director, Center for Research in Management Science, University of
California, Berkeley

IVAR BERG
Professor of Industrial Relations and Behavioral Sciences, Graduate School
of Business, Columbia University

ALLAN M. CARTTER
Chancellor, New York University

G. HOMER DURHAM
Commissioner and Chief Executive Officer, Utah System of Higher Education

MARK GERZON
Author and formerly Graduate Student, University of Chicago

W. LEE HANSEN
Professor of Economics and of Educational Policy Studies, University of
Wisconsin

C. ARNOLD HANSON
President, Gettysburg College

LOUIS HAUSMAN
Formerly Executive Associate, American Council on Education

PEGGY HEIM
Coordinator of Institutional Planning, Bucknell University

THEODORE M. HESBURGH, C.S.C.
President, University of Notre Dame

WERNER Z. HIRSCH
Professor of Economics and Director, Institute of Government and Public
Affairs, University of California, Los Angeles

ALEXANDER M. MOOD
Director, Public Policy Research Organization, University of California, Irvine

KERMIT C. MORRISSEY
President, Boston State College

SELMA J. MUSHKIN
Director, Public Services Laboratory, Georgetown University

HAROLD ORLANS
Senior Fellow, The Brookings Institution

ALLAN W. OSTAR
Executive Director, American Association of State Colleges and Universities

WALTER PERRY
Vice-Chancellor, The Open University, England

ALBERT H. QUIE
Representative from Minnesota, United States Congress

PAUL C. REINERT, S.J.
President, Saint Louis University

VALERIE A. RIDDICK
Student, University of Maryland

EDWARD SANDERS
Research Fellow, Claremont University Center

CLARENCE SCHEPS
Executive Vice-President, Tulane University

VIRGINIA B. SMITH
Assistant Director, Carnegie Commission on Higher Education

FRANK STANTON
Vice-Chairman of the Board, Columbia Broadcasting System, Inc.

LOGAN WILSON
President Emeritus, American Council on Education

DAVID R. WITMER
Director of Institutional Studies and Academic Planning, Board of Regents, Wisconsin State Universities

Contents

ix

Foreword

WHENEVER "UNIVERSAL" HIGHER EDUCATION IN THE 1970s IS CONSID-
ered, it immediately evokes a variety of responses. They range from the
totally optimistic aspirations of the uninformed to searching analyses
of the needs of the nation and its members individually for this form of
postsecondary education endeavor. As satisfaction of "needs" implies
benefits, consideration of "universality" must be accompanied by projections of expected returns, both social and economic, to the nation and
to the individual.

The American Council on Education, in its fifty-third annual meeting, explored the topic "Higher Education for Everybody? Issues and
Implications" in a series of papers that generally affirmed desirability
and, under certain circumstances, feasibility. The approach was to define anew the potential student populations, diverse as never before, and
the pros and cons of accommodating them within broadened institutions and through alternative means.

The fifty-fourth Council annual meeting continued discussion of the
topic, but, both by design and force of circumstances, the approach became more practically evaluative. Among the authors whose papers
make up this volume, many offered research studies as a basis for viewing the possibility and feasibility of wider access to higher education.
Of social benefits, one author said, "If our changing, complex technological society is to remain open, pluralistic, and democratic, we will
need to become a nation of men and women who possess the qualities
demonstrably stimulated by higher education." In economic benefits,
there are to be accounted not only value in dollars, but also the supply
of a wide variety of manpower so educated and trained that it can adapt
to the changing needs of the country.

Another author points out that "Fundamental to any decision about
who should pay for higher education is the recognition that society, as
a whole, does nothing for an individual as an individual. Nor should
it. What is done for the individual by society is done only as it is perceived to be necessary or beneficial to the society as a whole." Thus any
serious investigation of moving toward "universality" in higher education must soon turn to estimates of costs and possible ways of financing.
Again, research studies guided discussion of patterns of federal aid that
might offer incentives to other forms of support, and also suggested proportions for public and private sharing in the costs of higher education.

Two sections of the meeting were devoted to "getting more education for less money." The subject also threaded through many of the other discussions, induced by financial stringency in institutions, the economic situation in the nation, competing demands in our society, and the federal government's policy of reducing support for research and other programs in universities and colleges. Institutional planning, analysis of cost trends, and coordination among institutions to avoid non-productive duplication were repeatedly discussed and urged as necessities.

Optional means of moving toward universal higher education were presented in a factual study of open admissions at City University of New York and the differential access system in California, through a description of Britain's new Open University, and a theoretical discussion of what its author terms "a radical rearrangement of our system of higher education," including "Video University." All, of course, drew the strong criticism, favorable and adverse, that frequently characterizes reaction to innovation in higher education.

I wish to express appreciation to the authors for their contributions and to the Council's Board of Directors and executive staff for suggestions that shaped the content of the meeting. For his concentrated effort in helping to conceptualize the meeting's main concerns, in searching out competent participants, and in coordinating their assignments, Louis Hausman is owed particular thanks for his role during the period he was with the Council.

This volume will, I believe, help those who make policy for American higher education and who, in so doing, must cope simultaneously with the expanded demands for education and the financial limitations constantly present. The findings and views set forth in this book, both theoretical and practical, will throw light on problems and processes that are still far from resolution.

LOGAN WILSON, *President Emeritus*
American Council on Education

Preface

THE PAPERS WHICH MAKE UP THIS VOLUME WERE, WITH TWO EXCEPTIONS, prepared for the fifty-fourth annual meeting of the American Council on Education, held in Washington, D.C., October 6–8, 1971. The views range widely, for their authors come from public and private colleges and universities and the organizations of higher education, from the congressional and executive branches of the federal government, from state and regional education systems, and from public life. Overall, they present a rounded view of the thinking about open access to higher education—desirability, necessity, hazards, benefits, means, financing.

The general sessions were addressed by the Honorable S. P. Marland, Jr., the Rev. Theodore M. Hesburgh, William J. McGill, Frank Stanton, and Walter Perry. Nine papers—by Louis Hausman, W. Lee Hansen and David R. Witmer, Kenneth Keniston and Mark Gerzon, Frederick E. Balderston, Selma J. Mushkin, Allan M. Cartter, Virginia B. Smith, A. J. Jaffe and Walter Adams, and Alexander Mood—were commissioned and distributed in advance of the meeting to registrants and to selected knowledgeable persons who were asked to prepare commentaries to be presented at the meeting.

Two papers that appeared in the *Educational Record* but were unconnected with the meeting are reprinted here because of their pertinence: "The New Orthodoxies in Higher Education," by Logan Wilson, Spring 1972 issue, and "Perspectives on Open Admissions," by Jerome Karabel, Winter 1972 issue.

It gives me pleasure to join Dr. Wilson in giving acknowledgment to Louis Hausman, whose essay opens this volume. He ably guided the preparation of the papers for the meeting and suggested an organization for this volume. And I am happy to acknowledge our thanks to the authors for their cooperation during the process of readying both the background papers and this volume for publication.

O.M.

LOUIS HAUSMAN

Pressures, Benefits, and Options

A WIDELY HELD ASSUMPTION IS THAT HIGHER EDUCATION AT some unspecified time will involve every high school graduate. This is an assumption by no means universally accepted. Yet both those who believe, and those who question the desirability and wisdom of such a goal, unanimously ask, "Who is going to pay for it? How will (or should) these payments be made?"

But there are considerations antecedent to these questions. These considerations have a rough parallel in the problems faced by an architect in designing a house. Before contemplating what kind of house to design, the architect needs to know his client's resources, his present and future needs, his mode of life and status aspirations. Some of these matters are completely rational and demonstrable. Others are emotional—perhaps even irrational—but no less determining. Only after understanding these factors can the architect begin his design, circumscribed by his client's ability to pay. But even finances are not fixed. They can be expanded or contracted depending on the client's perception of values, his attitude toward debt, his willingness to do without some things to obtain others.

Similarly, there are considerations to be explored before attempting to answer who should pay for higher education. One item is the nature of *pressures* for higher education existing in our society; another is an assessment of who *benefits*. In other words: Who wants higher education? Who profits from it? An exploration of the extent and validity of both these questions intends (by inference, at least) to illuminate the question of who should pay. Such explorations will also serve to undergird recommendations for the distribution or redistribution of fiscal responsibility. They may help answer the question whether students or their families, government or private organizations should pay more or less of the costs of higher education than they now pay. Or maintain their support at present proportions. Investigation of these and associated issues is required before any

1

long-term public policy can be propounded. "Long term" is emphasized in the belief that public support for higher education will be only temporarily slowed by the current reactions to campus unrest. The assumption is that the long-standing and deeply rooted respect for education (and its corollary: the more education, the better) will, at some point in the future, reassert itself. The present climate—creating as it has a hiatus in the wide support for a greater public investment in higher education—may, in fact, represent an unrecapturable opportunity to prevent the institutionalization of existing patterns of support.

A DEFENSIVE ASIDE

This paper, as well as those which follow, discusses the financing of universal postsecondary education in the framework of higher education as it currently exists. The threshold question of what is meant by "higher" education is never fully explored or answered except inferentially.

Clearly, what kind of education, for whom, and for how long involves important philosophical and practical considerations. They become almost crucial when one considers the characteristics of the students who in the past have not been considered reasonable prospects for higher education. Yet the enrollment of such students—chiefly from families of lower socioeconomic status—will be required if universal postsecondary education is to be approached.[1] In this connection, Joseph Froomkin, in an unpublished paper, estimates that, by 1975, students from the lowest income quartile will represent one in 14 of the total undergraduate population as compared with the 1960 ratio of less than one in 20. Their number in this fifteen-year period will have quadrupled; those in the third quartile will have tripled whereas those in the two highest quartiles will have increased 2.7 and 2.4 times, respectively.

1. Currently, nine out of ten high school graduates in the top 40 percent of the College Entrance Examination Board's SAT enroll in college within five years after high school graduation *provided* their families are in the highest socioeconomic quartile. Among equally able graduates (based on SAT scores) from the lowest socioeconomic quartile, only half join their peers as college freshmen. Almost independently of academic ability, the proportion of high socioeconomic graduates who enter college is larger than that of the most academically talented from the lowest socioeconomic quartile. Robert H. Berls, "Higher Education Opportunity and Achievement in the United States," in *The Economics and Financing of Higher Education in the United States: A Compendium of Papers Submitted to the Joint Committee, Congress of the United States* (Washington: Government Printing Office, 1969), pp. 146–50.

Encouraging high school graduates from lower socioeconomic (SES) families to matriculate and stay in college means that institutions of higher education will need to create patterns of teaching under which such students can learn. This includes also a determination of the nature of the mix of liberal arts and sciences with career-oriented training. (Similar discussions have been going on for a long time in designing curricula for engineering students and for teachers destined to teach in elementary and secondary schools.)

As in peeling an onion, at least two more questions are exposed. (1) Is a college education to be defined as the "standard" liberal arts and sciences: a little history, a smattering of philosophy and biology, the novel from Beowulf to Camus, one or two foreign languages, some courses in appreciation of fine arts from Cro Magnon to Oldenburg—the sanctified courses leading to certification of an educated person? (2) If the answer is yes, how do we propose to teach these subjects so that students will be motivated to learn?

Resolution of issues such as these might be useful in answering the complaints of students from high SES families. For the rebellion against college draws its support from the children of middle- and upper-middle-class families. It is they, primarily, who have raised the issue of relevancy—not those from a group in the past described as lower class.

The economic viability of institutions of higher education may well require a redefinition of the role of higher education. Is the function of higher education to sort out and label people or to advance the state of the arts and sciences? Is it to cope with social problems or to train citizens or accountants? Is it to socialize the students or to educate them about the past so they may have greater wisdom to cope with the present?

Can any one institution do all these jobs without eliminating a number of other objectives? Should each institution limit its goals, ceding some of its ambitions to other institutions? Quite obviously, higher education is not a single product. Clearly it will have to be far more diverse than it presently is. Perhaps—and contrary to the current trend—many of the tasks which higher education has taken on belong to other institutions: museums, public libraries, correspondence schools, medical centers. These activities are lumped in the budget of many institutions under the heading "Public Services"; they include programs in the dance and music, support of art galleries and special ethnic exhibits, dentistry clinics, and so on.

At any rate, there is no use in waiting for answers to these questions and then waiting for them to be implemented. More than sixty-five years ago, Nicholas Murray Butler challenged the status quo when he said, "The Faculty of Columbia College say explicitly that to prescribe graduation from a four-year college course as a *sine qua non* for the professional study of law, medicine, engineering or teaching is not to do a good thing, but a bad thing." And he went on to say, "Any culture that is worthy of the name and any efficiency that is worth having will be increased, not diminished, by bringing to an end the idling and dawdling that now characterize so much American higher education." *Plus ça change.*

Despite lack of answers, the idea of universal postsecondary education will not be turned off. We need to examine why it is not a disposable idea, how—in terms of equity and effectiveness—it can be financed. And by whom.

PRESSURES FOR UNIVERSAL HIGHER EDUCATION

Motives for seeking higher education range from the usefulness of an A.B. in getting a job as a salesman for General Foods to the desire of the 82-year-old Boston grande dame to learn Hebrew so that she could talk to her Maker in his own language. Young men go to college (or want to) in order to become doctors or lawyers or scientists; to postpone going to work; to play football; to earn more money; to stay out of the army; or just because they like to learn more about literature or history or philosophy. Women go to college for many of these same reasons and additional ones as diverse as getting a secretarial job in a fancier office to meeting college-educated men who prefer to marry college women. (Women's Lib to the contrary.)

Satisfying the desires of individuals does not automatically determine who should finance higher education—and how it should be financed. The pressures exerted by the family, by the business community, and by society[2] itself, represent forces to be considered and evaluated in constructing an equitable and efficient approach to the financing of higher education.

---

2. For purposes of this discussion, "society" is defined as the electorate which, through the franchise, supports or rejects legislative or administrative practices—local, state, or federal—designed to extend or restrict the activities of its members. Such "consents" result in items as varied as parking regulations and child labor laws, enactment of appropriations for housing and support of bond issues for education. Given or withheld, they measure what society considers desirable or necessary. Private institutions, though less dependent on legislation in shaping their activities, are not uninfluenced by society's perception of their goals and means of achieving them.

Family Pressures. Most college-educated parents assume implicitly that their children should go to college. They're afraid that failure to go to college will result in "downward mobility" for their children. (This is a condition actively sought by many children of middle- and upper-class families. In a sense it may represent an expiation of guilt feeling for having been born to privileged parents.) Equally, parents who have *not* gone to college are determined to have their children receive the benefits of higher education, get the things they didn't have. They want their children to go to college to become middle class. But, in general, you can't get to college if you're not middle class to begin with.

Even though parents frequently are not too clear about the benefits of "a college education," these benefits are assumed. Since truth is often what is believed, this parental association of special virtue with higher education represents a powerful pressure.

Employer Pressures. Not least among the pressures is that exerted by employers. College education is, in effect, a certification that says to employers, "those with college experience will become more valuable employees than those without it." This is an assumption of doubtful validity. Except for certain organizations which rely on more sophisticated testing (insurance companies, for example), the fact of college attendance is a widely used and handy screening device.

Societal Pressures. Finally, there is the pressure exerted by society itself. Despite the current backlash created by campus disorders, people at almost all levels believe a college education is of value to the individual and to the nation. (And the further you go down the socioeconomic scale, the greater the lack of discrimination as to *which* college, *what* curriculum, *what* quality of education.) In addition, it is widely and traditionally held that society as a whole benefits from an enlarged universe of college-educated citizens in at least two ways. One benefit cited is economic: since college-educated people earn more money, they pay more taxes, they consume more goods, and thus contribute to a larger GNP. Another benefit is social: college-educated persons exercise their franchise more regularly and with greater discrimination; they commit fewer crimes (an economic as well as a social benefit to society) ; they share common experiences which may contribute to the development of a more egalitarian society, and so on.

A Fourth Force

The needs of the economy for a significantly larger body of college-educated workers are more difficult to substantiate. The difficulty stems not from a paucity of data on manpower needs for the future, but from the inability to demonstrate unequivocally that certain job categories require postsecondary education—particularly if the nature of this education remains undefined. As it does.

For example, the U.S. Department of Labor estimates that, by 1980, employment by state and local governments will rise 52 percent and that in service occupations (personal, professional, business) will increase by 40 percent. These two "industries" are expected to account for 6.7 million additional workers. They represent the two fastest-growing industries when compared with a growth of 23 percent for all industry.[3] Peter Drucker asserts that "the U.S. needs, for instance, a million computer programmers between now and 1975—as against 150,000 to 200,000 we have to date."[4]

Manpower needs such as these reinforce family and individual pressures to seek postsecondary education. The more widely they are publicized and discussed, the more desirable postsecondary education will appear, particularly to those who, lacking it, will conclude that they will be left out of the mainstream of our society unless they can continue their education beyond high school.

Parallel with the Past

These are some of the pressures which appear to be moving us toward universal higher education. Fifty years or so ago similar pressures extended the age for compulsory school attendance and in effect created universal secondary education.[5] These forces—individual, family, corporate, and societal—are powerful, rooted as they are in the conviction that a democratic society requires widespread education.

Up to now we have supported mass education largely as an article of faith. Experience has justified this faith: we now have secondary education for virtually everyone, our economy has grown steadily and enormously, and our democratic society has functioned and has been stable. Is universal higher education a factor essential to the extension of these happy circumstances? If it is not (or even if it's questionable), political realities may make it undesirable to attempt to reverse the trend in the face of the widely held assumption that it is desirable and necessary.

As we examine each of these issues, all manner of other questions

3. U.S. Department of Labor, *U.S. Manpower in the 1970's: Opportunity and Challenge* (Washington: Government Printing Office, 1970).
4. Drucker, *The Age of Discontinuity* (New York: Harper & Row, 1969), p. 27.
5. The proportion of each generation completing the twelfth grade rose from 5-10 percent of those who were eighteen in 1880 to an estimated rate of about 80 percent in 1970.

are revealed. There is the further question of the validity of answers—any answers—when they are projected against a college population two or three times larger than the present level. How do you satisfy the status aspiration of blacks if you tell them vocational education will serve their children better than college? In a New York City study conducted as part of the Coleman report, 96 percent of the black parents, compared with 79 percent of the white parents, wanted college education for their children. Can alternative status satisfactions be created?

Perhaps even more critical is the effect on our society created by a split between those who can go and those who cannot go on to college. It is all very well and neat to hold out the opportunity for higher education to all who want and can profit from it. Profit from it on whose terms? By what standards? W. W. Willingham, in his *Free-Access Higher Education,* summed up the issue when he wrote "It is insufficient that opportunity [for higher education] simply be available; it must be available in a form and under conditions that are likely to attract students."[6]

WHO BENEFITS FROM HIGHER EDUCATION?

Does the individual, the employer, the nation as a whole benefit most—in economic and social terms—from college education? Because so large a portion of an individual's decisions and behavior are conditioned by employers' requirements, let us look first at the attitudes employers hold toward higher education in selecting employees, and the presumed benefits which underlie these attitudes.

Benefit to Employers

Given the choice, both industry and government generally prefer to hire college-educated persons. How widespread this tendency is would probably be difficult to determine accurately. Employers might be reluctant to admit that they demand college-educated persons (or even give preference to them) to fill jobs as typists or gas station managers or soap salesmen. Yet in many fields attendance at college is rapidly replacing a high school diploma as a job requisite.

The prejudice in favor of college-educated employees—even for

6. New York: College Entrance Examination Board, 1970. P. 5.

Edward F. Denison, a senior fellow of the Brookings Institution, is critical of discrimination in the expenditures of public funds for higher education and concludes "that in education we grossly violate the concept of equality of opportunity for no sufficient reason." "An Aspect of Unequal Opportunity," *Brookings Bulletin,* Winter 1971, pp. 7–10.

unlikely jobs—starts with our traditional bias toward education, our belief that educated people will perform more efficiently. A college education then becomes an easy way to identify more competent employees. It also represents a perfectly legal form of discrimination against those who are less well educated than the personnel director or the manager or the bureaucrat doing the hiring.

The validity of the assumption that more education does, in fact, equal better performance is more difficult to establish. (How, for example, can the growing incidence of autos that don't function and repairmen who can't repair them be reconciled with the increased proportion of better-educated persons making and servicing these products?) Numerous studies and analyses have examined the correlation of education with performance. Their findings vary widely.[7] Would additional studies be more conclusive? Could a study be developed to indicate what *kind* of higher education produces what level of efficiency for what type of jobs? Would such studies serve to reverse the trend toward *higher* education as a job requirement? Is such a reversal desirable?

Unless this trend is reversed, and until such time as a college education becomes accepted as an irrelevant condition of employment (except for obvious occupations such as teaching or medicine), parents are going to press for higher education for their children.[8] Forget, for the moment, the pressure of the very poor. Consider only the factory worker who wants his children to get white-collar jobs in industry or GS 11 ratings in the federal service. Can society tell him, "Those are false requirements. Your children don't need to go to college for these jobs. Have your girl learn typing; let your son take a correspondence course in advertising or computer programing"?

The education establishment, in a different way, may not be wholly

7. Ivar Berg analyzes the performance of Federal Aviation flight controllers and concludes that personnel with "no college" performed demanding and technically complex duties requiring a high degree of judgment at least as well as did controllers with various years of college work. *Education and Jobs* (New York: Praeger, 1970), pp. 167–75.

The opposite conclusion is reached in a citation by Roger E. Bolton of large-sample studies by Gary Becker and by Weisbrod and Karpoff of Bell System employees which demonstrated that educational experience itself is the predominant explanation for higher earnings resulting, presumably, from greater competence. "The Economics and Public Financing of Higher Education: An Overview," in *The Economics and Financing of Higher Education*, p. 31.

8. The *New York Times* (Aug. 30, 1970) reported that Soviet sociologists say that 85 percent of secondary school seniors want to go to college. The *Washington Post* (Sept. 1, 1970) reported that only 180 (6 percent) of 3,000 Moscow secondary school graduates did not opt for college, despite heavy government publicity that blue-collar workers earn more than industrial engineers and economists.

guiltless in its rigid insistence on a bachelor's degree for entrance into graduate work. Illustrative is a recent conversation with the newly appointed dean of the graduate school of social work at a major university. He was concerned that many potentially valuable social workers are being screened out of the opportunity to study for a master's degree in social work—a requisite to advancement in this field— by lack of a baccalaureate degree. A former social worker, professor, and federal executive, he was persuaded that a bachelor's degree is not essential. His chances of reducing this requirement are very remote— even though the Carnegie Commission and others have made similar suggestions.

Benefits to the Individual

The evidence is reasonably consistent that those who go to college earn more than those who finish only high school. The latter, in turn, earn more than those who drop out of secondary education. The figure of $200,000 is widely accepted as the average net incremental lifetime value of a college degree. And those who attend college for less than four years earn more than those who have never attended institutions of higher education.

Most of those who dispute the claim[9] do not question the correlation between education and earnings. They do, strongly, question the assumption of a direct causal relation between college and earnings. They say, in effect, greater motivation and higher intelligence are the prime factors in higher earnings—not education. They dispute the validity of the greater efficiency of college-educated persons imputed by employers. And, buttressed by Berg, they question the need for college education to perform even highly technical assignments.[10]

Under the current state of affairs, it doesn't much matter whether such a causal relationship does, in fact, exist. In actual practice, college-educated persons find it easier to get jobs and frequently are paid more for performing the same duties than those who haven't gone to college. What would be the effect on the pressure exerted by individuals to seek college education if conclusive evidence were developed that a causal relation between education and earnings did *not* exist? Probably very little. A reversal of current hiring practices—a precondition to reducing the individual's desire for college—would

9. There are some who are concerned about how "forgone income" is used in the development of these incremental benefits and cast doubt on the entire concept. See John Vaizey, *The Economics of Education* (New York: Free Press, 1962), especially chap. 3.

10. Berg, *Education and Jobs*, pp. 152–53, reports on Air Force and Navy conclusions.

require a highly unlikely exercise in rationality. Despite vaunted claims of efficiency, business and government are only slightly more prone than individuals to make decisions based exclusively—or even chiefly—on cost-efficiency analyses. Ask the U.S. Bureau of the Budget (now the Office of Management and Budget) how successful it has been in its efforts to get federal agencies to develop cost-benefits of individual programs in housing, education, transportation, welfare.

In constructing a long-term policy of financial aid for higher education, it would be useful to know the relation between college education and earnings when (and if) 75 or 85 or 90 percent of all 18–24-year-olds have gone to college. Would individual economic benefits still obtain? Of what order?

Educational Upgrading of Occupations

Added to the questioning of economic benefits attributable to college education, there is the concern that the output of college-educated people will exceed both the demand and the need for them. Some persons contend that if there are too many college graduates, numbers of them are forced to take jobs which underutilize their educational skills. Presumed result: a greater incidence of job dissatisfaction, unacceptable rates of job turnover, and so on.

A counter to this fear is developed in *Human Resources and Higher Education:*

> The additional college graduates over and above those needed for replacement and occupational growth are available to raise the educational level of occupations. A large part of this educational upgrading . . . is occurring in managerial, sales, and professional occupations where college graduation has not been in the past a requirement for obtaining a job.

The authors recognize that "we don't know enough about the economic benefits associated with the educational upgrading of an occupation to be able to say just when educational upgrading of an occupation ceases to add to economic productivity." They *do* report that there will be a shortage of somewhere between 2.0 million and 2.8 million college graduates by 1975 on the basis of estimated needs for additional college graduates to meet projected national goals. They also point out that,

> The cost to the economy of an inadequate supply of educated persons is probably greater than the expenditures of resources in creation of an excess of graduates beyond the needs of the economy, and in this

sense an overexpanded educational system is less costly than an under-developed one.[11]

Benefits to the Society

What advantages accrue to the society from a larger universe of college-educated persons? How do benefits to society differ from the benefits to the individual? To industry? For purposes of examination, let's sort the discernible societal benefits into two broad categories: economic and social.

As already noted, many of the economic benefits to the nation flow directly from the greater earnings of college-educated persons.[12] College-educated persons make indirect, though no less real, contributions to the economy; they appear less frequently on relief rolls, occupy fewer jail cells; they have fewer auto accidents; are healthier; have a lower absentee rate. And so on.

Can these economic benefits be quantified: the net dollar benefit to society of a college education? It would be useful to know the value to society of one million additional persons with two years—or four years—of college. Can an "added-dollar-value-per-person-per-year-of-college" price tag be developed?

How much does *exclusion* from higher education cost the society? Attendance at institutions of higher learning is heavily skewed to the middle and upper income sectors—even though it is generally accepted that intelligence, defined as the capacity to learn, is fairly evenly distributed across all socioeconomic levels.[13] How many potential Nobel Prize winners, scientists and poets, industrial and government leaders is the nation depriving itself of through failure to cast the net of higher education far enough and deep enough?

It would be instructive if we could make concrete the shadowy claim that "education is an investment." Indication of the relative economic benefits of higher education to the individual, the state, and

11. John K. Folger, Helen S. Astin, and Alan Bayer, *Human Resources and Higher Education* (New York: Russell Sage Foundation, 1970), pp. 41, 38, 42. Chap. 2, "The Market for College Graduates," discusses society's needs for college graduates.

12. Society pays for only about 30 percent of the total annual investment in higher education. For 1969–70, society's share (government subsidies, private grants to institutions, scholarships, etc.) was estimated at $11 billion. The students and their families invested about $27 billion: $9 billion for tuition and other expenses; $18 billion in forgone income (at $3,000 per student).

13. Jensen and others have questioned this assumption: they have pointed out that genetics are also affected by environment, for example, that children and grandchildren of lower-class ancestors have lower intelligence than those from the upper and middle classes. Arthur R. Jensen, "How Can We Boost IQ and Scholarship Achievement?" *Harvard Educational Review*, Winter 1969, pp. 1–123.

the nation would assist the determination of who should pay. And in what proportions.

Toward a More Cohesive Democracy

Higher education benefits the society in ways other than economic. Some of these have been statistically demonstrated. Others may be capable of quantification. Still others exist as part of our culture. Taken as a whole, they may well be not only the most persuasive reasons for wide tax support of higher education, but also the most valid to ensure a functioning democracy.

As Berelson and Steiner summarized it: "The higher a person's socioeconomic and education level—especially the latter—the higher his political interest, participation, and voting turnout."[14] *How* college-educated persons vote should also be assuring to those who, influenced by the proliferation of campus violence, may have come to equate higher education with radical and destructive advocacy. Yet, "within each social class, the upper strata are more likely than the lower to hold conservative views."[15] On another tangent: it has been estimated that more than half of all volunteer activities are performed by college-educated persons. The value of a large body of such persons to our society is self-evident and, increasingly, essential.

Wider exercise of the franchise, more informed political judgments, greater participation in volunteer activities, and a myriad of other political and social "goods" are the cement holding a heterogeneous society together. The correlation between college education and these acknowledged benefits to the society is amply demonstrable.

It might be argued that these desirable patterns are a function of income rather than of higher education. This relationship is unimportant as long as the close relation between education and earnings continues. What *is* important is recognition and wide acceptance of such patterns of behavior as a central factor in determining public policy toward higher education.

Beyond these and similar benefits to society are the fundamental

14. Bernard Berelson and Gary A. Steiner, *Human Behavior: An Inventory of Scientific Findings* (New York: Harcourt, Brace & World, 1964), p. 423.

Specifically, in the 1968 national elections, only 61 percent of men with only an elementary school education reported voting, compared with 85 percent of those with four or more years of college education. And similar disparities occurred in the voting patterns of women in these elections. U.S. Bureau of the Census, *Current Population Reports: Population Characteristics*, "Voting and Registration in the Election of November 1968," Series P-20 (Washington: Government Printing Office, 1969), No. 192, Table 4.

15. Berelson and Steiner, *Human Behavior*, p. 427.

values inherent in higher education. Though not quantifiable, they are no less real. They were described by Berelson in an unpublished "White Paper on Higher Education" which he wrote in 1964:

> American society depends upon American higher education. This has always been true but in recent years it has become more widely recognized and probably more widely applicable. As American society has become more complex and more interdependent, the burdens upon the institutions of higher education have become heavier—the burdens to provide intellectual leadership for the society, to transmit the higher learning from generation to generation, to advance knowledge, to apply knowledge through professional practice, to recruit, screen, and develop the leading talent of each generation. The great society of the modern world rests upon trained intelligence, and the institutions of higher education are its sources of renewal.
>
> Just as American society depends upon American higher education, so does the educational system depend upon the society—for appreciation of purpose, for academic freedom, for vitality of recruits, for absorption of products, for financial support.

Fundamental to any decision about who should pay for higher education is the recognition that *society, as a whole, does nothing for an individual as an individual. Nor should it. What is done for the individual by society is done only as it is perceived to be necessary or beneficial to society as a whole.*

Youngsters are taught to read at public expense so that they may be drafted into the armed forces; or make out income tax returns or driver's license applications; get jobs and fill similar requisites of our society. The fact that they may enjoy reading—pornography or Proust or *Reader's Digest*—doesn't enter into the federal government's concern and support of programs to improve reading skills. Even such public programs as housing, or medicare, or roads are tax-subsidized because it is more costly to the community *not* to support them. It is irrelevant that an individual is happier if he doesn't live in slums, can get taken care of when ill, or can drive his car to the mountains for a holiday. But it is important to society if people riot because they find living conditions intolerable, or if sickness becomes epidemic, or if lack of roads inhibits the economic distribution of goods.

The extent of society's responsibility to ensure universal higher education depends on higher education's capacity to help attain a number of generally acknowledged goals. A check list of such goals would include increasing the GNP, improving the democratic process, reducing unemployment,[16] enriching the quality of life, and satisfying widespread and deeply held individual ambitions. To the degree that higher education helps realize such goals, individual benefits become secondary to society's. It can be argued, of course, that there are other ways to allocate a nation's resources to attain a number of these goals: more money for housing, more funds for low-income families through a negative income tax, and so on. *But none of these alternate allocations would lead the individual to participate as directly in the process of upward mobility; to achieve as a result of his efforts; to participate more meaningfully in the society.*

How to Get from Here to There

Assuming that society chooses universal higher education as the best means for meeting certain goals it selects, there are a number of ways to achieve and pay for universal higher education. Any method (or combination of methods) must face at least these tests: efficiency, affordability, equity, and effectiveness. And, far from least, it must be politically realistic.

Except for mandating universal higher education[17]—probably both unaffordable and politically unrealistic—virtually no avenue has been unexplored. Suggestions include variations of the GI Bill of Rights and proposals for vouchers for $2,500 a year for students to continue their education for at least two years. They range from carefully structured, actuarially based proposals to permit an individual to pay for a college education over a lifetime of earnings to unrestricted institutional grants. A number of states—California and Florida, in particular—have sought equal educational opportunity through widespread establishment of two-year colleges.

These and other suggestions (and combinations of them) are familiar to those who have thought and read about the issue of financing universal higher education. The authors of the papers which fol-

16. It is useful to recall that one of the pressures which contributed originally to the passage of the Social Security Act was the desire to take persons out of the labor market. Even though income received through dividends, interest, and rents did not reduce or eliminate an individual's social security benefits, payments were reduced and eliminated if he received wages or salary.

17. A variant of this approach to universal higher education would be to project the nation's skill needs in the future—biochemists, economists, mechanics, teachers, and so on—and then to educate the numbers of people to fill these needs. Such an approach, while theoretically inviting, would stumble on the questions of accurate projection of needs, of selection of which students to be educated for which skills. And it would certainly be viewed as contrary to our concepts of freedom and egalitarianism.

low examine these issues and proposals as well as the pressures for and benefits of universal higher education. A number of the items cannot be definitively explored without extensive and new investigation. Answers to other questions and issues will depend on value judgments.

The importance and timing of such an examination and discussion is almost self-evident: Our nation today stands at a crossroads in its attitude toward higher education. It is unclear just which roads lead where. Our needs for the future are obscured by issues of race, economics, shifting social values, worldwide unrest, and conflict.

The decisions about the direction and scope and financing of higher education have their parallel in the decisions of the past which activated the land-grant colleges and in massive federal aid to elementary and secondary education. Those decisions were not arrived at in a sudden and unanimous flash of divine revelation. No more will these. Philosophers and political scientists as well as economists and administrators will have a role in illuminating our goals and the means to attain them. The final decision will rest with the general public on whose good sense all our progress must depend. It is their perception of goals that will be the final determinant of which way we move. The educational establishment must and will fill the leadership role in helping the public arrive at wise and equitable conclusions.

PART ONE

Benefits of Universal Higher Education

W. LEE HANSEN and DAVID R. WITMER

Economic Benefits of Universal
Higher Education

WHO WILL BENEFIT FROM "UNIVERSAL HIGHER EDUCATION" AND
by how much? And what will it cost? These questions underlie any
serious consideration of implementing universal higher education. The
answers are difficult because they must call on experience and must
also project from experience into the future. An immediate complica-
tion is the lack of an agreed-upon definition of "universal higher
education." [1]

To provide contexts for speculation about benefits and costs, we
begin by sketching several alternative conceptions of universal higher
education. Next, we discuss the nature of economic benefits and costs
of higher education, review the historical evidence of the magnitude
of economic benefits, and look at the job market potential for the
1970s. Finally, we indicate how economic benefits and costs are likely
to differ under alternative conceptions of universal higher education.

ALTERNATIVE CONCEPTIONS OF UNIVERSAL HIGHER EDUCATION

The idea of universal higher education as public policy can be
traced to the report of President Truman's Commission on Higher
Education in 1947. The Commission's study of the Army General
Classification Tests administered during World War II indicated that
twice as many young men had the aptitude to do college level work, at
prewar standards, as were enrolled. The Commission was led to
conclude that (*a*) "At least 49 percent of our population has the

1. W. Todd Furniss, ed., *Higher Education for Everybody? Issues and Implications* (Washington: American Council on Education, 1971).

mental ability to complete 14 years of schooling with a curriculum of general and vocational studies that should lead either to gainful employment or to further study at a more advanced level"; (b) "At least 32 percent of our population has the mental ability to complete an advanced liberal or specialized professional education," and (c) 16 percent has the capacity for graduate study. The Commission's aim of making higher education equally available to all regardless of race, religion, or wealth, to the extent that "their mental capacity warrants further social investment," has come to be widely known as universal higher education.[2]

Much has happened since the Commission's statement to sharpen our thinking about the concept of universal higher education. The post-World War II surge of enrollments provided a new and successful, though short-lived, experience with huge numbers and a vastly different mix of students. The growing importance that most Americans assigned to college attendance led to an unprecedented rise in the proportion of the 18–21-year-old population seeking postsecondary education, from about 16 percent before World War II to approximately 43 percent during the late 1960s. Moreover, since the mid-1960s great efforts have been made to open up college-going opportunities to minority students and to lower income students generally. Massive increases in state funding have facilitated these developments. In particular, the complex higher education systems (for example, in California, Florida, and Wisconsin) evolved junior and vocational-technical college systems that have dramatically altered the old conception of higher education. Meanwhile, federal support assisted the expansion of physical facilities and student financial aid.

Despite all these changes, important barriers to college-going still exist, as revealed by the widely cited Project Talent data and the Little-Sewell data for Wisconsin. These data indicate that the higher a family's socioeconomic status, the more likely its children are to plan on attending college, to actually attend, and later to graduate.[3]

2. President's Commission on Higher Education [Truman Commission], *Higher Education for American Democracy, Vol. I: Establishing the Goals* (New York: Harper & Bros., 1947), pp. 1–49.

3. For an excellent survey of this literature, see Robert H. Berls, "Higher Education Opportunity and Achievement in the United States," in *The Economics and Financing of Higher Education in the United States: A Compendium of Papers Submitted to the Joint Economic Committee, Congress of the United States* (Washington: Government Printing Office, 1969), pp. 145–204; William H. Sewell and Vimal P. Shah, "Socioeconomic Status, Intelligence, and the Attainment of Higher Education," *Sociology of Education,* Winter 1967, pp. 1–23.

These data also reveal that many talented young people who are unable to take advantage of opportunities for higher education are concentrated in families of lower socioeconomic status.[4] More recent evidence indicates that a policy of public subsidies through below-cost tuition tends to favor groups of students who on average come from higher income families.[5] Whether the barriers to college attendance are largely economic or social in nature remains unresolved, but it is apparent that college-going opportunities are unequally distributed.

The combination of the tremendous expansion of higher education and recognition of inequality in the distribution of benefits has led to a number of different conceptions of what is meant by universal higher education. These involve several elements. The first concerns "universal": whether it refers to the *results*, as reflected by attendance or completion of higher education, in contrast to *opportunities*, as reflected by the promotion of mechanisms that facilitate attendance or completion possibilities. The second concerns "higher education": whether it embraces only those instructional activities carried out at institutions commonly classified as colleges and universities, or also includes other forms of postsecondary activity, such as job training, that may help young people achieve their individual goals of enriching their lives and at the same time adding to their production potential. The third concerns the time span: whether it embraces two years beyond high school or even longer. And the fourth, ordinarily given less attention, concerns financing mechanisms that must be an integral part of any serious proposal:[6] financial aid to institutions versus financial aid to students, and, in either case, how to take account of student financial need.

What are the major types of proposals for universal higher education?

Mandated universal attendance and free tuition for the first two years of college. The most extreme conception of universal higher education calls for legislated compulsory attendance at college for two years beyond high school graduation. Logically, under such a plan, public funds should pay for instructional costs; hence, there would

---

4. W. Lee Hansen, "Financial Barriers to College Attendance," in *Trends in Post-Secondary Education* (Washington: Government Printing Office, 1971), pp. 31–55. On social factors, see Leo A. Munday and Philip R. River, "Perspectives on Open Admissions," in *Open Admissions and Equal Access*, ed. River (Iowa City: American College Testing Program, 1971), pp. 75–100, especially p. 86.

5. W. Lee Hansen and Burton A. Weisbrod, "The Distribution of Direct Costs and Benefits of Public Higher Education," *Journal of Human Resources*, Spring 1969, pp. 176–91.

6. The work of the Carnegie Commission on Higher Education is filling these gaps.

be no tuition charge to students, and enrollments would increase sizably. This approach has never been fully developed or explored.[7]

Expanded access through free tuition for the first two years of college. An alternative assumes that universal higher education means a zero tuition charge for the first two years of college, with attendance voluntary. This approach is used in several state-supported systems of junior and vocational-technical colleges. A few years ago the Educational Policies Commission of the National Education Association recommended tuition-free education for the first two years beyond high school graduation,[8] and the Automation Commission made a similar recommendation in 1966.[9] More recently, the Carnegie Commission has recommended that there be no tuition or very low tuition for the first two years at public institutions, including community colleges, state colleges, and universities.[10] The effect of the proposal would be to increase enrollments and greatly increase the public costs of higher education.

Expanded access through proximity to two-year colleges. Willingham, in a recent study, reported that more than 500,000 high school graduates annually do not continue their education simply because no college is accessible. He suggests that building 375 additional colleges in key locations would put two-thirds of the population in most states near an accessible institution. He defined *accessible* as (*a*) accepting most of the high school graduates who apply, (*b*) charging no more than $400 tuition, and (*c*) being within reasonable commuting range (established by a time-distance formula).[11] This plan would not only lead to an enrollment increase but also reduce somewhat the financial barriers for all students. The costs to the public treasury would be considerably higher than present levels.

Equalized access through full financial aid for qualified low income students. Another interpretation of universal higher education assumes that it means offsetting the financial barriers to college by making attendance financially possible for all qualified students. The present

7. In 1964, then-Secretary of Labor W. Willard Wirtz called for two more years of free compulsory schooling. Whether he was referring to high school or post-high-school education was not fully clear. "Remarks" in *Proceedings of a Symposium on Employment* (New York: American Bankers Association, 1964), p. 16.

8. Educational Policies Commission, *Universal Opportunity for Education Beyond the High School* (Washington: National Education Association, 1964).

9. National Commission on Technology, Automation, and Economic Progress, *Technology and the American Economy* (Washington: Government Printing Office, 1966), I, 46.

10. *The Capitol and the Campus: State Responsibility for Postsecondary Education* (New York: McGraw-Hill Book Co., 1971).

11. Warren W. Willingham, *Free-Access Higher Education* (New York: College Entrance Examination Board, 1970).

tuition structure might be left unchanged, but grants—or, alternatively, a "financial aids package," of grants, loans, and employment—would be made available to meet the out-of-pocket costs of college attendance for lower income students. Financial aid might be restricted to the first two years of college, though most discussions concern the four-year undergraduate program.[12] An immediate stumbling block is in generating sufficient additional funds to meet the financial needs of lower income students.

Equalized access through a "GI bill" or endowment plan for all postsecondary education and training. Though a large proportion of young people may be able to benefit from further education of some sort, it is not clear that formal schooling represents the best alternative for everyone. Higher education might then be viewed more broadly to make all opportunities for postsecondary training and education open to all young people.[13] Training opportunities of the apprenticeship variety, special courses taught by proprietary schools, on-the-job training experiences, and the like would qualify for the same level of public subsidies now provided through colleges and universities. Under one proposal, every young person would be eligible to draw on an endowment sometime during his life to use however he sees fit to enhance his own development for a more productive life.[14] The costs would be very high, because the endowment would be available to everyone. To counter this difficulty, the endowment might be income-conditioned and limited to only two years of training. Many variations are possible.

We have now considered various conceptions of universal higher education and the important ways in which they differ. Because of the wide differences, the predicted effects of universal higher education cannot be discussed in the abstract. Each approach leads to a different number and mix of students (by ability, family income, and so on), which, in turn, affects the magnitude of both the benefits and costs of universal higher education. We shall return to this matter.

---

12. For one example, see W. Lee Hansen and Burton A. Weisbrod, "A New Approach to Higher Education Finance," in *Financing Higher Education*, ed. Mel Orwig (Iowa City: American College Testing Program, 1971), pp. 117–42.

An important variant to student financial aid grants is deferred loan plans. Examples are the Educational Opportunity Bank, the Yale University Tuition Postponement Option, and the newly announced plans for financing higher education in Ohio. For an analysis, see Robert W. Hartman, "Student Loans for Higher Education," in *Financing Higher Education*, ed. Orwig, pp. 177–99.

13. W. Lee Hansen and Burton A. Weisbrod, *Benefits, Costs, and Finance of Public Higher Education* (Chicago: Markham Publishing Co., 1969), p. 78.

14. James Tobin and Leonard Ross, "A National Youth Endowment," *New Republic*, May 1969, pp. 18–21.

ECONOMIC BENEFITS

Regardless of how universal education is defined, the heart of the matter is its efficacy in producing benefits for individuals and for society. Frank Bowles has stated the issue well: "Universal higher education is not, in itself, a goal for our educational system. The goals are intellectual, social, economic, cultural, political—the enlargement of knowledge, an open society, the advancement of the culture, freedom of opportunity, freedom of conscience and political expression—aspirations that are individual and aspirations that are collective." [15] Since many of these goals are not directly measurable, we must search for measurable evidence of outcomes that reflect the extent to which these goals are achieved. After these outcomes are identified and measured, the society will be in a position to determine whether, in the words of President Truman's Commission, "further social investment" in higher education is warranted.

What are the "economic benefits" of higher education? The term itself is not precise inasmuch as a variety of dimensions of benefits may be regarded as economic and the line separating what is and is not "economic" often is blurred.

It is useful to distinguish in other ways the various dimensions of both benefits and costs. For example, there are *monetary* and *nonmonetary* benefits. Monetary benefits—higher earnings—are economic benefits; moreover, they can be measured, though not always easily, in dollars. Nonmonetary benefits—including the joys and pleasures derived from one's education—might or might not be classified as economic; some nonmonetary benefits can be expressed in monetary equivalents but others are difficult or impossible to quantify. Further, there are *individual* benefits and *social* benefits, that is, the benefits which are captured by individuals as contrasted to the total benefits, including individual benefits, which accrue to society. The usual term for the difference between individual and total benefits to society is *external* benefits—those benefits produced by education but which cannot be captured by the individuals who obtained the education. Both individual and external benefits have a monetary and a nonmonetary component.

Before economic benefits can be discussed, it must be decided whether to consider them on a net or gross basis. The distinction is simple. Gross benefits consider only the benefits derived from higher education. But because costs must be incurred to realize benefits, it

---

15. Frank H. Bowles, "Observations and Comments," in *Universal Higher Education*, ed. Earl J. McGrath (New York: McGraw-Hill Book Co., 1966), p. 237.

becomes necessary to focus on *net* benefits, that is, gross benefits minus the costs of gaining the benefits. Here too, some difficulty is encountered because, although the benefits may accrue to individuals (as is the case with the higher earnings levels associated with more schooling), the costs of obtaining that schooling are usually shared by the student, his parents, and other taxpayers. Net benefits vary, therefore, depending on the vantage point, and thus the method of financing higher education has a direct bearing on the size of the net benefits as viewed by individuals and by society. Further, just as there are monetary costs of higher education, so may there be nonmonetary costs, only some of which fall on the individuals being educated.

We shall now turn to the available evidence on the major economic benefits of education and of higher education, specifically.

One often-cited piece of evidence is the relationship between occupation and educational attainment. The general notion is that more education opens up opportunities for individuals to enter better-paying occupations. In general, the higher-ranked occupations—ranked by income, prestige, and the like—are filled with people who have invested more heavily in education. Professionals tend to have completed college; managers, clerical and sales workers, and craftsmen have completed four years of high school; operatives, service workers, laborers, and farmers have completed less than high school.[16] Of course, there is wide variation within each group, but the relationship between educational attainment and occupational attachment is positive.

The economic benefits from higher education (not universal higher education) are best reflected by the strong association between level of educational attainment and income. Data for 1970 show that schooling beyond high school yields large economic benefits for male income recipients twenty-five years of age and over.[17] Whereas males who had completed four years of high school received a median income of $8,772, those with one to three years of college received $9,879 and those with four or more years received $12,681. The differentials, to degree holders in particular, are substantial, especially because these differentials persist over most of the individual's working life. Note, however, the much smaller differential for persons with one to three years of college. Although an unknown portion of these differences is likely attributable to other factors, such as ability, motivation, family

16. U.S. Bureau of the Census, *Current Population Reports: Population Characteristics*, Series P-20 (Washington: Government Printing Office), No. 207, Table 6, p. 27.
17. U.S. Bureau of the Census, *Current Population Reports: Consumer Income*, Series P-60 (Washington: Government Printing Office), No. 78, Table 7, p. 6.

background, and the like, efforts to identify and quantify these other factors, so as to provide a more accurate statement of the effect of schooling on income, have not been highly successful.[18] In summary, then, school and the factors closely associated with it appear to have a strong impact on the economic rewards provided to individuals in our society; in addition, there are other satisfactions—consumption benefits—which are not adequately reflected in money earnings.

Another indicator of the economic benefits produced by education (all levels) is provided by research studies on the relationship between investment in schooling and economic growth.[19] The pioneering work of Schultz and Denison indicates that improvements in the quality of the labor force resulting from rising educational attainment explain 16–23 percent of the growth rate of the economy over the period 1929–57.[20] Denison's more recent estimate for the 1950–62 period is a bit smaller—approximately 16 percent.[21] The Jorgensen-Griliches study for 1945–65 places the proportion of the growth rate explained by education at a still lower level—approximately 10 percent.[22] The successively smaller value these studies place on the contribution of education to economic growth injects a cautionary note in extolling the economic growth benefits of more education, even though most people believe they exist.

Despite such cited results, neither economists nor educators pretend to have any well-developed theories that explain exactly how and why increased schooling facilitates occupational entry, enhances worker productivity, increases earnings, and ultimately helps to account for a more rapid rate of economic growth. The vast gaps in our knowledge also dictate caution about relying heavily on the magnitude of the *economic* benefits of education or of higher education as a major rationale for public financial support.[23]

There remain, of course, the external, social benefits of higher

18. Henry M. Levin et al., "Social Achievement and Post-School Success: A Review," *Review of Educational Research,* February 1971, pp. 1–16.

19. For a review, see Mary Jean Bowman, "Education and Economic Growth," in *Economic Factors Affecting the Financing of Education,* ed. Roe L. Johns et al. (Gainesville, Fla.: National Educational Finance Project, 1970), II, 83–120.

20. T. W. Schultz, *The Economic Value of Education* (New York: Columbia University Press, 1963), pp. 42–46; E. F. Denison, "Education, Economic Growth, and Gaps in Information," *Journal of Political Economy Supplement,* October 1962, Part 2, pp. 124–28.

21. E. F. Denison, *Why Growth Rates Differ* (Washington: Brookings Institution, 1967), pp. 192–94.

22. D. W. Jorgensen and Z. Griliches, "The Explanation of Productivity Change," *Review of Economic Studies,* Autumn 1967, pp. 249–83.

23. For further evidence, see W. Lee Hansen, ed., *Education, Income, and Human Capital* (New York: National Bureau of Economic Research, 1970).

education that have been enumerated by Howard Bowen[24] and that are taken up in some detail in the Keniston and Gerzon paper in this volume. Ideally, these effects would be laid out in such a way that they could be quantified and valued in dollars. While the consensus is that the magnitude of these external social benefits is large, any reckoning must consider both the external social benefits *and* the external social costs of higher education.

Yet another approach to the estimation of the economic returns to education, from the standpoint of both individuals and society, calls for a measure of the net economic benefits of education. Such a measure would permit us to combine costs (which are concentrated over a brief span of years in early adulthood) and the stream of benefits (which is spread over most of the remainder of a lifetime) by calculating the internal rate of return. This requires that future benefits be "discounted" to allow for the fact that far-distant benefits are valued less highly than benefits just a few years off in the future.

The internal rate of return generated by this procedure may be likened to the rate of return or the rate of interest received from placing funds in a savings bank, buying government bonds, or investing in corporate securities. Individuals will find it beneficial to invest in more higher education if the internal rate of return to education for the individual exceeds the rate of return to other types of investments. Whether society as a whole finds it efficient to invest in more higher education will depend on the size of internal rates of return to education received by society relative to other investment opportunities open to it.

The analysis here deals with two kinds of internal rates of return: The first is the individual rate of return, which summarizes the future benefits and costs as perceived by the individual. The individual benefits are equal to the extra income received over what would have been received with less schooling. The costs include the income that is forgone while in school and the costs of books, tuition, and incidental expenses connected with college-going. The second is society's internal rate of return, which summarizes future benefits and costs as perceived from the standpoint of the economy as a whole. Thus, costs include not only the costs to the individual but also the subsidy provided by taxpayers through below-cost tuition. Later sections of this paper refer to these costs as *total resource costs*.

On the basis of a variety of studies, it appears that over the past

24. Howard R. Bowen, "Finance and the Aims of American Higher Education," in *Financing Higher Education,* ed. Orwig, pp. 168–70.

several decades the individual rate of return on investing in education through the completion of high school has for males averaged about 20 percent. This is well above the rate of return of about 10 percent to nonhuman types of investment. The individual's rate of return to investment in a four-year degree program has averaged about 12–14 percent, again well above alternative investment opportunities in the economy. The individual's rate of return to the completion of two years of college, however, has more often than not been less than 10 percent; hence, it compares less favorably with the return that can be earned in other investments. In short, the magnitudes of rates of return confirm that the completion of high school represents a wise economic decision and that a four-year or college education pays off. But the efficacy of two-year college programs is less clear-cut.[25]

Society's internal rates of return look somewhat less favorable inasmuch as they must reflect the taxpayers' share in underwriting the costs of undergraduate education. Here, the rates of return to the total resources spent by society—students, their parents, and taxpayers—are lower by 1–4 percentage points. Hence, whereas investment by society in four-year degree programs may still look favorable, investment in two-year programs is relatively less attractive.

HISTORICAL EVIDENCE ON BENEFITS

The purpose of this section is to indicate the extent to which the net benefits from higher education, as well as from secondary education, have changed under the onslaught of rapid enrollment increases. The benefits might be expected to decline as more people seek them out, yet the record is quite different: the individual rates of return have held roughly constant in the face of the universalization of secondary education and the growing participation in higher education.

Expansion of College Education, 1939–68

We have assembled data on the individual's rates of return to undergraduate education for the period 1939–68. The results, though not based on exactly parallel data and techniques, nevertheless provide a useful basis for comparison and are shown in Table 1.

In 1939–41, enrollments in higher education approximated 1.5 million per year, equal to less than 16 percent of the 18–21-year-old age group. The rate of return to college investment was rather hand-

25. For sources of data, see Table 1 of this paper. The discussion draws heavily on the framework set forth by Gary S. Becker, *Human Capital* (New York: National Bureau of Economic Research, 1964).

TABLE 1: *Rates of Return to Undergraduate Higher Education, U.S. Males, 1939–68*

Year	Percentage Rate of Return	
	1–3 Years of College	4 Years of College
1939..................	10	15
1949..................	6–8	12–13
1959..................	7–12	10–15
1968..................	9	11

Sources: Gary S. Becker, *Human Capital* (New York: National Bureau of Economic Research, 1964), chap. 4; W. Lee Hansen, "Total and Private Rates of Return to Investment in Schooling," *Journal of Political Economy*, April 1963, pp. 128–40; Giora Hanoch, "An Economic Analysis of Schooling and Earnings," *Journal of Human Resources*, Summer 1967, pp. 310–29; Fred Hines et al., "Social and Private Rates of Return to Investment in Schooling by Race-Sex Groups and Regions," *Journal of Human Resources*, Summer 1970, pp. 318–45; and David R. Witmer, *The Value of College Education . . .* (Ann Arbor: University Microfilms, 1971), vol. I, chap. 6.

some, exceeding 14 percent for individual investments, and it compared favorably with other kinds of investment opportunities which yielded a 10 percent rate of return.

This favorable outlook was not expected to continue, however, as evidenced by the conclusions of Kotsching and Harris, both writing in the 1940s.[26] They variously hypothesized that as the nation approached universal higher education, (*a*) college graduates would be in oversupply relative to the occupations they would seek to enter, with fewer and fewer uneducated people to do the less glamorous work; (*b*) the earnings of college graduates would fall relative to those of less-educated groups; (*c*) widespread unemployment of college graduates would result because of the nontransferability of skills; (*d*) idle, frustrated intellectuals would foment social revolution; (*e*) larger proportions of unqualified students would be enrolled in colleges, and as a consequence, (*f*) the social benefits to investing in college training would decline. Neither author supported all of these hypotheses, and some of the hypotheses were mutually exclusive, but each hypothesis had adherents. The following quotation from Cohn in the late 1940s captures the predominant tone:

> There will soon be more college graduates than there are jobs for them in their chosen fields. By 1950, for example, close to 50,000 engineers will be graduates, as against an annual replacement need of 7,000. Lawyers will become a surplus commodity with few takers, yet they continue to flock to college although many members of the class of

26. Walter Kotsching, *Slaves Need No Leaders* (London: Oxford University Press, 1943); Seymour Harris, *The Market for College Graduates* (Cambridge, Mass.: Harvard University Press, 1949).

1948 are jobless. There is still room for chemists and psychologists but only if they have a graduate degree. There are already too many personnel men. The fields of physical education, social science, and English are crowded.... Would ... men who had undergone rigorous disciplines of study in order to get a degree just sit and take it when they found themselves jobless? Or, embittered and frustrated, would they become enemies of society as it is at present; fanatical advocates of some form of authoritarianism, more dangerous since they are ambitious, trained, and resentful?[27]

Did these dire predictions materialize? By 1950, college enrollments had almost doubled, jumping to 2.7 million. Though the direct individual rate of return fell by about 20 percent, to roughly 12–13 percent, the rate still compared favorably with other investment opportunities. This decline still suggested that there might be something to the dire warnings; if so, even more dramatic declines in the rate of return could be expected to occur during the subsequent decade. The decade of the 1950s saw a continued, though slower expansion of higher education, with enrollments increasing to 3 million, equal to one-third of the 18–21-year-old population. Nevertheless, by the end of the decade the individual's rate of return held constant, at somewhere between 10–15 percent. Thus, the predictions did not materialize.

In the 1960s, enrollments increased at an accelerated pace, to more than 6 million students, or 43 percent of the 18–21-year-old population. By 1968, the individual rate of return was roughly 11 percent for holders of the bachelor's degree. Furthermore, the same general pattern emerges for those with two years of college, for whom, traditionally, the rates of return have been considerably lower but have moved in much the same pattern over time.

In summary, then, over the past three decades a dramatic shift toward more universal higher education has been accomplished without any great change in the rate of return on investment in the college-educated. True, the rates have oscillated somewhat in response to changing market conditions, but overall have changed far less than most reasonable observers might have predicted. In short, the market was able to assimilate the newly educated with comparative ease.

Some may argue that these results are testimony to the persistent and pervasive effects of "credentialism." According to this view, earnings associated with more schooling do not really reflect greater individual productivity; rather, salaries are tied to educational attain-

27. David L. Cohn, "Who Will Do the Dirty Work?" *Atlantic Monthly,* May 1949, pp. 45–48.

ment and people are hired on the basis of their credentials.[28] Although this view has some appeal and there is evidence that credentials and tests are often unrelated to job performance, it is difficult to believe that employers did not long ago discover that they were paying for more than they were getting in output. Disparities between test results, certification, and credentials on the one hand and genuine productivity on the other, we believe, do not long persist. Hence, we are inclined to accept the results presented above as a general indication of the economic returns to investments in schooling.

Transition to Universal Secondary Education

Let us look now at the nation's transition from universal elementary to universal secondary education for whatever light it may shed on a transition to universal higher education.

At the close of the nineteenth century, three-fifths of the labor force was engaged in agriculture and in nonfarm unskilled labor, and opportunities for the uneducated and unskilled to find gainful employment were abundant. The National Association of Manufacturers and other business groups criticized the schools and deprecated the value of college education. Children generally left school at age twelve. Fewer than 11 percent of the 14–17-year-old population attended secondary school; only 4 percent of the 18–21-year-old population attended college.

The rate of return to individual investment in high school education, as we have crudely estimated it, may have been about 10 percent at the turn of the century. The rate of return apparently rose to about 18 percent for high school graduation in 1909, but then fell sharply, dropping to under 10 percent and holding at that level for 1919 and 1929. Yet in 1939 the rate of return on private investment in high school education stood at roughly 16 percent, a handsome return by any test. By this time high school enrollment exceeded 7 million students, representing 73 percent of the 14–17-year-old population, and so the transition to universal secondary education was by this time nearly complete.

Since 1939 we have moved into what some call a "postindustrial society." Only 5 percent of the labor force is unskilled. Opportunities for employment in service, technical, managerial, and professional occupations have increased more than 300 percent in one generation.

28. A provocative exposition of this view is Ivar Berg, *Education and Jobs: The Great Training Robbery* (New York: Praeger, 1970). Hiring on the basis of tests and educational credentials may soon be ended as a result of the recent decision, Griggs et al. vs. Duke Power Company, 39 LW 4317 (1971).

Knowledge has become the central economic resource. Society seeks to identify potential talent of many sorts and to furnish opportunities for these talents to reach fruition through education. Nonetheless, the rate of return to individual investment in high school education stands at about 17 percent, having continued at a high level ever since 1939.

Note that *the transition from universal elementary education to universal secondary education did not force down the rates of return on investments in high school, did not increase unemployment of high school graduates, did not cause wages of high school graduates to fall, and did not foment social revolution.* By analogy, one might argue that the transition to universal higher education will also be smooth.

Returns to Noncollege Types of Training

Any thinking about the scope of universal higher education should give some attention to the returns to investments in other forms of education and training. Knowledge about the payoffs, or rates of return, to apprenticeship, on-the-job training, proprietary training, and the like is extremely limited.[29] Yet the long-standing market for such forms of training suggests that they pay off financially and may even produce some external benefits as well. The continued lack of knowledge about these activities not only hampers assessment of the relative economic benefits of important alternatives to college-going, but it may also overemphasize college-going simply because something of its economic effects is known.

THE OUTLOOK

Following the review of the past, the next step is to examine the outlook for the educated manpower market for the 1970s. The temptation is to extrapolate recent trends into the future. But the period of the 1960s, particularly, was one of rapid economic expansion, combined with a relative scarcity of young people entering the labor market either after graduation from high school or college. Thus, during this period of buoyant demand there was no dearth of job opportunities, starting wage rates were bid up rapidly, and there was little unemployment among people who had completed high school or gone to college.

The decade of the 1970s is likely to be different, although it seems

29. J. Robert Warmbrod, *Review and Synthesis of Research on the Economics of Vocational-Technical Education* (Columbus, Ohio: ERIC Clearinghouse, 1968), Research 16.

reasonable to expect a continuation of the rapid rate of economic growth. In contrast with the last decade, there will be a relative abundance of new young entrants into the labor force. Because of the post-World War II baby boom and the tremendous increase in the number of births throughout the 1950s, there have been anywhere between one-third and one-half more entrants into the labor force each year since the late 1960s, and this pattern will continue through the 1970s. At the same time, more of the entrants than ever before will be educated beyond the high school level. These developments suggest that the competition for educated young men and women is likely to be relatively less vigorous than in the 1960s. The result is that the relative monetary returns associated with college-going are likely to fall somewhat, just as they increased in the 1960s.

All of this further suggests that extrapolation will not do; judgment is called for in estimating the benefits from higher education over the next five to ten years. In our analyses, therefore, we are choosing a very cautious position for several reasons. First, no one has a firm enough understanding of the interaction between the college market and the labor market to provide a sound basis for projections. Second, and not insignificant, is the fact that other people have in the past attempted to look ahead but with less than complete success. We shall take up the second point first.

A review of the past twenty years shows that Seymour Harris' prognostications were far off the mark: until the last year or two, the market for college graduates has been booming. Admittedly, recessions have slowed the demand at times, and the recession of the late 1960s and early 1970s, combined with a reallocation of government expenditures, has reduced the rate of increase of demand for college graduates. Were Harris' prognostications to be published today, they would doubtless generate a sympathetic readership, much as they did during the 1949 recession.[30] But it is debatable whether current and analogous statements, such as those by Faltermayer, reported in the press in the spring and summer of 1971, should give us great cause for concern about the next twenty years.[31]

Looking ahead, we note that U.S. Bureau of Labor Statistics projections of industrial and occupational manpower needs generally

30. Harris, *The Market for College Graduates.* The author still claims that the impact of rising numbers of college graduates depresses earnings and that the highly educated then respond by deserting the market or accepting positions below their expectations. See Seymour E. Harris, "Book Reviews," *Journal of Higher Education,* January 1971, p. 81.

31. Edmund K. Faltermayer, "Let's Break the Go-To-College Lockstep," *Fortune,* November 1970, pp. 98–103, 144; *Time,* May 24, 1971, pp. 49–59.

indicate the continuation of long-term trends toward services rather than dramatic or sudden shifts during the 1970s.[32] Needs for professional and technical workers are expected to increase about 50 percent —faster than any other occupational group in the labor force. The downward trend, since 1900, for blue-collar workers will continue so that by 1980 they may constitute a third of all workers. Nonetheless, by 1980, 80 percent or more of all jobs will require fewer than four years of college.

The demand for college-trained high school teachers will not grow rapidly during the coming decade because the school-age population will remain roughly constant in size. Nor will the need for new college teachers be great, for much the same reason. It appears there will be a continuing need for most other professionals, and that *most* college-trained individuals will be able to make their way into the wide variety of occupations they have sought out in recent decades. On the assumption, however, that the occupations typically filled by college graduates do not increase quite as rapidly as the proportion of college graduates in the total adult population, then *more* college-trained people will have to seek positions in other occupations. This, however, has always been the case. Whether or not college graduates will be eagerly sought for these other occupations depends in part on the types of skills and training they bring with them. And so, while relative numbers are of great importance, of even greater importance is the potential productivity associated with college attendance and the extent to which college training increases people's adaptability to perform in a wide range of occupations.

Let us turn now to our first point—the extent of knowledge of how the labor and the education markets work. Here we recommend Richard Freeman's newly published *The Market for College Trained Manpower: A Study in the Economics of Choice*.[33] Freeman examines how college students, as a population and as students in selected fields, respond to changing economic incentives. He finds that students respond quickly to changing economic opportunities, and shift their field of interest in response to probable rewards awaiting them after college. Freeman's analysis suggests wariness in accepting projections of the occupational distribution of the labor force and the implica-

32. Russell B. Flanders, "Employment Patterns for the 1970's," *Occupational Outlook Quarterly*, Summer 1970, pp. 2–6; "The College Graduate—1980 Job Prospects," *Occupational Outlook Quarterly*, Fall 1970, p. 5; E. B. Sheldon, *Indicators of Social Change* (New York: Russell Sage Foundation, 1968).

33. Cambridge, Mass.: Harvard University Press, 1971. 264 pp.

tions for education as typically drawn. These projections are based on largely unchanging relationships between output growth and occupational distributions; they also assume unchanging relationships between jobs and earnings in different occupations. But to the extent that relative supplies of people with different types of training do not coincide with requirements, shifts in the rewards associated with different jobs and training will be induced. In turn, individuals will alter their choices, and in this way readjustments will occur to help equilibrate supply and demand. Of course, if there is a general "glut" of educated persons, the market may not be able to respond rapidly and fully enough. But gluts occur only if individuals are unresponsive to the earning differences associated with college-going and if they do not seek other noncollege routes to higher earnings.

In our look ahead, then, we do not assume that the differential earnings to college graduates will automatically fall either slowly or precipitously. They may decline somewhat overall and certainly will decline in some fields. At the same time, these changes can be expected to trigger reassessments by young people contemplating their educational and career choices.

THE QUESTION OF PRIORITIES

The economic returns to investment in higher education have been substantial; annual earnings increase as years of schooling increase; this favorable relationship between earnings and educational attainment has persisted through the years, even though the amount of formal schooling attained by the population has greatly increased. The potential for further returns to additional investment exists. How shall we—students, parents, other taxpayers; that is, the nation—make this further investment? Which approach to universal higher education holds the greatest promise? In entering this discussion, we are disregarding, as outside the domain of this paper, any priority rankings with other social programs as a guide to public policy.

We approach the analyses through the relative benefits to be gained from allocating more resources toward the achievement of universal higher education. To the extent that universal higher education involves an *expansion* of attendance in terminal programs of the traditional types offered by two-year colleges, it is probably not wise to spend resources in this way because the rates of return to individuals and to society are already below the rates of return available elsewhere in the economy. Indeed, given the greater returns to secondary education and to four-year college programs, greater gains could be had by directing more resources, particularly public resources, to these levels rather than to two-year terminal programs.

Do these conclusions have to be altered in light of the several different conceptions of universal higher education outlined earlier? Probably yes, for each leads to different increases in enrollments and produces different mixes of students, as reflected by ability, family income, and the like. Consequently, either or both the costs and benefits may change and cause, in turn, changes in the rates of return to both the individual and society. Moreover, each involves a somewhat different degree of sharing the costs of higher education, as between students, parents, and taxpayers in general.

Consider first the approach to universal higher education involving *expanded access through free tuition for the first two years of college.* Lowering the tuition charge would attract additional students to colleges, students who cannot now afford to attend. In our estimation, the quality of these added students will probably not differ appreciably from the quality of those already enrolled. Hence, both the average total resource costs of educating them and the benefits they could expect to receive from their education would approximate those for today's conventional students. As a result, the rate of return to society on the resources invested in additional schooling would not differ appreciably from what it is now. Hence, we would be investing additional resources in higher education, because of the added enrollments, while earning the same low rate of return on these resources.

But there is another change, and an important one. By lowering tuition, not only for the newly attracted students but also for the conventional students enrolled in the first two years of college, we would shift a larger portion of the total resource costs of higher education onto taxpayers. Thus, our enrollment increase and the low rate of return it produces comes at the expense of an increase of about $1 billion in public funds to finance the reduction in tuition. Inasmuch as college students on average come from families with above-average incomes, additional subsidies are provided to higher income families. Does this approach represent wise public policy?

If, instead, public policy opted for *expanded access through proximity to two-year colleges,* enrollments could be expected to rise because of the reduced out-of-pocket costs of attendance. The average total resource costs associated with this enrollment increase would probably exceed somewhat the present average costs of educating students because of the smaller size of these new institutions. Since no significant difference is expected in the quality of the additional students attracted to college, their future benefits would be much like those for present students. If anything, then, costs may rise a bit relative to benefits, with the result that the rate of return to society on the additional resources would drop slightly below that already prevailing. Again, for the added costs of making available new student places in local communities, the nation would receive a rather low return on the total resources invested.

Next consider *mandated attendance for two years of college, with free tuition.* This approach combines elements of the two approaches just discussed. The costs per student of such a program would likely be greater than present costs, not only because instructional costs would be greater for these less-motivated students, but also because many additional new campuses would be required. The benefits per student are likely to be less than present benefits, largely because a majority of the students who do not now attend college probably realize that its potential benefits for them are small. The upshot of this dramatically different conception of higher education would be to produce a lower average rate of return on society's investment of additional resources in higher education. As in the previous example, substantial resources would simply be transferred from taxpayers in general to college-going students and their parents. On balance, then, the mandated attendance approach is especially unappealing from an economic standpoint.

If *equalized access through full financial aid for qualified low income students* would reduce, if not eliminate, the financial barriers to college attendance, a different picture could emerge. Assume that financial aid grants based on ability to pay are available to qualified students, defined as those in the top half of the ability distribution. Because of these grants, more lower income students would enroll. The average total resource cost of educating these additional students would, since they come in with no ability disadvantages, be roughly similar to that required for present students. Inasmuch as the added students would have an average ability exceeding that of present two-year students, the potential benefits for the added students could be expected to exceed the potential benefits for presently enrolled students. Thus, with no difference in the average costs but larger average benefits, the rate of return on society's additional resources going into higher education would exceed the current rate of return to the society. If so, this approach to universal higher education appears promising as a means of maximizing the benefits from additional investment in higher education. The financing of these additional students would be costly, involving a large transfer of funds from taxpayers to lower income families of students.[34] Paradoxically, this plan, which would be beneficial to society from an economic standpoint, has some obvious political disadvantages.[35]

Finally, the idea of providing *equalized access through a "GI bill" or endowment plan for all postsecondary education and training* is more difficult to evaluate. The benefits from noncollege types of training may be high, and with the "endowment" many students now barred from such programs by financial barriers would gain access to them. Moreover, some students now attending college might opt for other forms of training that would be more beneficial. While we can only speculate, the average benefits for the large expected numbers of additional participants might well exceed the average benefits for those young people now in two-year college programs. And on the assumption that the costs of these programs would not be any higher, the rate of return on the total resources allocated to achieve this broader scope of universal higher education could be greater than that for students now in two-year programs. Again, however, by offering everyone an endowment, the cost to taxpayers would be considerable, but there is a distinct possibility that much more might be achieved by this approach than by mandated or other approaches to universal higher education.

In summary, on average, the *net gains* from attempting to implement universal higher education are not as high as on other alternative expenditure opportunities. At the same time we have tried to indicate to what extent this conclusion would have to be modified, depending on which approach to universal higher education is considered. It appears that a plan calling for endowments to be available for any of a variety of forms of education and training may have the greatest economic payoff, and that a system of financial aid grants based on ability to pay—or lack of it—is likely to be the next most attractive.

34. For more on this point, see Hansen and Weisbrod, "A New Approach to Higher Education Finance."

35. Running through this discussion is a countertheme, namely, the financing scheme underlying any of these proposals has certain redistributive effects. That is, by reducing average tuition costs or providing an endowment to all young people, resources are transferred from all taxpayers to those who qualify for the tuition reductions or endowment grants. In some cases the beneficiaries will be higher income families; in other cases they may represent a cross section of all families. In any case, the fact that these transfers do occur is bound to affect society's perceptions of the more narrowly defined benefits and costs that have been discussed in this paper.

A FINAL COMMENT

What is our overall conclusion? We believe that universal higher education, when it is viewed as an expansion of what we are now doing, will produce some economic benefits but at high cost. Rather than seeking only to expand access to higher education, we urge that greater consideration be given to equalizing access, not only to what is now known as higher education but also to other forms of education and training that may be appropriate to the differing needs of our young people. These efforts to equalize access will require a different set of policy instruments, instruments that must be tuned more finely to take account of individual needs—both financial and education training needs. Only by keeping these needs clearly in mind can an effective plan be devised to promote universal higher education— one that will serve individuals and society by producing significant overall economic benefits and at the same time making these benefits available to those young people most able to profit from them.

Higher Education and the Job Market

IVAR BERG

CREDIT FOR THE MOUNTING ENTHUSIASM REGARDING HIGHER EDUCATION IN the United States in recent years must go in fair share to her economists. During the latter half of the 1960s, their studies of the returns accorded to well-educated Americans (a few are cited by Messrs. Hansen and Witmer) significantly reinforced the energetic arguments supporting the expansion of opportunities for college and higher degrees.

Even those with the loftiest ideas about the meaning and uses of the higher learning could take comfort, in a pragmatic society, from the extraordinarily high proportion of economic growth attributed to education, and from the high social and personal returns purportedly generated by investments in education. Few educators would quibble about whether "qualitative" improvements, as signified by income differences among employees, are associated directly with their efforts in classroom, laboratory, and seminar.

As often happens in science, however, novel and imaginative analyses are followed by studies in which subtleties and details are pursued that escaped consideration in the first approximations. The typical sequence is that more cautious estimates, produced by more refined and sophisticated methods and the application of more critical intelligence, replace the assessments initially reported. It is a pleasure to note that the Hansen and Witmer paper is representative of this latter phenomenon. Its cautious tone and careful reasoning may lessen the danger that the initial overstatement of education's economic benefits would contribute to an already uncritical euphoria about education's capacity to solve problems and to be all things to all men.

I sincerely hope that Professor Hansen and his colleagues will continue to probe the complexities of the problem; one may confidently expect that their sense of caution will grow with each new assessment. It was Mr. Hansen who prepared a highly significant study, a few years ago, of higher education in California that demonstrated the inequalitarian implications of an educational and tax apparatus under which the greatest subsidies for higher education flow directly to those in least economic need. The present paper reports that successive recent studies give reduced estimates of returns to education, and it also presents evidence of declining returns over time.

One may have misgivings especially about comparisons of the returns on investment in higher education with those available from other investments. Many studies infer public policy implications rather too readily from the very components of economic studies of education that are least amenable to tests of reliability and validity—use of indirect data, extrapolations into the future, and arguments by analogy from the past.

Thus, one ought not be sanguine about the implications of the authors' observation that it "has always been a case" that increasing numbers of college graduates seek positions other than those typically filled by college graduates. Social quantities have a way of becoming social qualities with which we must ultimately contend, and the discrepancy between supply and demand in the market for educated manpower may well now have passed the critical point at which small statistical differences become significant social magnitudes. The hope, expressed optimistically by the authors as an expectation, that even slowly declining rates of economic return to degree holders will simply "trigger reassessments by young people contemplating their educational and career choices" might best be expressed prayerfully as another of the consummations devoutly to be wished.

In my own labors I find little to sustain an uncritical faith that the mismatches between supply and demand in the markets for well-educated employees will be as small or responded to as quickly as the authors imply. Of course, for three decades the market has adjusted to the flows of educated manpower; indeed the statement is a truism. It is also true that the "adjustment" of people to markets has been relatively unattended by the serious political and social protest anticipated by earlier worrywarts.

There are risks in overlooking some serious strains on our campuses that have been more than slightly attributable to the occupational and career problems facing young people. If one examines direct relationships between actual education needed on jobs and the educational attainments of the work force, he begins to suspect that well-educated employees in general, and well-educated women in particular, will indeed find themselves in occupational posts well below those our society has led them to expect as their reward for years of "forgone income" and long study. It may simply not be wise to gainsay the frustrations and disenchantments readily observable among those who feel themselves substantially "underutilized."

In the short run, direct estimates of actual educational requirements are closer to reality than the indirect relationships studied by economists. The latter, which examine the relationships between education and income, assume economic rationality among employers responding to market forces that are virtually perfectly competitive. Under such theoretical conditions the higher incomes of the better-educated population represent the differences between their higher ability—greater productivity—and the ability of less well educated employees, whose economic returns are more modest.

Currently direct estimates of job requirements are flawed, particularly those estimates of the economy's requirements for different amounts, levels, and kinds of education. The available assessments of "real" requirements are based on job requirements as translated by skilled analysts, not in terms of degrees or years of schooling, but in terms of qualitative criteria which have been coded into a six-point scale of "general educational development" (GED).

For example, I recently worked with multiple translations of job requirements thus conceived and applied a series of more or less critical assumptions about the meaning of equivalencies established between the GED scale and different clusters of years of formal schooling. I concluded that, even after giving the translations full credibility for the considerable elevation of educational requirements since the mid-1950s, a considerable portion of job requirements since 1966 result from employers simply upgrading jobs, rather than from essential changes in the jobs themselves.

Similar conclusions appear in a newer study, in which Census Bureau classifications of workers according to educational achievement were cross-tabulated with the educational requirements for jobs listed in the U.S. Department of Labor *Dictionary of Occupational Titles:*

> For professional, technical and managerial workers . . . the distributions of G.E.D. and educational achievement [i.e. jobs and people, both treated in terms of education] bear some resemblance to each other, both for males and for females. For males in farming occupations and machine trades the distributions are again similar. Beyond this, however, it is hard to imagine two more dissimilar distributions. . . . If we accent the two sets of data [on educational achievements cross-tabulated with educational requirements] at their face value, that is, disregard the questionable elements in each, it is hard to escape the conclusion that the high level of educational attainment in this country reflects a much broader set of social values than those related to purely occupational requirements.[1]

And in another careful study by demographers, we read that

> calculations for a static labor force size indicate that our colleges are producing graduates at a rate that is considerably above the rate of change in the occupational structure. When labor force expansion is added to the rate of change in the occupational structure, then the rate of educational upgrading . . . is much lower in the 1960 to 1970 period, but it was substantial for the 1950 to 1960 period, and is expected to rise again in the 1950–1960 rate in the 1970 to 1980 period.[2]

I sought, with colleagues, to examine the productivity-performance link that presumably accounts for the long-time, well-documented association between education and income in the United States. We considered thousands of jobs at all levels of the occupational structure, from piece workers in Mississippi textile operations to management's best scientists and engineers in the heavy electrical equipment manufacturing industry. We found education and performance to be either uncorrelated or negatively correlated.

Messrs. Hansen and Witmer, in their paper, regard such studies as provocative, but they are provoked to the same sense of equanimity as in the case, already noted, of the adjustments of supply. Discussing the view that a pervasive "credentialism" may have entered into the hiring process in this country, they write that

> although this view has some appeal . . . , it is difficult to believe that employers did not long ago discover that they were paying [in practicing "credentialism"] for more than they were getting in output. Disparities between test results, certification, and credentials on the one hand and genuine productivity on the other, we believe, do not long persist. [P. 31]

1. Ann Miller, "Occupations of the Labor Force According to the Dictionary of Occupational Titles," mimeographed (Philadelphia: University of Pennsylvania, February 1971), p. 39.
2. John K. Folger, Helen S. Astin, and Alan E. Bayer, *Human Resources and Higher Education* (New York: Russell Sage Foundation, 1970), p. 39.

I can assure the authors that their disbelief could be easily dissipated in almost any company, for we found only one among twenty firms whose managers even *asked* themselves questions about the wisdom of upgrading job requirements, let alone sought to "discover," in the authors' words, whether "they were paying for more than they were getting."[3]

I am obviously concerned, on behalf of higher education, that we not rest too comfortably on analogies between the nation's capacity to make socially productive and personally satisfying use of the enormous historical increase in elementary school graduates, and its capacity to do so with college graduates in evergrowing numbers over the long pull. Indeed, if the authors are correct in asserting that employers will not long be fooled by credentials-for-their-own-sake, then we, as educators, had best be concerned that national policies do not produce a disenchanted, underutilized population.

I do not fear revolution on the part of those whose educations are not "needed." Rather, I deplore the malaise and disappointment of frustrated people whose alcoholic and other mental health problems are not without costs. I will not comment on the feelings of blacks— whose incomes lag behind those of whites in every category of educational achievement—toward the education establishment in a society where economic policy evidences doing little more than helping job opportunities (barely) keep pace with population growth. It is by no means clear to me that minority graduates will distinguish between economic policies that bear on job opportunities and educational policies that would presumably open opportunities when they discover the market "adjustments" to which the authors refer so lightly.

My concern is that we embark on universal higher education thoughtfully and with careful definitions of society's various needs. I am pleased to endorse the authors' conclusions about the particular plan that makes the most sense: "we urge that greater consideration be given to equalizing access, not only to what is now known as higher education but also to other forms of education and training that may be appropriate to the differing needs of our young people." I wish I could join in the optimism in some minor sections of the paper, but the cautious tone that characterizes most of their analysis has persuaded me to join them, without qualification, in their most sober assessments.

Finally, we may all recognize that no injustice is done to the cause

3. As a former dean, I cannot avoid making the same comment about our pay scales for junior and senior faculty, as reassuring and self-serving as it would be for me to believe that now that I am back in teaching and research, I am more productive than my young colleagues in lower ranks.

of higher education by the authors' carefully drawn consideration of its economic costs and benefits. Indeed, we may applaud the authors for braving the criticisms of those who would raise red herrings in preference to careful analyses that, to use a statistician's term, partial out one or another aspect of higher education's place in American cultural, social, political, and economic life.

Weighing Economic and Social Benefits

JOHN D. MILLETT

THE PAPER PREPARED BY MESSRS. HANSEN AND WITMER HAS THE VIRTUES and the limitations inherent in the concept of economic benefit to be obtained from higher education. It is obvious that cost-benefit analysis remains an imperfect tool in the search for rational decision making in the allocation of the economic resources of society and in the budgeting of the public sector of our economy.

Necessarily and properly the authors begin their discussion with the search for an operative definition of universal higher education. This part of the paper I find most helpful and worthy of even more extended development. The critical issue here is the concept of ability standards to be applied in providing access to higher education. It is simple to assert that young people, regardless of socioeconomic status, should have access to as much higher education as they can handle. Such a statement of social objective offers little in the way of an operative definition. What are the cognitive, skill, and affective components of that learning experience which we label "higher education," and what expected standards of performance in this learning determine what each individual student "can handle"?

My impression is that the authors are in fact endorsing the generalized proposals of the Truman Commission on Higher Education in attempting to find a definition of universal education. Whether or not this proposal is now acceptable because of the experience of the past twenty-five years, I cannot tell from the paper.

The second issue that the authors must confront is how to define "economic benefits." Here, again, is an elusive concept. Admittedly there are nonmonetary as well as economic benefits to be derived from higher education. Admittedly there are social benefits as well as personal economic benefits. The authors concentrate their attention on investment return to the individual in the form of future earnings as a measure of economic benefit, although they acknowledge there may also be a benefit in terms of growth in output of the entire economy.

The most important aspect of the paper is its implications or recommendations for public policy. Here I find myself in agreement with some recommendations and in disagreement with others. First, I endorse wholeheartedly the proposition that our major concern at present should be with equalizing access to higher education for students of appropriate ability from low income families rather than seeking to expand general access to higher education. Second, I agree that we should expand our concern with equalized access through full financial aid for students of low income families. I am not at all sure that a plan of this kind has "obvious political disadvantages." And I view with the same abhorrence as the authors the prospect of a legislated compulsory enrollment of youth in grades thirteen and fourteen.

On the other hand, I question whether the analysis really does prove that it is an unwise use of resources to expand student enrollment in two-year programs. I suggest that the need for technicians is a major hope for expanding the productivity of our service economy, and that the economic returns to these persons may be much greater than any extrapolation of past experience would currently indicate.

My major problem with the paper arises from its omissions rather than its content. It is, of course, unfair to criticize any author for the things he does not say, and within this brief compass I cannot present an alternative paper. My chief point is how essential it will be in the decade of the 1970s to seek answers to two overwhelming problems. The first problem is to define what we as a society expect to achieve as the external or, as I prefer, the social benefits of higher education. Let us assume that we accept the idea that the role of government is to use tax revenues to pay that part of the cost of higher education which produces social benefit. What then are these social benefits, and what part of the total enterprise of higher education do these social benefits include?

Second, must the per-unit costs of higher education continue to rise throughout the 1970s? We are compelled today to undertake the kinds of analyses presented by Drs. Hansen and Witmer because of the increased expense of higher education during the 1960s. Such analyses will become even more compelling if costs continue to rise in this decade, and everyone should be properly forewarned.

On balance, the authors have contributed substantially to the advancement of our knowledge and our analytical technique in the continuing assessment of higher education as a social institution. I am sure that the authors would agree with me that their knowledge is imperfect, that their forecasts are at best reasonable expectations, and that decision making remains a challenge for educators and politicians.

Public and Private Investment in Higher Education

KERMIT C. MORRISSEY

MESSRS. HANSEN AND WITMER, IN DISCUSSING PRIORITIES, CALL FOR emphasis on high school and baccalaureate experience as representing the most effective allocation of resources in the pursuit of universal higher educational opportunity. The authors indicate that an expansion of enrollment in two-year programs would be unwise because the rates of economic return are already below the rates available from other forms of investment. At the close of their paper, however, the authors have made the following statement, "Rather than seeking only to expand access to higher education, we urge that greater consideration be given to equalizing access, not only to what is now known as higher education but also to other forms of education and training that may be appropriate to the differing needs of our young people." The positions above are somewhat contradictory, but that is probably the necessary fate of any effort to apply reliable economic indicators to the shifting problems and possibilities of American higher education today.

The authors have set forth five possible routes for enlarging higher educational opportunity and have indicated an expansion of existing financial aid policies as representing the best economic solution available. The authors assume that financial aid grants for those in the top half of the ability distribution will substantially increase the number of lower income students seeking to enroll. That assumption may be correct, but I find it to be in striking contrast to the reality of rising enrollment statistics in recent years. The greatest enrollment increases in higher education have been in two-year public community colleges, where a disproportionate number of lower income and lower ability students are present. The authors assume that the cost of educating additional students from low income families would be similar to costs for other population groups. Colleges and universities that have recruited students from disadvantaged backgrounds have discovered that the cost is substantially higher to educate such students because the level of their preparation differs from that of other groups and requires that compensatory programs be provided.

Another quotation from the background paper indicates some misunderstanding about possible consequences of increasing the proportion of qualified enrollments from low income families: "Inasmuch as the added students would have an average ability exceeding that of present two-year students, the potential benefits for the added students could be expected to exceed the potential benefits for presently enrolled students." This comment suggests that the authors are totally unaware of what has been occurring over the last decade in the restructuring of American higher educational opportunity. In light of the excellent economic returns from high school and baccalaureate experience, the two-year college is viewed as a less desirable economic investment. The two-year college is here viewed as an institution that will reduce the economic return of higher educational degrees and not as a new form of education "that may be appropriate to the differing needs of our young people."

It is not clear whether the authors exclude the community college from higher education as a matter of preference or whether the exclusion is an automatic consequence of the differing rates of economic return from different forms of higher education investment. In any case, they cling to the high school plus baccalaureate combination because it has in the past provided the highest rate of economic return. Given the substantial criticisms of that model as expressed in the past half-dozen years, the older rate of economic return might well not continue against massive consumer disaffection. Perhaps some new ways of measuring economic returns are required, as has been suggested for the modern measurement of gross national product; for example, one suggestion is to incorporate the annual cost of pollution in measuring economic advance, with a deduction made for the ultimate cost of the pollution created. A similar device might be applied in measuring rates of return from various forms of higher education. The rate of economic return from investment in a comprehensive two-year public college in an urban area would be substantial, I judge, if appropriate allowance were made for the cost of other alternative social and educational policies. The presence of the two-year public college permits increasing minority enrollments rapidly, particularly in the city. Moreover, diversified program offerings provide greater possibilities for success for the individual. In this perspective, the rate of return to the individual who completes two years of a community college might well be less than 10 percent, but the social, political, and economic return to the entire community is substantial and irreplaceable.

The views of Mr. Hansen and Mr. Witmer assume a re-creation of higher educational models that are now twenty years out of date.

Given the shortage of resources upon us, I do not share their enthusiam for the regeneration of older practice.

Higher education is one vital form of public and private investment, but there are other substantial claims on the total pool of capital in American society. Looking ahead, one may conceive of a relative decline in the economic return from higher education and relative increases in other forms of investment, such as pollution control, recreation, new governmental forms for the urban areas, and so on. Moreover, the taxpayer resistance to constantly rising educational expenditures being evidenced may have a substantial impact on the economic organization of American colleges and universities in the years ahead. Discussion of deferred loan plans in both the public and private sectors of American colleges during 1971 is a clear recognition of this fact.

The Yale Plan is designed to ensure alumni support by amortizing the actual cost of higher education over a long period of time. The commitment of the individual is achieved through a contractual relationship that makes repayment for higher educational benefit a high priority charge against the future income of the person receiving the benefit. This plan is a step away from the voluntary, charitable, personal loyalty history of college giving and is a recognition that the real cost of higher education must be met out of a lifetime of earnings rather than as fees at the admissions gate.

In the public sector, Governor John Gilligan of Ohio has attempted to combine the idea of social benefit from public investment in higher education with individual responsibility for the personal benefits that also derive from higher education. The Yale Plan and the Ohio Plan are two sides of a single thrust to meet rising costs in public and private colleges and universities. In both cases the social benefits of higher education are acknowledged through the postponement of the payment of the full cost for the service. Under the Yale Plan the individual defers repayment until after college with the specific amount determined by his or her earning power. In the Ohio proposal, the taxpayer advances funds for higher education that are later to be repaid at fixed rates following completion of the degree. These two suggestions, if adopted on a wide scale in future years, would substantially affect the rate of economic return from higher education.

KENNETH KENISTON and MARK GERZON

Human and Social Benefits

ONE COMMON AMERICAN WAY TO JUSTIFY A CONTROVERSIAL
enterprise is to argue that it makes or saves money. Concepts like
"worth" or "benefit" are quickly translated into quantities and dollar
signs. When the value of an enterprise is questioned—be it the war
in Indochina or higher education—its defenders pull out their slide
rules and begin cost-benefit calculations. Effectiveness in warfare is
commonly measured in terms of body counts, sorties flown, kill ratios,
"bang-per-buck," bombs dropped, cost-per-casualty, or whatever else
can be counted. Similarly, the benefits of higher education are considered to be such gains as lifetime income increments to the individual, contribution to the percentage rate of increase in the GNP,
or—if all else fails—increases in the number of hours spent "in the
presence of culture."[1] The implicit and unchallenged assumption
throughout these calculations is: The more the better.

In an early proposal for the 1971 Council Annual Meeting, "pecuniary benefits" were considered first. Paralleling pecuniary benefits,
a category labeled "nonpecuniary benefits" was established, and we
were asked to address this subject. The very term "nonpecuniary"
suggested that we were being asked to occupy a wastebasket category,
rather like those millions of Americans called "nonwhite." The value
of more money is debated by very few Americans: pecuniary benefits
therefore seem clear, clean, and conveniently all-inclusive. Lest we
might rely too much on intangible benefits, our instructions directed
us to "quantify" whenever possible. After all, no one enjoys vague,
subjective, and imprecise discussions. But if we could demonstrate
that higher education produced *measurable* nonpecuniary benefits,

---

1. Bernard Berelson, "In the Presence of Culture," *Public Opinion Quarterly,*
Spring 1968, pp. 1–12.

We are especially indebted to Louis Hausman, of the American Council on
Education, for his bibliographical assistance and editorial comments.

then these benefits would at least possess the legitimacy of quantification, though they would not be quite as solid as money.

Since the assumption is widespread that pecuniary benefits are in
some ultimate sense more "real" than less "tangible" human and
social benefits, we begin this discussion of human and social benefits
by considering two different concepts of benefit and the two distinct
components of higher education to which they correspond. We next
turn to an examination of empirical studies of the effects of college
attendance on students. Finally, we argue that the human and social
effects of higher education constitute benefits and, increasingly, prerequisites for the maintenance of a society that is not only technological and prosperous, but also open, pluralistic, and democratic.

Two Concepts of Benefit, of Education, and of Rationality

How we judge the benefits of higher education obviously depends
on how we define "benefit" in the first place, and our definition of
benefit in turn rests on usually unspoken assumptions about what is
most real and important. Much recent discussion of the costs, benefits,
and effectiveness of higher education rests primarily on pecuniary or
economic assumptions. But it has turned out to be poor rhetorical
strategy to put all of one's eggs into the pecuniary basket, however
solid it may initially have seemed. For example, if we start discount-
ing money invested in higher education, the pecuniary benefits of
higher education to the individual's lifetime earnings begin to vanish.[2]
And as for higher education's influence on economic productivity and
GNP, a clear cause-effect relationship is difficult to demonstrate.[3]
Since the pecuniary defense of higher education appears to be slightly
shaky, most defenses of higher education generally include some concept of "nonpecuniary benefits"—even though they seem less tangible
than money.

2. James N. Morgan and David H. Martin, "Income and Education," *Quarterly
Journal of Economics*, August 1963, pp. 423–37; Burkhard Strumpel, "Higher Education and Economic Behavior," in *A Degree and What Else? A Review of the Cor-
relates and Consequences of a College Education*, ed. Stephen Withey et al. (Draft
prepared for Carnegie Commission on Higher Education, pp. 96–143; New York:
McGraw-Hill Book Co., forthcoming). Strumpel notes that "higher education as an
investment, at least in the United States, does not match up to widespread, mostly
exaggerated notions about its profitability in dollar terms" (p. 105).

3. Walter McKibben, "The Benefits and Burdens of Higher Education" (Draft
prepared for Carnegie Commission on Higher Education, June 1970). McKibben's
intention is to demonstrate the indirect effects of education on GNP, but his argument is necessarily inferential.

But to make pecuniary benefits primary, including human and social benefits only as a kind of dubious "fall-back" position, reflects the prevalent assumption that what is real and important is what is measurable—preferably in dollars and cents. To challenge this assumption requires us to contrast two distinct conceptions of cost and benefit, two components of education, and two definitions of the rational assessment of effectiveness.

Milton Friedman exemplifies the narrowest form of pecuniary analysis when he insists that inasmuch as the individual is the primary beneficiary of higher education, he should be its purchaser.[4] Friedman explicitly derides discussions of the nonquantitative benefits of higher education, contending that "these are always vague and general, and always selective in that negative external effects are never mentioned." He adds parenthetically that campus demonstrations "suggest that there may be negative as well as positive training for 'citizenship.'" And he summarily dismisses all analysis of the nonpecuniary benefits of higher education until these are systematically identified "in such a way as to permit even a rough estimate of their quantitative importance"—ideally, in terms of dollars and cents. The logic of Friedman's argument is clear: if a benefit cannot be measured in pecuniary or quantitative terms, it is "vague and general," and a discussion of it does not belong in a "rational" consideration of the benefits of higher education.

It is ironic that not only Friedman's supporters, but also many of his critics have accepted his basic assumptions. Thus McKibben, in a tightly reasoned critique of Friedman's position,[5] argues that even after one has accounted for all of the known determinants of increases in the American GNP, a significant increase remains that can be attributed only to the influence of higher education. This remainder is quantifiable, and therefore permits us to calculate the pecuniary value of higher education to society as a whole. McKibben concludes that since society as a whole benefits economically from higher education, it should share the costs of higher education with the individual student.

Such a counterargument is a useful corrective to Friedman's definition of pecuniary benefits as exclusively individual benefits. But by accepting a monetary definition of "benefit," the counterargument risks winning a battle at the expense of losing the war. For if the "real" benefits of higher education are financial, higher education

---

4. Friedman, "The Higher Schooling in America," *Public Interest*, Spring 1968, pp. 108–12.
   5. McKibben, "Benefits and Burdens of Higher Education."

should be subjected to a narrowly defined cost-efficiency scrutiny that would, we believe, destroy much of what is valuable in it. To place primary emphasis on the monetary benefits of higher education does violence to the motives and hopes with which most students enter college, to the central effects of higher education, and to its most important benefits to the individual and society.

In a recent discussion of definitions of the costs and benefits of social policies, the British philosopher Stuart Hampshire has contrasted a Benthamite (or "technist") conception of rationality with a looser and broader conception.[6] Discussions based on the technist conception ultimately strive for complex equations in which factors that cannot be quantified are deemed unreal, "subjective," and irrelevant—or simply ignored. The broader concept of rationality, in contrast, emphasizes those individual and social characteristics that do not readily lend themselves to quantification: human values, feelings, desires, loyalties, and motives; social cohesion, cooperation, and morale; political pluralism, tolerance, democracy, and diversity; and so on. Seen from this perspective, a calculus limited to dollars or to quantified social indicators is not rationality at all, but a constricted analysis which achieves rigor at the expense of truth.[7]

These two concepts of rationality are related to two different kinds of education. Most discussions of the costs and benefits of higher education consider higher education as one definable experience, and treat the educated as a unitary group. But, in fact, there are as many kinds of higher education as there are student-institution pairs: 8,000,000 students times 2,500 institutions equals approximately 20 billion different potential educational experiences in America today. For our purposes here, however, these educational experiences can be classified as containing two distinct and sometimes opposing components which we will call *technical* and *critical* education.[8]

Two Components of Education

The *technical component* of education focuses primarily on preparing students to become economically productive citizens by training them for established occupational roles in technological, administrative, or industrial enterprises. Its aim is to transmit a body of

6. Hampshire, "The Autobiography of Bertrand Russell, Vol. III," *New York Review of Books,* Oct. 8, 1970, pp. 3–8.

7. For a critique of the application of narrowly pecuniary cost-benefit analyses to higher education, see Michael W. Miles, *The Radical Probe* (New York: Atheneum Publishers, 1971).

8. These two ideal types are further explicated in Mark Gerzon, "The Children's Revolution" (MS).

existing knowledge in order to enable its recipients to apply it productively to a defined range of technical problems. It can appropriately be termed professional "socialization," for it attempts to impart to students the formal competences required for a specific occupational role, along with the informal skills needed for attaining success in that role. Such education logically assesses its own effectiveness in terms of the number of its students who accede to positions of wealth and eminence as defined by quantifiable indices of income, rank, number of subordinates, pages published, and so on. Technical education exists at all degree levels, and throughout all fields of education.[9]

The *critical component* of education, in contrast, attempts to expose students to multiple and conflicting perspectives on themselves and their society in order to test and challenge their previously unexamined assumptions. It strives to create conditions which stimulate students' intellectual, moral, and emotional growth, so that they may ground their skills in a more mature, humane framework of values. Critical education deliberately tries to stimulate the student to reformulate his goals, his cognitive map of the world, the *way* he thinks, and his view of his role in society. Thus the more successful critical education is, the more difficult that success is to measure, for its aim is the transformation of persons and of the purposes to which they devote their knowledge.

In practice, of course, no individual's education is either totally technical or totally critical. Even in those rare institutions that concentrate exclusively on high-level technical training, students are likely to ask questions of themselves, others, and their society. And conversely, no matter how emphatically an institution encourages a critical reexamination of self and society, all American colleges and universities also attempt to teach students defined skills, methods, and knowledge. A totally technical education would produce unreflective automatons incapable of even cooperating with their colleagues. A totally critical education would produce students with many high-

9. Throughout this paper, we take largely for granted the very real benefits to the individual and society of the technical aspects of higher education. Quite apart from its measurable pecuniary benefits, a technical education, by providing the individual with extremely high level skills, makes it possible for him to take a more responsible job, to do more complex work, to work with less supervision, and so on. Strumpel, cited above, demonstrates that the more highly educated are more likely to show job stability, less likely to lose work time, more likely to have long vacations, more likely to seek "meaningful, interesting activity" as contrasted with "security," more likely to find their work enjoyable, and the like. Virtually every direct and indirect indicator of job satisfaction and work morale favors the college-educated. Here, however, our primary objective is to emphasize the effects that are more closely related to that kind of education which promotes critical abilities.

minded purposes but no competence with which to achieve them. In fact, the real experience of real students always falls along a continuum between these two poles. But any consideration of the consequences of higher education requires that we distinguish between the relative impact of the technical and critical components of education, for their consequences are not only different but in some cases opposite as well, and so are the standards by which they should be measured.

This point may be illustrated by two students, both capable college graduates with outstanding training in business administration and law. The first student, encouraged by his primarily technical education, accepts a job offer from a major consulting firm which promises the highest starting income and the fastest promotions. His personal earnings and spendings increase enormously, and his outstanding work increases the earnings of his firm as well. The second student, equally capable in the field, is led by a more critical educational experience to choose a different path. Seeking to use his skills for the purpose of demilitarizing the American economy, he joins a small, shoestring operation of young businessmen and lawyers who are trying to demonstrate that a changeover to nonmilitary production is economically feasible and politically urgent. His personal income is low, and his group also earns little. Even if his efforts are successful, the GNP will at best remain roughly the same. The first student's education, therefore, is a tremendous cost-benefit success, whereas the second's is a dismal failure. But given a broader definition of benefit, we would judge the second student's behavior rational and the effects on him of higher education highly beneficial.

Danger of Stressing Pecuniary Benefits

In general, the more the critical component is stressed in higher education, the easier it will be to demonstrate that, by a technist definition of rationality, it is ridden with gross cost inefficiencies and counterproductivities. For example, a liberal arts education, as compared with an education in engineering or industrial management, doubtless tends to reduce individual income increments. Judged from this perspective, many other kinds of higher education also have a negative effect upon the individual's motivation or ability to increase his income. Critical education in any field, but particularly in such disciplines as sociology, philosophy, political science, and history, often creates dissenters who not only earn little themselves, but espouse social and political ideas that would divert resources away from improvement of education's cost-benefit appearance as judged by technist criteria. From amongst a few economists and sociologists, one even hears talk of placing upper limits on profits, of nationalizing sectors of the economy, of diverting productive resources to improve the quality of human and social life, and of zero economic growth as an ultimate (if distant) goal.

By a pecuniary definition of benefit, we would have to conclude that any form of education which encourages such talk is extremely costly, and that it should be phased out as quickly as possible. Rigorous application of pecuniary criteria to the cost-effectiveness of higher education logically entails the systematic elimination of all but the most narrowly technical education. Liberal arts colleges would be the first to go; departments which produce students with a non- or anti-pecuniary mentality would follow soon after; and the final "rational" solution would be a system of totally technical manpower training and "channeling," geared solely to preparing students to fit into the most remunerative occupations or those which contribute most to increasing the worth of the GNP.

Finally, acceptance of the pecuniary concept of "benefit" neatly sidesteps and avoids all of the issues that are most controversial about higher education today. Public anxieties about higher education have very little to do with its influence on lifetime earnings or gross national product, but very much to do with its effects on the outlook, consciousness, and behavior of those who attend colleges and universities.[10] Topics like campus unrest, the "counterculture," the life styles, language, and dress of students, their sexual behavior, their use of drugs not used by most adults, and their disaffection from American society—these are at the heart of the controversy over the benefits of higher education. The technist discussion of higher education simply evades these issues by derogating them as vague, general, and unquantifiable.

In criticizing the pecuniary definition of "benefit" and the technist concept of rationality that underlies it, we are not deprecating the possible contribution of higher education to the individual's lifetime earnings or to increases in the gross national product. A decent standard of living for the individual and rising productivity for the nation as a whole are important goals, although not so important as to override all other considerations. And in stressing the importance of the critical component in higher education, we assume the value and

10. For a discussion of public anxieties on higher education and the facts, see Kenneth Keniston and Michael Lerner, "Campus Characteristics and Campus Unrest," *Annals of the American Academy of Political and Social Science*, May 1971, pp. 39–53.

necessity of a technical component as well. Nor do we object to efforts to assess and improve the effectiveness of higher education, provided effects other than financial reward are included in the assessment. Our purpose is to demonstrate that it is arbitrary to relegate "nonpecuniary" considerations to the realm of the "vague and subjective," and thus to judge higher education solely or primarily in economic terms. If higher education increases individual earnings or contributes to the growth of GNP, so much the better. But these are its added justifications—frosting on the higher educational cake—and not its main benefits.

THE EFFECTS OF HIGHER EDUCATION

When we turn from general considerations to a review of the current knowledge about the human and social effects of higher education, we immediately confront major methodological problems.[11] It is easy enough to demonstrate that college graduates differ in myriad ways from those who did not attend college. Graduates have different patterns of consumption, recreational and voting behavior, group involvement, health care use, media usage, exposure to "culture," and so on. But such findings are almost always correlational, and they therefore do not establish a *causal* relationship between college attendance and the subsequent characteristics of college graduates.

Four Problems in Assessing Effects

At least four major problems stand in the way of assuming that observed differences between graduates and *nongraduates* can be causally attributed to higher education. First, college graduates as a group share a number of other characteristics apart from attendance at college.[12] Each of these *other* characteristics of the college-educated may have important and truly causal relationships to the factors that

11. The most comprehensive discussion of the methodological problems involved in studying the effects of higher education is found in Kenneth A. Feldman and Theodore M. Newcomb, *The Impact of College on Students* (San Francisco: Jossey-Bass, Inc., 1969), especially chap. 3, "Problems of Interpretation." See also Nevitt Sanford, ed., *The American College: A Psychological and Social Interpretation of the Higher Learning* (New York: Wiley & Sons, 1962), passim; and Stephen Withey, "Problems in Assessing Impact," in *A Degree and What Else?*, ed. Withey et al., pp. 1–22.

12. For a review of studies of the "economic behavior" of college graduates, see Strumpel, "Higher Education and Economic Behavior"; on the life styles of college graduates, see Stephen Withey, "Some Effects of Life Style," in *A Degree and What Else?*, ed. Withey et al., pp. 141–65; on usage of mass media, see Berelson, "In the Presence of Culture," and John P. Robinson, "Mass Media Usage by the College Graduate," in *A Degree and What Else?*, pp. 166–91.

empirically differentiate them from the non-college-educated.[13] But almost all studies simply compare the "college" population with the "noncollege" population;[14] and many studies define the "college" population so that it includes everyone with more than twelve years of education—dropouts from two-year community colleges along with Ph.D.'s from Cal Tech.[15]

A second methodological problem inheres because college attenders are demonstrably different from nonattenders even *before* they enter college.[16] When we further note that, compared to nonattenders of

13. We will later summarize studies which demonstrate that a college education tends to have a "liberalizing" effect. But if high income, managerial position, and suburban residence all independently have a conservatizing effect, these latter characteristics may more than cancel out the effect of the college experience itself. The outlooks of college graduates as a group would then be found to be more conservative than those of non-college-attenders, but this fact would obscure the real impact of higher education. In fact, many studies have shown that where conservatism is indexed by such behaviors as voting Republican, college graduates tend to be more conservative in political behavior than non-college-graduates. Other studies show that when conservatism is measured by such behaviors as rejection of civil-libertarian attitudes, college graduates tend to be less conservative. See Elizabeth Keogh Taylor and Arthur C. Wolf, "Political Behavior," in *A Degree and What Else?*, ed. Withey et al., pp. 192–218.

Our explanation of the conservatism of college graduates on some issues involves a consideration of two factors: (1) other characteristics associated with college attendance (e.g., professional-managerial occupations) tend to exert an independent conservatizing effect; (2) the nature and impact of college attendance has changed in recent decades toward an increasingly "critical" emphasis (see below). We therefore anticipate that in the years to come the conservatism of college graduates will diminish as the liberalizing effects of critical education make themselves felt with new cohorts of college graduates. For a study which demonstrates the differential impact of more and less selective colleges on attitudes toward the war in Vietnam, see Philip E. Converse and Howard Schuman, " 'Silent Majorities' and the Vietnam War," *Scientific American*, June 1970, pp. 17–25.

14. See, e.g., most of the studies referred to in Withey et al., *A Degree and What Else?*

15. Studies that consider the duration of college attendance and the selectivity of quality of the college attended generally show that the effects of higher education are increased both by prolongation of attendance and by attendance at the more selective institutions. See, e.g., James W. Trent and Leland Medsker, *Beyond High School: A Psychosociological Study of 10,000 High School Graduates* (San Francisco: Jossey-Bass, Inc., 1968), especially chap. 6, "Factors Related to Persistence in College."

16. As a group, future college attenders get better grades in secondary school, perform better on aptitude tests, have a more "intellectual" outlook, come from more prosperous, more middle-class families, and tend to share the sociopolitical outlooks of their relatively more affluent parents. Future college attenders are also taller, stronger, and in better physical and mental health. Thus even if college itself has no effects, college attenders as adults should continue to differ from nonattenders in all the ways in which they differed before entering college. See, e.g., Jo Anne Coble, "Who Goes to College?", in *A Degree and What Else?*, ed. Withey et al., pp. 23–42; Feldman and Newcomb, *The Impact of College on Students;* and Elizabeth Douvan and Carol Kaye, "Motivational Factors in College Entrance," in *The American College*, ed. Sanford, pp. 199–224.

equal ability and background, college attenders possess a distinctive set of psychological characteristics and motivations,[17] the problem of attributing differences between graduates and nongraduates to the effects of college becomes even more complicated. Yet few studies have held the precollege characteristics of college attenders and non-attenders constant in order to focus on the independent effects of college attendance.[18]

A third difficulty in examining the impact of the college experience lies in the vagueness of the concept of "the college experience." We have argued that college experiences can be placed along a continuum that runs from "critical" to "technical" education. Other investigators have proposed other ways of categorizing educational climates.[19] But virtually all researchers agree that different kinds of colleges may have different effects on students. Studies that merely contrast graduates with nongraduates inevitably obscure these effects, and may therefore be misleading.[20] Yet once again, research that examines college characteristics as a separate variable is still in its infancy.[21]

Perhaps the most intractable methodological problem springs from the *interaction* between freshman characteristics and college characteristics.[22] If all students were assigned at random to all colleges, we could clearly attribute differences in the graduates of each college to the special characteristics of that college. But in fact, of course, students apply selectively to colleges; they are further selected by college admission offices. What complicates research is that these freshman characteristics tend to be highly congruent with the char-

17. See Trent and Medsker, *Beyond High School*, especially chap. 4, "Patterns of Employment."
18. *Beyond High School* is the most notable exception.
19. See C. R. Pace, "Perspectives on the Student and His College," in *The College and the Student*, ed. L. E. Dennis and J. F. Kauffman (Washington: American Council on Education, 1966), pp. 76–100; George G. Stern, "Myth and Reality in the American College," *AAUP Bulletin*, December 1966, pp. 408–14.
20. For example, if a "technical" education tends to consolidate acceptance of the social-psychological status quo, and if "critical" education tends to upset this acceptance, any study that lumps together students with a predominantly technical education and those with a predominantly critical education will result in findings in which equal changes in opposite directions are canceled out, supporting the erroneous conclusion that college has no impact whatsoever on acceptance of the status quo.
21. The most sophisticated research in this area is currently being done by Alexander W. Astin and his associates in the Office of Research, American Council on Education.
22. See George G. Stern, "Student Ecology and the College Environment," *Journal of Medical Education*, February 1965, pp. 132–54; Feldman and Newcomb, *The Impact of College on Students*, pp. 132–40. What Feldman and Newcomb call the "accentuation" effect springs largely from this correlation between initial freshmen characteristics and the characteristics of the college attended or the subgroups chosen by the student within the college.

acteristics of the colleges they choose to attend. Students seeking vocational training generally attend colleges that offer a predominantly
technical education; students with more intellectual and developmental goals usually attend colleges that offer more critical education.
This correlation between freshman characteristics and college characteristics creates complicated chicken-egg problems in the study of
college impact. Yet once again, studies which compare matched
groups of college attenders and nonattenders, while at the same time
studying the interaction between freshman characteristics and college
characteristics, simply do not exist.[23]

Such methodological problems have made it astonishingly difficult
to demonstrate unequivocally that colleges have had *any* effect on
students. For example, college attenders are more likely to go to
concerts and museums than nonattenders.[24] But from this fact alone
we do not know whether such cultural activities spring from higher
income of college graduates or the pressures of professional and
managerial suburban life, whether they result from the precollege
characteristics of the college attenders, whether there are differences
amongst colleges in their impact upon cultural activities, or some
combination of factors. The interested reader is referred to Withey's
excellent summary of such studies, *A Degree and What Else?*, for a
comprehensive and critical review of college and noncollege differences. In the discussion that follows, however, we shall not consider
these studies, since they almost uniformly fail to demonstrate that the
differences observed are causally related to college attendance.

Impact of College on Students

We will instead rely on the more rigorous research that has examined the impact of the college experience by studying changes in
students as they progress through college or as they appear in comparison with matched groups of non-college-attenders. In 1957, Philip
E. Jacob, in a comprehensive review of all studies on value and attitude change in college,[25] reported that most colleges did little more
than confirm the preexisting characteristics of their students. Jacob

23. Trent and Medsker, *Beyond High School*, compared matched attenders and
nonattenders, but did not study the effects of college characteristics. Astin and his
colleagues are currently studying the interaction between freshman characteristics
and college characteristics, but have no control group of nonattenders; for a preliminary report of findings, see Alexander W. Astin, "College Impact on Student
Attitudes and Behavior" (Paper presented at the American Association for the Advancement of Science, Chicago, 1970).

24. See Berelson, "In the Presence of Culture," and Robinson, "Mass Media
Usage by College Graduates."

25. Jacob, *Changing Values in College: An Exploratory Study of the Impact of
College Teaching* (New York: Harper & Bros., 1957).

in effect concluded that the attitude changes induced in college were ephemeral, and that most of the apparent "effects" of college attendance could be accounted for by the single principle of the reinforcement of preexisting student characteristics. For example, students who attend colleges that place great stress on social life tend to be more socially oriented to begin with; and after four years of college, these initial differences have merely been accentuated; intellectual students who attend highly selective colleges become even more intellectual during the course of college, and so on.

Jacob did note, however, one major exception to his otherwise pessimistic conclusions. He commented on the existence of a few "high potency" colleges (mostly small liberal arts colleges) which appeared to have a more "liberalizing" effect upon their students. Most of the research conducted since Jacob's review has focused on and confirmed the existence of such liberalizing effects.

Undoubtedly the most comprehensive single study conducted in the last decade is Trent and Medsker's study of 10,000 high school graduates. Their large sample allowed them to compare high school graduates of equal ability and social class who did and did not attend college. They found that, with ability and socioeconomic status held constant, college tends to have important liberalizing or "developmental" effects on students:

> What most distinguished the "experimental" group of college persisters from the "control" groups of withdrawals and especially nonattenders was the development of autonomy. Definitely there was a strong relationship between entrance to and length of stay in college and the growth of open-minded, flexible, and autonomous disposition, as measured by two scales designed to assess these traits. The fact that the carefully classified college withdrawals were more like the nonattenders than the persisters in their amount of manifest change indicates that the type of personality development measured continues to be associated with persistence in college beyond the early years. This held regardless of level of ability or socioeconomic status. . . . there was a tendency for the experience of full-time employment and particularly early ·marriage combined with full-time homemaking to be associated with a constriction of flexibility and autonomy. Complexity scores of the full-time employed and early married indicated an even greater tendency toward constriction in intellectual curiosity, interest in new experiences, and tolerance for ambiguity.[26]

Two more recent reviews of research on the impact of college have generalized the results of Trent and Medsker. Feldman and

26. Trent and Medsker, *Beyond High School*, pp. 176–77.

Newcomb, who in 1969 surveyed the entire literature on college effects, conclude:

> Declining "authoritarianism," dogmatism, and prejudice, together with decreasingly conservative attitudes toward public issues and growing sensitivity to aesthetic experiences, are particularly prominent forms of change—as inferred from freshman-senior differences. These add up to something like increasing openness to multiple aspects of the contemporary world, paralleling wider ranges of contact and experience. Somewhat less consistently, but nevertheless evident, are increasing intellectual interests and capacities, and declining commitment to religion, especially in its more orthodox forms. Certain kinds of personal changes—particularly toward greater independence, self-confidence, and readiness to express impulses—are the rule rather than the exception.[27]

In an even more recent survey, in 1971, Gerald Gurin comments:

> most studies show that students going through college increase their interest in aesthetic and cultural values, decrease their adherence to traditional religion and other traditional values, become more relativistic and less moralistic in their ethical judgments, take an increasingly liberal rather than conservative position on political and socio-economic issues, and become more "openminded" as measured by scores on authoritarianism, dogmatism, ethnocentrism and prejudice.
>
> ...on issues of liberalism, tolerance, openmindedness, and rationality, there is clear evidence of freshman to senior change, that this change is greater than it is for noncollege populations, that the change persists into the post-college years. This liberalization seems to reflect an impact of college generally, although it is also differentially affected by different colleges, and by different experiences within a college.

We earlier noted that studies which do not differentiate between the impacts of different educational environments are likely to obscure the different effects of technical and critical education. Gurin approaches this issue indirectly by commenting upon the differences between students who have a vocational orientation and those who do not. Admitting the paucity of data, he suggests that:

> students with a dominantly "vocational" orientation may change less than those of other orientations; in a sense, they may be less responsive to value and ideological issues not directly relevant to their vocational interest.[28]

27. Feldman and Newcomb, *The Impact of College on Students,* p. 326.
28. Gurin, "Impact During College," in *A Degree and What Else?,* ed. Withey et al., pp. 47–48, 93, 89.

Since other research shows that vocationally oriented students usually attend colleges that provide a more "technical" education, Gurin's observation supports our general thesis concerning the differential impact of technical and critical education.

Socialization versus Development

As Gurin notes, virtually the entire literature on the impact of the college experience has been organized around the single concept of "socialization"; most researchers have tended to interpret the college experience as an exercise in mass attitude change toward the dominant norms expressed within the college. Almost entirely neglected until recently have been all those other effects not so readily captured with the concept of socialization—effects which involve not merely attitude changes in response to group and institutional pressures, but truly "developmental" changes in the complexity, differentiation, and integration of cognitive, affective, and ethical aspects of the individual's personality.

This continuing emphasis on "socialization" is especially unfortunate since most of the recent research lends itself more readily to a developmental interpretation. To be sure, as Feldman and Newcomb demonstrate, some studies still support Jacobs' conclusion that college attendance accentuates the preexisting characteristics of those who attend college. But crosscutting and at times opposing this "accentuation effect" are those more general impacts commented on by Trent and Medsker, Newcomb and Feldman, and Gurin. We will term these other effects *liberalization*. By "liberalization" we do not mean the adoption of any particular set of sociopolitical dogmas or attitudes, but rather a more general reorganization of outlook, mind-set, and world view. We believe these effects can be interpreted only as a consequence of *developmental changes* during the college years, that is, of progressive and largely irreversible differentiations and integrations at a higher level of the emotional, intellectual, and moral components of the personality. And we consider these changes the predictable consequences of a *critical education,* as we earlier defined it. Only in this fashion can we make sense of the finding that college attendance yields demonstrable increases in autonomy, open-mindedness, cognitive relativism, independence of moral judgments, along with decreases in authoritarianism, dogmatism, ethnocentrism, prejudice, and adherence to traditional values.

The works of William Perry, Lawrence Kohlberg, and Nevitt Sanford provide at least the beginning of a theoretical framework within which the observed "liberalizing" effects of the college experience may be understood. Perry posits a sequence of intellectual and ethical development during the college years which closely parallels the more quantitative research we have summarized above. In Perry's view,[29] the student starts in high school or college from a stage of *dualism*— from the conviction that all questions have correct or incorrect, true or false, answers. But if confronted in college with classmates and professors who sincerely hold views other than his own, the student becomes aware of *multiplicity*—aware of a diversity of opinions, of areas of uncertainty, and of legitimate disagreements about crucial intellectual and ethical questions. If his confrontation with alternate points of view persists, he then moves to a stage of *relativism,* wherein he perceives knowledge and values as contextual and perspectival. Beyond this basically relativistic framework, Perry argues, it is possible to move to still higher stages of *commitment within relativism,* wherein the student accepts the responsibility for the affirmation of intellectual and ethical commitments *within* an epistemologically relativistic universe. This process of intellectual and ethical development in the college years clearly corresponds closely to some of the observed liberalizing impacts of college, for example, increasing relativization of knowledge, declines in dogmatism, greater open-mindedness, and so on.

Lawrence Kohlberg's theory of the development of moral reasoning in adolescence and early adulthood[30] provides a complementary way of understanding the liberalizing effects of higher education. Kohlberg asserts the child passes from an initially *premoral* stage of reasoning about moral issues to a stage of *conventional* moral reasoning, characterized by adherence to conventional social role expectations and to the immutable validity of existing community standards. During and after adolescence, however, he may move to a *postconventional* level of moral reasoning, which involves greater personal responsibility for moral judgments, now made either on the basis of considerations of the long-range good of the community or on the basis of more general, universalistic principles. This trajectory of moral development again overlaps with empirical findings on college impact, especially as these involve increasing independence of moral judgments, greater autonomy, decreased conventionality, and lessened adherence to traditional values.

29. William G. Perry, Jr., *Forms of Intellectual and Ethical Development in the College Years* (New York: Holt, Rinehart & Winston, 1970) .
30. Kohlberg, "State and Sequence: The Cognitive-Developmental Approach to Socialization," in *Handbook of Socialization Theory and Research,* ed. David A. Goslin (Chicago: Rand McNally, 1969) , pp. 347–48; Kohlberg, "The Child as Moral Philosopher," *Psychology Today,* September 1968, pp. 25–30.

In a number of recent works, Nevitt Sanford and Joseph Katz[31] have begun to develop a theory that stresses affective and ego development during the college years. In simplified summary, they emphasize such personality changes as the *freeing of impulse*, increasing *differentiation and integration of the ego* and the growth of *autonomy* as potential developmental effects of the college experience. These changes are seen not as transformations of beliefs and values, but as more basic reorganizations of personality. The correspondence between their theoretical account and empirical findings on college effects is once again a close one: recall the findings of increased flexibility, autonomy, independence, readiness to express impulses, and so on.

The work of Perry, Kohlberg, Sanford, and Katz indicates that the liberalizing effects of higher education cannot be adequately understood simply as "attitude changes" induced by peer pressure, social conformity, and professorial indoctrination, but must be seen as the reflections of developmental changes in personality structure and functioning. In general, developmental changes are likely to be irreversible, a fact that is consistent with the finding that the changes we group together under the concept of "liberalization" tend to persist long after college and to be relatively independent of the milieu in which the individual later finds himself.

The Changing Effects of College Education

Finally, our reading of the research on the influence of college leads us to hypothesize that changes in American society and American higher education have notably increased the overall liberalizing impact of the college experience during recent decades. Empirical data show that, other things equal, older college graduates tend to be less liberal than younger college graduates in almost every area measured. This lesser liberalism seems not to be the simple result of aging or true generational differences, but at least partly of different kinds of education received by college students in the past. Similarly,

31. Sanford, "Developmental Status of the Entering Freshman," in *The American College*, pp. 253–82; Sanford, "The Freeing and Acting Out of Impulse in Late Adolescence," in *The Study of Lives*, ed. Robert W. White (New York: Atherton Press, 1963), pp. 4–39; Katz, "Four Years of Growth, Conflict and Compliance," in *No Time for Youth*, ed. Joseph Katz et al. (San Francisco: Jossey-Bass, Inc., 1968), pp. 3–73. See also Marjorie M. Lozoff, "Autonomy and Feminine Role," in *College Influences on the Development of Female Undergraduates*, by Carole A. Leland and Marjorie M. Lozoff (Palo Alto, Calif.: Stanford University, Institute for the Study of Human Problems, 1969), pp. 28–100; Jane Loevinger, "The Meaning and Measurement of Ego Development," *American Psychologist*, 21 (1966): 195–206.

a recent comprehensive review of studies of authoritarianism demonstrates a slow but steady decline in authoritarianism scores amongst college students over the past decade.[32] In part, these changes doubtless reflect the growing liberalization of the cultural climate in America. But we believe that they are also related to specific, though subtle, changes in the educational experience, which at any given college has usually become less technical and more critical in recent decades.

William Perry's work suggests one reason for the apparent increase in the liberalizing effects of college. Perry argues that a prime catalyst for the development of a relativistic and postrelativistic orientation is confrontation with multiple perspectives on truth and morality. He examined Harvard College examination questions in the years between 1900 and 1960, rating them according to whether or not an adequate answer required the consideration of two or more frames of reference. He found that a perspectival outlook was required by less than 10 percent of all examinations in 1900, but by about 50 percent of examinations in the same departments in 1950–60. Taking into account shifting patterns of course enrollment and curriculum, Perry estimates an overall jump from 10 percent to 75–80 percent in questions demanding a relativistic outlook from 1900 to 1960.[33] Comparable changes have occurred, we believe, at most other colleges, although at different rates.

The inference is obvious: at the turn of the century, education was far more likely to involve only the "technical" mastery of a body of knowledge, be it the classics of the Western tradition or the principles of scientific agronomy; today, it is more likely to require the "critical" capacity to compare many perspectives on truth and morality. When we add to the curricular changes reflected in Perry's study of examinations the greater emphasis on personal, cultural, ethnic, and racial diversity within colleges, the great pluralism of values expressed in college and national life, and the increased exposure to different cultures made possible by the new technology of communications, it becomes clear that a major revolution in the direction of more "critical" education is occurring.

In sum, research on the impact of higher education clearly demonstrates that attending college has major effects upon students—apart from imparting skill and information. For one, college attendance

32. Daniel Albert Ondrack, "An Investigation into Changes in the Level of Authoritarianism among College Student Populations, from 1958–1968" (Ph.D. diss., University of Michigan, 1970) .
33. Perry, *Forms of Intellectual and Ethical Development*, pp. 3–7.

tends to accentuate the student's preexisting characteristics provided the student attends a college congruent with his prior characteristics. But overall, and increasingly clearly within the last decades, the college experience has a demonstrably liberalizing effect on most students: college attendance tends to increase open-mindedness, a perspectival view of truth, the individualization of moral judgments, psychological autonomy and independence; it decreases dogmatism, authoritarianism, intolerance, conformity, conventionalism, dependency, and so on. These effects, we have argued, can only be understood as developmental changes, as essentially irreversible transformations in the basic structures of the personality. Finally, these are precisely the kinds of effects we would predict as the consequences of critical higher education.

ARE COLLEGE EFFECTS BENEFITS?

Demonstrating that higher education has effects does not necessarily prove that its effects are benefits. Empirical research enables us to identify the liberalizing developmental impact of college attendance; it further suggests that the greatest liberalization occurs at those colleges that emphasize "critical" education. But political rhetoric and the mass media have selectively emphasized the disruption, conflict, and violence associated with higher education. As a result, a large segment of the American public, although perhaps vaguely aware of the liberalizing impact of higher education, is deeply concerned with its apparent social costs. The further question must therefore be directly confronted: Should the liberalizing effects of higher education be considered human and social benefits?

If stasis and stability were the highest human or societal goods, then the effects of critical higher education would almost certainly be deemed costs, for critical education helps generate social change and often temporarily increases psychological tensions. It deliberately challenges students to reexamine assumptions, convictions, and world views that they previously took for granted. It therefore creates psychological conflicts as an inseparable part of development; and these conflicts may produce personal anguish as the foundations of a dualistic world view are eroded, as conventional moral reasoning comes to seem arbitrary, and as dependence on authority is gradually relinquished for greater autonomy. Nor does critical higher education promote a conflict-free or unchanging society. In the last decade, American higher education has visibly helped produce millions of students who do not accept their society without question, who criticize corporations rather than simply serve them, who resist war-makers rather than fight for them, who challenge traditional American practices rather than follow them.

It follows that, if by "citizenship" we mean only unquestioning acceptance of the status quo, Milton Friedman is correct in claiming that higher education often produces "negative training" for citizenship. Furthermore, there are students for whom the confrontation with new frames of reference leads to regression or cynicism, and for whom critical education is not successful, but merely creates new prejudices and new rationales for the violation of human rights. Like any complex enterprise, higher education has real human and social costs, and any assessment of its effects must take them into account.[34]

Meaning of Citizenship

If, by "citizenship," we mean the responsibility of each generation to reexamine and redefine its own and its society's purpose and potentials, then higher education has overall positive effects on the individual and benefits the society as a whole. Consider first the impact of higher education on the individual. In its overall effects, higher education is remarkably responsive to the expressed goals of students upon entering college. A national survey of college freshmen conducted in 1969 by the American Council on Education indicates that nonvocational, nonpecuniary, and broadly "developmental" objectives are primary for most freshmen.[35] The ACE group asked incoming freshmen to indicate the "importance to you personally" of a series of possible accomplishments. The following accomplishments were rated as "central" or "very important" by a majority of all incoming freshmen:

	Percentage
Develop a philosophy of life	81.7
Raise a family	71.4
Have friends different from me	66.5
Help others in difficulties	66.5
Be an authority in my field	59.1
Have an active social life	59.0
Keep up with political affairs	51.4

34. Just as modern medicine, though beneficial overall to life and health, produces some iatrogenic illnesses, so higher education, though beneficial overall, produces a set of "pedogenic" problems for some students. A franker acknowledgment and study of these problems is needed if, as we believe likely and desirable, the critical component in higher education increases and access to higher education becomes more open.

35. John A. Creager et al., *National Norms for Entering College Freshmen—Fall 1969* (Washington: American Council on Education, Office of Research, 1969) .

In contrast, only 44 percent gave a comparable rating to "being very well off financially." These data indicate that, to freshmen, developmental, humanitarian, and interpersonal objectives have a higher priority than do vocational or monetary concerns.

Just as the distinction between technical and critical education is relative, so the emphasis students place on vocational and developmental goals is relative: most students have both, in varying ratios, depending on the student. But data like those from the ACE survey indicate that, from the students' point of view, developing a more complex and integrated world view—a philosophy of life—encountering different people and ideas, acting in a humanitarian way, and being socially and politically involved have an extremely high priority. If one benefit of college is to help students accomplish their expressed purposes, then higher education benefits its recipients.

But it might be objected that responsiveness to the needs of students is not an adequate criterion of individual, much less social, benefit. To confront this objection requires us to move from empirical data to the realm of ethical discourse, predilections, ideologies, and values. Indeed, the controversy over the benefits of higher education cannot be finally resolved solely by recourse to empirical data. The Nazi psychologist Jaensch, for example, argued that human qualities like open-mindedness, opposition to dogma, flexibility, a perspectival view of truth, direct expression of feelings and antiauthoritarianism, though praised in the degenerate democracies, were actually undesirable "Semitic" traits. He extolled instead "Aryan" qualities like decisiveness, impassiveness, certainty, unshakable faith, dislike of ambiguity, and unquestioning respect for authority.[36] Such an argument reminds us that research can only demonstrate the effects of higher education, not show their desirability.

But the finding that higher education tends to induce deep-rooted developmental changes supports the view that its effects are true benefits to the individual. We have argued that the impact of higher education on students is best understood as stimulating the unfolding of inborn but often unrealized human potentials. The research of Perry, Kohlberg, Sanford, and others has shown that the development of many men and women is foreclosed long before they reach the levels of autonomy, complexity, differentiation, and integration of which they are capable. Although higher education cannot guarantee human development, it demonstrably makes the unfolding of these emotional,

36. Cited in Theodore Adorno et al., *The Authoritarian Personality* (New York: John Wiley & Sons, 1964).

intellectual, and moral potentials more likely. Unless we are willing to argue that human development *should* be foreclosed at an early stage, we must count the individual effects of higher education beneficial.

We earlier suggested that the liberalizing effects of higher education seem to have increased in recent decades. This shift is reflected in studies like those of Yankelovich, who asked a national cross section of students to choose between two definitions of the purposes of higher education.[37] The first was clearly technical-vocational: 58 percent of all students agreed with this choice. The second definition was more broadly critical, developmental, and oriented toward social change: 42 percent of students agreed with this statement. Yankelovich calls the nonvocational students "forerunners," because their goals and values are coming to characterize a growing percentage of the student population. Other observers, arguing from an analysis of demographic trends, have noted a similar change away from vocational and financial objectives toward a concern with developmental and societal goals. Increasingly, students who complete higher education are showing more concern with humanitarian, social, and political objectives than in the past.[38]

Social Benefits to a Democratic Society

This shift in the nature of higher education and in the objectives of students themselves reflects major changes in the nature of modern American society. An analysis of these changes leads us to conclude that higher education not only benefits society but also is increasingly essential to it because a "critical" education strengthens human characteristics necessary if our highly technological, rapidly changing society is to remain open, pluralistic, and democratic.

In a more static, less complex society, it may have been desirable for the young simply to be "socialized" by families and schools into an uncritical acceptance of the skills, institutions, and cultural truths of their ancestors. In such a society, dualistic conceptions of truth, conventional levels of moral reasoning, and a high degree of dependence upon others for guidance and psychological security were probably

37. In "What They Believe: A Fortune Survey," *Fortune,* January 1969, p. 70.
38. Nevitt Sanford, "The College Student of 1980," in *Campus 1980: The Shape of the Future in American Higher Education,* ed. Alvin C. Eurich (New York: Delacorte Press, 1968), pp. 176–99; Alan E. Bayer, Alexander W. Astin, and Robert F. Boruch, "College Students' Attitudes Toward Social Issues: 1969–70," *Educational Record,* Winter 1971, pp. 52–59. Bayer et al. note: "the same liberalizing effects that have been observed in successive classes of entering freshmen also occur *within* each class during the undergraduate years" (p. 59).

functional. Higher education, insofar as it existed at all, could safely limit itself to passing on the inherited wisdom of the past.

But in a rapidly changing modern society, the mere acceptance of tradition becomes ever less adaptive. Virtually every observer of the industrialized nations has been impressed with their enormously rapid rates of technological, social, and cultural change.[39] In some highly technical fields, the half-life of methods and bodies of knowledge may be as short as five years; the life span of social institutions and cultural values is often shorter than the life span of an ordinary man or woman. One psychological requirement of rapid historical change is that individuals reorient themselves during their lifetimes to new technologies, new social institutions, and new cultural orientations. Rigid adherence to dualism leads to the inference that everyone else is in error except those who share one's own views; conventional moral reasoning leads to the view that those who reject the moral standards of one's own subculture are wicked; and absence of autonomy prevents the self-directed independence required in any responsible position today. If, as increasingly happens, technologies, definitions of truth, and conceptions of morality change within the individual's lifetime, ironclad adherence to one set of skills, to one view of truth, or to the present moral standards of one subculture will leave the individual stranded, isolated, and displaced before he reaches middle age. We already see the results in vocational obsolescence, human dislocation, and social alienation.

What Philip Slater has termed "technological radicalism"[40] is rapidly transforming every aspect of American life. New weapons of mass destruction make annihilation antiseptic and impersonal, and these have long required an ethic of personal and collective responsibility that transcends militaristic definitions of patriotism. Omnipresent mass communications make it essential to develop commitments within a world of competing, relativistic values and cultural assumptions. The imperatives of mass production in a technological society require highly specialized, fragmented public roles; to cope with them, all citizens must acquire high levels of self-integration and a coherent personal identity. The rapidity and scope of cultural change demands that modern Americans achieve a sense of personal values that transcends narrow commitment to the often parochial

39. See Alvin Toffler, *Future Shock* (New York: Random House, 1970) ; Kenneth Keniston, "Social Change and Youth in America," in *The Challenge of Youth*, ed. Erik H. Erikson (Garden City, N.Y.: Doubleday & Co., Anchor, 1965), pp. 191–222; and Margaret Mead, *Culture and Commitment* (New York: Natural History Press, 1970) .

40. Slater, *The Pursuit of Loneliness* (Boston: Beacon Press, 1970) .

moral injunctions of any particular subculture and time. In a world that is increasingly unpredictable and out of man's control, the greatest social need is for that kind of critical education which can help the individual develop a capacity to live in a world of rapid flux and to regain mastery over his own technology.

A closely related problem of contemporary American society is the problem of monitoring social, cultural, economic, and political change. In a nation that has rejected centralized planning and totalitarian controls, the relationship of individuals, social institutions, and political and economic forces to the public interest must nevertheless be constantly scrutinized. For this to occur, men and women must possess what can be called a "critical consciousness"—autonomy of judgment; a capacity to separate their individual identities from existing social institutions, cultural symbols, and political forms; an ability to compare existing policy to practice, creed to deed, actual to potential. Critical commentaries based on the concepts of equity and the public interest are of course often incorrect, uninformed, or unwise. But the existence of a group of men and women capable of making such commentaries or of accepting them as potentially valuable is necessary to ensure that social change be scrutinized in light of broader concepts of justice and the public good.[41]

STIMULATING CRITICAL JUDGMENT

Research on the effects of higher education indicates that it should help stimulate critical commentary, both positive and negative, on the existing social order. And, empirically, this has been increasingly true in recent years. For example, the debates over American involvement in Southeast Asia, over the persistence of racism in an allegedly egalitarian society, over the degradation of the environment, and over the quality of life in American society have been more vigorously conducted in colleges and universities than in any other institutions. Whether any specific argument put forward in these debates is valid or invalid is not the issue here. What is important overall for a society like ours is that there should *be* constant criticism, constant proposals for change, constant reminders of unfulfilled promises and unrealized human and social potentials. There needs to be, too, an audience capable of accepting such criticisms not as dangerously subversive but as potentially constructive, yet an audience capable also of responding

41. See Kenneth Keniston, "Responsibility for Criticism and Social Change," in *Whose Goals for American Higher Education?*, ed. Charles G. Dobbins and Calvin B. T. Lee (Washington: American Council on Education, 1968), pp. 145–63.

critically even to social criticism. Another benefit of higher education, then, is that it encourages this constant process of critical reexamination of the present society from the view of its ideals and potentials.

In brief, a technological nation like our own generates a series of new psychological, social, cultural, and political problems, all of which have increased in number and complexity in recent decades. Each of these problems makes unprecedented demands on the individual. Not only is modern society more complex than primitive society, but it has also created a technology and a life style that constantly inundate its citizenry with its complexity. The visual immediacy of electronic communications bombards modern men with alien events and ideas, from which their ancestors would have been shielded. Americans today are constantly assaulted by alternative truths, values, life styles, and political ideologies, often presented in their most provocative form by the mass media. Unless a significant and growing proportion of men and women possess a perspectival view of truth, and individualized conception of morality, and a high degree of psychological independence, the dangers of collective atavism and reaction are enormous.

At its best, critical higher education is a direct and necessary response to these new societal needs. As the modal "educated man" emerges from research studies, he is more likely to tolerate and enjoy the pluralism of modern society, to acknowledge the existence of alternative values and truths without feeling personally threatened, and to retain a sense of psychological integrity even in the presence of multiple roles and rapid social change. He is less likely to simplify the world into good and evil, black and white, to seek to "restore" social cohesion and cultural unity by turning back the political clock. He is more likely to tolerate ambiguity without demanding instant closure, to adhere to universalistic values that insist on the rights of adversaries as well as allies, to resist the appeals of authoritarian leaders and doctrines, and to be skeptical of all-or-nothing political and social programs. If, as we believe, the greatest threat to democracy in modern technological society is the danger of political reaction, critical higher education minimizes that danger.

Higher education is obviously not a panacea for psychological, social, cultural, or political problems. There are obviously highly educated bigots, fools, authoritarians, dogmatists, and criminals. And the human qualities stimulated by higher education are also found among millions of men and women with little formal education. The changes toward "liberalization" reported in the research literature are average changes, which neglect that important minority on whom education has de-liberalizing effects. All we can say is that overall, and for most of its graduates, higher education has effects that are humanly and socially beneficial in a democratic society.

Furthermore, the graduates of American higher education are only one part of a much broader matrix of people and institutions which affect the purposes and quality of life in America and throughout the world. Furthermore, the college-educated in America form a heterogeneous group that has never allied itself with any single sociopolitical faction. The human and social effects of higher education are subtle, often indirect, and almost impossible to quantify. Our claim is merely that if our changing, complex, technological society is to remain open, pluralistic, and democratic, we will need to become a nation of men and women who possess the qualities demonstrably stimulated by higher education. Seen in this light, the question is not whether we can afford universal higher educaton, but whether we can afford to be without it.

It is thus especially dangerous that today, when the need for critical higher education is most transparent and when the call for a probing examination of existing national priorities is most urgently felt, the impulse to reduce higher education to technical training is so strong. The experience of Nazi Germany and the Soviet Union illustrates that it is possible for a modern nation to develop an education system which, far from stimulating a development of critical consciousness, simply provides a high-level technical schooling, while indoctrinating most students in an unquestioning acceptance of the status quo. Today in America, strong pressures toward this more technical educational system exist, and they are often rationalized by an appeal to the narrowly pecuniary benefits of higher education.

It is all too easy for us to imagine how such a technical system of higher training could be implemented. The universal desire to make higher education more effective could be twisted into a narrow call for manpower training and channeling. The public's justified abhorrence of campus disruption could be diverted into an attack upon legitimate dissent and essential criticism. Gradually, public financial support for the critical component of higher education could be withdrawn. The funding of academic enterprises and individual students could be determined solely by technological needs or by the political requirements of controversial governmental policies. Disciplines that correspond to no easily definable corporate need or immediate political interest could be quietly "defunded" and finally phased out of existence. Dissenting professors could find their appointments terminated, while "protest-prone" students could be barred from the gates of higher education.

As a result, dissent would cease and the campus grass would grow tall and green. Higher education would no longer be a center of criticism of the society. The campus would be efficiently integrated into the existing man-power needs and priorities of the nation. The best human outputs of this training system might be superbly prepared for the complex occupational roles of a technological society. But we would have abandoned the only kind of education which can examine our potentially lethal priorities and work toward their humanization. Indeed, the only thing missing in this academic idyll would be the students: those who want an education would have gone off to found a university.

The Need to Redefine "Benefits"

G. HOMER DURHAM

THE VIEW OF HIGHER EDUCATION, ESPECIALLY BY MANY SCHOLARS, SOCIAL leaders of the nation, and so-called intellectuals generally, is too much focused on the university and universities. Too often the focus is on a particular university. To culture-bound creatures, the latter is often the one inhabited, or formerly inhabited, or the one desired for one's offspring.

National policy making for American higher education has tended to overreflect the university. Educational associations at One Dupont Circle tend to channel the views and experiences of university, liberal arts, or other college presidents.

The liberal arts college is the micro-image of what the most articulate intellectuals presume the university ought to be (and which in the case of "service station" state universities it is not), and liberal arts faculties and university presidents have dominated and shaped what the intellectual community generally regards as "higher education." But higher education as it is now known to increasing numbers of the American people, and especially to their elected representatives in state legislature, is far more than the university and the liberal arts college. As is well known, the university, more than any other segment of education beyond the high school, is in bad trouble with the "taxpayer," with the average legislator, and with growing segments of the population.

I do not question the immeasurable values of liberal higher education. The Keniston-Gerzon list of benefits could be lengthily extended. From my view, the key issue in their paper is whether the "liberalizing effects" of "critical" higher education are always more beneficial than not, and if beneficial, whether the values are an automatic, or a contrived, consequence. The question is something like Lord Morley's concerning the state: Is it a work of nature, or a work of art? If the benefits of higher education are a work of purpose and art as I presume them to be, and not automatic, undesigned consequences of congregating professors and scholars around some geographical point, we are left with the questions, How shall the presumed benefits be designed, cultivated, and produced? What benefits are most to be desired?

This commentary attempts some opinions in the area of these latter concerns. As a participant-observer in the politics of higher education, I observe that increasingly vocal elements of the community reject the notion that "critical" education, like a good cow, always produces sweet milk. Rather than ready acceptance that it is essential to strengthen "human characteristics [that are] necessary if our highly technological, rapidly changing society is to remain open, pluralistic, and democratic," there is a growing tendency to view some elements of critical education (which has its highest seat in the university) as unguided by carefully selected values and out of control financially. A statement in the paper with some appeal to these critics is "the greatest social need is for that kind of critical education which can help the individual develop a capacity to live in a world of rapid flux and to regain mastery over his own technology."

Most legislators I have recently met would delete the word "critical" from the phrase. They would argue that all necessary human pursuits are the legitimate concerns of education; that critical faculties of the mind can be developed in the application of intelligence and education to any skill, process, or human concern; that the arts, sciences, and "learned" professions must make more room in higher education for the mechanics, draftsmen, cosmetologists, and practical nurses; that more of the nation's resources must be devoted to the education of the latter, instead of allegedly "overeducating" some students at the universities. In response, some university presidents are being pressed to establish paraprofessional programs of all kinds. But can such programs flourish within the university?

The view of higher education as embracing more than the university or liberal arts college has been emerging in America for more than a century. Land-grantism, state colleges, technical and community colleges have marked its rise. But today, increasing numbers of alumni of the great land-grant universities believe that alma mater has been lost to the aristocratic, "critical" embrace of the university. And some educational politicians believe that if "the people" are to be served best, the nation and world saved, it must be done through "vocational-technical education."

One's own opinions force the judgment that society has been well served by the "critical" role of the universities. But the old ideas that only a few subjects are fit and suitable to cultivate the human mind and that only a few individuals have acceptable minds to develop has long since been discarded. The American state universities pioneered science and engineering through agriculture, and they came to acquire teacher education, business administration, huge stadiums, and pom pom girls.

As mass higher education beckons further (and as it has virtually come to exist in Utah, California, and some other Western states for decades), new institutions have arisen. In many regions the new institutions are capturing the hearts of legislative majorities. Meantime, intercollegiate athletics is hard pressed to help preserve community support for many Harvard-of-the-West-bound state universities.

As the financial requirements of higher education press, most of the states have responded with either the creation of statewide systems of higher education or with some type of coordinating mechanism. At the fifth annual meeting of the Educational Commission of the States this past summer, a resolution was adopted urging Congress to make further funds available to induce statewide planning for higher education in every state.

So, the politics of higher education has changed and is changing. The voices of single institutions and their heads are joined by others or are even muted in some state legislatures. Instead of going directly to the governor's office or to his finance director with the budget request, the university president finds himself more and more in the company of the statewide "coordinators" and of the technical, community, and state college presidents. The cut of his cloth, manner, and life style (including access to the better clubs and head tables) is not modified. But the university president's political presence is more and more *en famille* with "sister institutions."

In national circles, the Educational Commission of the States, and its staffs, responsive to statewide concerns, still commute from Denver. Permanent space at One Dupont Circle has not yet been acquired. And associations of statewide coordinators, commissioners, or chancellors have yet to assume the status and presence of associations of institutional presidents. But they are on the way. So, currently the view of higher education in America is increasingly the view from the statewide systems.

Whatever the measurable pecuniary or the nonmeasurable nonpecuniary benefits of higher education in America, the citizen mind sees it certainly as embracing the university. But other types of institutions loom larger and larger in the public mind. The citizenry want the benefits of the university, including the ancient values associated with its "critical benefits." But like learned ones such as Professor Friedman who suggest that negative aspects exist and may relate to nonquantitative benefits, the blue-collar and white-collar workers and clerks want good to triumph over evil. For good to triumph or at least have a chance, they want to see that the community, technical, state, and lesser colleges are financed and encouraged, want to see that their values have a chance in the "mix" with "all those university sociologists and liberal law professors." They want "teaching" to have its just rewards, as well as "research" and grantsmanship.

Keniston and Gerzon indicate that benefits accruing from the "critical" end of the continuum have key significance. I accept this on faith. But that faith also includes experience that critical education can have both good and evil effects. This experience has been reinforced before many legislative committees which presumably represent the democratic pluralism that critical education is believed to cultivate. The official public no longer accepts the notion that if money is made available "to the college of your choice," all thereafter will automatically turn out well. They no longer believe that professors and students somehow occupy a self-correcting universe in which *all* that issues forth is manna for soul, body, and society. The distinction between that which is more and less desirable—the choice between values—is the essence of their concern. For after the pecuniary benefits have been measured and paid for, the concern of nearly everybody, and the hallmark of participation and decision making in contemporary higher education, is confidence in higher education's ability—at whatever point—to separate good from bad, while preserving freedom under law and helping the good to flourish. Some aspects of Calvinism may have fled this country. But the concern that higher education's goals should approximate the building of God's Kingdom still flourishes at the grassroots. And *universitas* is no longer *civitas dei* in the public mind.

For higher education as a whole to emerge from the bear market, the influence and help of the universities' "critical education" is needed to join with the technical, community, state, and private colleges to convince the people that not only are "critical" values on the side of the angels, but also that higher education knows how to assist "the truth" to prevail. *Veritas, lux, et veritas* are still the watchwords. But today, truth is more than and different from what the universities appear to have recently proclaimed.

Matters of Measure

FRITZ MACHLUP

Mr. Gerzon, coauthor of the paper that I am to discuss, has informed me just recently that Mr. Keniston and he did not mean to plead for *college education for all* but, instead, to argue the case for "critical" rather than "merely technical" college education. I wish they had said this explicitly in their paper, for my critique of it assumes that it is a plea for critical *universal* college education.

My assumption was based on three grounds: first, the theme of the conference is "Universal Higher Education: Costs and Benefits"; second, the opening statement in the background papers refers to higher education involving "every high school graduate";[1] and third, an important proposition in the Keniston and Gerzon paper asserts a need, an "imperative," that *all* citizens in our complex society must acquire those mental attitudes that are fostered by the proposed kind of college education.

One gentleman in this audience charged me privately with being naïve if I believed that educators mean "universal" when they say "universal." I am sorry; it may be naïve, but I take educators seriously and assume that they mean what they say. There is no dictionary meaning of "universal" that allows us to make it mean less than all. No one who has had even one week of a course in logic can have any doubt about this.

It happens that the Carnegie Commission on Higher Education released this morning its newest report, on *New Students and New Places*. It predicts that college attendance will not increase beyond 50 percent of the college age population, and it adds: "We do not anticipate a further move to universal higher education in the sense of universal attendance; in fact, we consider this undesirable and believe that public and private policy should both avoid channeling all youth into higher education and create attractive alternatives to higher education."[2] I mention this as a testimony in support of my position, though I am for still greater selectivity and would like college enrollment to be far below the 50 percent figure.

1. Louis Hausman, "Pressures, Benefits, and Options," reprinted in the present volume, p. 1.
2. McGraw-Hill Book Co., 1971. P. 9.

After these preliminaries I turn to the critique of the paper, interpreting it, though perhaps wrongly, as dealing with the "Human and Social Benefits of Universal College Attendance."

In the second paragraph of their paper, Keniston and Gerzon tell of an early proposal that the paper should distinguish pecuniary and nonpecuniary benefits of higher education. This is a good and tried distinction. The proposed pair of opposites was replaced—perhaps at their behest—by a distinction between "economic" and "human and social" benefits. This is not a pair of opposites and makes little sense to one who knows what economics is all about. Economics deals with human and social choice; both individuals and society have to make decisions about using their resources for all sorts of things, material as well as intangible. For example, whether more of the available means should be allocated to education, to art, to music, to religion, to sport, or to quiet contemplation, the rational weighting of the pros and cons—benefits and costs—of all these and other options is called "economic decision making." The notion that economics deals only with material things and with money went out about a hundred and fifty years ago, if it was ever meant literally by the best of the earlier economists.

It is true, early classical economists made the naïve distinction between productive and unproductive labor according to whether it was employed to produce material goods or intangible services. This distinction is still used in the social accounting of Soviet Russia and some Eastern European countries, but virtually all non-Marxist economists have rejected it for over a hundred years. This statement can be documented by the example of an economist who explicitly included in his concept of wealth such intangibles as "distinction," "leisure," "benefits for acquaintances and friends," and contributions of "advantage to the public." The economist whom I have quoted is Nassau W. Senior, and the date of his book is 1836.[3] If we now, in 1971, are told that economists are not interested in "human and social benefits," an economist cannot help regarding this as hair-raising, no matter if he has as little hair as Milton Friedman or as long hair as your present reviewer's.

To set things straight: there are no "economic values," strictly speaking. *All values are human values.* They may be imputed to material things or to intangibles, to things for one's own benefits or for benefits accruing to others. Certain goods and services are sold and

3. *An Outline of the Science of Political Economy* (London: 1st ed., 1836; 6th ed., 1872), p. 26.

bought and thus have market prices; this concept is helpful to the economist, although he knows that some prices do not reflect all the costs that are incurred in production (for example, the pollution of the air we breathe) nor all the benefits that are afforded by the goods and services (as the beauty of a building enjoyed by outsiders or the peace and quiet of a residential street while the children are at school). Many services have no price tags; but it may still be possible to estimate their benefits in terms of money, though any such estimates are necessarily subjective. Keniston and Gerzon seem to think that the designation "subjective evaluation" is derogatory; this is a misunderstanding. If they or I make an evaluation, it is inevitably subjective, whereas if the evaluation can be read off a market report of what thousands of buyers have actually paid, it is called "objective." For things without market price, one can make only subjective valuations. There is nothing wrong with some economists' preference for sticking to recorded data, because they can thereby avoid making their own value judgments. Precisely herein lies the distinction between pecuniary and nonpecuniary benefits. For example, if some public program can be shown to have large pecuniary net benefits, the economic adviser to the government may have a relatively easy time convincing himself and others of its desirability. His task becomes more difficult and the outcome much less certain if he has to work largely with evaluations not supported by calculations that allow at least an ordering of magnitudes of the benefits potentially derived from the proposed and from alternative projects.

Keniston and Gerzon are not only suspicious of but downright hostile to cost-benefit analyses. So were the generals and admirals in the Pentagon when their favorite programs were turned down because of poor scores in cost-benefit estimation. Similarly, many inventors are furious when their ideas are rejected as uneconomical, and many engineers hate the economist who does not recognize that the benefits from their grand designs are large enough to warrant the required investment. Keniston and Gerzon's favorite program is University Education *for All*; they justify it by asserting great benefits for society, but they do not present a single statement about its cost or—which comes to the same thing—about the benefits from competing projects. There is always a long list of important projects to choose from, say, better transportation, better housing, better health service, better air, cleaner water, safer streets, and so forth. Keniston and Gerzon seem to be unaware of the sad but unquestionable fact that we cannot have everything that looks good to us, and that acceptance of their recommendations would exclude many things that society needs badly, per-haps much more urgently than University Education for All. Even if we were fully convinced that universal schooling until age twenty-two could yield all the benefits which their advocates promise, we might still find that society could not afford the cost of this program. The cost, estimated in money terms, stands for all the things that society would have to do without if this program were adopted.

I shall look briefly at the cost of the program before examining the claims made regarding the benefits it might yield. In looking at costs, I shall take the program seriously and assume that virtually every-body—or 90 percent of the age group—will take four years of full-time education beyond high school. Let us use the present size and age distribution of the resident population.

In 1970, the 18–21 age group numbered 13.1 million, of whom, in fact, only 75 percent had graduated from high school. But this surely must not be permitted in a Keniston world; "all" means 100 percent, and if we draft only 90 percent for education beyond high school we are already slackers. Thus, with 90 percent as the "full enrollment" target, 11.8 million should be in college. Actual enrollment, however, was only 4.5 million, a shortage of 7.3 million.[4]

According to recent studies for the Carnegie Commission, the in-stitutional cost per undergraduate student is roughly $2,000. This would mean $14.6 billion for the 7.3 million of the new recruits to tertiary education. Earnings forgone may be put at $4,500 per year for each person attending college instead of working on a paying job. For the additionally enrolled 7.3 million, the earnings forgone would be $32.9 billion. Disregarding the taxes forgone and other costs to society, we come to $47.5 billion as the cost of the program for 1970–71.

Some of us may have a hard time visualizing what $47 billion means. It looks small compared with a gross national product of a trillion dollars. We can, however, compare it with some other things, for example, with the total product of agriculture (including forestry and fisheries), which was only $25 billion; or with total residential construction, which was only $32 billion in 1969; or with total corpo-rate profits (before taxes) from manufacturing, which was $41.8 bil-

4. There were actually 7.2 million students enrolled in college in October 1970, but only 4.5 million were of the 18–21 age group, while the remaining 2.7 million were older. Some of the latter may have entered college late, which would reduce the shortage calculated for the age group. Most of them, however, were probably staying longer in college, professional school, or graduate school and thus were counted as enrolled also when they were members of the age group here considered as of "college age." We would have to know the composition of the enrollment in order to say what adjustment should be made of the "shortage."

lion, in 1969, and even lower, namely $34.1 billion, in 1970; or with total dividends of all corporations, which were $24.7 billion in 1969.

I can imagine that enthusiastic supporters of "universal university attendance" are not impressed by the high cost of their program and are willing to have it at any cost. I must therefore proceed to an examination of the benefits of the program. Keniston and Gerzon implicitly refuse to put a money value on the beneficial effects of their program, but they threaten us with dire consequences should we fail to adopt it. Avoidance of the bad consequences of not adopting it is then the minimum benefit of instituting the program. Now what are the consequences of nonadoption? According to Keniston and Gerzon, society may not get enough individuals who can "reorient themselves during their lifetimes to new technologies, new social institutions, and new cultural orientations"; or too many who may be left "stranded, isolated, and displaced before [they] reach middle age" (p. 70); and too few who have the "capacity to separate their individual identities from existing social institutions, cultural symbols, and political forms" (p. 71). As a result, society might be in "danger of political reaction" (p. 72) and might not "remain open, pluralistic, and democratic" (p. 73).

Keniston and Gerzon would hold that these dangers or their avoidance have no money value. Wrong. I can say how much of my income I would be willing to give up for the certainty of living in a free country, and so can most people. Many have actually made such choices, leaving wealth and income behind in their Hitlerized or Stalinized home country, to live, however poor, in a foreign but free country. (Some of these expatriates, I am sorry to say, have bitterly complained afterwards when their material sacrifice proved to be real; they probably had hoped that the trade-off between freedom and material comfort would be less exacting than their *ex ante* preference ratio seemed to justify.) In any case, to say that the benefits of life under particular political conditions are "invaluable" is only to admit that one has not cared to evaluate them. When no hard choices have to be made, rejection of such conscious comparisons is all right, but when decisions cannot be avoided, one had better begin to do some hard thinking about the comparative benefits to be derived from alternative courses of action.

My argument against "universal university attendance" is not only that the costs of the program are too high but also that the benefits are too low. Indeed, I expect no incremental benefits from universal schooling until age twenty-two. If really everybody were sitting in school for sixteen years and nobody started to work in gainful employment before his twenty-second birthday, the harm inflicted on our youth might be very serious. However, such a scheme could probably not be enforced: the dropout rate might rise to 50 percent. Compelling or pressuring all youngsters to stay in school for six, seven, or eight years beyond their puberty and physical maturity would be to invite anti-intellectual revolts; and in trying to make them take it without rebelling, we would have to transform our colleges into rock-and-roll camps. I do not believe that the effects on the character, the mentality, or the psychological makeup of the graduates would be beneficial, and they might be quite harmful.

I cannot resist the temptation to show some minor flaws in the arguments of Keniston and Gerzon:

1. They first criticize a production-oriented evaluation of higher education, but then contradict themselves by arguing (on p. 70) that universal higher education is needed to permit mass production: "The *imperatives of mass production* in a technological society require highly specialized, fragmented public roles; to cope with them, *all* citizens must acquire high levels of self-integration and a coherent personal identity." (The added emphasis is mine.)

2. The authors accept the finding that "college attendance yields demonstrable increases in autonomy, openmindedness, cognitive relativism, independence of moral judgments, along with decreases in authoritarianism, dogmatism, ethnocentrism, prejudice, and adherence to traditional values" (p. 62; similarly p. 66). Now, if this finding was established for a time when 20–30 percent of the age group went to college, it is by no means certain that it will hold when 50, 70, or 80 percent go to college. Standards cannot be the same, especially in what Keniston and Gerzon call "critical education."

3. The authors concede (pp. 64–65) that college was in former times *not* offering much critical education, but has improved in this direction. They also concede (p. 73) that universities under the Nazis and Communists did *not* offer much critical education. Yet, in calling for *universal* university education, they take it for granted that it will be of the critical type and have the liberalizing effects which they desire.

4. The authors accept as genuine and honest what incoming college freshmen mark on questionnaires as their "central" or "very important" objectives in choosing to go to college; and they make much of the fact that 81.7 percent of the respondents entered check marks at the line that stated they were seeking to "develop a philosophy of life" (p. 67). Keniston and Gerzon actually conclude that these students gave to "developmental, humanitarian, and interpersonal ob-

jectives" higher priorities than to vocational or monetary concerns. I find it naïve to derive such conclusions from answers to questionnaires. What does it cost the respondent to put a check mark to a phrase generally regarded as noble and high-minded? The question of genuine priorities can be answered only on the basis of preferences revealed through actual choices. How much personal income is the student willing to sacrifice for the benefit of developing a philosophy of life? Would he choose to go to college if he were certain to earn lower incomes than those who do not go to college? These are the criteria by which one has to judge the priorities in the students' objectives.

I want to conclude with a statement of an issue to which I have already alluded but which deserves top billing as a message of great significance in all such discussions as these.

One of the worst fallacies is to talk or think about the utility and benefit of anything without referring to the quantity in which it is available. If something is good, and more of it is better, the incremental benefits derived from additional quantities are never constant, or hardly ever. If eight years of schooling is good and ten years is better, this does not guarantee that twelve years is better still and sixteen years is still grander, and then thirty-two years and ultimately the whole life. Likewise, if sixteen years of formal education is good for 10 percent of the population, and also for 12 percent, and perhaps for 15 percent or even 20 percent, this does not imply that there would be benefits if 30, 50, 60, or 90 percent were exposed to sixteen years of schooling. Economists speak of marginal utility, marginal productivity, and marginal benefits, to indicate the influence of the quantities considered. This concept is not technical economics, which you may or may not accept; it is plain common sense, which no reasonable man can reject.

PART TWO

Financial Problems of Institutions

FREDERICK E. BALDERSTON

Varieties of Financial Crisis

MANY COLLEGES AND UNIVERSITIES ARE ALREADY FACING
several crises simultaneously: a crisis of internal governance and control; a crisis of confidence with major external constituencies; a crisis
of philosophy and mission; a crisis of market position; and a crisis
of money. We can, in fact, expect that a sufficiently serious state of
stress in any one of these areas will be communicated to the others,
particularly to the financial area. And, the realities being what they
are, ability to address problems in the other areas of deep concern
in the hope of overcoming them will often depend on whether money
problems can be solved or at least alleviated.

This paper will examine the various forms of financial stress that
academic institutions may face. The term "stress" is preferred to
"crisis" because the latter implies a peak of tension and then its end:
death, or transfiguration, or sudden discovery of gold at the end of a
money-raising rainbow. Most students of higher education finance are
agreed that there is only one source large enough and powerful
enough to help all of the institutions now facing financial stress. His
name is Uncle Sam. To produce a permanent easing of financial stress
in higher education, the federal government would have to change
its policies for educational finance in some very basic ways that would
add up to several billions of dollars per year of federal money. An
example would be the changes in federal policy generated by a decision calling for the immediate adoption of the major portion of
the various Carnegie Commission recommendations or of the recommendations of the Rivlin Report.[1]

1. *Toward a Long-Range Plan for Federal Financial Support for Higher Education: A Report to the President* (Washington: U.S. Department of Health, Education, and Welfare, Assistant Secretary for Planning and Evaluation, 1969) .

The author acknowledges with thanks the research assistance of Constance
Holton and the help of L. M. Furtado, C. J. Courey, and Burton I. Wolfman in
securing information. George Weathersby, Earl Cheit, Virginia B. Smith, John
Wheeler, and Margaret Gordon read and criticized drafts of the manuscript. The
author is responsible for interpretation and errors.

87

We can all hope that as the executive branch and the Congress move during the next couple of years to review the financial problems of higher education, key elements of these recommendations will indeed be adopted. Yet no college or university president should simply wait for that to happen. A more reasonable forecast is that, whatever the improvements and changes in federal policy, we will see no basic change in the structure of higher education finance but rather a number of piecemeal ameliorations. The basic pattern of financial stress will likely persist through the present decade.

FINANCIAL STRESS DEFINED AND EVALUATED

How did financial stresses accumulate in a variety of types and sizes of institutions? Why did these stresses show themselves suddenly and almost simultaneously within the last three years or so, especially since the early 1960s had not revealed obvious evidence of financial trouble in most colleges and universities? What are the specific varieties of financial crises to which the institutions concerned and their constituencies must seek solutions?[2]

As Defined by Cheit

Earl F. Cheit arrived at a particular definition of financial stress in his recent Carnegie Commission monograph, *The New Depression in Higher Education*.[3] Many public institutions are required by law or state financial regulation to keep current expenditures within current income; in other words, they are not allowed to run an operating deficit even though they may find their financial resources seriously inadequate. Some private institutions do, from time to time, dip into capital or reserves—run an operating deficit—without feeling that they are in long-range financial difficulty. Cheit cites the academic truism that each institution may expect to spend for current operations up to its current income. Neither good financial stewardship nor effective academic management generally requires an institution to more than "break even" each year.

Cheit therefore felt that the presence or absence of an operating deficit is not a good litmus test of financial difficulty, and that the right test is the adequacy of resources in relation to the institution's mission. He said, "For purposes of this study, an institution is judged

---

2. Virginia Smith's paper, "Institutional Economies," explores some of the possibilities in alleviating these financial maladies. My task here is limited to that of diagnosis.
3. New York: McGraw-Hill Book Co., 1971.

in financial difficulty if its current financial condition results in a loss of services that are regarded as a part of its program *or* a loss of quality" (Cheit's italics, p. 36). He points out that his definition accepts the institution's own definition of its educational mission and academic quality standards. If its resources are inadequate to sustain it in that mission and at that quality, then it is in financial stress. Given the wide variety of institutional types, sizes, and missions in American higher education, it is hard to set forth an external, objectified measure to replace the self-definitions of financial situation given by the individual institutions. Thus, we have no convenient and operational test of financial viability to apply directly to the observable accounting picture of an institution.

Cheit's findings are aptly summarized in the title of his monograph, *The New Depression.* . . . He assembled data on costs, income, and enrollment trends and also gathered detailed interview information on a total of forty-one institutions classified into six groups, ranging from seven "national research universities" to five "two-year colleges." He conducted most of the interviews that comprised his field work, and was assisted by several people, including myself, who interviewed presidents and other senior officials at some of the institutions. Although he emphasizes that this study cannot purport to be a strict statistical analysis applicable to all of American higher education, it was a serious effort to assess the situation for a group of institutions representing all of the major types.

Cheit recently summarized for Representative Edith Green's Special Subcommittee on Education what he found:

> Almost three-fourths of the schools studied (71 percent) were either in financial difficulty or headed for it. The Carnegie Commission staff estimates (by a national projection of my sample) that two-thirds of the nation's colleges—enrolling three-fourths of the nation's students— are in financial difficulty or headed for it.
>
> My study found that all types of institutions are affected. The major private universities have been hit first, but the others are not far behind. Public and private alike are facing increasing financial trouble. No class of institution is exempt from the problem or free from financial trouble.[4]

He went on to describe the logic of the cost-income squeeze—a gap of several percentage points in the trend of cost per student per year

4. Testimony of Earl F. Cheit before Special Subcommittee on Education, Committee on Education and Labor, U.S. House of Representatives, March 29, 1971.

versus income per student per year—facing different types of institutions, and suggested that

> the nation's colleges and universities need between $300 and $700 million in additional operating income. When we recall that this would come from federal, state, local, and private sources in 50 states, it is hardly a frightening sum.

And he concluded by urging the need for new federal programs both to assist the student and to provide institutional support.

According to Rivlin

Alice Rivlin, in still more recent testimony before the same congressional committee, posed the question whether there is really an emergency or crisis in higher education finance, and then said:

> Hard facts are difficult to assemble in this area. My own impression from available studies and conversations with higher educators is that there is no *general* [her emphasis] crisis of higher education finance.

She noted:

> There are several sets of factors affecting various kinds of institutions in various ways at the same time, some permanent and some temporary.
> 1. Some major research institutions are suffering from cutbacks in federal research programs or federally funded graduate programs. . . .
> 2. Some, but by no means all, state-supported institutions are suffering from smaller than usual increases in state support. . . .
> 3. Some institutions, especially private ones, are finding themselves over-extended as a result of ambitious attempts over the last decade to improve the quality and variety of their programs. . . .
> 4. Some institutions are suffering the combined effect of recent recession and inflation. Private institutions are the hardest hit. Private gifts have dropped sharply, although they seem likely to recover somewhat this year. Students are less likely in a recession to pay the difference between public and private tuition. At the same time, wages, salaries, and other costs have continued to rise steeply.
> 5. Some institutions no longer offer what students appear to want. . . .[5]

Dr. Rivlin concludes this litany of woes with the observation:

> It is certainly not obvious that a program of general support for higher education is the appropriate answer to all or even most of these varied financial problems.

5. Testimony of Alice Rivlin, Brookings Institution, before Special Subcommittee on Education, Committee on Education and Labor, U.S. House of Representatives, April 1971.

These different, or differently shaded, views of the nature and trend of financial position are cited to show the differences in judgments of qualified experts on the economics of higher education, and they also point the way toward what may be needed for further diagnosis of the "varieties of financial crisis."

FIVE MODELS OF STRESS

First, I offer several conceptually different models of financial stress and discuss each of them briefly:
1. Expanded academic aspiration
2. Time passing
3. Stabilization after growth
4. Conscientious overcommitment
5. Income tapering

Each of these is a stress model for the individual institution of higher education, and any one institution may have some combination of these stresses accumulating at the same time. After commenting on each model, I shall take up trends in unit prices and volumes used of the different kinds of institutional resources. Next, I shall apply the lessons about trends in costs to the various types of institutions, and then join the observations about cost structure with comments about income trends and problems.

At that point, I shall hope to have arrived at an answer to each of the following questions: (1) Have cost trends affected the several types of institutions in different ways? (2) Have income trends affected these institutions differently? (3) What aspects of their financial stresses will be temporary, and what aspects will be permanent—last until at least 1980!—in the various types of institutions?

Expanded Aspiration. Here is what an institution needed to do to achieve the first kind of stress: It established a number of new programs in areas of hot competition and (almost by definition) recruited key faculty from a limited supply, ahead of enrollment growth. It developed new programs especially in areas of growing prestige—doctoral programs requiring heavy library or laboratory investment and substantial fellowship funds to enable it to compete successfully for good students who would redound to the prestige of the program and the institution. This was done in many program areas in order to move the institution upward in academic status, but also, inevitably, moving it outward toward the fiscal cliff.

Time Passing. This model is closely related to the stress from *stabilization after growth*, which might also be labeled "rising fixed commitments." It is almost breathtakingly easy to experience stress from *time passing*, for two reasons: aging of the institution, and differentially growing cost factors that push up institutional costs relative to income. Consider the institution having, say, in base year 1960, three components of operating expenditure: *A*, amounting to $500,-000; *B*, amounting to $250,000; and *C*, amounting also to $250,000. Let component *A* grow in cost at the compound annual rate of 4 percent, component *B* at 6 percent, and component *C* at 8 percent. By 1970, the $1 million total budget back in 1960 will have grown to a total budget of $1.74 million, with *no* change in actual operations or their productivity. An annual rate of income growth of 5.75 percent would have been just sufficient to offset the cost rise. But if in a second institutional example the three components had been equal in 1960 at $0.33 million each, and if the growth in costs had been the same as in the first example, the budget would have grown to $1.83 million, or 5 percent more than in the first case.

These differences in cost structure are not chosen accidentally, nor are the different rates of cost growth. Component *A* could well be faculty wage bill, component *C*, maintenance of fixed plant plus library, and component *B*, all other overhead. The first example above could be an undergraduate college, and the second (the example of three equal components in 1960), a university.

"Simple aging" is the other aspect of the model of time passing: the increase of age and rank distributions of faculty, increase of seniority of administrative staff, increased age and maintenance requirements of buildings. To avoid upward cost pressure over time in each of these categories, an institution would have to put into effect some positive policies that are very difficult for it to conceive and enforce. To illustrate the issue of aging of faculty, let us assume that the institution has gone through a period of expansion in which mostly junior people were added to faculty so that at the beginning of the decade 50 percent of the faculty was nontenured, 10 percent consisted of associate professors, and 40 percent were (youngish) full professors. Now let ten years pass, with *no* change in the total number of positions. In each year, let us say, one-fifth of the nontenured faculty comes up for promotion to associate professor, of whom three-fourths make it and one-fourth are replaced by new assistant professor appointments; one-fourth of the associate professors comes up for promotion to full professor, and three-fourths of them make it; the rest remain as associate professors; and among the full professors (because the faculty is young), nobody reaches retirement age.

By the end of the tenth year, here is the situation: the rank distribution is 10 percent assistant professors, 15 percent associate professors, and 75 percent full professors.

Stabilization after Growth, or Rising Fixed Commitments. This model of financial stress can be seen as one in which the potential for trouble is primed by a substantial interval of past growth—growth in which significant numbers of new faculty and staff were added, mostly at the junior levels, and capital facilities in copious quantity were added while no old buildings were torn down (pressure of growth forced continued use of old buildings). Underlying the expanded institution is a rising level of budget for administration, for libraries, and for computer centers. With this priming force, the cost structure of the institution and the age distribution of its faculty and capital facilities can hardly fail to produce later rapid increases of costs. Here is the basis of crisis—the cost increases will not have been foreseen at the time of the expansion because the early budget years of the expansion could be financed at low entry costs.

There is an interesting corollary to this model of stabilization: if the institution had been able to keep growing, it could have put off the evil day. But to do so, it would have had to grow at more than a linear rate in total faculty, total building space, and so on, and keep income growing at least proportionally with enrollment growth. And what institution can do all that indefinitely? Correspondingly, we can predict that any institution that has been growing will begin to be hit by the stresses of stabilization shortly after its growth tapers off.

Conscientious Overcommitment. This model is also a familiar one. In recent years, many colleges and universities increased their financial aid to students, not only to offset for needy students the effects of rising tuition, fees, and other costs of attendance but also to attract black, Chicano, and other minority students previously excluded from college-going opportunities. Once entered into, the commitment to the individual student cannot be cut back, and the institution's first-year program commitment grows rapidly with each new group of students admitted. These financial aid budget obligations, as Cheit points out, are a major source of cost increase for many colleges and universities.

Again many colleges and universities, particularly in urban areas, have sought, or had thrust upon them, increased community responsibilities. These, too, are sources of budgetary strain.

Conscientious commitments of an institution need not constitute a large fraction of the budget to produce a financial crisis. If the costs are enough to produce imbalance when added to ongoing budget, and particularly if they grow at a more rapid percentage rate than other costs, they are enough at the margin to cause severe financial stress.

Income Tapering. The preceding types of crisis deal with the dynamics of prices, costs, and expenditures. This last model is concerned with trends in income and the possibility that some income components are not sufficiently responsive over time to enable an institution to keep up with its cost pattern.

Cheit noted in his study of forty-one institutions that, overall, income trends had failed to keep pace with expenditure trends. Private institutions are hit by two basic income problems: the hazard of pricing the institution out of the market through tuition increases, and the declining purchasing power of endowment income. The latter may be offset by increased annual giving and by new capital gifts, but in recent years increasing tensions between private institutions and their alumni and other donor constituencies have dampened income growth from gifts. Potential market resistance to increases in attendance costs—tuition, fees, dormitory charges, and other costs of attendance—is especially serious for private institutions that encounter increasing competition from publicly supported colleges and universities with lower fees and with enrollment spaces and political commitment to take all of the new applicants who meet their admission standards.

Universities face an additional problem. In the past few years extramural research funds from federal agencies and foundations have grown more slowly, or, for some universities, have actually declined. Most seriously affected are institutions that have counted on a portion of the direct costs of research to buttress academic salaries (and now must find other funds to meet these basic commitments) and those that have come to depend on the overhead (indirect cost recovery) rate as the budgetary base for other major institutional services—from libraries and computer centers to building space and general administration.

Cost Trends in Academic Operations

What are the various activity and program components in an institution's cost structure? To be considered are: the unit price of each type of resource used in the activity, and the trend in that unit price; the trend in the quantity used of each resource; and, because productivity rates of some resources improve over time while others may decline, the effect of productivity changes on the amount of service that the activity or program actually contributes to the institution.

There are, of course, many serious problems of data, of interpretation of the measures of both quantity and quality of each resource used, and of measures of the quality and quantity of services contributed. Academic institutions vary greatly from one another and differ from other types of economic institutions in their location in labor and other resource markets, in their uses of resources, and in their perceptions of the quality and quantity of the services produced in their activities and programs. The best that can be offered here is a series of clues and judgments about the financial stresses caused by cost trends.

Trends in Unit Prices

We can look first at the trends in unit prices. Labor costs, according to the traditional rule of thumb, account for about 80 percent of an academic institution's operating budget, and so will be examined first. The general trend of faculty salaries has been recorded in the annual surveys of the American Association of University Professors. Salary trends for other categories of personnel in higher education have not been studied in the same detail, however, and are difficult to examine on an appropriate comparative basis because of wide differences in the definitions of administrative and staff positions and differences in labor market conditions throughout the country.

Committee Z (Economic Status of the Profession) of the AAUP reported in April 1970 that average faculty salaries for all ranks had risen, after correction for inflation by only 1.1 percent for the year from 1968–69 to 1969–70. (By contrast, in various years from 1955 to 1967, real faculty purchasing power had shown growth rates ranging from 3.2 percent to 4.4 percent per year.)[6] In the latter 1960s institutions were having trouble keeping up with cost-of-living increases, and most professorial ranks—both in public and private institutions—were affected. Preliminary information reported concerning the 1970–71 status of the profession showed that all-ranks average compensation failed to keep pace with the cost-of-living rise from 1969–70 to 1970–71.[7]

One measure of institutional labor cost is the average faculty salary across all ranks and disciplines and the average salary of administrative staff across all ranks and types of jobs. This measure,

6. "Rising Costs and the Public Institutions," *AAUP Bulletin*, June 1970, p. 177.
7. *At the Brink: Preliminary Report on the Economic Status of the Profession, 1970–71* (Washington: AAUP, April 1971), p. 48.

unfortunately, combines the effect of changes in salary at each rank or position with the effect of a change in the roster of personnel and the percentage composition of the work force.

Salary Trends for Various Types of Labor

In order to explore the change in unit price *for a given type of labor,* I have put together Table 1, based on the experience of my own institution, the University of California. The university's faculty salaries have been adjusted, over the years, to keep pace with a peer group of major universities; nonacademic salaries have been adjusted in accordance with findings of the California State Personnel Board studies of wage rates in comparable classifications in business and industry throughout the state.

TABLE 1: *University of California Salaries, 1950–70,*
and Compound Rates of Increase

Labor Category[a]	Salary[b]			Compound Annual Rate of Increase (Percent)	
	1950	1960	1970	1950–70[e]	1960–70
Academic year faculty[d]					
Average faculty salary.......	$ 6,284	$10,255	$15,505	4.2	3.6
Assistant professor, II.......	5,040	7,536	10,700	3.8	3.6
Professor, II...............	8,190	12,900	17,900	4.0	3.3
Teaching assistant, half time..	1,200	2,365	3,447	5.4	3.8
Monthly administrative salary[e]					
Average administrative salary.	313	432	645	4.1	4.1
Principal clerk, minimum....	230	376	530	4.3	3.5
Accountant, minimum.......	370	676	1,048	5.8	4.5
Principal engineer, minimum.	560	950	1,475	5.0	4.5
Librarian, I, minimum.......	240	415	627	4.9	4.3
Librarian, III, minimum.....	370	584	820	4.2	3.5
Campus librarian, yearly.....	10,800	20,325	35,000	6.05	5.6

[a] Roman numerals indicate steps in the salary schedule within the given labor category.
[b] Salary is stated in current dollars for each year, *not* corrected for changes in purchasing power.
[e] For the University of California, no salary range adjustment was made from 1969–70 to 1970–71. For the years 1950–51 to 1969–70, the compound rates of increase were: Average faculty salaries, 4.4 percent; Assistant professor, II, 4.0 percent; Professor, II, 4.1 percent.
[d] Nine-month, academic year salary.
[e] Salary per month, not per year.

Table 1 shows that weighted average administrative salaries over the twenty-year period rose at just about the same compound annual rate as average faculty salaries, but the latter's rate of rise in the 1960–70 decade was lower than that of nonacademic salaries. The averages are an amalgam of the respective job classification wage rates and the (possibly changing) mix of people in the various job classifications. Therefore, we have also shown the compound rates of increase for three administrative job classifications. These rates are significantly higher than those for academic position salaries (see Table 1, rates for both 1950–70 and 1960–70).

We have also shown the salary of teaching assistants for the years in question, where the compound annual rate of increase was 5.4 percent for the 1950–70 interval and 3.8 percent for 1960–70. Finally, three classifications in the library staff are shown. All three librarian positions showed higher rates of salary increase from 1950–70 than did any of the faculty positions.

Two Inferences

Two inferences can be drawn from these data. First, an institution that had a greater-than-average proportion of its employees in the administrative and subfaculty categories in 1950 *and* maintained these proportions from 1950 to 1970 has experienced a greater-than-average upward pressure on its costs. In addition, as we all know from observation of both nonacademic and academic personnel practices, there has been a tendency to upgrade jobs and create supergrades in order to provide opportunities for salary advancement beyond the cost-of-living adjustments. Thus, the average salary of individuals has risen by more than the rates of increase shown in Table 1.

The second inference is that *faculty* have become cheaper, at given ranks and steps, between 1950 and 1970, relative to teaching assistants and administrative staff of given ranks and steps. Institutions have some choices in determining whether to substitute one form of labor for another. Some institutions experienced little increase in the complexity and technology of their operations between 1950 and 1970. If so, and if they had an optimal balance of faculty with other staff in 1950, the sensible policy over the years would have been to hire relatively more faculty than administrators and, where feasible, substitute faculty labor for the kinds of administrative labor whose costs were increasing faster than faculty salaries.

I have pursued this analysis of unit costs and trends because it counters conventional explanations of the last two decades about cost problems and rational responses to them. According to the conventional argument, faculty salaries are a major cost item, faculty salaries have been rising, and therefore colleges and universities should be finding ways to substitute other kinds of labor for faculty labor. Yet in at least one major institution, the cost of other kinds of labor has increased faster than faculty costs.

Trends in Commodity Prices

As we turn to costs of operation other than labor, again we look for changes in unit prices. Our first objective is to observe what has happened to unit prices *of the same items*. After that, we can look at quality upgrading and increases in volume of various items. The wholesale price index of industrial commodities rose 19.6 percent in total from the base period of 1957–59 to 1971. Individual components of the index show large differentials, however: rubber and plastic products rose only 6.1 percent and furniture and durables rose 10.5 percent, whereas, at the other extreme, metals and metal products rose 29.4 percent and general-purpose machinery and equipment rose 33.4 percent.

When these price increases for various types of purchased commodities are stated in terms of compound annual rates of increase from 1957–59 to 1971, shown in Table 2, the figures give us greater comparability with the rates of increase of wages in higher education. As shown, prices of purchased commodities have apparently risen over the decade much less rapidly than wages in higher education. Increases in number of commodity units required, relative to other factors, and increased demand for more complex items may, nevertheless, have caused more cost pressure from these components of expenditure than indicated by Table 2. Further, the impact of increased costs may have been particularly strong during the entire last three years of the 1960s, influenced—as was the entire U.S. economy—by the inflation resulting from the Vietnam war. Thus, the relative influence of cost rise in certain types of items has been increased.

TABLE 2: *Wholesale Prices, by Major Commodity Groups*
(1957–59 = 100)

Commodity	Price Index, 1971	Compound Annual Rate of Increase (Percent), 1957–59 to 1971[a]
All commodities	119.6	1.38
Rubber and plastic products	106.1	0.46
Furniture and durables	110.5	0.77
Metals and metal products	129.4	2.0
General-purpose machinery and equipment	133.4	2.2

[a] 1958, mid-point of base period, assumed for start of calculation.

Various types of institutions are, of course, affected differently by the differentials in commodity price increases. However, we can reasonably suppose that the types of institutions that have experienced rapid capacity growth have also experienced the largest amount of exposure to increases in machinery prices.

Prices of Library Materials

Price trends in library books and serial publications have exerted an influence on budgets in all types of higher education institutions. Unit prices of library books, periodicals, and services have risen at different average rates from the base period of 1957–59 to 1969, books having gone up a total of 77.1 percent, while periodicals rose 89.2 percent and serial services, 98.0 percent over the same interval. These represented, respectively, compound annual rates of 5.3 percent, 6.0 percent, and 6.4 percent.

Recent inflationary pressures hit all three sectors of library acquisition costs. In the one year from 1969 to 1970, the U.S. periodicals index rose from 189.2 to 211.6, or by nearly 12 percent over 1969, and a combined index of serials services rose by 8.4 percent.[8] In the same period, an index of the prices of hardcover books, ranging by field from agriculture to travel, rose overall by 22.7 percent; this same index showed a rise of 38.3 percent during 1967–70, with the greatest increase occurring during 1969. Also during 1969, mass market paperbacks rose in price only 2.1 percent, whereas the more selective, "trade" paperback category rose by 29 percent.[9]

As striking as the average price increase in each category is the great variation among categories in the amount of increase. A few examples of periodicals and serials will illustrate. While business and economics periodicals rose from 1957–59 to 1970 by a total of 82.1 percent, chemistry and physics periodicals rose in price by 233.2 percent, engineering by 123.5 percent, literature by 63.1 percent, and history by only 56.1 percent. Thus, an institution having a heavy periodicals commitment in the hard sciences and engineering would have found more inflationary pressure on its library costs over this interval than one which concentrated on the humanities. Even more striking interfield differences were shown for the serials services, those in law having risen since 1957–59 by 155.7 percent; business, 66.5 percent; science and technology, 554.2 percent; and U.S. documents, 48.7 percent. Here again, the specific effects of the increases in unit prices of library materials will depend a great deal on each institution's mix of programs.

EDUCATIONAL RESOURCES USED

Now to be examined are, first, the increases in quantity used of each type of resource for higher education and, next, such fragments of information as we have concerning changes in productivity for each type of resource. In his study, Cheit converted each category of expenditure to expenditure *per student* in each institution, in order to obtain a basis of comparability among institutions. This approach,

8. Helen W. Tuttle, Norman B. Brown, and William H. Huff, "Price Indexes for 1970, and U.S. Periodicals and Services," *Library Journal*, July 1970, pp. 2427–29.
9. *Publishers' Weekly*, Feb. 8, 1971, pp. 53–54.

of course, combines the effects of prices, quantities of a resource used per student, and productivity. It is very difficult to go beyond this approach because dates are scant.

Increases in Personnel

Use of faculty labor has, of course, risen enormously with increases in enrollment in all types of institutions. At the same time, however, student-faculty ratios have apparently increased—that is, *fewer* faculty are being used per thousand students—in all types of institutions.[10] It may be questioned whether the increased number of students per faculty member actually represents an increase in the amount of teaching output per faculty member. Some evidence suggests that in many institutions during the 1960s the number of faculty teaching contact hours per week in regular classes decreased but was accompanied by increases in the amount of faculty time spent in supervising graduate students and increases in class size.

Cutting the problem another way, we find that the total number of faculty in some institutions increased dramatically. At Stanford, for example, the number of members of the Academic Council went from 427 in 1955 to 1,031 in 1970, an increase of 141 percent, compared with an increase of enrollment from 7,870 to 11,600, or 47 percent. But there was a sharp change in the composition of the student body: graduate students accounted for 36 percent in 1955 and 45.5 percent in 1970. Staff other than faculty increased by 161 percent, from 2,220 in 1955 to 5,802 in 1970. Stanford was transformed in those fifteen years by plentiful federal research funds, the generosity of its benefactors, and the drive of its leadership. From 1955 to 1970 its total operating budget rose by 572 percent, the instruction budget rose by 632 percent, the research budget by 669 percent, the library budget by 634 percent, and plant operations by 551 percent. Other major research universities had similar growth, and some public institutions grew even more in total budget and enrollment.

Note that staff other than faculty increased by a greater percentage than did faculty, that both grew by much more than enrollment (because of growth in research and increased relative emphasis on graduate instruction), and that all of the dollar budgets grew by percentages far greater than either the enrollment growth or the faculty and staff growth. (An increase of 600 percent in fifteen years represents growth at a compound annual rate of 13.9 percent.)

Table 3 illustrates the recent experience of the University of

10. R. Radner and L. S. Miller, "Demand and Supply in U.S. Higher Education: A Progress Report," *American Economic Review*, May 1970, pp. 326–34.

California. During this period, the university's enrollment increased from 65,945 to 95,259 FTE (full-time equivalent) students, or by 44.4 percent.

Educational institutions which have the specified mission of providing the first two years or four years of postsecondary instruction, and which have been constrained by their own policies or by jurisdictional allocations from accumulating research and graduate instructional responsibilities, have experienced growth in enrollment and thus in total faculty (though student-faculty ratios have increased over the past twenty years). They are not, however, as likely as universities to have experienced as costly a *relative* expansion in non-faculty personnel.

TABLE 3: *Growth of Full-Time Faculty and Staff at the University of California, 1962–63 to April 1969*

Labor Category	1962–63		April 1969		1969 as Percentage of 1962–63
	Number	Percent	Number	Percent	
Clerical and administrative.....	17,600	65.1	30,600	67.8	173.9
Teaching assistants...........	1,100	4.0	1,500	3.3	136.4
Faculty....................	3,800	13.9	6,600	14.6	173.7
Total employees.............	27,100	100.0	45,200	100.0	166.8

As academic institutions have grown in size over the past decade or two, they have had available to them some economies of scale in administration resulting in increases in the number of administrative staff less than proportional to growth. For example, the budgeted cost for general administration and institutional services at the several campuses of the University of California in 1969–70 was 3 percent of total state budget at Berkeley, with 27,300 students, 4 percent at Santa Barbara with 13,300 students, and 6 percent at Irvine with 4,300 students. At the same time, we know that colleges and universities have become more complex institutions to administer over this period, and, as cited above, some have expanded administrative staffs relative to academic staff. Such increases have introduced another independent source of cost increase, for often the increases in proportion are in precisely those types of personnel whose costs rose the most rapidly.

Library Growth

Let us now consider the increase in quantity of library resources. The previous discussion of unit price trends showed that book, periodical, and serial prices rose at a more rapid rate than salaries, and the major research universities experienced enormous expenditure increases for library materials through the past two decades. But in public two-year and four-year institutions which experienced major enrollment growth, especially in the 1960s, a frequent budgetary device has been to provide funds for a certain number of books per FTE student. Quite natural desires to improve library resources have led to increases in the budgeted factor over time. From 1965–66 to 1971–72 (estimated), the California State College System will have increased the number of volumes per FTE student from 27 to 35.5. In this same seven-year period, total library holdings more than doubled, from 3.2 million volumes to 7.5 million volumes.

Equipment

Expansion of the equipment base of academic institutions was also rapid during the enrollment upsurge of the 1950s and particularly the 1960s. The mechanical core of buildings became more expensive and more elaborate. One simple example is air conditioning: in 1960–61, only 14 percent of the University of California's total building area was air-conditioned; in 1970–71, after a huge expansion of total space, 40 percent was air-conditioned, with large cost consequences not only in initial capital outlay but also in subsequent maintenance and utilities expense. In addition, numerous colleges and universities, to conserve scarce land, have had to build high-rise buildings. Again, basic construction methods and more mechanical equipment make these more expensive per square foot at the time of construction, and also result in higher maintenance costs in subsequent use.

Scientific equipment has also increased in complexity. Electron microscopes cost about $30,000 in 1960, and, with improvements and design conveniences, about $50,000–$60,000 in 1970.

Computers are an example of equipment whose unit cost has fallen rapidly and continuously with technological advance, but the decreases in unit prices have been much more than offset by increases of usage. In a ten-university study of rising costs, published in 1967, computers were shown to represent 0.3 percent of operating budget in 1961–62, 1.0 percent in 1966–67, and were projected to be 1.7 percent in 1972–73.[11]

Although we have concentrated on prices and quantities of operating resources in this paper, it should at least be noted that new construction has had a high and rising rate of increase. In the past three years, depending on the type of construction, the cost index has risen at 10–12 percent per year.

11. *Study of Rising Costs at Ten Universities* (Ithaca, N.Y.: Cornell University, September 1967).

Security Cost Rise

In the past three or four years, insurance premiums, fire and other damage losses, and personnel costs for security have risen very rapidly. Fire and casualty insurance rates have risen throughout the economy, but, with the spread of student unrest, academic institutions became a new kind of risk. To keep dollar premium rates from rising too high, institutions have been forced to increase the deductible limit for each occurrence—an action that, in turn, forces them to absorb fire and other damage losses from their own resources. Cheit cites these expense increases as a common theme among most of the institutions he surveyed. He finds that total costs of "campus disturbance" —insurance, security, property maintenance and repair increases, and diversions of staff time—amounted to 4.746 percent of educational and general expenditures in 1969–70 at one institution; and he offers the judgment that one percentage point of the cost push in each of the past three years came from this source alone.[12]

Student Financial Aid

Increased financial aid to students is a final element of important growth in the cost structure of many institutions. Those public institutions which have sought, successfully, to secure added appropriations for student aid and especially for education opportunity programs have experienced offsetting increases in both income and expense from this activity. But many private institutions which have increased their income by raising tuition have felt obliged to devote a significant portion of the new revenue to financial aid for needy students, and many have also accepted new financial responsibilities toward minority students formerly underrepresented in their enrollment. It has been of great importance to American society that our colleges and universities, both public and private, undertake these new responsibilities. But their discretionary resources are clearly not adequate to do the job of redressing deep imbalances in the previous distribution of income, assets, and educational opportunity. There is a strong case for new federal finance to meet this need.

AN APPRAISAL

We must now step back from details and appraise the overall consequences of the cost push and the failure of institutional income to keep pace with costs. Many of the figures cited go back one or two decades and show that the seeds of financial difficulty for higher edu-

12. *The New Depression in Higher Education*, pp. 108–10.

cation were germinating for a long time. The inflation associated with the Vietnam war has clearly accelerated the cost push of some major elements. The growing competition for the federal and state program dollar has worsened the lot of research universities and public institutions. The private institution, worrying about whether to raise tuition still further, faces market resistance to the prices it must charge.

The rate of inflation may be moderating. Cheit and others point to the hope that some of the effects of unrest on institutional expenditure may be tapering off. Many colleges also hope that they are repairing the breach of confidence with legislative and private funding constituencies, with possible beneficent effects on future income.

Provost William G. Bowen of Princeton University has suggested a fundamental relationship which may pertain to all of higher education: that higher education may be a constant-productivity "industry" surrounded by other sectors of society whose productivity is rising several percent per year.[13] Bowen shows long-term comparisons (1905–66) of direct costs per student in higher education with an economy-wide cost index, as well as detailed cost experience of a sample group of major universities. The data seem to show a continued *relative* cost rise for higher education. To get out of this trap, academic institutions can try to gain whatever economies of scale are available to some of them and also use more capital and technology per staff member *where this might cut costs per student.* But Bowen raises a problem that, in the absence of significant productivity gains in the use of resources for higher education, could be dealt with only by cutting the quality of educational operations as we have known them, by reducing the real wages of those who earn their living in higher education, or by continuing to raise the tuition cost and the public subsidy to higher education.

Not much progress has been made in measuring educational output or educational quality.[14] With the development of such measures and with a new address to the improvement of the productivity of higher education, there might be some hope of moderating the cost

13. "Economic Pressures on the Major Private Universities," in *The Economics and Financing of Higher Education in the United States: A Compendium of Papers Submitted to the Joint Economic Committee, Congress of the United States* (Washington: Government Printing Office, 1969), pp. 399–439. In his paper, Bowen drew on his *The Economics of the Major Private Universities* (Berkeley, Calif.: Carnegie Commission on Higher Education, 1968).
14. The author contributed an essay, "Thinking about the Outputs of Higher Education," to a seminar on this subject which included as well a number of interesting contributions, reported in *The Outputs of Higher Education* (Boulder, Colo.: Western Interstate Commission on Higher Education, 1970).

push. These approaches will take a great deal of time, money, and—above all—courage.

Meanwhile, for the balance of the decade, continued cost pressures must be anticipated with the continued growth of total college enrollments. It seems likely that the public two-year colleges are the type of institution whose cost structure will be least vulnerable to further rapid increases of operating cost per student because they rely most heavily on academic personnel, not other types, and they face fewer urgent needs in other areas of rapid cost increase such as library expansion. To the extent that two-year colleges find that they must expand their higher-cost-per-student technical-vocational programs more rapidly than their academic programs, however, they too will have new cost pressures; and those community colleges which have a vital role as gateways to new educational opportunity face intense demands for counseling and other educational services.

Beyond the 1970s there will be, for many institutions, a new problem of living with absolute retrenchment, for total college enrollments will probably fall for several years in the early 1980s.

This paper has dealt with cost and income influences on institutions with stable or growing levels of activity. This has been and, for the 1970s, will be the environment of most institutions. As institutions look some years ahead to the problems of adjusting to possible future decreases in the size of their operations (as indeed some of them are already having to do in research areas), it will be necessary to consider, by means of analysis that is beyond the scope covered here, how to plan the withdrawal of resources from each domain of the institution's activity.

EPILOGUE

Additional evidence concerning trends in expenditures and income has become available through the courtesy of Dr. Hans H. Jenny, co-author with G. Richard Wynn of *The Golden Years*.[15] They will soon publish *After the Golden Years . . . ?*, an updating of income and expenditures in forty-eight four-year colleges.[16]

For the full decade of the 1960s, Jenny reports that these colleges had compound annual rates of income growth per student of 6.4 percent, while the like rate of growth in expense per student was 6.8

15. *The Golden Years: A Study of Income and Expenditure Growth and Distribution of 48 Private Four-Year Liberal Arts Colleges, 1960–1968* (Wooster, Ohio: College of Wooster, 1971).
16. In preparation; to be published by the College of Wooster.

percent; thus, for the decade, the "gap" was 0.4 percent per year. This rate is less than the average shown by Cheit in his study of forty-one institutions of several types. Jenny finds, however, that his very recent figures, for 1968–70, show a much larger gap—income growth of 6.8 percent per student per year as against 8.2 percent yearly growth of expense. Student aid expenses had much the most rapid growth rate of all the expense categories. He has also calculated the year-to-year marginals—the changes in income and expense—and finds that for 1960–61 about eight cents of each dollar of extra tuition and fee income went to student aid, whereas for 1969–70, thirty-two cents went to student aid.

Dr. Jenny has provided the author with some conclusions and observations, summarized here as follows: (1) There are real differences in the economic pressures on different types of institutions, and, in particular, the four-year colleges have limited room for maneuver on both the cost and expense sides. (2) Among all categories of operating expenditure, student aid expense has had to grow the most rapidly, and that total is approximately the total size of the "subsidy" gap in the forty-eight colleges he studied. (3) In addition to the focus that he, Cheit, and the present author have all had on operating income and expense, there should be detailed study of the capital accounts of higher education, an area which has unfortunately not received detailed analytical treatment.

Relating Costs and Income

JOSEPH A. KERSHAW

DR. BALDERSTON HAS PREPARED A PAPER THAT ONE READS WITH PLEASURE and profit. He is one of a small, but growing group of economists who are bringing careful analysis to bear on the complex questions of resource allocation in higher education. He is a practitioner as well as an analyst, having served in a central decision-making role in one of our largest and most complicated institutions. What he says, therefore, is worth heeding, and although I take issue with him on a couple of points, I agree with most of it.

The author's principal contribution is a close look at how institutions of higher learning came to the precarious financial condition in which they now find themselves. The most interesting aspect of this discussion perhaps is how problems can be generated, grow, and become acute while no one is looking. When relationships among the variables as they change over time are examined in detail, the consequences of seemingly innocent decisions can be seen as sometimes devastating. One shudders to contemplate the consequences of some decisions recently taken under pressure—entry into black studies, urban studies, environment—as they come home to roost in coming years.

I found particularly interesting, but unpersuasive, Dr. Balderston's "stabilization after growth" model. He asserts that growth is beneficial while it is happening, but that an institution will find itself in trouble, not only when its growth stops, but when the rate of growth begins to slacken. This view seems akin to the economist's acceleration principle, and I wish he had demonstrated what he had in mind. The tapering-off of growth *may* bring trouble, but I think the outcome would depend entirely on what had happened to the relationship among the key variables during the growth process. If growth is used as the occasion to achieve an appropriate value for such things as size of faculty, salaries of faculty, size of student body, and level of tuition (in the private institutions) or the place of students in the support formula (in the public institutions), then a viable, steady, stable situation seems to me not at all impossible. I do not argue that arriving at this state is simple; indeed getting there may not be half the fun, but it *is* the basic management challenge.

My own model of why higher education is in trouble is not in conflict with any of Balderston's five. It has elements of most of his and is probably much more simple-minded. It may fit the private institutions better than the public ones, but I think it has applicability to both. It might be called the "income determines expenditure" model. For twenty years, roughly until 1968, institutions generally had growing incomes, and their prime fiscal decision was how to allocate that income each year. There was no great pressure to minimize costs; indeed the successful administrator in a sense *maximized* his costs within an ever-growing income, because he and his peers assumed a one-to-one relationship between cost and quality. The "best" institution had the highest cost—high salaries, low faculty-student ratios, and so on; the administrator's primary function was to get more income and thus get his costs even higher.

Then, for reasons we are familiar with, beginning in the late 1960s, income—in terms of both money and purchasing power—became less easy to get. Many early decisions turned out to be irreversible (you don't stop heating those new buildings and you don't cut salaries). Those expenses that could be cut bore the whole brunt, and the retrenchment seemed even more drastic than it was. Allocating increments to budgets is *much* easier than parceling out cuts, even when the cuts are moderate. This is why deficits, which are generally rather small in relation to total budgets, seem to be causing so much trouble. This model may be somewhat more optimistic than is warranted; it implies, for example, that many educational institutions have it in their power to set their houses in order if only they make the right difficult decisions, even without massive federal entry.

I want to comment briefly on Professor Balderston's findings that faculty salaries at the University of California have been growing less rapidly than salaries of administrative staff and teaching assistants. From that analysis, he argues that the university should be substituting faculty for nonfaculty to the greatest possible extent, a course that is the opposite of the conventional wisdom.

Two things seem to me to be wrong with this conclusion. First, faculty represent a much greater financial commitment than their salaries indicate. Not only do their fringe benefits tend to be higher (children's tuition scholarships, sabbatical leaves, and promotion to tenure come to mind) but also many other expenditures tend to be closely related to numbers of faculty—library and computer expenditures are examples. Second, it isn't rates of change that ought to determine intelligent substitution, but the relative size of the costs. Even though incomes of teaching assistants may be growing more rapidly than salaries of regular faculty, their use is still economical so long as it costs less to use a teaching assistant than a faculty member. I believe this point to be of central importance since the major way in which costs can be brought under intelligent control is in the way faculty are used. Mr. Balderston's argument pushes us in just the wrong direction.

The paper is useful in bringing together data on what is happening to costs of library acquisitions, computer operations, and insurance premiums, among other things. The information is not encouraging. I agree that perhaps the most difficult to digest will be the runaway costs of student aid, which turned up so sharply just a few short years ago. I agree too that the case for federal subsidy for this budget item is both more persuasive and more urgent than for any other. The consequences of institutional cutbacks on aid to disadvantaged students are not pleasant to contemplate; and present resources are no match for the way this item is exploding.

The View from Negro Institutions

HERMAN H. LONG

MY COMMENTS ON DR. BALDERSTON'S PAPER WILL BE FROM THE VIEWPOINT of the historic Negro institutions of higher education, and are based on eight years' experience as president of a small private college. The paper is exceedingly useful in applying five models of financial stress to explain a variety of typical institutional experiences. According to the author's analysis, the normal condition in most of our institutions is now one of financial *stress*—not yet necessarily crisis—that has been reached simply by virtue of continued operation. The situation described appears to prevail in the institutions that historically have served the generations of black students who have sought the opportunities of higher education.

In the black institutions, the underlying difficulty is the low and narrow economic base of their constituencies—students, alumni, families and relatives of students, and indeed the Negro community itself to which the institutions are most immediately though not exclusively related. Throughout their hundred or so years of existence, they have never had a sufficient flow of income and support to discharge adequately either the quality of educational mission or the heavy burden of educational responsibility which has been almost singly theirs over the years. The fact that they have continued to exist, to increase in size and in the quality of program, and to produce about 80 percent of all Negro students who receive undergraduate degrees in this country and who proceed to graduate and professional programs and to careers in community service, is in the nature of a miracle whose full story is yet to be told. I think the late Charles S. Johnson, then president of Fisk University, was right when he said that what the black institutions have to contribute most specially in the diffusing processes of integration in higher education are the values that lie in the experience of struggle and survival.

Recent estimates from the Office of Civil Rights in the Department of Justice indicate that there were some 379,000 black students in higher education, representing about 6.5 percent of total enrollments. Of these black students, 40 percent were enrolled in the 111 historically Negro institutions; thus 5 percent of the nation's colleges and universities were carrying 40 percent of the burden of educating the largest economically dispossessed segment of the population. It is pertinent that Negro income, nationwide, has averaged only about half that of white income, even during the recent periods of high increase in national income and wealth; and, of course, this continuing and gross disparity is reflected in the ability of students and their families to pay their share in the rising costs of higher education. McGrath a few years ago stated the disparity as follows: "Estimates indicate that over three-fourths of all families nationally with children in college may earn over $6,000 a year. Fewer than a third of the students surveyed at Negro colleges reported a family income of that magnitude."[1]

The question then arises whether the weak basis of constituency support for the historical Negro institutions is to any adequate degree being equalized through income from state and federal sources and from foundations, corporations, and individual donors. Although the information on private giving to Negro higher education is limited, the evidence appears to be convincingly in the negative. For example, the report of the Federal Interagency Committee on Education, issued in 1970, presented the dismal picture that only 3 percent of the collective education funds in all agencies of the federal government go to support programs and services at the black institutions. On the side of private giving, only two of the 111 black institutions have been able to raise endowments of as much as $30–$40 million, and the majority have endowments of only $3 million or less. The situation for the private institutions is far more critical than for the state-supported colleges and universities, which receive direct operating and capital funds from state appropriations.

Both the public and private Negro institutions face, in addition to inadequate constituency support, the indirect but powerful factor of color or racial discrimination which exists in America as a subtle and pervasive cultural norm. Higher education in this country carries a high prestige value along with a corollary exclusiveness value. In the competition for financial and other forms of support, there clearly exists an institutional prestige hierarchy in which the high-ranking institutions are favored. Since the Negro in America suffers generally from systematically ascribed low prestige status, the institutions that have grown out of his identity and experience—particularly the institutions of higher education—uniformly occupy the bottom rung of the prestige ladder. The popular view is that all black institutions are ipso facto inferior to any and all white institutions. To the extent that these evaluations influence the decisions and priorities of both public

1. Earl J. McGrath, *The Predominantly Negro Colleges and Universities in Transition* (New York: Teachers College Press, 1965), p. 39.

and private sources of support, racial or color discrimination becomes an effective economic factor related to financial stress. The history of state appropriations to the public Negro colleges, especially under the separate but equal doctrine, reveals an assumption of a differential on racial grounds; it is not clear at present whether that assumption has disappeared. For the private college, only minor gains have been achieved in the continuing fight for federal and private support on a level commensurate with both their need and the disproportionate burden of social responsibility they carry.

The United Negro College Fund, established some twenty-five years ago as the first national united educational fund effort in this direction, bears special mention in these comments. It is the major source of private giving to some forty private Negro institutions of higher learning, with accreditation required as a basis of membership. The annual campaign returns from this effort constitute a kind of living endowment for the colleges, and the highest amount raised to date in any campaign was a little above $7 million. Institutions sharing in this effort realize in income from the private sector amounts ranging roughly from $100,000 to $200,000, as based on a formula of distribution. The current campaign goal is $10 million, although as measured against the need and mission involved, the national effort should be aimed at something in the range of $100 million of private giving each year.

This brief summary, unhappily, is but part of the story of financial crisis facing the Negro institutions, for not only do they lack basic income and constituency support, but also they are victims of the same economic factors of rising costs and inflation that characterize the higher education scene generally. They present in several ways classic cases of Balderston's models of "expanded academic aspiration" and "conscientious overcommitment." Under pressures of accreditation and of both student and public expectation, they have added new programs, including community service projects, which greatly strain their resources. In addition, under the terms of federal support for innovations in curriculum, teaching, and counseling, they have undertaken additional responsibilities for which there is no assurance of continued funding. In this respect, they fall into Balderston's analytical model of "time passing." They certainly are overcommitted in terms of student aid insofar as their own resources are concerned and insofar as they must meet the matching fund requirements of federal programs. In one group of private colleges with which I am associated, more than 80 percent of the students were receiving financial assistance in order to remain in college, and about 70 percent of students came

from families earning less that $7,500. It seems safe to say that the differential effect of the economic factors producing financial stress in higher education institutions generally works out to be an added and disproportionate factor in the case of the black institutions.

My role in this discussion, I am relieved to say, is not to prescribe solutions, even if I had the wisdom to do so. It seems apparent that nothing approaching a solution to the problems of financial stress in the historic Negro institutions can be achieved in the absence of a drastic reordering of priorities in the state, federal, and private sectors— a reordering that will take into account the special burden these institutions carry in responding to the national goal of providing equality of educational opportunity for all youth.

A Time for Realism

PEGGY HEIM

DR. BALDERSTON HAS APTLY OBSERVED THAT THE END OF FINANCIAL CRISIS for colleges and universities is not yet in sight. He foresees that the basic pattern of stress will persist through the present decade. I see no reason for a brighter forecast. The balance among forces will change, but the net effect will still be one of stress. If anything, the stress may become progressively greater, and gains in cost reduction may well be offset by increased difficulties on the income side.

Is federal aid a solution? Dr. Balderston implies that large infusions of federal aid, say several billion dollars a year, would produce a permanent easing of the stress. I am not that sanguine. His five models of stress—expanded academic aspiration, time passing, stabilization after growth, conscientious overcommitment, and income tapering— reveal much of the reason that, without other developments, nothing less than escalating levels of government expenditures would suffice. For most of higher education, government aid would merely postpone the evil days. Of course, to say that federal aid alone would be insufficient to the need does not mean that it is not indicated.

Varieties of financial stress. Dr. Balderston's major contribution lies in his formulation of a variety of models. He has stripped them down to their fundamentals and laid them out for all to see. His message should serve as warning to many institutions, which, I suspect, are

The author is indebted to numerous colleagues for their helpful suggestions, and especially to Dr. John Harrington of the Wofford College faculty.

tripping along these paths. Even though they are engaging in long-range planning, they are failing both to calculate the full financial costs ahead and to analyze realistically their revenue prospects. For those who probe deeper, his comments will indicate the nature and scope of some of the hard, unpleasant decisions that may lie ahead before higher education can get its financial house in order again.

A microview. Dr. Balderston's approach is essentially a microview of specific cost and revenue factors that are functioning to cause the serious financial stress. He is quite right. An understanding of these factors is essential if practitioners are to avoid or correct the problem. But I hypothesize that there are other underlying causes, more basic than those he has depicted, that must also be understood before solutions are possible.

I shall turn now to a "macroview." The basic problem in the financial crisis appears to lie in the inappropriateness of the orientation, organizational patterns, and administrative techniques of higher education to the new economic environment.

The "community of scholars" and aversion to management. In the traditional faculty view, the community of scholars should determine educational policy even when it involves financial consequences. In a relatively favorable financial climate, this unwieldy form of organization works tolerably well. But in long periods of acute stress, this organizational pattern combined with an aversion to management and the techniques of management may well prove disastrous. On the one hand, a faculty turns crimson at the word *management.* On the other hand, it will not itself use advanced management approaches. (It should be added that the same failings hold for many administrators.) It shuns budgets, disdains sophisticated financial analyses, deliberates interminably, and avoids hard choices that may affect a segment adversely. In the past a faculty has taken its chances in muddling through as a "community of scholars." It has not realized that the odds have changed and that educational tradition must change too.

The transformation of integrating values. Prior to World War II, two coordinate values served as the integrating force in higher education: the education of the new generation(s), and the pursuit of knowledge. The pursuit of knowledge was relatively low-keyed. In the ensuing decades the emphasis on education receded in importance and the pursuit of knowledge was transformed into publications, best epitomized by "publish or perish" and academic prestige. The new duo came to dominate directly or indirectly the aspirations and thrusts of the profession *and* the institutions themselves.

The cost impact of the new values. In brief, emphasis upon publication and other forms of individual academic prestige caused faculty to seek conditions conducive to the goal, among others, bigger and better research facilities, secretarial help, graduate programs, released time, the option of teaching courses in their specialties, and the proliferation and growth of disciplines. All these augmented the servicing load—administration. Further, if publication output increased, library costs too must increase. Since faculty is to a large extent the institution, what faculty wants tends to become the desire of the institution. Colleges that might care little about faculty research still must compete in both sellers' and buyers' markets. Thus they are forced to imitate the ambitions of the universities.

Other cost-raising and revenue-shrinking forces. The forces described above converged with other forces—the tremendous growth in enrollment, the social upheaval that evoked new commitments on the part of institutions, alienation of donor constituencies (public *and* private), and inflation of both a general and structural nature. Structural inflation has been particularly severe in some major areas of expenditure. The result—the varieties of financial stress described by Dr. Balderston. What makes the economic environment new is the severity of some of the stresses, the convergence of many, and their persistence. Most institutions cannot work their way out merely by holding tight for a few years while revenues catch up with expenditures. Those which have not yet been severely affected are likely to be, and some, in anticipation, are already making changes.

What then might be a viable response, a workable prescription? (1) Faculties, administrations, and organizations must face up to a review of the mores, orientation, and patterns of administration and governance. (2) The same groups must see the need to acquire and use techniques of more sophisticated management. (3) Financial planning must be fully programmed to anticipate realistically the effect of both old and new forces on costs and revenues. (4) Faculties, administrations, and organizations must be prepared to institute and accept changes, painful though some may be. So must government and society. (5) Even with these considerable modifications, some private institutions will not survive and public institutions will experience hardship. (6) In the final analysis, the only way out lies in the axiom of the French Foreign Legion, "March or die!"

WILLIAM J. McGILL

Means and Ways in Private Universities

YEARS OF STUDENT UNREST FOLLOWED BY SERIOUS FISCAL
problems have produced a crisis of the spirit in our nation's universities. It is a morbid sentiment that descends upon large institutions
when their sense of security or purpose is threatened. The crisis is not
unlike the one the entire nation is experiencing; indeed, almost every
aspect of American life, good and bad, finds itself represented in one
way or another on campus. The university crisis, however, has elements of uniqueness that require special thought and attention. It is
now evident that the expanding responsibilities which modern society
has pressed upon the universities, ranging from scientific and technological education to broadened educational opportunity for the disadvantaged, have forced many institutions into deepening financial
trouble.

The temporal linkage between student unrest and fiscal crisis leads
immediately to speculation that these problems are somehow causally
related. Many critics seem to have concluded that support for public
and private institutions is diminishing as the larger society reacts to
the political and emotional excesses on campuses during the last seven
years. Without doubt, some public reactivity to campus disorders does
exist, but the financial troubles of universities are far more complex
and serious than that reason alone suggests.

The root of the troubles seems to be the large-scale and rapid university expansion stimulated by federal policy in the middle 1950s in
response to signs of Soviet technological advancement. Vast resources
were poured into universities for the development of new graduate
and professional programs and for physical facilities to support them.
Fiscal growth was stimulated by an understandable desire on the part
of each institution to retain its position of intellectual leadership and
by a fear that it might become second rate through the mere exercise
of civilized caution. The theory was that the expansion would be self-
supporting; but new buildings, laboratories, computer centers, and a

variety of other facilities produced ever-widening circles of support and maintenance costs that continuously inflated operating costs. The foundation practice of providing "seed money" to start new and innovative programs also contributed to a pattern of university growth, which had been set off by the growth of knowledge itself. Now the institutions are paying for it.

Suddenly the expansionist tide turned, and in 1968 contraction was clearly setting in. Federal programs supporting student aid, faculty research, and physical expansion began to level off or even decline. At the same time rampant inflation forced continuing increases in salaries and central costs. Universities were caught in a squeeze of limited resources, increasing commitments, and spiraling costs. But their problems are not limited to fiscal woes. The growth pressures that produced deficits and the dogged efforts at retrenchment also disenchanted many of the students. Student unrest and fiscal problems are probably not related in causal sequence. Both seem to be consequences of the vigorous growth that has made American higher education the best in the world. Now we are entering upon a climactic period.

THE CREDENTIALING FUNCTION

Universities are experiencing remarkable changes in structure and governance, which reflect some equally remarkable stresses and contradictory and conflicting currents in the American society itself. Universities have thus been forced to spread themselves steadily thinner in order to accommodate to the changing requirements of mass education in a technological age.

Ever since World War II, the expanding scope and difficulty of higher education have placed serious stresses on students that few of us really understand. Increasingly, they seem to be repelled by the rigidity of undergraduate curricula and the pyramiding of course requirements that extend education further and further into adult life.

The rapid growth since 1945 of an advanced technological society in America has shaped an educational system in which advanced degrees are really avenues of entry into business and professional occupations. This view has been expressed by my colleague Ivar Berg at Columbia, and is confirmed by all my own hard-won administrative experience during the last four years. The difficulties and frustrations posed for students by an extremely competitive and not entirely rational occupational credentialing system, together with the university's role as the purveyor of the necessary credentials, seems—especially recently—to have been driving many students toward overt hostility.

The last decade has witnessed the growth of a campus-based counter-culture whose life style and values are placed in romantic and mystical opposition to the evils of what is called "the system." Somehow the occupational credentialing system and the counterculture must be seen as standing in reciprocal relation to each other.

It seems to me that these problems, whatever the students may say about them, derive from the sheer weight of higher education in a mass technology, and that the coming decade will be a critical one. Our universities, and colleges too, must find the ways to educate a new generation of managers and professionals without creating an educational structure so repelling that it drives inexperienced and genuinely curious students toward the dropout blandishments of the counterculture. Institutions must also find ways to educate a new generation of the economically deprived so that they can, for the first time, commence to identify themselves with the future directions of a society in which almost no occupation is simple and manual toil is fast disappearing as a form of gainful employment.

Our colleges and universities need to find the resources to provide adequately for the arts and humanities on campus lest we face a bleak future in which an Orwellian life style and Stakhanovite value system begin to replace the literary and cultural attainments that free men and women have always cherished.

FINANCIAL STRESS AND INSTITUTIONAL MISSION

Finally, institutions—both public and private—must find ways to do all these things while operating under conditions of limited resources and uncertain funding as well as probable deficits and program cutbacks.

We at Columbia believe that we have no more than ten to twenty years to find long-term solutions to our problems. We also believe that the university must undergo some contraction during this period in order to resolve the fiscal problems that confront us today. The precise character and amount of contraction are not yet clear although we have attempted several types of forecasts. Nationally, graduate education is experiencing considerable stress, and many studies predict an overproduction of Ph.D.'s extending well into the 1980s. Columbia must be exceptionally cautious as we seek an appropriate response, for we cannot risk the potential collapse of a complex system of graduate and professional education on which the health and safety of American society depend. Boom and bust operation is extremely hazardous to the functioning of delicate and sensitive institutions like universities. We have to avoid it.

Undergraduate education does not seem to display similar signs of contraction, nor are some of the major areas of professional education, particularly medicine and law. Thus, patterns of university adjustments to the harsh realities of the 1970s are likely to be complex and will almost certainly be determined to considerable extent by initiatives in governmental support as the nation's needs become clear. In this respect, the new era resembles the 1960s. Another cycle seems about to begin as the stresses of two decades of cold war competition force the nation to consider new directions for our society.

No one knows the way to assured safety in this uncertain future. Columbia and all other universities must discover new ways to finance quality higher education. Large endowment resources no longer guarantee safety under conditions of rapid expansion and run-away inflation. At Columbia, our present efforts are aimed principally at buying sufficient time to permit us to conduct our search for new directions thoughtfully and wisely. All universities ought to be talking more to one another about it. They should be using the rapidly contracting lead time for intense study, appeals to legislative bodies, and a joint national effort not only to portray the crisis confronting higher education but also to try to define what their new directions must be.

Columbia's most critical immediate need is for increased general purpose income. To obtain it, we need to become more effective in developing new forms of alumni giving and new corporate support, a task that offers the most difficult and elusive fund-raising problems. Nevertheless, Columbia experienced a number of signal successes in 1971 and we must redouble our efforts in the years ahead.

We may also be forced to contemplate increasing tuition charges. Here we are approaching a decisive stage in a sensitive area of Columbia's finances, for tuition is already so high that it cannot be raised much further without making Columbia inaccessible to all but the very rich.

We can realize modest savings by pursuing our rigorous cost-cutting efforts and by searching out more efficient forms of instruction. It is apparent, however, that the sophisticated instructional techniques demanded by modern technology will increasingly impose patterns of educational costs that are simply not commensurate with prior standards. For example, the current cost of educating a medical student at Columbia University is close to $11,000 per year. Tuition charges are $2,800, and many students must borrow to meet even this subsidized tuition figure.

The only sensible long-term solutions for the combined societal and fiscal problems now confronting Columbia and other large private universities must involve new forms of federal and state subsidy to help defray the heavy central costs and simultaneously provide support for increasingly expensive technological education that serves in the public interest.

All signs at Columbia point to the conclusion that the university's operating deficit is located principally in its central operating costs. In 1965, when our budget was last in balance, central costs (administration, libraries, computer center, buildings and grounds) were approximately $15 million. By 1970, central costs had climbed to $31 million whereas the general purpose income available to meet these campuswide needs was still about $15 million. Thus the source of Columbia's 1970–71 operating deficit is not difficult to identify: all signs point to a devastating inflation of central costs as the primary cause of our problems. We have also not done well in raising the new revenue required to defray our indirect costs.

If private higher education is to be rescued from a danger whose outlines grow sharper with each passing year, it appears that new federal programs will be almost obligatory to help meet central costs and provide funds for public service technological education. A precedent is found in the so-called Bundy funds provided by New York State to private institutions. A sound rationale underlies the subsidies: the state finds it less expensive over time to subsidize graduate and professional education in existing private universities than to construct the public institutions that would be needed if private universities were forced to curtail their public service professional training.

A SHARP LOOK AT INSTITUTIONAL MISSIONS

Universities will not get receptive hearings from federal and state legislatures unless they are prepared to cooperate in efforts to control costs. I have joined with other educational leaders in New York City and in the state to undertake serious regional planning to avoid expensive redundancy and to operate instead in ways that are mutually and educationally complementary.

Selective excellence in higher education in the state of New York implies that units of the State University and the City University should not seek to construct professional schools of medicine, dentistry, nursing, architecture, and engineering merely to fulfill self-defined prescriptions of their aspirations for scope and size. Development efforts should be undertaken only as part of a plan reflecting existing state resources and the manpower needs of the state and the nation. The state's resources include many facilities in the private sector, which surely must be recognized as operating in the public interest. A medical school offers professional training in the public interest regardless of whether it is public or private. Both types are vital state and national resources. No part of higher education, public or private, can fail to recognize that its value to society, and hence its capacity for survival, rests on the ability to work cooperatively so as to generate public confidence in its mission. The people of the nation must become convinced that investment of their resources in higher education is a sound investment in their own future.

Higher education will be effective in meeting the challenges posed by the increasing and almost insatiable demands of the world's most remarkable technological state, as well as the equally critical need to educate our entire population and not just a privileged elite, only by preserving a diversity of educational resources. The latter range from community colleges, four-year private institutions stressing educational innovation, large private universities stressing educational excellence, and large state universities stressing the new imperatives of national need. Institutions must find ways to work together, or face public disavowal.

A substantial mythology of recent years portrays universities and colleges as irrelevant to the needs of students and insensitive to the requirements of our society. Criticisms among students and in the larger public reflect some of the conflicting and contradictory directions in the society itself. Perhaps most administrators and faculty have reached a point of accepting the rhetoric in the realization that institutions are expected to absorb and sublimate the tensions of society. Yet they should not allow themselves to be mistaken or misled about what American higher education has achieved in the last quarter-century or what will come to be expected of it. Whatever its weaknesses, the higher education system as constructed is, in Robert Hutchins' words, not very good but simply the best there is anywhere in the world. Everyone involved must continue with the task of sustaining and improving it. The future will not be easy.

These are difficult days not only for Columbia but for all universities and indeed all of American life. We are caught up in a torrent of social change, civil unrest, and conflicting directions in the society. No one can foresee the future, but we are determined that our universities must continue and flourish. If anything has characterized the past year at Columbia for me, it has been the development there of a new courage and determination. We deal daily with dedicated revolutionaries, tough community groups, idealistic students, and all the ferment of an American society in transit to a new era. We are not afraid of it. In fact, we rather enjoy it. Some satisfaction comes with knowing that we live at a decisive time in history. Special meaning is given to our lives in recognizing that we are grappling with problems so vital that the future directions of American life depend in large degree on what we are able to do and how we are able to achieve solutions. I submit that the problems are many and that the cause is worthy of the expenditure of all our energies.

VIRGINIA B. SMITH

More for Less:
Higher Education's New Priority

FOR THE PAST SEVERAL DECADES, HIGHER EDUCATION HAS outstripped all believable predictions in providing its services to more and more of the nation's youth. At the same time, our colleges and universities have been using more and more resources per student. Costs per student in higher education have risen at a higher rate than costs in the general economy, and the warning is that this trend is likely to continue. In a nation that places expansion of educational opportunity high on its agenda, the proven ability to accommodate ever greater numbers of students is welcome. But when total costs for higher education become a major and highly visible portion of a public budget which must also respond to many competing and equally urgent demands, reluctance to accept the inevitability of sharply rising costs for higher education grows demonstrably.

The public still calls for more higher education; recent public actions, however, suggest an underlying belief that it should cost less. In New York City the public wanted and got an open admissions policy leading to a massive, instantaneous increase in enrollment; the budget was not, however, commensurately increased. Similar actions, if not so dramatic, have occurred in other states where legislatures have appropriated substantially less than institutions have requested but have somehow assumed that the same number of students could still be accommodated at essentially the same level of quality.

The initial, and still overwhelmingly the most frequent, response of colleges and universities to this new depression has been to seek additional revenues. To the institutions, the simplest and quickest solution to their financial problems would be to have their funds increased sufficiently to cover anticipated expenditures. But as the total financial needs of colleges and universities rise, there are gathering demands for more efficient use of resources, growing suspicions that less costly techniques may exist to accomplish institutional goals, and increasing challenges to some of the goals themselves. Indeed, convincing the public that resources are being handled effectively, both among and within institutions, is rapidly becoming an explicit condition to obtaining increased public revenues. Thus, the potential for achieving economies in our colleges and universities without reducing quality has assumed an importance equal to the search for new revenues.

It is this potential for economies within the institution and the difficulties in achieving them that I explore in this paper. Problems of increasing revenue or allocating resources within the system will not be considered, although these matters are certainly important to the solution of the new depression.

EFFICIENT USE OF RESOURCES

Certainly there is room for improvement in the management of higher education. In 1967, Alan Pifer, president of the Carnegie Corporation of New York, voiced what growing numbers of Americans had begun to think, that this nation can "no longer afford the luxury of an unplanned, wasteful, chaotic approach to higher education.[1] Although he was speaking of the system as a whole, the criticism is not totally inapplicable to the units that make up that system.

Few would argue that our colleges and universities are models of efficiency. Examples of apparent inefficiencies are not difficult to find. Perhaps the most obvious and also enduring example is the continuing proliferation of courses. In 1957 the President's Committee on Education Beyond the High School, concerned with the proliferation of courses, urged that all faculties "earnestly and periodically review their own curricula in the light of the students' educational needs, major objectives and institutional resources." The President's Committee hoped that a periodic review would stem somewhat "man's desire to categorize his ever-growing specialized knowledge."[2] Seven years later, Lewis B. Mayhew reviewed the same problem and suggested the situation was becoming more acute as institutions added more and more departments covering narrow areas of a discipline.[3]

The situation has not changed. Those concerned with efficient use

1. Pifer, "Toward a National System of Higher Education" (Paper delivered to the Association of American Colleges, Jan. 16, 1968).

2. *Second Report to the President* (Washington: Government Printing Office), p. 37.

3. Mayhew, "Curricular Reform and Faculty Well-Being," *Educational Record*, January 1963, pp. 53–61.

of resources still refer to the "lushness of the curriculum" and observe that "new courses spring into being every fall and they seldom fade away. Pruning is resisted and rare."[4] State agencies have been particularly concerned with underutilization of plant and equipment and have developed standards to achieve more efficient use, but idle periods continue to exist. And little direct attention has been given to the development of techniques for saving one of the most costly resources in the higher education process—the student's time.

The casual observer might easily conclude that American colleges and universities as they now operate provide substantial opportunities for increasing the effective use of both human and capital resources. Along with the laments about the present financial condition of higher education, there is one recurring optimistic theme: the state of financial stringency is conducive to the achievement of economies; with less to spend, institutions will learn to spend it more wisely. Is this optimism justified?

Is the New Depression Conducive to Economies?

Hundreds of colleges and universities are now well into a period of financial difficulty so that their responses to the situation will provide some evidence to support or refute the optimists' contention.[5] The most frequently reported immediate response to financial crisis is to delay expenditures (for example, defer maintenance, postpone capital projects, postpone expansion of existing programs or introduction of new academic programs). Delayed or deferred expenditures can and often do lead to net diseconomies over time: Rapidly rising maintenance and construction costs increase the cost of the same task undertaken later. Aborted capital and education projects

---

4. Edwin D. Etherington, "Help and Self-Help in Financing Higher Education," *AGB Reports*, May 1968, p. 9.

5. For descriptions of institutional responses to the present financial difficulty, see Earl F. Cheit, *The New Depression in Higher Education* (New York: McGraw-Hill Book Co., 1971), pp. 83–90; William W. Jellema, *The Red and the Black* (Washington: Association of American Colleges, 1971), pp. 9–10. Several periodical articles and newspaper reports provide additional indications of institutional response: "Cost Cutting Is Vigorous on Many Campuses," *College Management*, January 1971, pp. 16–17; "How Institutions Are Coping with the Financial Crisis," *College and University Business*, November 1970, p. 21; Andrew H. Malcolm, "Colleges over U.S. Cutting Services," *New York Times*, Feb. 22, 1971; William Delaney, "Georgetown's President and College Financial Squeeze," *Washington Star*, March 14, 1971; "To Meet College Crisis: Cuts in Faculties, Courses, Students," *U.S. News and World Report*, Dec. 14, 1970, pp. 54–55; Amitai Etzioni, "On the Art of University Pruning," *Science*, April 30, 1971, p. 429; William Trombley, "Private Colleges—Redding Keeps Getting Redder," *Los Angeles Times*, April 5, 1971.

result in waste of the staff time that has been devoted to planning and initial recruiting of staff or selection of architects and contractors. By its nature, the deferred expenditure is at best a temporary remedy that changes the input-output relationship only for the immediate period but leaves unchanged or increased the resource need for a given output in the future.

Inefficient Economies

"Tightening the belt" and eliminating the "extras" are economy measures available only to institutions that are still, to a degree at least, affluent at the time the acute financial stringency develops. Many institutions have learned to live without frills as a part of their normal state. Characteristically, in "economies" of this kind, human resources are substituted for capital resources, and the substitution frequently results in an uneconomic use of human—both student and staff—resources. For example, drastically shortening the time that libraries are open may lead to wasteful use of student time, particularly if the student body includes many students who work part time. Reduction in the number of copies of books placed on reserve for a course may prevent even the motivated students from being adequately prepared for class discussions.

Some institutions and some state legislative bodies have responded to the financial crisis with a variety of techniques designed to get more work out of faculty for the same price: adoption of specific, and in some instances increased, workload requirements; restrictions on the use of sabbatical leave; and staff reduction through attrition without commensurate reduction in tasks to be performed. These cost-reducing activities may have serious repercussions. One response is increased faculty interest in unionization and in the development of rigid contract provisions to protect themselves against further deterioration in working conditions.

Although financial distress within an institution may frequently be attributed to inefficient management, improvement in management is rarely reported as one of the initial responses to financial stress. Probably, however, administrators become more aware of the need for improvement in management during such a period.

For certain sized institutions and certain programs within institutions, unit cost may be reduced through exercising particular types of economies of scale: Some institutions have reported combining certain programs in order to reduce costs. A more common action is the elimination of all courses with less than a preestablished enrollment.

Some institutions, as well as some state systems, are reducing total expenditures by limiting enrollment. If an institution's instructional revenue is reduced by 10 percent, that institution may well consider cutting its enrollment by 10 percent. Yet this response may prove inappropriate at a time when equality of educational opportunity seems almost within reach. The unfortunate social consequences of limiting enrollments could be overcome if meaningful alternatives to college were available, but the nation has a long way to go before the concept of "meaningful alternatives" is a reality for its youth.

It is understandable that most institutional response to financial crisis, at least in the short run, takes the form of deferred expenditures and various types of retrenchment. These actions are largely within the control of the administration, can be undertaken fairly quickly, and usually do not require the input of additional resources. While they do reduce current expenditures, they may also lead to wasteful use of human resources, to increased expenditures in future periods, and to unwanted social consequences.

Increasing Productivity

In the present situation, reductions in expenditures are essential to balance budgets, but not all reductions in cash outflow qualify as real economies. To qualify as a true economy, an action should increase productivity; that is, after the action, more units of output will be produced with the same units of input. Under this definition, few of the institutional responses described above qualify as economies for, at best, they produce only limited and often temporary increases in productivity. As long as changes are confined to support functions (as they have been in many of the initial efforts of institutions to cut costs), the processes through which an institution carries out its central functions are, for the most part, left unchanged.

Substantial increases in productivity will likely be achieved only through changes in the educational process itself. Certainly the significant advances in productivity in industry have involved the processes of production rather than support functions. In higher education, such changes can occur only with experimentation and innovation in academic programs, in instructional techniques, and in the relationship of the student to the institution. Theoretically, an institution in financial crisis may have the motivation to undertake the experimentation, but it rarely has the risk capital needed. Ann Heiss, writing on academic innovation, observes that:

> Trustees and legislative committees are inclined to conserve or to cut back during periods of economic recess rather than to innovate or experiment with new educational ideas. In the absence of adequate

underwriting, colleges and universities are often forced to maintain a holding action or to effect economies by dropping special programs or fringe services from the curriculum. If auxiliary services, such as secretarial or clerical aid, are cut, or instructional loads are appreciably increased, an anesthetized atmosphere may develop with regard to reform or planning for future needs. Creative persons caught in these situations often leave the academic life and are thus lost as the stimulants to new programs. Some institutions have found it virtually impossible to regenerate interest in planning long after the financial crisis is abated. Many of the so-called emergency economies that are enacted in periods of economic crisis prove, in the long-run, to be costly or false. . . . The great Depression of 1929 was so extensive in its effects on higher education that practically no institution emerged from this period unscarred. . . . With growth funds non-existent, and operating funds drastically reduced, institutions of higher education were unable to find the risk capital to support reforms or innovation. It was a time for retrenchment and for the elimination of "frills."[6]

Thus, those who believe there is a silver lining in the financial troubles of higher education may be sorely disappointed unless the impetus provided by financial stress is combined with the much needed risk capital to permit experimentation with and evaluation of different educational approaches.

Even with additional resources, significant economies may be difficult to achieve because of certain characteristics current in higher education. Before discussing these characteristics, I shall review some proposals made for increasing productivity. An examination will, I believe, lead to the conclusion that the greatest potentials for savings lie in changes directly concerned with the educational process itself.

POTENTIALS FOR INSTITUTIONAL ECONOMIES

The most frequently mentioned possibilities for institutional economies involve economies of scale, better utilization of physical facilities, specialization and contracting, the move off campus, and program acceleration. Less frequently mentioned and still relatively unexplored in terms of cost effectiveness are changes in instructional and educational processes.

Economies of Scale

Some four hundred seventy institutions of higher education in the United States have enrollments under three hundred students. Many persons have argued that such institutions could achieve economies

6. Unpublished report on academic innovation, prepared for the Carnegie Commission on Higher Education.

of scale by increasing their enrollments, and their arguments are supported to some extent by facilities surveys showing excess capacity in physical facilities. But difficulties in comparing programs and outputs among institutions make it almost impossible to prove that economies of scale do, in fact, exist. And even if we do assume that economies of scale exist, a realistic assessment must be made of whether the smaller institutions can increase enrollments sufficiently to take advantage of substantial savings in cost per student—economies of scale. Three factors reduce the likelihood of such expansion.

1. *Pricing problems.* Most small institutions are private, and, as such, their ability to increase to a size that would afford economies of scale is limited by their comparative position in the market. The gap between tuition in private and public institutions has grown markedly in recent years. Small private junior colleges are perhaps the hardest hit because public community colleges offer very low or free tuition *and* their accessibility has increased with their rapid growth in numbers in the last decade. The pricing problem is demonstrated by the ratio of tuition levels in private and public institutions: in the four-year institutions, the ratio has changed from about 2.5:1 in 1939–40 to 4:1 in 1967–68; in the two-year institutions, the ratio in 1967–68 was more than 7:1.[7]

Full funding of federal student aid programs and adoption of tuition grant programs by states would improve the competitive position of the private institutions.

2. *Institutional style.* Even if the small colleges could compete on tuition, some, though by no means all, have institutional styles that no longer appeal to many of today's students. This style is characterized by *in loco parentis,* rules governing personal conduct, required residence in dormitories, and other restrictions on the individual's life style.[8]

3. *Educational philosophy and approach.* For many small colleges, the lack of a well-defined educational mission adds to the difficulty of attracting funds for expansion or more students. On the other hand, distinctive educational missions and goals selected by small colleges are likely to be the kind best achieved in a very small college setting and they may also require relatively high cost programs. Thus,

7. *The Capitol and the Campus: State Responsibility for Postsecondary Education,* A Report and Recommendations by the Carnegie Commission on Higher Education (New York: McGraw-Hill Book Co., 1971), pp. 78, 79.
8. For a description of the characteristics of many small nonselective four-year private institutions, see Alexander W. Astin and Calvin B. T. Lee, *The Invisible Colleges* (Prepared for the Carnegie Commission on Higher Education; New York: McGraw-Hill Book Co., 1971).

per student cost in such colleges is not a function of the size of the institution; rather, both institutional size and cost per student may be viewed as functions of the educational mission. Alice Lloyd College affords an example. In 1960, when its enrollment was 200, the cost per student was $600. Today the enrollment is 500, and the cost per student is $2,700. President William Hayes of Alice Lloyd College, testifying before Representative Edith Green's Special Subcommittee on Education, expressed the institution's deliberate decision in this way:

> Leadership and citizenship education for students with culture-based disadvantages requires heavy investments beyond the classroom and personal contact of teachers and students, guidance, counseling, language laboratory, media center, cultural programs, special services, and staff relating to dormitory governance and community involvement activities. These are not luxuries.[9]

Of the colleges with enrollments under 300, 212 are technical or special-purpose institutions that probably could not increase enrollments substantially without adding other subjects to their educational programs. And there is no assurance that a somewhat larger institution offering more subjects could operate at a lower cost per student than a smaller institution with only one specialty.

The above factors suggest that, although economies of scale may be possible, their potential cannot be determined by a gross examination of quantitative data. Only a careful analysis of each small institution would yield tentative conclusions on the possibility or desirability of its achieving economies of scale. Then would come the problem of how to increase the size of the institution, in large part through enhancing its appeal to students. Some small liberal arts colleges, such as Ottawa University in Kansas and at least fifteen others, are experimenting with returning to the students control of their educational programs through negotiated contract. Perhaps this and other innovative techniques will revitalize small institutions, but the relative cost effectiveness of such approaches is yet to be determined.

In some cases a merger may be a desirable solution for two or more small institutions that have geographical proximity and compatibility of educational philosophy and institutional control.

More likely savings from economies of scale could be obtained within large institutions by eliminating courses or programs with small enrollments and by changing instructional techniques to place

9. Statement before Special Subcommittee on Education, Committee on Education and Labor, U.S. House of Representatives, March 31, 1971.

heavier reliance on large lectures which are supplemented with materials prepared for use by several classes. Of course, these changes in instructional techniques may or may not have desirable educational consequences. I shall discuss later potential economies of scale through changes in instructional techniques.

Although not exactly an economy of scale, interinstitutional cooperation among small institutions may achieve savings. Obviously, the advantages of the new technologies are rarely available to a small institution and may prove too expensive for specialized instructional use even in a large institution. Cooperative endeavors, however, open up successful and economical use of closed-circuit TV, computer centers, and similar high cost equipment. For example, five Texas private institutions have recently developed a two-way closed-circuit television system that permits one professor to teach a class at the five institutions simultaneously. The few students in each class at each institution discuss the lecture with the professor through two-way television, and the professor can generate his class at any one of the five institutions; thus he can have not only the television contact but also "face-to-face" contact with each of his students in his scattered classroom at several points during the term. This technique enables the campuses in the closed-circuit network to pool their subject specialists, with a specialist on any one campus serving all five. Although the cooperative facility provides the service at a cost that would otherwise be considerably higher, it does require an initial input of funds to introduce the equipment and to develop the system.

The above is but one example of interinstitutional cooperation. Other possibilities for such cooperation include purchasing pools; joint or exchange use of library facilities; joint appointments of professors, particularly in specialized fields; and a variety of consortia for cooperative development of special programs or shared use of high cost equipment (for example, observatories).

Such cooperative efforts probably offer greater potential for improving the quality than for reducing the level of resources required for the basic educational programs of the participating colleges.

Better Utilization of Physical Facilities

A variety of efforts have been made to achieve better utilization of physical facilities. The technique most widely discussed currently is adoption of some form of year-round calendar. The possibilities and some of the ramifications may best be presented by recounting the experience of the University of California. While I was on the administrative staff there, I observed firsthand the adoption by the Regents of a year-round calendar and its initial implementation in

1967. I did not observe firsthand its demise, but that event was joyously reported by several faculty members who had been convinced that it would not work.

The primary motivation for adopting the year-round calendar was a belief that it would save money and assist accommodation of California's climbing enrollments at a lowered cost. Although an increase in current operating costs was anticipated, its level was estimated to be more than offset by long-range savings in capital outlays. To establish a year-round operation required other adjustments.

First, a shift from a two-semester system to a quarter system was necessary to create terms of equal length. The shift was not welcomed by most faculty, whose courses and life styles were geared to the semester. Second, all faculty pay scales, fringe benefits, and the like had been computed on an academic year basis. This pattern was not changed, and the normal faculty work year remained nine months. Fourth quarter teaching was considered extra employment. But when not all staff chose to work an extra quarter, additional staff had to be hired, and the staff expansion added a few costs. Third, the three campuses that implemented the year-round program encountered low summer enrollments. A dilemma resulted. When a full range of courses was offered, the unit costs were high. When course offerings were reduced, summer enrollment became less appealing to students who were pursuing a predetermined program.

When the university's budget was cut in 1969, the summer quarter was eliminated so that the funds could be allocated to the other three quarters. The quarter system—resisted by much of the faculty—remained as a souvenir of the experiment. Possibly, more experience with the year-round calendar and further modifications would have gained the advantages and savings originally predicted.

The University of California is still investigating ways to utilize the summer term effectively and also the possibility of returning to year-round operation. Its experience shows, however, that long-run savings are not attainable without adequate operating funds in the short run and that, in a complex system, any single change necessitates further multiple adjustments if the system is to work effectively.[10]

Specialization and Contracting

Most institutions feel that they must offer every element of their educational programs on campus or at least under their direct supervision. Perhaps institutions should view themselves as responsible for an individual's overall education program but not necessarily re-

10. Clifford L. Dochterman, "The California Experiment: A Case Study," *Compact*, December 1970, pp. 29–30.

sponsible for providing every one of the components. If there is an excellent computer programming school near a community college, does the college need to develop programming classes? Would it not be more economical for the community college to contract with the computer school to offer the instruction in programming?

Some forms of contracting for educational services already exist: occasionally between neighboring public institutions, among states through regional programs administered by interstate compact, for special types of instructional activities such as contracts for public school personnel to supervise practice teachers or other interns, and for special educational services such as aptitude and achievement testing.

A 1966 Oregon state study, "Education Beyond the High School," proposed greater use of the contracting technique, suggesting establishment of authorization for public school administrators to contract for service with the proprietary schools. The report stated, "Because the private school facilities exist without public investment, using them to supplement public vocational school curricula may make good financial sense."[11]

Contracting for particular courses or other educational services would seem advisable when: (1) development of the course on campus is not essential to the total educational program of the institution, (2) a high quality course is available in an institution accessible to the student, and (3) it would be more economical to contract for the course than to develop it on campus.

The Move off Campus, and Acceleration

Most of higher education has long been shaped by the conviction that only on-campus activities are legitimate parts of the student's program. Strong as the tradition has been, it has not prevented most institutions from recognizing certain off-campus activities as part of a college program: intern programs in social welfare and other fields, practice teaching in the public schools, organized field trips in archaeology, geology, oceanography, and the like. And some sixty institutions between 1911 and 1960 recognized the educational value of off-campus activities by developing cooperative education programs in which off-campus activities (usually work experience related to the student's major) were alternated with on-campus instruction.

In the last few years, the move off campus has picked up momentum. New York and Massachusetts are planning external degree

11. By Post-High School Study Committee (Duplicated).

programs, and similar efforts are under consideration by education systems in other states and some public and private institutions. Some colleges are revitalizing correspondence courses through the use of tape cassettes. Closed-circuit television is being used to take the college to industry. More than a hundred and forty additional institutions since 1960 have adopted some form of cooperative education program that makes some off-campus activities part of their curriculum, and more than three hundred colleges and universities have applied to the federal government in the last year for funds to plan or implement such programs. In its report *Less Time, More Options,* the Carnegie Commission urged greater experimentation with external degree programs and with the integration of relevant off-campus activities into a student's program of educational development. The Newman Task Force also endorsed many of these approaches.[12]

The arguments in support of the move off campus are couched in terms both of educational philosophy and of potential economies, although some supporters insist that the economies are simply fortunate spin-offs rather than central motivations for the proposals. Whether spin-off or motivation, the move off campus promises some economies for the student, the institution, and the system.

As pointed out by Frederick Balderston in his "Varieties of Financial Crisis" in the present volume, among the institutional accounts showing the most severe strain in this period of financial stringency is the student financial aid account. His assessment agrees with one of the major findings of a recently completed study of independent colleges in Pennsylvania.[13] Under a cooperative education program, the strain is substantially reduced. During the off-campus periods (as much as one-half of each year at Northeastern University) the student receives pay for his work; thus, a large measure of student aid is built into the educational process itself. In the external degree program, the student can pursue a degree at his own pace while continuing to work as much as he wishes or needs to.

Although external degree programs that rely heavily on independent study may require substantial faculty time for development of syllabi and course materials and for student evaluation, there can

12. *Less Time, More Options,* Special Report and Recommendations by the Carnegie Commission on Higher Education (New York: McGraw-Hill Book Co., 1971), especially pp. 11, 13–24; *Report on Higher Education* [Newman Report] (Washington: Government Printing Office, 1971), pp. 68–70.

13. McKinsey & Co., Inc., "Study of the Financial Condition of Independent Higher Education in the Commonwealth of Pennsylvania" (Duplicated; Feburary 1971), p. vii.

be substantial savings in faculty time as compared with conventional instructional programs. The British Open University, looked to as a model for some American experiments, is providing education at a per student cost approximately one-third that at the traditional British universities.

Capital savings are, of course, the most obvious fiscal advantage of external degree programs. And in cooperative education programs, if the student spends every other six months off campus, the college can accommodate twice as many students over a year's span as it could with a conventionally scheduled program. Somewhat similarly, students in technical or health service fields learn on the job to use equipment and gain proficiency in processes necessary to their profession, with the result that less laboratory space and equipment—both expensive—are needed than when both practice and theory must be taught on campus.

Various forms of acceleration are also being urged, again on grounds both of educational policy and of potential for economies. The Carnegie Commission proposes shortening the B.A. and the M.D. programs to three years. These changes could not be accomplished without some additional resources for adequate planning and development. Even with such inputs, however, estimates indicate that the changes could result in savings of $3 billion to $5 billion a year in operating costs by 1980 and a total of $5 billion in capital costs in the 1970s.[14]

Granting credit by examination both permits some acceleration and recognizes proficiencies gained off campus. Thus, on a reduced scale, this approach produces some of the same economies available through use of external degree programs and acceleration techniques.

Resistance to several of the approaches described above, particularly the external degree, is still sufficient to block their adoption in many institutions. Those who resist argue that only a part of the educational development achieved in a B.A. degree program, or even in a particular course, can be measured by an examination. And it is further argued that these educational impacts are not likely to occur in a program that takes place almost entirely off campus. Although benefits may be greater from a conventional on-campus degree program than through an external degree program, a student may choose to forgo such benefits for any number of personal reasons. In the absence of more overwhelming proof than now exists of the decided superiority of on-campus programs for all types of students,

14. *Less Time, More Options*, pp. 23–24.

it does not seem desirable to foreclose the student from the more flexible and lower cost off-campus options or to foreclose the society from the possibility of providing higher education to more students through such means—and at lower cost. In the past, flexible alternatives such as independent study have been a special favor reserved for only the best students. The goal now is to make these alternatives more broadly available to all students.

Changes in Instructional Techniques

The public generally perceives instruction as the central task of a college or university. Faculty salaries constitute two-thirds to three-quarters of instructional expenditures. It is inevitable, therefore, that any public pressure for reduction of costs in higher education will focus heavily on the amount and nature of faculty work. One suggestion is to shift noninstructional or nonresearch activities to administrative personnel. Not only would the amount of time released by such a shift be slight, but, as Dr. Balderston's paper suggests, administrative salaries may actually have risen more rapidly than faculty salaries in recent years.

Various proposals are based on the assumption that faculty members do not put in enough time on the job. Recent work load studies indicate that the average workweek of a faculty member is sixty hours. Thus, forced increases in certain elements of the faculty member's work would generally result only in a decrease of time spent on others.[15]

A recurring issue relates to precisely this question of allocation of a faculty member's time among tasks: whether research is being done at the expense of teaching. Forced change in the pattern of faculty utilization is one of the most sensitive and difficult ways to attempt to achieve economy. A recent University of California study on faculty effort and output suggests, in part, the reason:

> University faculty are scholars as well as teachers, and in their own fields of competence they are judged by other scholars' teaching and on the quality of their scholarship. Their own professional standards set limits to institutional resource management. These standards govern the national market place in which every university must compete for manpower. Scholarship is also an indispensable element of the content

15. Unpublished study of faculty effort and output at the University of California, presented to the Regents at its meeting, Jan. 15, 1970; preliminary findings of a national survey of faculty work load, presented by T. W. Keene at the American Association for Higher Education conference in Chicago, 1971; "Faculty Productivity Story," *From the Ohio Board of Regents*, November 1970.

and process of instruction, although the amount of research necessary to university-level teaching has been a perpetual policy issue.[16]

Work load studies do indicate that about thirty hours a week for faculty members at universities are spent in instruction and in preparation and evaluation related to instruction. It would seem, then, that efforts should be made to assure the most effective use of those thirty hours. Howard R. Bowen and Gordon K. Douglass have recently completed an excellent analysis along these lines. Comparative cost per student credit hour is analyzed for six different ways of organizing teaching-learning in a liberal arts college.[17] The method of analysis proposed by Bowen and Douglass should prove useful to college administrators, and the analysis itself may help convince some of those reluctant to experiment with new patterns of instruction that substantial increases in productivity are possible if faculty are willing to take a cost-conscious and fresh look at how their instructional activity is organized.

PROBLEMS THAT BLOCK THE POTENTIAL

Changes in the educational process offer the greatest potential for increases in productivity in higher education. Yet such basic changes are generally more difficult to achieve than are modifications in more peripheral processes and activities or in the support functions of the institution. Since these basic changes involve an alteration in the way people relate to their activities and possibly to one another in the organization, they are subject to all of the forces that make change difficult in any organization. And, according to many researchers, the university is the most resistant of all organizations to change. I suggest, however, that a change motivated in part by the desire for institutional economy suffers several additional and quite pervasive handicaps.

1. *The generally held notion is that institutions which have the highest resource input per student are the highest quality institutions.* In higher education, this view is more than a particularization of the common feeling that you "get what you pay for." In many other activities we have learned to recognize good bargains. We have also learned to recognize marked differences in efficiency. But in higher

16. Unpublished study on faculty effort and output at the University of California, cited above.

17. Bowen and Douglass, *Efficiency in Liberal Education* (Prepared for the Carnegie Commission on Higher Education; New York: McGraw-Hill Book Co., 1971).

education we suffer from an inability to find other suitable yardsticks for determining quality. Goals have not yet been clearly identified; therefore, measures for ascertaining the extent to which goals have or have not been reached are lacking. In the absence of well-defined goals and measures, the tendency is to assume that high-input institutions must be better and, thus, that any reduction in per student cost may actually bring a reduction in quality. Determinations of institutional quality usually rely on criteria that are only once removed from direct financial input—number of Ph.D.'s on faculty, number of volumes in library, faculty-student ratio, and so on.

2. *Perhaps an even greater deterrent to the introduction of more efficient educational processes is the feeling that attention to costs is somehow unrespectable.* In the last few years there has been a flood of literature on innovation, much of which describes particular experiments that change institutional programs, structure, or process. Few of the studies include comparative cost information. Only rarely have institutional task forces charged with the task of institutional self-study included any focus on the costs of the proposed reforms. Some reviewers of the Carnegie Commission report *Less Time, More Options* were upset by the reference to possible financial savings from the proposed reforms. They felt that proposals for reforms should not stem from reasons of economy; educational policy should be the sole motivating force. There are, however, many ways to improve present educational processes, but the special significance of many of the proposals in *Less Time, More Options* is that they would not only result in improvements but could also lead to institutional economies.

3. *Most tenured and senior faculty in universities are committed to the university setting because of their interests in research. The training received by prospective university faculty does little to stimulate their interest in the educational process as such.* Without either a primary commitment to teaching or a background of expertise or interest in the process, many members of the university faculty, although certainly not all members, have understandably engaged in little activity to improve the educational process. It is also understandable that many changes in educational process have originated at institutions that do not have a strong research component.

4. Even if faculty members were to become interested in the relative costs of various educational processes, *certain further impediments are inherent in administration in a university or college and in the budgeting process. Program development is often sharply separated from administrative responsibility for securing revenues for the final budget developed.* As a result, at the primary unit level,

budget construction rarely involves any total analysis of the costs of the program; rather, the budget is simply a statement of justification for additional requirements. In other words, once the basic budget is determined for a given unit within the institution, later budgeting for that unit is arrived at on an accretional basis, and only in rare instances is the unit required to consider the costs of its program from a zero base. The question is rarely asked, What should it cost to accomplish what we have decided to do? In some departments the budget may actually be prepared by an administrative assistant who is only remotely attached to the educational process of the department and is merely supplied the necessary "accretional" information to build into the next year's request. Thus, personal incentives work against the achievement of economies, and no savings are realized within the department. Where such a system prevails throughout an institution, a reduction in expenditures may actually work to the disadvantage of an exceptional department when it makes its next budget request.

Thus, the budget, which could be a device for analyzing the effectiveness of the operation in terms of cost, is rarely coupled with measures of the program's educational effectiveness. Early hopes for the introduction of PPBS (Program Planning and Budget Systems) techniques into higher education have not yet materialized, perhaps because the specificity of goals essential to the PPBS process is lacking, perhaps because the budget-makers, the users of PPBS, are not the ones directly involved in the educational process. Heavy reliance is still placed on various inputs (enrollment, student credit hours) to determine the support funds to be allocated, rather than on output measures (degrees, value added, or measures of effective progress toward specified goals).

As Professor Brown of Miami University puts it,

> Too long higher education has trusted the canard that ". . . college is good for you and benefits the nation" and has neither defined objectives nor measured response. . . . Timely it is for educators to define objectives precisely . . . to develop measurement devices . . . and to offer a quantitative model for judging the success or failure, the efficacy or inefficacy, of higher education in achieving desired goals. . . . To construct meaningful measures, statements of objectives must precede.[18]

18. Ben Lawrence et al. (eds.), *Outputs of Higher Education: Their Identification, Measurement and Evaluation* (Boulder, Colo.: Western Interstate Commission for Higher Education, July 1970), p. 27.

Measurement of Output

Research on the relative impacts on students of different types of institutions and different instructional techniques does exist. One recent study, utilizing data from ninety-one studies completed between 1924 and 1965, concluded: "These data demonstrate clearly and unequivocally that there is no measurable difference among truly distinctive methods of college instruction when evaluated by student performance on final examinations."[19] Another study examined three instructional procedures—television, lecture, and discussion—as well as various class sizes, and found no differences in achievement or critical thinking among the various methods.[20] The research to date suggests that "recall of knowledge is as readily achieved in large group lectures as in small group discussion sections."[21] Affective learning as well as cognitive learning is an important dimension of the educational experience, and a recent study attempted to test the influence of class size on both kinds of learning. The conclusion was that large group lectures combined with small group discussions appeared to be as effective as conventional classes of fifty to sixty students in both the affective and cognitive domains.[22]

Still other research suggests that superior students are no better off in highly selective institutions or high quality institutions than in less selective ones; their intellectual development proceeds equally well at either type of institution. Conversely, the few average or below-average students who manage to enter highly selective colleges do not seem to become unduly intimidated or discouraged, and their dropout rate is only slightly greater than that of typical bright students in such institutions.[23]

Studies of students transferring from two-year colleges to four-year colleges suggest that if ability is controlled, students transferring from a junior college do approximately as well at the four-year institutions as students who began at the four-year institutions.[24]

19. Robert Dubin and Thomas C. Taveggia, *The Teaching-Learning Paradox* (Eugene: University of Oregon, Center for the Advanced Study of Educational Administration, 1968).
20. F. G. Macomber, ed., *Experimental Study in Instructional Procedure* (Oxford, Ohio: Miami University, Oct. 1, 1957).
21. Kenneth H. Hoover et al., "The Influence of Class-Size Variations on Cognitive and Affective Learning of College Freshmen," *Journal of Experimental Education*, Spring 1970, p. 39.
22. Ibid., pp. 42–43.
23. Astin and Lee, *The Invisible Colleges*.
24. Leland L. Medsker and Dale Tillery, *Breaking the Access Barriers* (New York: McGraw-Hill Book Co., May 1971), p. 59.

On first consideration, these research conclusions suggest that experimentation with the educational process gives little hope of improvement in educational effectiveness. If the research is valid, one might ask why the faculty shouldn't continue to use their customary organization and techniques, with which they feel comfortable. Unquestioning continuation would, however, indulge in dangerous complacency, for the research cited leads to what may be a disastrous conclusion: that significant reductions in cost without decreasing quality could be obtained by using the least costly type of institution and the least costly technique. In other words, if there are no measurable differences in the product, then isn't it sensible to move toward the "least cost" solution? As we all know, there are differences in the costs. One governor recently stated his own adoption of the "least cost" solution by declaring, "Since it costs four times as much to educate a lower division student at the university than it does at a community college, why not send them all to community colleges?"[25] And if large classes and other less costly instructional techniques are as effective as somewhat smaller classes, why continue to use anything but the lowest cost approach?

It is particularly encouraging, therefore, to note growing questioning of research such as that described. In an excellent review of the literature, Ohmer Milton suggests that most of the research has lacked the refinement essential to shed light on the learning process and particularly on differences among individual learners, but, rather, has focused for the most part on relatively timid experimental influences.[26] As for impact of different types of institutions, it is not always clear what should be measured. For instance, although community college students who transfer to four-year colleges may do approximately as well as students who began at four-year colleges, other studies show that students entering four-year colleges as freshmen are four times as likely to complete their bachelor's degree.[27]

Current research using the concept of "value added" suggests new measures of success or failure. One researcher comments that the "most important index of college success and its social contribution may be the quality of its dropouts, not the quality of its graduates."[28]

Systems techniques are also providing new guidance to the problem

25. William Trombley, "Education Budget Fight Looming for Governor," *Los Angeles Times*, Oct. 13, 1969.
26. Ohmer Milton, "Teaching or Learning?", *Research Report Number 6* (Washington: American Association for Higher Education, May 1, 1971).
27. John K. Folger, Helen S. Astin, and Alan E. Bayer, *Human Resources and Higher Education* (New York: Russell Sage Foundation, 1970), p. 174.
28. Arthur W. Chickering, "The Best Colleges Have the Least Effect," *Saturday Review*, Jan. 16, 1971.

of output measurement. A recent conference sponsored by the Western Interstate Commission for Higher Education included a number of thoughtful analyses and conceptual frameworks for moving closer to output measurement.[29]

In this decade, one of education's highest priorities will be to move from research and discussion of approaches to usable techniques that will help measure effectiveness among various instructional techniques, among programs, and among institutions. It is an essential precedent to more effective handling of higher education resources.

Needed: A Scholarly Approach by the Scholar to His Own Activity

Theoretically, it is possible to meet the top priority of higher education's agenda for the 1970s—"To provide more for less." To do so, however, will require availability of resources for experimentation and innovation, a more precise definition of goals, and the development of output measures. As a part of this effort, faculty members will have to apply to their own activities the same intellectual curiosity and analytical approach that they use in pursuing their disciplines. Questions must be asked:

1. How effective are the traditional instructional means in enabling higher education to reach its goals?
2. Will continued laissez faire for each professor in choosing instructional techniques constitute an excessive cost?
3. Should a new approach to recruitment be considered; for example, should faculty be hired to use their instructional time in accordance with their particular instructional talents?
4. Does continued reliance on the course as the unit of instruction and on the credit as the unit of achievement impose undue constraints on organization of the educational process?
5. Would an analysis of present program content suggest possibilities for (a) deletions and combinations, and (b) for optimum fitting of instructional techniques to the various elements of the program?
6. Are there organizational approaches to permit use of different instructional techniques for different students within programs?
7. Has the absence of clear goals made it too easy to see the traditional process as an end in itself rather than a means?

Higher education is suffering a crisis of funding which many say results from a crisis of confidence. Unless administration and faculty together are willing to direct their talents to a thoughtful reassessment of some of the basic assumptions questioned above, both these crises may be with us throughout the 1970s and beyond.

29. Lawrence et al., *Outputs of Higher Education.*

Elements in Economy Measures

C. ARNOLD HANSON

"MORE FOR LESS" EXPLORES POSSIBLE ECONOMIES IN THE EDUCATIONAL enterprise and some impediments to attaining savings potentials. Recognizing that colleges and universities tend to resist innovation and hence cost cutting, Miss Smith urges the academic community, and particularly the scholar, to analyze the teaching-learning process in order "to provide more for less." Her analysis is indeed useful. My comments will offer additional observations and emphases that may reinforce or enlarge on some of her considerations.

There are those who believe—and act accordingly—that the financial pinch being experienced is temporary and that the steps in response can be of a short-run and relatively painless character. In my view, such a course of action is not sensible. There is evidence that all sources of income for higher education not only will be increasingly unwilling to provide or increase support but also will attach more conditions to that support. This generality applies alike to state allocations, gift income, and tuition payments. Although tuition may remain the most readily adjustable source of income, those who pay it are increasingly insistent about the quality of their return. It follows that efforts to decrease costs and to increase income are unquestionably necessary, but that these must be lasting efforts directed toward genuine economies and the generation of greater and more dependable income for the educational institution. It is useful, therefore, to explore further some of the influences that will bear on the analysis urged by Miss Smith.

Her paper correctly implies that the institutional budget is composed in large part of faculty salaries and that the average faculty member gives generously of himself to his institutional responsibilities. Consequently, while economies in faculty salary budgets are likely to be sought, these efforts will encounter considerable internal opposition. The opposition will stem not only from valid differences in educational philosophy but also from growing involvement by faculty in determining the conditions of their employment. Thus, as college and university faculties assume hard-line collective bargaining attitudes, opposition to increased faculty loads will be reinforced. Moreover, most academicians hold the continuing conviction that, among the categories of professionals, those engaged in higher education are still at a disadvantage vis-à-vis compensation. Examples now abound, particularly in the public sector, of the effectiveness of teachers joining in concerted bargaining action. There is reason to believe, therefore, that faculties will resist economies achieved at their expense and will indeed continue their efforts to advance the rank of educators on the professional compensation scale.

Some, possibly many, institutions concerned with economy measures may have to modify their views about institutional growth and absolute size. Private colleges that are competing for students and institutions that face budget cuts cannot readily improve unit costs by adjusting the number of students involved. Cost reductions, if they are to be made at all, will doubtless come chiefly from painfully paring expenditures and introducing bona fide efficiencies. In such cases, those responsible might be wise to disclose in detail the institution's fiscal circumstances in order to enlist the cooperation of faculty, and possibly student representatives, in determining and carrying out economy measures. Indeed, some believe that only under conditions of broad involvement are economies at all possible. Moreover, it appears that, with full disclosure and greater involvement, a better case can be made for increased support from customary sources. There is, finally, the proposition that economies recommended by concerned faculty are more apt to be achieved than those suggested or imposed from without.

It is important to underline Miss Smith's plea for scholarly analysis of what scholars do. We know precious little about the process of learning, and we frequently fail to apply what we do know. Many in the academic community have clung to notions about teaching which have little sound evidence to support them, and at the same time they turn away from proposals for experimentation and for the testing of devices which might enhance the effectiveness of teaching. Education and its support no longer occupy a favored position with legislators, individual donors, and the general public. A new realism now marks the approach of those who provide educational support. This same realism can usefully be applied by the educational enterprise to itself.

A View from a Private University

PAUL C. REINERT, S.J.

VIRGINIA SMITH HAS OFFERED US IN HER PAPER NEW INSIGHTS AND perspective to truths that we all must recognize. It sheds new light on the interrelationships of the various elements that bear on the financial crisis of higher education, and is a commendable work.

Still it is clear that the shading and weighting of these elements and interrelationships issue from the perspective of the large public institution. I shall try to augment what Dr. Smith has said and offer my view from the perspective of the moderate-size private, *urban* university.

Early in her paper Dr. Smith states that "there is no question that the simplest and quickest solution to the financial problems facing our colleges and universities would be to increase funds sufficiently to cover their anticipated expenditures." I suspect that the large public institution is still looking to increased revenues as the most promising solution to its fiscal problem, but I can assure you that there is now no easy way for the private urban university even to maintain its present level of income, to say nothing of increasing it. Such institutions are in a competitive squeeze from neighboring public universities which are able to market their wares at a fraction of the cost of the private university. Tuition rate increases often result in declining enrollment—particularly in the undergraduate liberal arts college of the university, where the competition is most intense—and an offset in the increase in total tuition income.

Even while enrollments stabilize or increase slightly, the costs of education escalate. For example, at Saint Louis University from the 1960–61 academic year to 1969–70, the number of full-time equivalent students rose from 7,166 to 8,869. This is not a dramatic increase, but the total cost per full-time equivalent student rose from $1,685 to $4,220. Furthermore, over the nine-year period, the increase in cost per student accounted for almost 90 percent of the total increase in expenditures. Of all items of expenditure, the most significant increase was in the university's contribution to student aid, where the increase was at the annual rate of 12.4 percent compounded over the period.

However undesirable, clearly for Saint Louis University the only feasible way to place budgets more nearly into balance is to reduce expenditures, for it is this area over which the administration has control. As Dr. Smith correctly points out, although these economy measures "may lead to wasteful use of human resources, to increased expenditures in future periods, and to unwanted social consequences," it becomes the function of good management to plan the reductions in such a way that there is minimum damage from these side effects to the quality of the institution. In this regard, Dr. Smith's remarks on the need for good, objective yardsticks by which to measure quality are particularly pertinent and timely. It would be tragic indeed if academic institutions were forced to approach the all-important question of quality in higher education in the same crass manner as commercial competitors who ask themselves: How much oatmeal can be added to the hamburger before the public no longer will buy the hamburger?

But there is a deeper aspect to expenditure reduction that should be stressed. In my view, the dilemma faced by private universities, and probably by all of higher education, is that revenues and expenditures exist in an intimate "feedback" relationship, and efforts to reduce expenditures often result in offsetting reductions in revenues. Some universities that have tried to solve their financial crisis by eliminating costly programs have been shocked to see the benefits of their efforts disappear in a wave of revenue losses produced elsewhere within the system by the actions intended to reduce expenditures. Fundamentally these institutions are overcommitted, and the overcommitment extends down to every unit and subunit within the institution. Thus, as the institution struggles valiantly to reduce its commitment by chopping off large segments, what remains is still overcommitted with respect to itself. The absolute reduction in commitment may turn out to be a benefit in the long term, but the short-term situation is often worsened. Such cases reinforce the view that what is needed is a scalpel, not an ax, and that reductions must be applied judiciously and only after careful planning and full assessment of all the side effects.

At best, the economy measures can only be looked upon as a short-range solution to the immediate problem of keeping the institution from sinking in a sea of deficits. The victory will be short-lived, however, unless it is accompanied both by broad-scale institutional planning and redesign and by the search for innovative educational approaches and techniques that must be conducted on more fundamental levels if there is to be a real increase in productivity. It is particularly true for private institutions that few have the risk capital needed to mount meaningful experimental programs. Perhaps the appropriate role of private foundations is in providing expanded support for this activity.

At Saint Louis, we are finding some beneficial aspects to the financial crisis besides the obvious one of forcing us to reassess our goals and priorities. First, we see that the implementation of difficult economy measures has helped us to regain the confidence of our corporate benefactors upon whose gifts a private institution like ours depends. No individual or corporation wants to contribute to a sinking ship; neither do they want to contribute to an institution that is incapable of exercising the internal discipline needed to save it.

Second, the crisis has indeed forced us to sharpen our management skills because the margin for error is small. We now carefully monitor faculty productivity—insofar as we can define and quantify productivity—and we use this tool in our budgeting and planning. We have moved away from the "incremental" budgeting approach, where one has only to justify the additions to existing budgets, to a system of nearly full review and justification of the total budget from ground zero. We are reevaluating our fiscal policies in an attempt to give the heads of our budget divisions the added flexibility that is particularly needed in tight times when there is no fat in the budget.

We are developing more sophisticated procedures for analysis of financial and operational data and are using them in more effective financial management decision making. And we are beginning to develop and apply management techniques based on the concepts of marginal finance. As one example, we are determining the various cost plateaus associated with the addition of varying amounts of students in varying mixes. That is, we are determining up to what level there would be virtually no additional costs, at what level added faculty and staff would be required, and at what level major expenditures for new facilities would become a factor. This approach—an analysis of fixed and variable costs—can be applied to many aspects of university finance and, in our case, is closely related to the question of a state tuition equalization program.

I am convinced that higher education not only can but also must offer the American public "more for less." Virginia Smith has outlined in a small compass most of the sensible methods whereby this objective can be achieved. For many of us, there is not much choice: either we offer "more for less" or we will have nothing to offer.

Sharing Responsibility for "More for Less"

CLARENCE SCHEPS

I AGREE WITH MISS SMITH THAT THERE IS A POTENTIAL FOR ACHIEVING economies in our colleges and universities without reducing quality. I would, however, state the proposition more emphatically by stating that there is an absolute necessity that substantial economies be achieved in our institutions of higher education—and soon! I concur, also, in her analysis that meaningful economies are to be associated more with increased productivity than merely with postponed or reduced expenditures. Put simply: costs based on student credit hours must be reduced.

Her review of several proposals of ways to increase productivity provided support for her conclusion that significant advances in productivity depend fundamentally on changes in the educational process itself and cannot be confined to supportive functions. In my judgment, an equally fruitful way to economize is to improve systems of allocating resources and functions among the institutions of the nation, the regions, and the states. Expensive and unnecessary duplication would be eliminated, and the nation's educational dollars would stretch further than is now possible.

Until recently, I was among those who contended that only through greatly increased revenues could the financial ills of higher education be cured. I no longer believe this. I am now convinced that both sides of the equation must be pursued vigorously and imaginatively: at the same time we strive to make our systems of higher education and our individual institutions more efficient, we must also energetically pursue additional sources of revenues. These two goals are clearly interrelated because, as Miss Smith points out, our inability to produce sufficient additional revenues at this time is due in part to the crisis in the confidence of those who would provide the funding—state legislatures, private donors, the federal government. Some of the erosion in confidence was caused by the widespread belief that higher education has not managed itself efficiently.

Progress, expansion, and enrichment in higher education in the past two decades have been great. However, our individual institutions as well as our systems of higher education were expanded with little thought of a future day of reckoning or of the costs of such expansion. In a real sense we were living in a dream world.

In my judgment, we cannot continue on a "business-as-usual" basis. We urgently need improved planning mechanisms in the individual institutions, in regional and statewide coordination, and in the formulation of federal policy. There are now twenty-six hundred institutions in the nation, of all types and sizes, many with more or less parallel programs. There are more than fifty separate systems of state-supported higher education. In Louisiana, for example, there are at least three competing systems of state-supported higher education with more or less independent jurisdictions, as well as a fourth system composed of competing privately supported institutions. So far, there has been little attempt at real coordination. Although diversity among institutions and the right of institutional autonomy have been vigorously defended as absolute virtues, the exigencies of the times are so great that some compromises in these positions will have to be made.

It is imperative that the goals and objectives of each institution be reexamined critically, and that objectives be realigned in conformity with the resources realistically available to the institution. Despite the difficulties so ably pointed out by Virginia Smith, it is imperative to slow down the ever-decreasing productivity that has characterized our institutions. Small class sizes, low teaching loads, course proliferation—much maligned terms in higher education—must be looked at anew.

There is obvious danger that increased efficiency may impinge on the quality of the educational process, and this hazard we shall have to guard against at all times. On the other hand, reduction in the number of degree programs, modest increases in class sizes, improved utilization of physical facilities, savings in the length of time that students spend in higher education, better statewide planning, these may not necessarily lead to a decrease in quality.

Miss Smith, in one extremely significant statement that I would like to underscore, points out that an important impediment to increasing productivity has been the nature of institutional administration and the traditional budgeting process. In most institutions, program development is sharply separated from the administrative responsibility for securing program support. Development of academic programs is largely in the hands of the faculty, who have little or no responsibility for raising the funds and frequently have minimal knowledge about the budget as a whole. The budgeting process must be reformed so that the faculty member will feel a sense of responsibility for the entire budget process and be able to help judge the financial impact of programs and activities he has advocated.

At the risk of being repetitious, I would like to emphasize once more the absolute necessity for those in academic administration to find ways to exercise better academic management. New programs should be added only in the full knowledge of what they will cost and how the funds to finance them are to be obtained. In approaching the difficult problem of allocation of resources within the institution, all segments of the institution, including the faculty, should share responsibility not only for the introduction of new programs but also for the effort required in obtaining the resources to initiate and to perpetuate them.

In commenting on "more education for less expenditures," I may not have stressed sufficiently my conviction that, along with increases in efficiency, the obtaining of additional sources of support will be essential to avoid chaos and continuing crises in our colleges and universities. This support must come from the student who is able to pay, from the private philanthropist, from the state governments, and—perhaps most important—from the federal government in the form of general institutional support.

PART THREE

Financing Universal Higher Education

SELMA J. MUSHKIN

Public Financing of Higher Education

PROPOSALS OF PATTERNS FOR ADDING TO THE TAX SUPPORT BASE
for financing higher education are only now emerging: the major
studies of the Carnegie Commission on Higher Education are being
published; state commissions are reporting to governors and state
legislatures; the administration and the Congress are developing policy
positions. The policy options thus far are for the most part standard
—aid to students, or to schools; aid for construction, or for operation.
Those options give little hint of the drama of an institution in transition and of the financial support required to facilitate, not impair,
wanted changes in operations and programs. Titles of the Carnegie
Commission studies indicate some of the directions proposed for higher
education programs: *Less Time, More Options, A Chance to Learn:
An Action Agenda for Equal Opportunity in Higher Education;
Change in Educational Policy: Self-Studies . . . ;* "What's Bugging the
Students," . . . *Socialization as a Function of Higher Education.*

Generally lacking are counterpart financial patterns that are imaginatively designed and appropriately structured to build on the base of
tax revenues for higher education estimated for 1972 at $6 billion in
federal funds and $7 billion in state and local funds. The federal gov-
ernment has enunciated its policy of vastly expanded student aid. In
addition, the administration, on an initial round, accepted the concept
of formula assistance by suggesting "cost of education" subsidies to
the institutions selected by students receiving federal aid, with the
amount of subsidy to be related to the amount of student aid.

Among the states, proposals vary greatly (a not uncommon situation in our federal system). Initiatives include extending state aid to
private colleges and universities and restricting subsidized tuition to
needy students. For example, in the Wisconsin proposal, tuition for
students from families with income below a specified level would be
reduced or forgiven; under a North Carolina plan, more and larger

153

scholarships would be granted and, concurrently, tuition charges would be levied on a full-cost basis.

Few debate the prescription of *more* funds, especially more federal funds, to help colleges and universities meet some of their critical financial problems in educating students. Further, the idea of more federal funds for general support (with less emphasis on categorical aid) and more state support for both public and private institutions indicates that some past concerns, such as federal control over education, have been laid to rest—at least temporarily.

In any event, new patterns of federal aid to higher education are needed. Whatever the new formulas, they need to incorporate incentives for other forms of support.

Proposals for broad federal aid to institutions—free from ties to narrow "public interest" activities such as research or manpower training in specialized fields—mark a departure from past policies. Appropriately, the proposals for noncategorical aid follow a course taken by the administration in another context, namely, the proposal for fiscal reforms through revenue sharing with states and localities. With general support aid, institutional expenditure decisions would be freed from restrictive federal conditions but would, nevertheless, have feedback effects on other sources of university and college support.

On their part, the institutions need to help guide the formulation of federal financial policies and to assure that the methods for financing encourage and facilitate new directions in higher education. Financial policies must be far more comprehensive and thoroughgoing than simply stimulating add-ons of piecemeal adaptations of existing educational programs such as open-door colleges, "sandwich courses," or shortened years of study. The various financial options that have been advanced require analysis to examine their potential effects on the entire higher education program. And those effects can be tested only when the "mission" for higher education is made plain.

Use of federal tax revenues to subsidize higher education—directly or indirectly, by student aid, or institutional aid; by expenditures, or such tax methods as credits and deductions—underscores anew the apparent absence of concern in the higher education community about the price for involvement of federal dollars in university governance. Nevertheless, federal aid does carry a price: financial uncertainty and instability, and, for the future, "accountability" in terms of federal purposes not yet defined.

Federal financial policies can encourage more private giving to colleges and universities, or less; they can stimulate the states and localities to do more, or discourage such further financing. Diversity in institutions that gives students greater choice in educational programs and methods of learning can be nurtured, or not. Higher educational institutions can be stimulated, or not, to apply their talents and knowledge to pressing social issues and to sources of information for open public debate that draws on the unique competences of the university. In turn, the states, by their practices, defeat, or aid, some federal purpose, variegate the college and university system, or impose great uniformity.

In the pages that follow, questions are raised: How much by way of resources to higher education? By what governments? and, With what incentives toward what purposes?

Resource Requirements and the Governments

As recently as the 1950s, the major single determinant of college-going of youth was the educational attainment of the parents.[1] By 1971, however, a U.S. Bureau of the Census survey showed that 61 percent of those enrolled in college came from families whose head had, at most, completed high school.[2] This fact alone indicates that the yardstick of past performance is not necessarily a good measure for assessing the resource requirements of higher education in the 1970s. Other changes too are influential: the boundaries of "higher education" have come to be expanded to "education beyond the high school," including "learning by working" and "learning by doing." Thus enrollments have vastly expanded, and many of today's "students" in higher education do not fit the conventional definition. If higher education is restructured to become a base for continuing education for those in the midstream of their working life, rather than exclusively a preparatory institution for the young, enrollments in the future will become even more uncertain. Total resource requirements under these uncertain circumstances are especially difficult to quantify.

A 1968 Carnegie Commission report, using institutional costs as the base for measurement, estimated total institutional expenditures would rise by 1976–77 to $41 billion, or about 3 percent of the gross national product (GNP), from about 2 percent of GNP in 1967[3]—a

1. Harvey E. Brazer and Martin David, "Social and Economic Determinants of the Demand for Education," in *Economics of Higher Education*, ed. Selma J. Mushkin (Washington: Government Printing Office, 1962), pp. 21–42.

2. U.S. Bureau of the Census, *Current Population Reports: School Enrollment, October 1970*, Series P-20 (Washington: Government Printing Office, June 28, 1971), No. 222.

3. *Quality and Equality: New Levels of Federal Responsibility for Higher Education*, A Special Report and Recommendations by the Commission, December 1968 (New York: McGraw-Hill Book Co., 1968), pp. 5–8.

percentage-point increase in line with the growth of higher education expenditures as a percentage of GNP from 1957 to 1967.

Taking a different route, I have asked: How would expenditures for educating students[4] in institutions of higher education increase in the years ahead if the institutions make a minimum accommodation to expansion in enrollments and to inflation? On this basis, I estimate expenditures for student education for 1975–76 will amount to $18.5 billion, or 1.2 percent of the GNP, compared with $8.3 billion in 1967–68, which was less than 1.0 percent of the GNP. The following elements enter into my calculations.

My projections for expenditures make no allowances for changes in the quality of education provided.

For the period ahead, projections indicate that increased enrollments and inflation will produce an average 10 percent rise per year in the cost of student education. Of the total outlays for student education projected for 1975–76, public institutions would spend $13.4 billion. By 1979–80, again combining projected enrollment growth under existing institutional patterns and projected price inflation, student higher education expenditures would rise to over $25 billion, of which almost $19 billion would be spent by public colleges and universities (Table 1).

In making these projections, I applied an aggregate economic model, assuming: (a) a 1.8 percent per annum growth in the labor force, (b) a 4 percent unemployment rate after 1973, (c) a gradual transition in rate of increase in productivity per person employed from the present rate to a longer-term rate of 3 percent per annum, and (d) a check in price increases over time to a 2.5 percent rise per year. These assumptions yield the following projections for the *gross national product*: 1970, $977 billion; 1976, $1,505 billion; and 1980, $1,994 billion. My projections also assume that full-time equivalent (FTE) *enrollments* will grow as projected by the U.S. Office of Education, that is, by 5.2 percent per year between 1967–68 and 1975–76 (contrasted with 8 percent per year in the decade preceding 1967–68). By 1979–80, a further decline in the rate of enrollment increase is expected. As to the division of increase of *enrollments in public and private institutions*, I have assumed the Office of Education projections

---

4. *Cost of educating students* is here defined as "student higher education expenditures": includes instructional costs and that part of library expenses, plant and maintenance, and administration attributable to teaching. It excludes from the U.S. Office of Education expenditure category "education and general" (current fund expenditures) the following items: organized research, organized activities related to educational departments, other sponsored programs, and extension and public service.

from academic years 1967–68 to 1975–76: public institutions are expected to grow at an annual rate of 6.6 percent, which is many times the expected rate of 1.5 percent for private institutions.

My projections are for minimum *expenditure levels.* Even so, the $13.4 billion projected for public institutions in 1975–76 would incur a deficit estimated at $3 billion, and the $19 billion projected for 1979–80 would cause a deficit of $5 billion. Deficits can be expected for private institutions as a consequence of student response to the high subsidies in public institutions, a feedback effect that is not reflected in the estimates shown in Table 1.

Capacity of the States to Respond

Can the states meet the predicted deficits by additional state taxes? The question is asked often, but the record of the past must cause us to pause before answering. In the 1960s, the states accepted the challenge and met the demands for college-going opportunities. As the number of youth of college-going age mounted, the states responded by expanding existing institutions and by adding new branch campuses. A number of state institutions (for the sake of economy) became larger—up to forty thousand students—and more impersonal. The states increased their general revenues for student higher education, provided state scholarship support for students in private colleges and universities, and developed cooperative programs with local governments for two-year community colleges.

Much of the responsibility for providing the additional places for the vastly increased number of eighteen-year-olds fell on the states and the public institutions. About four and a half times as many places for freshmen were created in public colleges and universities as in private institutions, and of the added places for degree-credit freshmen, eight out of ten were in public institutions.

Moreover, the states faced the unprecedented demands for education during a period of great expansion of other public services—welfare, transportation, health and hospital care, and local schools, services that within our federal system are traditionally provided by states and localities. Despite other pressing demands, higher education claimed an ever larger share each year of the mounting state tax load. New levies and higher tax rates were imposed by the states to meet those demands. During the decade 1957–58 to 1967–68, state tax revenues rose by $21 billion, to $36.4 billion. New state levies for student higher education account for about 12 percent of the rise in state taxes, or the equivalent of $1 out of each $2 rise in state personal income taxes, and $1 out of each $3 rise in general sales taxes.

Table 1: Amount and Sources of Student Higher Education Funding, 1967–68, with Projections for 1975–76 and 1979–80

(In millions of dollars)

Source of Funding	All Institutions			Public Institutions			Private Institutions		
	1967-68	1975-76	1979-80	1967-68	1975-76	1979-80	1967-68	1975-76	1979-80
Total required	*$8,250.4*	*$18,459.8*	*$25,828.3*	*$5,280.3*	*$13,356.6*	*$19,287.6*	*$2,970.1*	*$5,103.2*	*$6,540.7*
Tuition and fees	$3,260.8	$6,501.1	$8,787.3	$1,107.4	$2,801.2	$4,045.1	$2,153.4	$3,699.9	$4,742.2
Endowment income and gifts	595.1	1,030.3	1,319.5	74.8	157.7	209.1	520.3	872.6	1,110.4
State and local funds	3,594.3	6,315.6	8,371.6	3,551.4	6,240.2	8,271.7	42.9	75.4	99.9
Federal funds	338.1	712.9	944.9	287.5	606.2	803.5	50.6	106.7	141.4
Other	462.0	1,004.0	1,393.2	259.1	655.4	946.4	202.9	348.6	446.8
Total	$8,250.3	$15,563.9	$20,816.5	$5,280.2	$10,460.7	$14,275.8	$2,970.1	$5,103.2	$6,540.7
Deficit	—	*2,895.9*	*5,011.8*	—	*2,895.9*	*5,011.8*	—	—	—

Source: National Center for Educational Statistics, U.S. Office of Education, *Financial Statistics of Institutions of Higher Education: Current Funds Revenues and Expenditures; Physical Plant Assets, 1967–68* (Washington: Government Printing Office, 1970).

States have been forced in the past dozen years or so, according to the President in his February 1971 message to the Congress on revenue sharing,[5] to institute new levies or raise old ones on four hundred and fifty separate occasions, with a resulting heavy burden on many tax-payers with moderate or low incomes. Higher education contributed importantly to those levies and to the plight that has led to the new proposals for federal revenue sharing.

If tax subsidy requirements for higher education grow only in line with normal expansion of the tax bases, such as the dollar value of state retail sales in response to economic growth, the added resource requirements pose no special fiscal problems. It is the growth in excess of normal expansion that will necessitate new levies and higher tax rates. Over the past decade, state and local subsidies to higher educa-tion for teaching rose 13.6 percent per annum, whereas the normal expansion rate of state and local taxes was 6.4 percent, or at about the rate of increase of the GNP during that period. (Past experience sug-gests that, for every 1 percent rise in GNP, there tends to be a 1 percent rise in state and local tax revenues without the addition of new levies or higher tax rates.) As the estimates in Table 2 suggest, about $1.7 billion of the $2.6 billion addition to state and local funds for higher education over the ten-year period 1957–58—1967–68 (from $1.0 billion to $3.6 billion) required new tax levies.

TABLE 2: *State and Local Funds for Student Higher Education*

(In billions of dollars)

Academic Year	State and Local Funds			Approximate Percentage Growth per Annum from Base Year 1957–58	
	Total	Share Attributed to Economic Growth	Share Attributed to New Taxes	State and Local Funds	GNP
1957–58	$1.0	—	—	—	—
1961–62	1.2	$1.2	$0.0	5.0	5.0
1967–68	3.6	1.9	1.7	13.6	6.4

Source: The methodology used here is based on Selma J. Mushkin and Gabrielle C. Lupo, "Project '70: Projecting the State-Local Sector," *Review of Economics and Statistics*, May 1967, pp. 237–45.

Residents in the states and localities taxed themselves heavily to keep pace with the demand for higher education opportunities. The rate of increase was greater than the 12 percent per year needed to

5. U.S. Department of the Treasury, Office of the Special Assistant for Public Affairs, *General Revenue Sharing* (Washington: Government Printing Office, February 1971), pp. 7–19.

accommodate enrollment increases and price and salary inflation,[6] and accelerated especially from 1962 through 1968. The margin for quality improvement was small, about 1.5 percentage points per year, small, that is, when considered from the perspective of the major tensions in the decade's interaction of campus and society.

Local Tax Loads

Some of the states, in order to relieve their tax loads, turned to local governments to share the responsibility and costs of providing opportunities for higher education through the creation of community colleges. The community college was intended (1) to bring college to the student, and thus lower the cost of college-going, and (2) to promote access to college for new groups of students, either through two-year terminal education or as a step toward the four-year college.

Enrollment growth in two-year institutions has outstripped that in four-year colleges. With the shift of a considerable responsibility to the community colleges, the states have caused local governments to become involved in ways that mark essential changes both in traditional institutional structure and in the financing of higher education. For community college current income, local governments (principally out of property taxes) contribute about one-third; states contribute out of general revenues an approximately equal one-third share, and the remainder is financed by tuition and from other sources.

This pattern of financing higher education in the same general way as elementary and secondary education poses sharp issues for the future. It places an overload of tax burden on property owners, similar to the tax load for the two lower levels of education, which is already causing some states to shift their financing in the opposite direction— toward enlarged or exclusive state funding.

Comparative Effort and Capacity

The states and localities certainly cannot be faulted for their record in providing vital public services. They met the challenge of population growth, increasing density of population, impact of new technologies, rising expectations, and demands for services. Among other things, they financed the post-World War II rise in number of pupils in elementary and secondary schools as well as the subsequent wave of enrollees into colleges and universities. Since World War II, the share of GNP claimed by state and local governments for public services has

6. Selma J. Mushkin, "A Note on Higher Education Finance: Directions and Projections," Paper prepared for the 1970 annual meeting of the Southern Economic Association, Atlanta, Ga., Nov. 14, 1970 (processed).

been going up, making a larger and larger claim on the nation's resources for services, among which education ranks high. To support these services, local and state taxes in 1969 accounted for more than 11 percent of all personal income, compared with 8.5 percent in 1957. The performance of the states has not been uniform. The states, however, cannot get very far out of line in their comparative tax efforts lest high income residents and business firms move. Tax effort thus tends to be kept in alignment among the states despite differences in economic resources, industries, population characteristics, and traditional policies on higher education—public and private. Those states that are pressured by urgent public demands to increase their tax efforts out of line with neighboring or competitive states are in fiscal difficulty. In a sense, they are the "fiscally poor" states despite earlier concepts of fiscal capability. California, for example, with an effort already greater than its neighbors, increased its tax claim on income by 4.1 percentage points between 1957 and 1969. New York State increased its share of income for taxes even more—by 4.6 percentage points. Those two fiscally troubled states combined in 1968 to account for 23.5 percent of degree-credit enrollments in public institutions of higher education in the nation. The incremental change in tax effort for higher education in the ten years 1958–68 in California was equal to the national average (0.3 percent); in New York State, it was in excess of the national average (0.4 percent). Lest the small percentages be deceiving, it is well to note that, for all states combined, one percentage point change is equal, at 1970 income levels, to $8 billion.

Share of State Support

State appropriations to finance educational opportunities at subsidized amounts have been the primary instrument of state policy in the past. State and local funds for higher education are shown in Table 3, along with current income from other sources for all institutions—public and private combined.

Between 1957–58 and 1967–68, all expenditures for student higher education rose 250 percent, from $2.4 billion to $8.3 billion. To pay for this, tuition and fees have risen 281 percent; gifts and endowment earnings, 72 percent. Paralleling these figures, all government support has risen over 250 percent—state and local funds have increased 259 percent, federal support (excluding organized research, public services, and construction), 254 percent. Over this period, the percentages contributed by the respective components have shifted very little, with

TABLE 3: Source of Current Income for Support of Student Higher Education, in Colleges and Universities, 1957–58 and 1967–68

(In millions of dollars)

Source of Funds	Amount		Percentage Increase 1957–58—1967–68		Percentage Distribution	
	1957–58	1967–68	Total	Per Annum	1957–58	1967–68
Total...................	$2,363.9	$8,250.4	249.0	13.3	100.0	100.0
Tuition and fees...........	$ 856.1	$3,260.8	280.9	14.3	36.2	39.5
Gifts and endowment earnings....	346.8	595.1	71.6	5.5	14.7	7.2
State and local funds.........	1,001.3	3,594.3	259.0	13.6	42.4	43.6
Federal funds..........	95.5	338.1	254.0	13.5	4.0	4.1
Other..........	64.2	462.0	619.6	22.0	2.7	5.6

Source: Estimated from data on higher education finance, U.S. Office of Education, *Financial Statistics of Institutions of Higher Education, 1957–58 and 1967–68* (Washington: Government Printing Office, 1960 and 1970).

162

tuition and fees rising somewhat while the share from gifts and endowment income dropped.

State Support of Private Institutions

Not without historical precedent, state aid becomes urgent as the financial plight of many small institutions grows.

In a history of 19th century college financing, it was found that many colleges have had large injections of state funds added to their resources, and those additions had a crucial role to play in the financial life of the college. Bowdoin, Columbia, Dickinson, Hamilton, Harvard, Union, Williams, and Yale were among the 19th century recipients of state grants, and there is some evidence that loans by state governments to church related colleges made it possible for many of those colleges to survive in the 1840's and 1850's.[7]

The amount of state appropriations and funds for student aid in private institutions was reported for 1967–68 by an Office of Education Survey;[8] with the exception of the following eleven states, the amounts were under $100,000:

	Millions		*Millions*
New York	$32.8	New Jersey	$0.7
Pennsylvania	24.6	Alabama	0.6
Illinois	3.3	Texas	0.4
Florida	1.3	Michigan	0.2
Maryland	1.2	Rhode Island	0.1
California	0.9		

Various methods of granting money are reflected in public funds to private institutions. Contractual payments are made under interstate compacts for state residents to attend private institutions in other states. The direct grant to private schools has been traditional in Pennsylvania for many years. More recently, general formulas for institutional grants have been adopted. For example, the New York State legislature has adopted a program of general formula institutional grants that provide private nonsectarian colleges and universities with annual grants of $400 for each undergraduate degree granted and $2,400 for each graduate degree.[9] Illinois now has under

7. Frederick Rudolph, "Who Paid the Bills? An Inquiry into the Nature of Nineteenth Century College Finance," *Harvard Educational Review*, Spring 1961.

8. National Center for Educational Statistics, U.S. Office of Education, *Financial Statistics of Institutions of Higher Education: Current Funds Revenues and Expenditures; Physical Plant Assets, 1967–68* (Washington: Government Printing Office, 1970), pp. 14–72.

9. John I. Kirkpatrick, "Financing Higher Education: The Role of the State," *College Board Review*, Spring 1971, pp. 22–25.

consideration a similar general formula grant to private institutions based on the number of state scholarship and grant recipients enrolled in each institution and the number of all other FTE undergraduate students. State aid to private institutions, however, has most often been of a limited purpose or categorical nature, such as aid for construction purposes, mostly through extending a tax exemption on public securities to private institutions. Connecticut, Illinois, Massachusetts, Michigan, New Hampshire, New Jersey, New York, Ohio, Pennsylvania, South Carolina, and Vermont have programs that essentially permit private institutions to borrow on a tax-exempt basis.

State support of private institutions has created a new set of policy considerations in recent years. A New York State study reviewing such aid notes: "State aid should be available only for the support of education which is at least equal in quality to that provided in public institutions of higher education in the state . . . public funds must not be used to sustain at subsistence level institutions which would be better dissolved or merged."[10] Thus, institutional grants are leading states to establish standards of educational quality, and "accountability" is beginning to accompany such aid.

The most common form of state aid to private institutions is scholarship aid to students. Most states that have state scholarship programs permit students to choose between private and public institutions. A recent Carnegie Commission report estimates that in excess of $150 million of state-funded scholarships and grants was received in 1969–70 by students attending private colleges and universities.[11]

The Superior Federal Position

Perhaps, if the slate of past history were to be wiped clean and higher education, both public and private, were initiated anew, the states would be called upon to play a smaller role in the financing of higher education. Both tax and economic reasons suggest this alteration. Federal taxes are more efficient and equitable than are the taxes of the states, and the collection costs are lower, both to the administrative agency and to the taxpayer. Federal taxes conform more nearly than do state taxes to the realities of our national economy and to national markets. It is important, too, that federal taxes are far fairer in their burden on income groups than are state taxes, and have fewer

10. Bundy Committee Report, cited in Kirkpatrick, "Financing Higher Education: The Role of the State," p. 24.
11. *The Capitol and the Campus* (New York: McGraw-Hill Book Co., 1971), p. 87.

adverse economic incentives (on business location, land use, and property investment) built into their structure.

Economic research has revealed the value of the public benefits (externalities) of higher education by finding that the discovery of new knowledge and its diffusion increase worker productivity and earnings even for those without college education. From the perspective of our society, the public benefits accruing beyond the individual benefits (increased productivity and earnings of the college-educated) are such as to override placing sole reliance on the individual's calculus of the costs and gains in college education and thereby unduly lowering the investment in higher education. The amount of investment in tax subsidies, in concept, would match the external benefits; in practice, these amounts are difficult to quantify. In a federal system of government, moreover, it is not efficient to rely exclusively on the states to finance subsidies, for frequently the public benefits are external to the state's boundaries. Federal funding makes for a more equitable allocation of resources.

On educational policy grounds, I suspect the nation would opt for the state college and university system to safeguard academic freedoms and to foster diversity in missions and institutions. State provision of higher education is not synonymous, however, with state subsidies out of state tax funds. States do need help in financing higher education. Their fiscal capacity will not stretch to finance the many requirements for public services and new deficits for student higher education. Even if all of the state allotment funds proposed by the administration in its revenue-sharing proposal were pledged to the student higher education deficit, the amount would still fall short.

The Federal Record

Despite the pattern of general aid through land grants, which antedates the Constitutional Convention—a pattern reinforced by the Morrill Act of 1862—almost all federal support of higher education now takes the form of categorical aid. Among the categories are the array of research grants and contracts and grants for research equipment and construction, student aid, and aid for teaching, libraries, and public service activities. There are available to colleges and universities, as public and nonprofit agencies, somewhere between two hundred and two thousand special federal grant programs (the number depends on how the count is made and how a "program" is defined).

Federal outlays for higher education grew from about $1.3 billion in 1962 to $5.1 billion by 1970. Of the $5.1 billion total, $2.1 billion represents student support; $1.5 billion, research; and $0.8 billion, construction and equipment. The remaining $0.7 billion represents federal funds to institutions for current operations. The year-by-year federal outlays for all higher education purposes since 1962 are as follows: 1962, $1.3 billion; 1963, $1.6 billion; 1964, $1.7 billion; 1965, $2.0 billion; 1966, $2.7 billion; 1967, $3.6 billion; 1968, $4.4 billion; 1969, $4.4 billion; 1970, $5.1 billion; 1971, $5.8 (budget estimate); and 1972, $6.0 (recommendation).[12]

Since World War II, research and public services have increased significantly as a share of college and university activities, but in the immediate past have leveled off. For all private universities and colleges, organized research activities amount to 50 cents for each $1 of student higher education. Research has a somewhat smaller role in the public universities and colleges, where, for each $1 of student higher education expenditures, 30 cents goes for organized research.

Organized research of colleges and universities amounted to $18 million in 1930; a decade later it was $28 million. By 1950 it had risen tenfold and continued a rapid increase for much of the following decade. Two-thirds to three-fourths of that growth was federally encouraged and financed. Rates of growth of federal funding were destined to fall off; not only did the rates of growth drop but also total funds were just about stabilized between 1970 and 1971, with the consequence that, during this period of marked inflation, in real terms federal support declined.

Student aid claims the largest share of federal support of higher education. At present, new initiatives are proposed by the administration that would greatly enlarge the numbers of students aided and the support given. Additional federal budget outlays projected for 1972 for student aid include funds for expansion of work-study programs and NDEA loans.

PURPOSES AND INCENTIVES

During the past quarter of a century, ad hoc solutions often were applied by the states and national government to facilitate the financial accommodation of colleges and universities to the vastly expanding student demand. The practices adopted then have contributed to today's financial crises. Yet the search for new remedies has not included consideration of fundamental corrective actions that would

---

12. *Special Analyses, Budget of the United States Government, Fiscal Year 1972, Special Analysis I: Federal Education Programs* (Washington: Government Printing Office, 1971), p. 118.

give the structure the reinforcement it requires for new remedies to work.

Added Federal Funding and Fund Instability

The amount of federal funds has changed from year to year, with uncertainty as the result. Yet the aggregates do not necessarily reveal the full picture because shifts in federal aid programs have varying effects among institutions. Furthermore, differences in allocation techniques under each aid program and disparate granting methods make for marked variations from year to year within any given institution.

In many ways, the contribution that higher education receives from the federal government is the least stable of all its revenue sources. The amount depends on competing claims made on the budget by the wide variety of other national objectives. In a federal budget totaling about $200 billion, higher education outlays, even at $5 billion, are a mere 2.5 percent of the total. Fiscal policy objectives and the political configuration as it happens to shape and color itself in the kaleidoscope of partisan debate make for more (or less) funds for higher education—public or private—without heed to the planning required by those institutions.

Within institutions, the uncertainties generated by changes in programs and funds spill over from the directly affected unit to other units of the campus. Often, institutions, having gone to considerable expense to recruit highly valued talent for research projects, attempt to maintain the faculty after research outlays are reduced, and do so at the price of student education. Another example is to be found in the cases of the medical schools. After the 1969–70 period of critical shortages in institutional support, originating in part at the federal level with program reassessments and cutbacks in some programs and realignment of others, the medical schools have been jarred into understanding the consequences of fluctuating federal resources. One university president, appearing before a congressional committee in 1971 in favor of medical school aid, stated the situation: "The key to a better system is provision of a basic level of support by the Federal government in recognition of the national nature of the system. This support should be provided without strings, and it should be stable— without sharp swings either upward or downward."[13]

Uncertainty about levels of funding, and fluctuations in those levels, in the words of a Carnegie Commission report, "make it extremely

13. Testimony of Charles E. Odegaard, president, University of Washington, on behalf of the Association of American Universities, before the Subcommittee on Health, Senate Committee on Labor and Public Welfare, May 10, 1971.

difficult for our colleges and universities to achieve real savings"[14]—and, I would add, "to plan." In new proposals for federal funding, greater weight is likely to be given to continuity and stability of funding—assurances, that is, that teaching and other institutional programs are not made pawn to national fiscal policy reviews or priority assessments that have little to do with higher education finance.

As the responsibility of the national government for funding higher education increases, so will the concern about the price of that increase. A precursory proposal looks to basic financial support, support that would be substantial in amount and would be provided on a continuing basis.

It may become necessary to insulate colleges and universities from the pressures of federal budgetary policy. One option to consider is the establishment of a grants commission or academy, whose distinguished members are appointed for long periods (perhaps for life, to free the commission of outside influence or charges of such influence). The grants commission would have among its duties: (1) to receive federal funds, (2) to evaluate methods of allocation of the federal funds, including assessment of the effects of those methods on the structure and purposes of higher education, (3) to report on those evaluations to the Congress and the public, and (4) to distribute the federal funds among colleges and universities either in accord with the purposes that the grants commission has determined, or, if the Congress has by law adopted a formula for grants distribution, in accord with that formula. In addition, the grants commission would be authorized to receive corporate donations to higher education and to allocate monies, along with federal funds, equitably and efficiently.[15]

State Correctives to Perverse Price Incentives

Stable federal funding will not alone yield institutions the safeguards against financial crises that they seek. An important source of instability is the perverse incentive set in motion by low or zero tuition in the public institutions and the advancing tuition price in private ones. Between public and private, the average tuition and fees per student differ markedly, as illustrated in Table 4. Also markedly different is the share of current costs covered by tuition payments. In 1967–68, in public institutions, tuition represented approximately 21 cents of each $1 of student higher education outlays, graduate and

14. *Quality and Equality: Revised Recommendations* (New York: McGraw-Hill Book Co., June 1970), p. 30.
15. This final suggestion has been made by David B. H. Martin.

undergraduate combined; in private colleges, tuition amounted to $2.2 billion of the approximately $3 billion for student higher education expenditures, or 72 cents out of each $1.

TABLE 4: *Tuition and Required Fees per Full-Time Undergraduate Student in Universities, 1957–58—1969–70*

Year	Control		Ratio, Private to Public
	Public	Private	
1957–58..............	$205	$ 798	3.89
1960–61..............	250	994	3.98
1962–63..............	268	1,149	4.29
1964–65..............	298	1,297	4.35
1966–67..............	360	1,456	4.04
1967–68..............	366	1,533	4.19
1968–69..............	377	1,638	4.34
1969–70..............	402	1,795	4.47

Source: U.S. Office of Education, *Basic Student Charges* (Washington: Government Printing Office, annual series).

Low or zero tuition stimulates enrollment in public institutions; in private institutions it is likely to make for uncertainty about enrollments and to aggravate their financial plight. It increases the pressure on state and local tax dollars for academic opportunities, and, as will be indicated later, adds to the accumulating financial deficits in the public institutions. If the private college is to continue, it will be forced to look toward state subsidies or more federal funding—or both. And unless these added subsidies are provided, the public college student load will be enlarged, requiring more state monies, or more federal monies, or both. The remedy lies in narrowing tuition differentials and more nearly revealing the cost to students by tuition charges when they choose among colleges. (Student aid under such a system is discussed below.)

Aid to Institutions as a Corrective

Institutional support, which now constitutes a relatively small proportion of federal categorical aid, is actively being urged to relieve the financial crunch. Aid to institutions, rather than students, is urged in order to: (1) assure that the funds do not go in undue proportion to the more prestigious institutions that presumably would be selected by students, (2) reduce the administrative costs of the method of support, and (3) provide a stimulus to the institution to enhance quality.

But the idea of institutional support also raises familiar questions: (1) What should be the total amount of institutional aid from tax sources? (2) Which institutions should qualify for aid (public, private, both)? (3) How should the aid be distributed among eligible institutions? (4) What requirements or conditions should be imposed on recipient institutions?

Much of the consideration of institutional aid has come to center on the criteria for formulas for distribution of funds. In perhaps oversimplified form, these criteria and their primary consequences are noted below.

Criteria or Measure of Fund Allocations	Consequences
All enrollments	Benefits would be larger for public institutions, and less favorable to small, high-cost colleges
Enrollment of holders of economic opportunity grants and doctoral fellowships	Favors institutions with large numbers of needy students and graduate students of outstanding ability
Amount of scholarship supplementation and fellowships	Favors institutions with large student assistance resources, and those with strong graduate programs
Institutional expenditures	Ignores economies of scale; provides a relatively larger part of the funds to relatively rich institutions; may reward inefficiency
Level and rate of growth of expenditures	Favors relatively rich institutions, those that increased their outlays, and institutions that have had large additional research support
Degrees awarded	Relatively favorable to degree-granting institutions; may be unfavorable to two-year colleges unless they award degrees

What of stability of financing, however? If higher education were priced more nearly at cost (except as national purposes dictate education and training in high cost curricula such as medicine), the demand by students, as evidenced by their tuition payments, would be the best safeguard of stability.

The components or characteristics of a stable funding base need to be defined carefully. Stability surely does not mean locking in inefficiency or wasteful practices that were encouraged by expansion, overlooked in the momentum of growth, but uncovered in the depressed period. Nor does it mean a subsidy amount that is insulated from changes in demand for higher education, changes in demand for curricula, or changes in methods of teaching and technology in higher education. It does mean forward planning to be able to adjust program and quantity of offerings to meet student demands.

Prometheus' woeful words were these:

One thing being certain, that no victory Is his who wars 'gainst that which Needs must be.

". . . that which Needs must be" by way of added federal institutional aid ought to be responsive to student demand and responsible to the taxpayer. States can maintain low tuition at the cost of further deficits in their own colleges and universities, and at the cost of permitting private institutions in increasing numbers to become disadvantaged by the "student market" and forcing them to turn to state government and federal government for support. Or, states can raise the tuition at public institutions to provide a more competitive market with private institutions, and do so with smaller rather than larger subsidies by creating student incentives more favorable to institutional diversity.

Clearly, the contrasting tuition policies adopted in the past and carried into a period of even greater contrasts cannot be sustained without endangering the fabric of higher education—the balance of public and private institutions, the diversity that has been characteristic throughout our history. If public institutions continue to increase their share of enrollments, at some point in the process the forces will culminate in loss of balance and diversity.

Views are strong on both sides of the issue of tuition in public institutions. One consideration sometimes overlooked was emphasized years ago by former Secretary Folsom when he noted: "If education is dispensed as a commodity, all the laws of the market must apply, and we shall wind up offering, not the kind of education we believe to be valid, but the kind that will sell." If institutional support is intended to stay the forces that are propelling higher education toward more enrollments in public institutions, it becomes necessary to assess how each aid formula would work to mantain quality-price trade-offs so that students may make efficient choices.

Perhaps federal aid to institutions might be made conditional on competitive tuition charges among institutions or charges reasonably within a margin of competition. Another option is to require the states to (a) determine the effect of differences in tuition charges between public and private institutions (both immediate and long run), and (b) publicize the finding for public consideration and debate.

Student Aid and Equity

In responding to her teacher's query: "Is this not a prosperous nation?" Dickens' Sissy answered:

"I thought I couldn't know whether it was a prosperous nation or not, and whether I was in a thriving state or not, unless I knew who had the money . . ."

Equity, or "who gets the money," is a theme that pervades many discussions of the federal role in higher education, perhaps because it constitutes a clearer national purpose.

As indicated earlier, there are many who prefer student aid over institutional support. They argue that it permits the government to target the aid, that is, to so bound the eligibility requirements as to confine the aid to those for whom it is a condition for further study, and to restrict its amount to the minimum necessary to maintain access for needy students. Accordingly, debates on forms of aid make much of the problem of equity and the possibility of targeting the funds. If tax funds are to be used to subsidize education, particularly education that will have a continuing favorable effect on future income, then clearly equity demands that the subsidies go to the most needy students. Their arguments for aid to students as a method of channeling funds to higher education include: (1) Student choices help to assure efficient use of the added funds ("efficiency" is defined as use that accords with the student's desires). (2) Aids can be targeted. (3) Continuing competition among institutions is better assured through the channeling of funds to the students, who then choose an institution and a course of study. (4) Educational institutions and programs tend to respond to the student-consumers, who decide how they will spend the subsidy amounts.

Increased student aid will improve the financial condition of a college or university only to the extent that it either frees institutional money for other uses or supports a rise in tuition. Some proposals for student aid, such as the Educational Opportunity Bank, clearly intend that tuition shall be increased as a consequence of the aid. Other proposals would severely limit loans in order to keep tuition down.

Scholarships, work-study payments, and subsidized interest on loans, both federal and state, are intended in principle to provide the lower income student with an amount of aid related to family income.

National statistics show that some 2.7 million undergraduate and 200,000 graduate students[16] already receive federal student aid. Improved access to federally guaranteed loans under the proposed National Student Loan Association is estimated to help an additional one million students. The 1970 amount of federal student aid is reported at $2.1 billion. The latest institutional account data (1968–69) show a total of about $600 million in student grants, divided among classes

16. *Special Analysis I: Federal Education Programs*, p. 128.

of institutions so that more goes to public institutions than private ones, more to universities than to four- and two-year institutions. And as a percentage of student tuition revenues, student assistance also favors the public institution. See Table 5.

TABLE 5: *Student Aid Grant Revenues of Colleges and Universities, 1968–69*

(In millions of dollars)

Institutions	All Student Aid Revenues		Federal Aid	
	Amount	% of Tuition	Amount	% of All Student Aid
All institutions...............	$578.8	15.1	$303.4	52.4
Control:				
Public....................	299.4	21.4	176.2	58.9
Private..................	279.4	11.5	127.1	45.5
Level:				
Universities................	346.1	20.2	197.7	57.1
Four-year colleges...........	206.6	11.5	91.8	44.4
Two-year colleges...........	26.2	8.2	13.9	53.1

Source: Unpublished data from the U.S. Office of Education on financial statistics of higher education.

In the wake of sharpened concerns about equity, not only are federal aid proposals scrutinized for their fairness, but also tuition policies in the states are being assessed. However, the usual question of equity as the education community has usually addressed it needs to be broadened and deepened lest some persons gain upward mobility while others become relatively poorer. Equity for three groups is at issue: (1) those denied by circumstances an approach to access to higher education, (2) those of working age whose earlier circumstances denied them access to higher learning, and (3) those who pay, by taxes, for the education of persons more affluent than they. And questioning is not sufficient. Blinders have obscured the vision of the higher education community to neglect the evidence on the basic nature of the problem of high school dropout. The problem originates, not in the immediate financial inability to go to college, but in longer run disparities with consequences on (1) child development and ability to learn, (2) motivation to continue in school through high school graduation, (3) capacity for access to the best of the institutions of higher education, and (4) incentive to continue through the years of higher education to graduation. The higher education community, when it broadens its concerns, may prevent wastage of human resources in the approaches to access to higher education, as well as losses in the course of direct access after high school graduation. What are the national priorities in resource allocation between higher education and intellectual development generally? What are the priorities between these two courses in the use of public funds? Although more consideration has been given in the past to "lifetime" education and to a second chance for post-high-school education for those who were bypassed on the first round by accident of timing, the added resources have not been sufficient to reorder the priorities in public expenditures.

College Enrollment Disparities among States

High school graduation opens access to college, and yet among the states the proportion of young persons who graduate from high school varies greatly. Table 6 shows that in the ten lowest income states, measured by 1970 per capita income, eight reported less than 75 percent of their ninth-graders made it through to graduation from high school three years later, and in two states—Kentucky and Mississippi— less than 70 percent of ninth-graders graduated three years later. Thus, by their elementary and secondary programs, these states deny college opportunities to large numbers of their young people. In contrast, in the ten highest income states, which include the developing states of Alaska and Hawaii, only one state—Nevada—was below the 75 percent level, and in half of these highest income states, 80 percent or more of the ninth-graders graduated.

How much would these disparities be affected by college scholarship or institutional aid? By very little, clearly. But what would be the effect if, in addition, child development and educational allowances were paid on behalf of the poorest families to providers of such services as child care, preprimary education, teaching of basic reading-writing-arithmetic skills and of more advanced studies as the child grows into the ninth grade? These questions require consideration, if not for fairness sake, then because the education of teachers is an important function of higher education generally.

As indicated in Table 6, children from the lowest income states have less chance of completing high school; in relatively smaller proportions they go on from high school to college. Again, of the ten lowest income states, six had fewer than one-half of their high school graduates in full-time higher education studies in 1968, whereas among the ten highest income states, only Alaska fell below the half proportion. Seven out of each ten New York State high school graduates were enrolled in higher education full time, and in California an even larger proportion of high school graduates are enrolled. For those in New York and California who have no opportunity for higher education, the problem of equity still remains. To draw on Dickens' Sissy's response in a similar vein:

TABLE 6: *Comparative Access to Higher Education, by State*

States, by per Capita Income, Low to High, 1970	Ratio		
	First-Time Enrollments[a] (Full Time), to High School Graduates, 1968	Undergraduates,[a] to 18–21-Year-Olds in State, 1968	Public High School Graduates, 1968–69, to Public School Ninth-Graders, 1965
United States	*.58*[b]	*.41*[b]	*.79*[c]
Mississippi	.64	.33	.68
Arkansas	.54	.34	.70
Alabama	.47	.32	.70
South Carolina	.39	.20	.71
West Virginia	.42	.33	.73
North Dakota	.62	.48	.86
New Mexico	.50	.39	.75
Tennessee	.46	.31	.71
Kentucky	.49	.31	.68
Louisiana	.49	.35	.70
South Dakota	.55	.47	.88
North Dakota	.41	.24	.67
Idaho	.62	.51	.84
Utah	.57	.53	.85
Maine	.34	.26	.82
Oklahoma	.62	.46	.79
Georgia	.41	.25	.66
Montana	.58	.45	.82
Wyoming	.70	.52	.76
Vermont	.34	.34	.84
Texas	.61	.37	.71
Arizona	.98	.48	.73
Florida	.65	.38	.71
Virginia	.47	.26	.76
New Hampshire	.45	.35	.83
Missouri	.56	.40	.75
Oregon	.64	.48	.84
Nebraska	.56	.45	.87
Iowa	.53	.46	.90
Wisconsin	.48	.44	.85
Colorado	.61	;43	.83
Indiana	.46	.36	.79
Minnesota	.52	.45	.93
Kansas	.64	.45	.84
Pennsylvania	.43	.40	.86
Rhode Island	.67	.39	.86
Ohio	.51	.38	.82
Washington	.73	.46	.89
Michigan	.51	.41	.82
Delaware	.48	.31	.83
Maryland	.52	.36	.79
Massachusetts	.66	.49	.85
California	.75	.50	.88
Illinois	.68	.47	.78
Hawaii	.64	.32	.91
New Jersey	.59	.46	.83
Nevada	.54	.27	.74
Alaska	.46	.14	.78
New York	.71	.52	.77
Connecticut	.67	.51	.81

Source: *The Capitol and the Campus: State Responsibility for Postsecondary Education,* A Report and Recommendations by the Carnegie Commission on Higher Education (New York: McGraw-Hill Book Co., 1971), pp. 45–46, 133–34, 139–40.
[a] Residents of state enrolled as undergraduates in any state.
[b] Includes District of Columbia.
[c] Excludes District of Columbia.

175

. . . I thought it must be just as hard upon those who were starved, whether the others were a million, or a *million* million.

When relative state and local effort is measured by amount of state and local funds (including state scholarship aid) as a percent of personal income, many low income states spend a larger percentage of their residents' personal income on higher education (both public and private institutions) than do many high income states. For example, I computed that, for 1967–68, four of the ten states with the lowest personal income spend 1–1.2 percent of their taxable resources to support higher education; five spend 0.7–0.9 percent; and only one of these states spends as low as 0.6 percent. Contrast this support with the effort made by the ten top income states. Only one (Hawaii) spends as much as 1.0 percent, and five made an effort of 0.6 percent or less, of which two (New Jersey and Massachusetts) had an effort of 0.3 percent. Stated differently, these two states devoted three-tenths of one percent of their personal income resources to subsidizing higher education out of tax funds.

It is apparent that low income states—despite spending a relatively high percentage of their personal income for higher education—continue to have higher dropout rates from high school and low college enrollments compared with high income states. This imbalance, in my opinion, results from low expenditures of some states for primary and secondary education and their relatively high expenditures for college education. If students were better prepared at the elementary and secondary levels, more of them would be likely to enter college and thereafter less likely to drop out.

Purposes and Processes

Consideration of educational finance proceeds on two levels. One level encompasses the old debates—I was tempted to call them ancient —such as the time-worn issues of aid to institutions or to students; bricks and mortar aid versus aid for current expenditures including faculty salaries; student loans versus grants; and so forth. The other level recognizes the processes of reassessment and reconstitution in higher education now under way and seeks to view the problems of finance in that context.

Lack of clarity of educational objectives nationwide complicates the design of means to accomplish such objectives. When purposes are defined, processes can follow. Many avenues are open to the federal government in carrying out its roles in higher education. Suppose the governments (federal and state) and the institutions agreed that a multiplicity of revenue sources yielded a wanted objective—autonomy in college and university governance. In principle at least, many methods are available to achieve that multiplicity. I cite a few without intending to suggest either feasibility or desirability. Gifts and endowments to colleges and universities could be increased by (*a*) reducing legal margins on stock purchases, (*b*) offering large tax deductions or credits for institutional gifts against corporate income taxes, personal income taxes, and estate taxes. Institutional income from investments could be increased by such federal measures as: (*a*) subsidizing interest rates on bonds held by institutions of higher education, (*b*) guaranteeing classes of high-risk, high-yield private investments, (*c*) creating a new high-yield federal security available only to colleges and universities. State and local funding can be encouraged by (*a*) federal revenue sharing with states and cities, (*b*) federal grants to the governments restricted to higher education uses, (*c*) credits against the federal income tax for state and local taxation, (*d*) federal grants to public colleges and universities, (*e*) federal loans and federal guarantees on loans, and so forth. Suppose, to give another example, a policy was advanced of one-third federal funding, one-third student funding, and one-third state funding to gain (*a*) a desired educational program (which I do not try to define) and (*b*) an optimum allocation of resources to education. How would the higher education community know whether (or not) the financial policies proposed serve their educational objectives, or whether skim milk is masquerading as cream?

The Carnegie Commission on Higher Education now serves a vital purpose in analyzing some of the major organization and financial policies in higher education. Recommendations of the commission, however, require further analysis and review. The state and private higher education agencies, in my view, would greatly advance the progress toward a new campus role in society by developing capability for examining the many financial proposals and assessing them in terms of a defined set of educational goals. If the state higher education agencies would create offices for educational policy analysis (including analysis of methods of financing and related organization processes), the work of those offices would give added meaning to the $100 million commitment to the new design proposal of the administration for a National Foundation for Higher Education, an independent federal agency that would provide funds to colleges and universities to experiment with new educational forms and techniques.

Processes examined carefully can help secure the goals of higher education. "And" (with Mr. Dickens), "if we didn't get to Heaven that way, it was not a politico-economic place, and we had no business there."

Federal Contributions to Higher Education

HAROLD ORLANS

"I KNOW WHERE I'M GOING, AND / I KNOW WHO'S GOING WITH ME," Wendy Hiller once sang (if I remember correctly, it was to Scotland, with a handsome young man). Selma Mushkin's larger point is that we should know where we are going in higher education—the "purpose" of that unfree enterprise—in order to finance it intelligently, in ways which get us *there* (to Scotland, not Wales) economically.

She tells us that the educational consequences of alternative financial methods "can be tested only when the 'mission' for higher education is made plain." And "Lack of clarity of educational objectives nationwide complicates the design of means to accomplish such objectives." That is true enough, but it is a truth which we had better accept if the task of analysis is to understand the world, not to simplify it, and if the task of policy making is to satisfy people, not planners.

For, of course, the difficulty with clarifying "the" purpose of higher education is that it is not singular but multifarious: to learn some things and to forget others—habits as well as knowledge; if possible, to leave home, make friends, have a good time; to find—or lose—oneself. And the government's purpose is almost as multifarious as the student's: in addition to the conventional objectives enunciated by economists, it includes all the good and bad political purposes of reducing the labor force, keeping the domestic peace, placating discontented constituencies, and shoring up our ruins and our hopes. If we devised a separate system to finance every separate system to finance every separate public purpose of higher education, we would end up with pretty much the system we now have, from which the higher education community is trying so hard to escape.

But how hard is it really trying? We may recall a painful truth uttered by Lee Dubridge in his anguished effort to serve loyally both his president and his scientific colleagues (I paraphrase): "Everyone talks about 'policy' but all they mean is 'money.'" Surely, the main reason for the silence Daniel Moynihan complained about in October

1970 in St. Louis, with which the President's March 1970 higher education message was greeted,[1] was simply that there was so little new money in it. In Washington, at any rate, it may appear that the academic community is less interested in ideas for their own sake than for the money that comes in their train.

I shall turn now to a few detailed comments on Dr. Muskin's paper, and apologize if the circumstances lead me to put them too categorically.

Dr. Mushkin's effort to separate the cost of "educating students" from other higher education (especially construction and research) costs is brave but, in large measure, futile. As a single instance: 35 percent of the academic year salaries of faculty at Massachusetts Institute of Technology comes from federal research funds,[2] which she excludes from her calculations. It would be more realistic—financially, educationally, and politically—to take these funds into account, as does the Carnegie Commission. In that event, the federal contribution would, of course, rise substantially and the showing for private universities would come off somewhat better.

I appreciate the logic that leads her to stress the importance of raising tuition at public institutions; few refrains recur more often in the liturgy of economists. But too much attention is given to averages and not enough to the diversity we praise more than we foster. In my day, it was said that City College was for the poor and bright, Columbia for the rich and bright, and New York University for those who were neither. Now that public institutions enroll so many (which, of itself, is no calamity or threat to the private sector), why not introduce a wider range of fees at different kinds of public institutions, from an Ivy League level at a place like Santa Cruz to nothing at most community colleges? The classless college offers such vast economies that it should be possible for any serious and intelligent person to receive a reputable bachelor's degree for virtually nothing, through a system

1. See Daniel P. Moynihan, "On Universal Higher Education," remarks at the American Council on Education's opening general session, St. Louis, Missouri, Oct. 8, 1970. "One would like to report that the response of higher education was positive with respect at least to this proposal [for a National Foundation for Higher Education], but I fear this was not the case. Here and there approval was expressed. Here and there suspicion. But on balance there was no response. . . . A major presidential initiative that, right or wrong, was at very least the product of some thought and some analysis was greeted by silence on the part of precisely those institutions that are presumably devoted to thought and analysis." In *Higher Education for Everybody: Issues and Implications*, ed. W. Todd Furniss (Washington: American Council on Education, 1971), pp. 252–53.

2. The figure is for fiscal 1969 (*Creative Renewal in a Time of Crisis*, Report of the Commission on MIT Education, November 1970, p. 45).

of external examinations. Unfortunately, students at SUNY's new campusless, classless Empire State College, which opened in fall 1971, pay the standard $550 undergraduate tuition.[3]

If we are going to push educational costs and debts up—excuse me: tuition and loans—two statistics might usefully be added to the cost-benefit computations: (1) average professorial salary per classroom hour (it may range from less than $10 at many public institutions to more than $100 at Harvard); and (2) individual student-faculty contact hours per hundred dollars tuition (reckoning an "individual" contact, where there is no other, as the fraction of class size; this range may be smaller, from perhaps $100 tuition per faculty hour at large state universities to $300 or so at Harvard).[4] Thus, lawyers are not so expensive after all, and call-girls are a bargain.

I believe, with as much resignation as pleasure, that institutional grants are an idea whose time has come. We have had them for years at medical schools, and who has complained about that? The idea can be defended on grounds of administrative and political convenience without gainsaying the waste it entails (many other government programs give money to those who do not need it in order to get some to those who do), the political intrusion it is likely to engender at *some* time at *some* institutions, or the continued need for countless categorical programs which will *and should* account for the bulk of federal higher educational expenditures. But the idea of importing a University Grants Committee to allocate peacefully vast sums which the bumbling Congress can raise but not dispense is fanciful. The United Kingdom is a quaint but un-American country, full of people whose economy is more backward and whose life is more civilized than ours, who preserve a degree of community and civility that we lack, and who—most un-American of all—do not go around killing one another. In that wonderland, the University Grants Committee works well, though its public accountability has grown and categorical research grants have had to be increased to counter the monasticism of the dons. But anyone who thinks that such a committee can today be transported and function meaningfully here should think again. The short history of the proposed National Foundation of Higher Education already provides suitable food for thought.

Those who come to Washington seeking financial security and a clear sense of national purpose, when there is all too little financial security or common purpose anywhere in the nation, are bound to be

---

3. Reported in *Higher Education and National Affairs*, July 9, 1971, p. 2.
4. These are the grossest order-of-magnitude estimates; I hope some economist will prepare accurate figures.

disappointed. To ask the government, in this season of our discontent, to relinquish major legislative and budgetary powers to a permanent, independent commission is to ask it not to govern. That is neither realistic nor wise.

Effects of Raising Tuition

ALLAN W. OSTAR

IN COMMENTING ON DR. MUSHKIN'S PAPER I SHALL REFER TO OTHER published statements to reinforce my positions.

I remain unalterably opposed to raising tuition as a means of financing higher education. The concept of public education as a commodity to be sold for a price that the market will bear is anathema to our democratic principles.

The current tuition controversy is reminiscent of the arguments over the establishment of public high schools in the mid-nineteenth century, as described by Ann Rosenthal. In 1890, less than 6 percent of the children of high school age were enrolled in secondary schools; by 1960, over 86 percent were so enrolled. Compare the trend as it applies to higher education: in 1900, only 4 percent of the 18–21 population was enrolled in college;[1] now, nearly 58 percent of high school graduates enter college.[2] As high school enrollment increased, the rationale did not shift to require students to finance their own secondary education. Similarly, as enrollments in higher education increase, the nation should not reverse its historic commitment to the responsibilities and benefits of educating all its children to the highest level of ability. It is unthinkable that this generation should be the one to cut back or deny public support of higher education by shifting the burden to the student in the form of higher tuition. Must we be reminded by Henry Steele Commager that "The United States—the richest country—is also almost the only one which requires university students to pay tuition"?[3]

Can anyone seriously challenge the benefits of public support under the GI bill, which sent about 4.5 million veterans to college at a fed-

---

1. "Tuition-Free College: Parallel and Perspective," *Educational Record*, Fall 1966, p. 510.
2. Russell I. Thackrey, *What's Behind the Rising Cost of Education?* (Washington: American Association of State Colleges and Universities and the National Association of State Universities and Land-Grant Colleges [1971]), p. 3.
3. "Tuition Charges Are a Mistake," *New York Times*, Feb. 25, 1971.

eral cost of roughly $12 billion?[4] The benefits to society in increased income and availability of technological and professional skills acquired by the veterans resulted in an impressively large return on the government's investment. The return, through increased federal taxes paid by veterans, is estimated at $100 billion. In addition, society gained one million college-trained businessmen, 750,000 engineers, 300,000 medical personnel, 200,000 scientists, and 400,000 teachers, to cite a few categories.

Tax money spent for education is not a burdensome outlay down the drain, but a magnificent productive investment. Indeed, contrary to the Mushkin remedy, movement toward free tuition would be more desirable.

Myriad reasons argue against tuition increases. I shall focus on only a few. (1) Between 1959 and 1969, tuition and required fees in public degree-granting institutions doubled, while those in public two-year colleges increased by 93 percent. College charges for instruction and related purposes has risen at a rate more than three times as high as the consumer price index because students are being charged a higher proportion of costs.[5] (2) Even if colleges made no charge for tuition, students and their families would still be paying more than 70 percent (five-sevenths) of the cost of education.[6] When incidental expenses and forgone income are included, students are paying three-quarters of the cost of education.[7] (3) Tuition represents a tiny fraction of the total cost of higher education—less than 10 percent. Moderate expansion or contraction of tuition would not change the system decisively.[8] (4) Higher tuition obviously discourages low income and minority group members. Increasing fees for public education flatly negates the American dream of equal opportunity.

Howard Bowen comments: "If one argues that the rich are not paying their share of higher educational costs, the remedy is not necessarily to raise the charge to the level of full cost but to revise the tax system." Joseph Pechman makes a similar point: "We do not ask the wealthy to pay higher fees for police or fire protection or for any other public good; similarly, there is no reason to extract from them a larger

4. Cost figure provided by the Veterans Administration, Justin Lewis.
5. Thackrey, op. cit., p. 6.
6. Joseph A. Pechman, "Distributional Effects of Public Higher Education," *Journal of Human Resources*, Summer 1970, p. 9.
7. Howard R. Bowen, "Society, Students and Parents—A Joint Responsibility," in *Financing Higher Education: Alternatives for the Federal Government*, ed. M. D. Orwig (Iowa City: American College Testing Program, 1971), p. 161.
8. Howard R. Bowen, "Who Pays the Higher Education Bill?" in *Financing Higher Education*, p. 285.

payment for the external benefits of higher education than is made by others. The way to handle the equity problem is to be sure that the tax system is progressive, not to levy user charges to pay for the external benefits directly." What would the people say? A public opinion poll in *Life* magazine about two years ago showed Americans placed highest priority on education in the use of tax money.

It is untrue that the public institutions threaten the private sector by their increasing enrollment. M. D. Orwig explains: "Although the *proportion* of students in private colleges and universities declined significantly, the *number* of students in private institutions increased approximately 86 percent from 1954–1969, in spite of the rapid increase in private tuition during the same period. Furthermore, the number of private institutions has not declined during this time. . . ."[9] The public institutions are not cutting into the pie of the private sector; rather, the whole pie is growing. The sharp increase in the public sector has occurred because more students seek postsecondary opportunity. Public institutions, particularly junior colleges, have responded to this demand. Minority group and low income students—those who might not otherwise attend college—have seized the opportunity offered by low tuition at these public institutions.

Proposals such as the Educational Opportunity Bank are another means of shifting the cost of higher education to the student. I oppose this scheme because it fails to serve the very people solicited. Minority and low income students would be loath to assume an indebtedness of from $5,000 to $20,000 for higher education. This device does not open the door to education. It opens the door to indebtedness. A student borrowing $2,500 a year at an annual interest rate of 9¼ percent repayable over a twenty-year period faces the prospect of paying up to $27,822, including interest, over the period of the loan. That is enough to frighten away the middle income student too.

In the past, the low and middle income groups received help in the form of federally guaranteed student loans at subsidized interest rates. The debt incurred by students was bearable as long as colleges kept their charges down through assistance from federal and other sources. Reduction or elimination of direct federal aid to our institutions will result in higher than normal increases in tuition and fees, making these loans an intolerably expensive burden.

Every generation has sacrificed to provide educational opportunities for its young people. Are we now to say to the next generation, "We

9. M. D. Orwig, "The Federal Government and the Finance of Higher Education," in *Financing Higher Education*, p. 341.

are looking out for ourselves—if you want an education, hock your future and get it yourself"?

As a partial remedy to the patent unfairness of raising tuition to meet costs, some suggest student aid for low income families only. Such a scheme places a severe burden on middle income families. They could not qualify for student aid, nor could they afford the higher tuition.

I wish particularly that diversity in higher education be preserved in the face of strong pressures to wipe it out. Our society needs institutions with a variety of missions, responsibilities, and educational philosophies—from multipurpose universities with wide ranges of graduate and professional programs to highly specialized single-purpose institutions and junior colleges. Each institution should have an identity, a mission, and a commitment to excellence and quality. Assuming diversity is desirable, forcing public institutions to become more akin to private, by raising tuition, has the effect of making our colleges and universities proprietary schools. Add to this the argument that private schools should receive public funds and the irony is compounded.

There are other areas of diversity not yet fully explored. It may be time to redefine higher education to include all forms of postsecondary education. This concept is particularly important when tax support dollars (federal and state) are gathered from all the people. Yet we have no reliable data concerning the number of students served or the number of dollars spent. For example, it is estimated that there are 7,000 proprietary schools serving about 1.5 million students, but the Office of Education has no data on this area of postsecondary education.[10] We can say: (1) There are many more students involved in postsecondary education than have ever been taken into account in the various economic models (including Dr. Mushkin's). (2) There are many more dollars being spent (primarily private dollars). (3) Most of these students and dollars, ironically, probably represent the lower income families. If all of postsecondary education is brought into consideration, the dimensions of the financial problem are much greater and its nature is considerably different.

The inequality of state efforts is mentioned by Dr. Mushkin. Her proposed solution appears to suggest that California, which has low tuition and high effort (and 80 percent of high school graduates going to college), should raise tuition and reduce effort and thus become more nearly equal in providing opportunity with those states that do not fund higher education adequately and have lower proportions

10. Unpublished figures provided by Kenneth A. Young, vice-president, American College Testing Program.

going to college. I suggest the reverse would be more suitable. States like New Jersey should become more like California rather than having California copy New Jersey.

What financing do I favor? In a panel before the U.S. Senate Subcommittee on Education in 1968, the American Association of State Colleges and Universities, together with every major higher education association, believed the next major move the federal government must make was for general institutional support. There was also unanimity that the federal government should do everything in its power to help all institutions, private and public, to keep their charges down.

I support the concept of general federal assistance to higher education, provided such assistance: (1) is paid directly to the institutions; (2) is provided in such a manner as to assure that cutbacks of existing levels of appropriations will not take place at either state or federal levels; (3) is based on easily available and measurable data, for example, the number of full-time equivalent students as of some fixed date; (4) provides a graduated level of support that recognizes the increased cost of instruction, beginning at the two-year level, and advancing to the highest costs for doctoral and other advanced professional degrees.

As Wayne Morse states: "The concept of opportunity to all, regardless of race, religion, or economic circumstances, has been firmly placed in our system of values as a good thing. It is a prime tenet in the theology of the democratic approach to social order."[11] The first objective of higher education must be to equalize educational opportunities and ensure that every qualified student proceeds to the limit of his ability. He will repay society, not only through his increased taxes, but through his contributions. Jonas Salk attended college only because it was free and accessible. Society made an investment in him which he repaid through the elimination of polio. How do you put a price tag on elimination of a dread disease? How many more Jonas Salks merely await the opportunity for low cost, accessible higher education? Who can reasonably deny them that opportunity?

National Priorities and Learning

ALBERT H. QUIE

STUDENTS OF HIGHER EDUCATION POLICY HAVE IN RECENT YEARS IMPROVED our ability to ask good questions. Here the question is on the nature of public support. No clear consensus on this issue has yet emerged.

11. From material prepared for the National Commission on the Future of State Colleges and Universities.

Dr. Mushkin's paper articulates very well some basic considerations and possible alternatives. My comments are meant to supplement her scholarly analysis with some practical political considerations and personal judgments.

I shall begin with these givens: (1) new departures from present policy will be "add-ons" or a realignment of existing programs; (2) the *total* amount of federal aid to higher education is likely to increase *gradually*; and (3) the erratic levels of support for the many existing categorical programs will continue as the mood of Congress changes from year to year.

New departures in policy will be add-ons because of the extreme difficulty in repealing existing authorities. First, each senior member on a congressional committee has a few favorite programs, many of which he was instrumental in getting passed and therefore is reluctant to see curtailed. Second, the authority for present programs is spread among several congressional committees, each jealous of its own jurisdiction. Third, interest groups have built up strong protective lobbies for even some of the smallest programs. And finally, the higher education associations have shown no inclination to make hard decisions about which programs have outlived their priority or usefulness and which should be given greater support. To date, the plan has been to give *more* support, albeit in varying amounts, to *all* programs.

Even though there now exists a certain amount of disaffection with higher education (temporary, it is to be hoped), it is difficult for the Congress consciously to cut back its support in any major area of social welfare below the level of the year before. The size of the increase tends to be the issue.

There is no way to predict the size of these increases. The childlike faith placed in our institutions of higher learning to discover solutions to our problems has eroded. That expectation was unreasonable to begin with, but it did in years past contribute to a federal willingness to pour large sums of money into our colleges and universities. The public also questions the wisdom of significant increases in aid to a structure of higher learning that is increasingly under attack by those who provide the very breath of life to that structure—its faculty and students. But the more important reason it is difficult to predict levels of support from the federal government is the competition for funds among increasingly popular programs in health, welfare, housing, environmental control, crime, and other socially desirable areas.

Finally, the Congress must view education—as well as all other areas—within the broadest perspective. Increasing amounts of research indicate that one's socioeconomic background is perhaps the most important factor in intellectual development. And that the importance of the first three or four years of one's life is so much more crucial to future development than we had ever imagined. And that we will soon be graduating more college seniors than there will be jobs requiring a college degree. These are only a few of the considerations which must go into planning for higher education.

Personally, I find few who disagree with me in putting a higher federal priority today on early childhood education and on what has come to be called occupational or career education. More federal support must be given to higher education. But much, much more must be done in these other two areas. The number of those who terminate their education at twelfth grade unqualified to get a job is discouraging to say the least.

When one considers national priorities and learning, he must look beyond education. Could recent studies be suggesting that decent shelter, adequate food, and competent medical care for every American are perhaps equally compelling needs if the educational level of our society generally is to be raised?

I do not intend to skirt the issue, but only to point out that the President and the Congress are forced to see the issue in a much broader perspective than tends to be prevalent on the campus. Which raises another point. Too much of the discussion about the financing of "higher education" concentrates on some eight million students scattered among some 2,500 institutions. In fact, there are at least another eight million people engaged in some form of postsecondary education *outside* these institutions. It is time to focus more on providing every adult with continuous opportunity for learning in our urban, technological society, and less on how we preserve 2,500 college and university campuses. They are the core, to be sure, but separate institutions with separate buildings and separate communities of students and faculty are only one approach to learning. The federal role has, to date, been focused on these institutions. Should the focus be broader? I think it must.

This point provides an opening to agree especially with that portion of Dr. Mushkin's paper dealing with student assistance. Although, for reasons I have already discussed, federal support of higher education will continue to flow in many forms, I tend increasingly to favor student aid as the best of these forms. There are several reasons. First, one of the objectives should be to give each individual maximum choice in the type of higher learning he wishes to pursue. Second, institutions old and new, large and small would compete for federal funds, not through grantsmanship but through creating programs attractive to a larger number of students. Third, student aid is least likely to raise constitutional questions in light of the Supreme Court decisions in the summer of 1971. And finally, this form of assistance will, in the long run, have fewer federal strings attached than either institutional aid or categorical aid.

I have for some time supported the concept of general aid as part of the federal mix. In considering the matter of general aid last spring, one of the few questions in the House Special Subcommittee on Education which received a unanimous positive response was whether we wanted to support private higher education. (We have—along with most people—neglected to consider how much public support a private institution can accept and still be private.) At the time of this writing, no decisions have been made on this issue in our committee. But it would be a grave disservice to higher education if we promised huge sums of money for general aid, only later to appropriate but a small sum or to have the law declared unconstitutional. Whatever the outcome this year, I personally would prefer to have higher education look to student aid rather than institutional aid for its greatest federal support.

If this policy were followed, the result would undoubtedly include higher tuitions at public institutions. That is something we might as well get used to. I see no other alternative if a substantial mix of private institutions is to be maintained. I am not sure what portion of full cost tuition should ideally cover. Between 60 percent and 80 percent at most institutions seems a reasonable long-range target. I suggest this with full confidence that we can maintain our commitment to seeking equal opportunities for all who can benefit to pursue some form of postsecondary education.

I believe the chances of increasing federal appropriations to keep pace with inflation and increasing enrollments are much better by means of student aid than by any other form of assistance. One problem with funding so far is a lack of consensus on the proper federal role in higher education. Some measure of stability in funding, which institutions now lack, would then be determined by their level of enrollment. New institutions should also be able to count on the same aid to the extent they could attract students.

One last comment. It is well to remember that the states should and probably will continue to play the major role in the support of higher education. It is becoming increasingly important that federal policy making be done in cooperation with the states. I expect that matter to be a major concern in the decade ahead. For many of the same reasons mentioned above, I hope that states put more of their money in student aid. If that becomes the case, closer state-federal coordination will be mandatory.

ALLAN M. CARTTER

Student Financial Aid

THE FINANCIAL IMPLICATIONS OF UNIVERSAL HIGHER EDUCATION are so dependent on the definition of "universal" that it is appropriate to distinguish among several alternative versions. For the purposes of this paper, I pose three quite different definitions, although there are many other possible gradations:

1. Equal opportunity with merit constraints (that is, higher education serving some fraction of the eligible age group, with selective admissions)
2. Universal access to postsecondary education
3. Universal college education

The distinguishing characteristics among these variants are commonly understood. Under the *equal opportunity* definition, it is presumed that society commits itself to the further education of only some fraction of the potential pool—perhaps the upper one-quarter or one-half as measured by some ability standard. Only twenty years ago it was generally assumed that not more than a quarter of the population were "educable" at the collegiate level. Ten or fifteen years ago policy goals set by several national commissions suggested the upper 30–40 percent. Today, with the expansion of differentiated systems of higher education, the responsibility of *four-year* collegiate education is still often defined at these levels of opportunity, with a more universal role assumed for the two-year college.

Universal access has traditionally existed in several states that have admitted all high school graduates to their respective state universities, but the term today more commonly presupposes a network of two-year colleges to serve the bulk of the population either in college-parallel or vocationally oriented programs. Fifty years ago when only about 17 percent of seventeen-year-olds graduated from high school, universal access of high school graduates to collegiate opportunities implied selective (partially self-selected) admissions. Today, when

189

high school graduation has lost its special meaning as a way of identifying talented youth, and progression through the grades is more nearly a function of years spent in school, universal access clearly implies nonselective admissions. The most persuasive argument for universal college access is the failure of the public schools in disadvantaged localities—many rural areas as well as urban ghettos—to overcome environmental and neighborhood obstacles to learning. Although the attrition rate implied by universal access is dishearteningly high, the success rate of many who, by ordinary aptitude and high school performance criteria, would never have had the opportunity to pursue postsecondary education is frequently dramatic. *Universal access*, as I use the term here, implies continuing high standards for college graduation, and assumes reasonably high attrition rates and the further development of subbaccalaureate terminal points.

Universal college education, as used here, is the continuation of the primary and secondary school pattern. Some advocates argue that in the modern industrial age it is important to attempt to carry every young adult through to the level of education usually associated with the baccalaureate degree. It could even be imagined that, by the end of the present century, age twenty-one might become the legal school-leaving age. In effect, this pattern would shift the responsibility for specialized education and for selective progression into graduate or advanced professional school—just as, fifty years ago, college assumed this primary role when universal high school education was implemented. Universal college education, no matter how ardently we might wish to the contrary, implies a modest diminution in standards for the representative institution and probably also implies even greater variation in quality standards among institutions than now exists.

EQUITY VERSUS EFFICIENCY

The educational and social implications of these different versions of universal higher education differ greatly; the three alternatives cannot be viewed as merely different points on a continuous spectrum. The usual debates on this subject invoke considerations of both equity and efficiency. It seems quite obvious that efficiency, as measured by society's return on investment, is served best by equal opportunity with merit constraints, and is least well served by universal collegiate education. It also seems evident that equal opportunity with merit constraints would be a much more efficient system than that which we have traditionally experienced, although over the last decade substantial progress has been made toward attaining this goal.

It could also be argued that the third alternative, which largely forsakes merit principles at the prebaccalaureate level, carries higher education beyond the point of diminishing returns, and quite possibly carries it to the point of diminishing absolute returns. Several of Astin's studies, which indicate that bright students perform outstandingly in what are thought to be poor institutions as well as in the prestigious ones, might seem to dispute this conclusion.[1] However, the degree of universalism implied in the third definition, especially if it should be reinforced by compulsory attendance, might reverse Astin's conclusions. The experience of mediocre public high schools, where the weight of numbers of untalented and disinterested students creates an environment that stifles intellectual development, is not encouraging in this respect.

On the other hand, equity considerations are probably better served by the second and third definitions than by the first. This proposition would not necessarily be true if equal opportunity implied a policy of *exclusion* as well as inclusion. Ordinarily, however, equal opportunity is thought of as requiring minimum guarantees, while still permitting the student from a relatively affluent family to attend some collegiate institution and thus to get some of the benefits that a degree (or even college attendance) provides. Although it is easy to overstress the inequities imposed by a "credentialist society," nonetheless privilege *is* bestowed upon many who could not qualify by ability standards alone.

On the other hand, while the higher education system may be nonexclusionary, individual institutions frequently are. Prior to World War II privilege was a much more common factor in determining admissibility. Affluence, parental alumni status, and knowing someone in the right place influenced decisions even in the most distinguished institutions. Far from being negative features, many private colleges and universities took it as their task to maintain loyalty to alumni families and to train those who seemed destined to positions of importance in government, business, cultural affairs, and the professions. Today, however, the most prestigious private colleges and universities are among the more exemplary institutions in pursuing an admissions policy based primarily upon academic per-

1. Alexander W. Astin, "Undergraduate Achievement and Institutional Excellence," *Science*, Aug. 16, 1968, pp. 661–68; and *Predicting Academic Performance in College* (New York: Free Press, 1971).

formance. During the 1950s and 1960s, intellectual homogeneity, as a prime characteristic of student bodies, largely displaced social homogeneity in the more selective private as well as public institutions. The one area in which institutions have made little progress is athletics, where academic and need considerations are frequently secondary to athletic prowess.

I believe that the growing public support of universal higher education—by whatever definition—is largely attributable to the unwillingness or inability of higher education to exclude those short on talent and motivation but long on affluence or influence. In today's social and political climate it is less and less acceptable to guarantee the means of attending college only to the high aptitude but economically disadvantaged student, while at the same time making room for the low aptitude but economically advantaged student. Our structure of higher education, divided between public and private, and giving a considerable degree of autonomy to individual institutions, is not designed to provide a merit-based equal opportunity performance that satisfies equity considerations. Without the practice of exclusion—much more common in the British, French, and Russian systems—it appears unlikely that the equal-opportunity-for-the-talented goal will ever be satisfactorily attained. The high cost of universal higher education may be the price we shall have to pay for our nonexclusionary tradition.

THE NUMBERS INVOLVED

Under the three definitions of "universal," above, somewhat different magnitudes are involved. Rough approximations can be made which give some indication of the implications for student aid.

Under the "equal opportunity" variant, one might take as a target the entrance into college of at least 90 percent of the top 40 percent of students as measured by ability. (In the early 1960s, according to Project Talent data, about 90 percent of high-income, high-aptitude youth entered college in the year after high school.) Using Project Talent follow-up data, the talent loss from the upper two aptitude quintiles from the lowest three income quintiles was about 100,000 students, or roughly 16 percent of the entering college class in 1960.[2]

2. See John C. Flanagan and William W. Cooley, *Project Talent One-Year Follow-up Studies*, Cooperative Research Project No. 2333 (Pittsburgh: University of Pittsburgh, 1966) ; John K. Folger, Helen S. Astin, and Alan E. Bayer, *Human Resources and Higher Education* (New York: Russell Sage Foundation, 1970), pp. 309–12.

It can be assumed that sufficient headway has been made over the last decade so that the equal opportunity target as defined here would probably involve a 10–12 percent increase in undergraduate-level enrollments.

Alternatively, one might take as a goal bringing the percentage of high school graduates in families in the lowest three income quintiles (those who ordinarily would need some degree of financial aid) up to the same percentage of attendance as in the next to the highest income quintile (where financial need usually disappears as a limiting factor). Table 1 gives an estimate, based on Project Talent data for 1960 high school graduates, of the expansion in entering enrollment that might be expected if the third, fourth, and fifth SES quintiles had the same college entrance pattern as the second quintile.

TABLE 1: *Percentage Increase in College Attendance of 1960 High School Graduates If Lowest Three SES Quintiles Had the Attendance of Second Highest SES Quintile*

Group Brought up to Target	Percentage Increase in Enrollment
30 percent of students with highest aptitude.	6.7
60 percent of students with highest aptitude.	12.0
80 percent of students with highest aptitude.	17.0
All aptitude levels.	24.3

If we accept high school graduation and scholastic aptitude as appropriate and adequate measures in the pattern for admissions to higher education, and if in 1960 we had been primarily concerned with the top 30 percent of the talent pool, then we were within 6.7 percent of accomplishing a reasonable target. And if, in 1960, the top 60 percent of students had been the concern, that goal would have required a 12 percent expansion from the lower SES talent pool.

It seems highly likely that these targets are even closer to our reach today than they were a decade ago, although, as measured in Table 1, the targets themselves shift upward as the upper income groups experience higher attendance rates. Nonetheless, it seems reasonable to assume that perhaps a 5 percent or a 10 percent expansion of students from low income groups would equalize opportunity respectively for the top 30 percent and the top 60 percent as measured by merit. *If funds could be targeted to present nonattenders,* and if it could be assumed that students from middle and low income families would need about three-quarters of their costs underwritten through tuition subsidies or student aid, such goals would involve a commitment of additional funds in a magnitude of $0.5 billion and $1 billion respectively today. (As a rough measure, I used $14 billion as the approximate total student educational expenditure of institutions of higher education for 1970–71,[3] and took three-quarters of 5 percent and 10 percent of that expenditure.)

Some will argue not only that financial inducements for initial attendance must be provided, but also that low income students have a higher attrition rate which must be compensated for. Project Talent data do not support this conclusion. Entering students from low SES families have a higher college completion rate than that of the economic groups in the second and third aptitude quintiles. Further, when compared with middle income groups, their performance is equal or better at all aptitude levels.

Universal access to higher education would probably entail an increase in college attendance approximating the last line of Table 1. This assumption would hold if, as assumed in Table 1, the second highest SES quintile is essentially free of financial need and its attendance pattern is duplicated by lower SES groups when financial barriers are removed. The 24.3 percent estimate for 1960 has probably declined to about 20 percent today. If academic standards are maintained, however, attrition rates would be significantly higher for the lower aptitude students than it is with today's student mix. Therefore, the increase in total undergraduate enrollment implied by a universal access policy would probably be about 15 percent. If aid—either direct or through indirect subsidy—could be *targeted* on this group, the cost of expansion would probably be a little over $2 billion.

Finally, *universal higher education,* implying an adjustment of educational standards to the level of the representative student, would probably mean an enrollment expansion of 20–35 percent if voluntary and about 65 percent if compulsory. Costs become harder to compute as the increments become larger, but if attendance is voluntary, would probably involve a targeted cost of $2.5–$5 billion. Compulsory attendance implies free tuition, and would probably have a price tag for the public purse of at least $10 billion.

All of the above estimates are in 1970 prices and take no account of the general inflation in educational costs likely in the future or of the added personal costs of the residential student. Even so, the cost of *compulsory* universal higher education is so high, and so

3. National Center for Educational Statistics, U.S. Office of Education, *Projections of Educational Statistics to 1979–80* (Washington: Government Printing Office, 1971), p. 102. The $14 billion is defined as including "general administration, instruction and departmental research, extension and public services, libraries, operation and maintenance of the physical plant, and sponsored activities such as training institutes and related sponsored activities which were specifically financed by outside sources."

evidently wasteful in both human and economic terms, that I shall dismiss it in the remainder of this paper. It would run counter to all the present trends of conferring adulthood at age eighteen and of encouraging the assumption by young men and women of decision-making powers over their own lives.

It should also be emphasized that *the approximations above assume the targeting of incremental aid only to those students not now attending college.* In practice, such targeting is impossible, and the costs of the various alternatives would be correspondingly higher. If additional aid is offered equitably to all potential students in low income groups, there are several likely consequences. First, the contribution by low income students now attending college through various forms of self-help (jobs, loans, and parental sacrifices) will undoubtedly diminish. Second, to the extent that institutions and voluntary agencies are relieved of part of the burden of supporting low income students, there will be a tendency for some portion of these funds to be redistributed to middle income students with partial need. While both of these adjustments may be socially desirable, the need for a shotgun rather than a rifle shot approach would probably raise the cost of a public program of direct aid to students (or parents) by about one-half under an equal opportunity program, and by a third or more under broader noncompulsory programs.

FINANCIAL AID IN A PLURALISTIC SYSTEM

There is a perennial debate over the relative merits of direct aid to students on the one hand, or the subsidization of institutions on the other. The problem is exacerbated by the dual structure of higher education. Public institutions traditionally have charged very low student fees (in some instances, zero), and have been directly subsidized by public—predominantly state—agencies. Private colleges and universities have traditionally subsidized the cost of education to the extent possible from gifts and earnings on endowment, and have aided a fraction of students through scholarship grants. It is possible to equalize opportunity and provide universal higher education either under a student subsidy or an institutional subsidy structure, although at the present time there are inadequate resources to achieve this goal by either method.

Today there are not more than a handful of private colleges or universities that can make admissions decisions without *any* concern for financial aid consideration. There are no public systems that have sufficient resources to provide *full* opportunity for every high school graduate in their state—although several states, led by California, come reasonably close to this goal. What is even more discouraging is evidence that, with the rapidly rising burden of health, welfare, and other social program costs, higher education may lose ground in the future if it has to rely on traditional public sources of revenue. In almost all areas of social welfare, public aspirations are outstripping the ability of governmental units to meet expectations. The situation is further complicated for higher education in that support now comes from a variety of sources, and thus no one source is in an effective position to attempt to rationalize the whole system. The federal government, with its national perspective and revenue base, is in the best position to ensure that higher education achieves national objectives, but is today the minor partner in the general support of education. It has become a substantial partner in health education, it has complemented institutional programs in graduate education through research and fellowship support, it has steadily increased its involvement in aiding the disadvantaged, but it contributes only an infinitesimal portion of support for ongoing operating expenses of colleges and universities. Unlike the situation in most other nations, where the central government plays the commanding role, the Congress has left this responsibility largely to the states and to private agencies.

The pluralism in higher education has many advantages in encouraging diversity and permitting a higher degree of autonomy than might otherwise exist, but it is not conducive to an orderly approach to making educational opportunity more universal. A move such as the 1970 decision for open admissions to City University of New York was made without the full support of the state (which had to fund 50 percent of the cost), and implementation of the decision as a unilateral action could ultimately destroy some private institutions in the metropolitan area. The sharp federal cutback in research and development and in graduate fellowship and training grants is imposing a devastating cost on many universities, both public and private. The current GI bill, by contrast with its post–World War II counterpart, almost automatically eliminates independent colleges from sharing in the education of returning veterans. Each of these examples, picked only to illustrate the dangers of pluralism, could be described as irrational (in the economist's sense of the term) because the decision-making unit did not have to take full responsibility for the consequences of its decisions. I doubt that any one of these decisions would have been proposed if the deciding agency had had to concern itself with the total universe of affected institutions and accept the total financial responsibility.

The dangers of pluralism are most evident in a period of severe financial constraint, for agencies that provide only partial support tend to feel much freer about reducing their support level. Perhaps the clearest example is the federal government, which induced the considerable expansion of graduate and research capacity in the nation's universities in the 1957–68 period, but today exhibits little concern for the continued welfare of its partners in the endeavor.

STUDENT AID—DIRECT VERSUS INDIRECT

Direct aid to students has some clear advantages: it maximizes the freedom of choice of the student, and it encourages the fullest use of available facilities, both public and private. Subsidy to institutions rather than students tends to result in indiscriminate benefits going both to the advantaged and the disadvantaged. Whether or not low public tuition redistributes income in favor of middle and upper income groups (the Hansen-Weisbrod—Pechman debate),[4] it can be argued that low tuition is an inefficient means of distributing aid. The total educational and general expenditure of collegiate institutions today is approximately $14 billion, but subsidies (from public revenues and from private endowments) pay for nearly $8 billion of this cost, and financial aid (including various forms of campus self-help) accounts for roughly another $2 billion. Thus students and their families pay only about $4 billion (not including living and incidental costs) —less than one-third of educational expenditures by institutions. *It seems evident that were these total direct and indirect resources equitably distributed, all current financial needs of students could be met.* To do so would require a drastic restructuring of higher education, with all institutions charging graduated prices to students from different income groups, *or*, alternatively, charging moderately high fees to students able to pay and giving generous support to students from lower income backgrounds. Were colleges and universities all public or all private, such a goal would be more easily attainable. Our divided system, however, is an almost insuperable obstacle to accomplishing such an objective.

Lest the preceding statement be misunderstood, let me attempt to clarify it. I believe that New York State—to use the example I know best—could "spin off" all public colleges and universities as

4. See W. Lee Hansen and Burton A. Weisbrod, *Benefits, Costs, and Finance of Higher Education* (Chicago: Markham Publishing Co., 1969) ; Joseph A. Pechman, "The Distributional Effects of Public Higher Education in California," *Journal of Human Resources*, Summer 1970, pp. 361–70; Robert W. Hartman, "A Comment on the Pechman—Hansen-Weisbrod Controversy," *Journal of Human Resources*, Fall 1970, pp. 519–23.

autonomous institutions, and provide even broader educational opportunity for all its citizens, *if* it were willing to continue to spend
nearly $1 billion annually to give direct support to students. (The
$1 billion is approximately what the state and municipalities now
spend supporting various higher educational activities.) Instead,
nearly a third of the college students in the state pay zero (CUNY),
a little more than a third pay about one-fifth of the cost (SUNY), and
approximately a third pay from one-half to nearly full cost in the
private sector. A visitor from Mars (or most other countries on earth)
would have good grounds for thinking us quite mad. We, however,
defend the system with strong emotion for its real (or imagined)
virtues.

An alternative to divesting ourselves of public institutions would
be to recognize the public nature of all institutions of higher education, and to devise a common pricing system which would appropriately subsidize students in relation to their real need and institutions in relation to their function. Such a system would be closer to
the British pattern. I believe that it would be possible, within the
sum of resources now devoted to higher education, to bring about
such a reordering of the system *if* we could overcome the doctrinaire
attitudes of local, state, and federal agencies on the one hand and
private bodies on the other. Furthermore, I believe that we shall not
be able to make the educational system both equitable and universal
(by whichever definition) without such a reordering. Within the
bounds of the present divided system, we could achieve universal
access, but it will cost a great deal more and be likely to have a
corrosive effect on the quality of education.

SHARING THE BURDEN OF COLLEGE COSTS

Everyone has his own explicit or implicit philosophical view of
how the costs of college education ought to be borne. As author of
this paper, my views should be stated explicitly, for they influence
my reasoning about what would be an "ideal" situation.

I believe that society should bear a part of the cost both because
there are obvious social benefits of living in a society with an
educated citizenry, and because I would like to encourage individuals
to consume more education than they ordinarily would if they themselves had to pay for its full cost. Encouraging the consumption of
higher education through modest subsidies (to use the economist's
phraseology) I view as sound public policy, just as I believe the
taxing of alcoholic beverages and tobacco is desirable to discourage
their use.

On the other hand, I believe that adult educational experiences are largely undervalued (and frequently wasted) when one does not have to make some personal sacrifice. Therefore, I believe that a student or his parents should contribute to educational costs, although such expected contributions should be adjusted to ability to pay. Full-cost pricing assumes too great a rationality on the part of students and their parents, and I therefore reject it as a reasonable alternative; free tuition, on the other hand, places such a burden on the tax system that I believe it is not a desirable alternative when more than a small, select fraction of potential students is being educated.

If I were to delineate an ideal system of financing higher education that would assure equal opportunity or universal access to higher education, it would be a system where costs of education were roughly divided into fourths. One-fourth would be covered by federal grants either to students or to institutions; one-fourth would be in the form of subsidies from state and local governments and from private gifts and endowments; one-fourth would be paid by parents, amount adjusted to ability to pay; and one-fourth would be assumed by students, either in current self-help or in long-term loans.

A Federal Role. One-fourth financing by the federal government might be in the form of institutional aid based on a formula differentiating between the costs at various levels of education (perhaps even differentiating by area of study). In this form it would tend to keep tuition levels down; if students carried the aid with them—as many state scholarship programs provide—the nominal tuition level would be higher than in the case of direct institutional support.

Federal aid to institutions might be devised to approximate one-fourth of the cost at various levels for a representative institution of quality, and aid to individual institutions would be that amount or one-fourth of their actual costs, whichever was smaller. Such a formula for 1971, based on number of full-time equivalent (FTE) students at various levels, might be: $400 per lower division student; $600, upper division; $800, master's; and $1,400, doctoral. A college which had lower than average educational costs would receive somewhat less than these amounts (that is, 25 percent of its *actual* expenditures), whereas an institution that spent more on educational services would receive the formula amounts. The support levels could be made to reflect changes in annual costs of higher education, and approximately every five years an in-depth study could be made to reevaluate the cost ratios reflected in the formula.

If the federal government is to become a more dominant partner in higher education—which I believe it will, and which it must become if real equality of opportunity is to be attained—a formula program may be much more satisfactory than a host of categorical programs. The federal government today spends about half as much in general education and student support as is envisioned here, and it targets these expenditures through a variety of programs for disadvantaged students, veterans, graduate students, training programs, and so on. Both the federal and the institutional staff functions which service these programs could be largely eliminated with a simpler formula support mechanism.

State and Local Share. These levels of government today finance slightly over 50 percent of the cost of education in public institutions. Given both the limitations of revenue sources and the current inadequacies if we are to achieve full equality of opportunity, I doubt that most states will be able to finance adequate support to higher education. The entrance of the federal government through a general support formula, and greater reliance on an efficient pricing arrangement, would gradually relieve the states of part of their burden. As I envision it, the absolute contribution would probably stabilize, and other sources would increasingly shoulder the added costs of expansion and rising costs.

In the case of the independent institutions, private gifts and endowment earnings play a role somewhat comparable to that of state subsidies for public institutions, although at present these revenue sources account for only about 15 percent of educational costs in private colleges and universities.

Parental Participation. The one-fourth contribution by parents (or the emancipated student) would be adjusted to reflect ability to pay, using a system such as the College Scholarship Service provides. As chairman of a panel of economists and financial aid officers which has just completed a two-year review of that system, I am impressed by the improvement in equity that has resulted from the CSS effort. If parents, on the average, are to pay one-fourth, the nominal price to the parent would be set somewhat higher to provide tuition waivers for students from less affluent families.

The Students' Share. Student contributions to their own education—either in present or future earnings—are usually the most controversial subject. The principle of sharing part of the burden for one's own education is appealing, particularly because it is likely to make an individual value the opportunity in a way that is unlikely if the education is a "free good." It is also likely to encourage the individual student to make a more rational choice than if he is attending college only to please parents or just because it is a costless way of living for several years before entering the world of work.

Reliance on loans to meet the financial need of students who come from low income families, however, builds a continuing inequity into the system. I doubt that many educators would be opposed to either jobs or loans as a substantial part of financial aid if every student had to assume the same burden.

Sweden perhaps comes closest to devising a higher education system where the student carries a significant part of the burden. Students are determined to be "emancipated" at the time of entering the university, and are expected to pay their own way. Whatever resources society provides to educate a university student, he or she must repay *in real terms* out of future earnings. Interest is waived, but a former student must return the same amount of real resources that he or she drew from society at the time of his education.

I am persuaded that a long-term contingency repayment loan, somewhat like that proposed several years ago by Professor Zacharias, would be advantageous, particularly if it became *mandatory* for all students.[5] In the form in which the Educational Opportunity Bank was originally proposed, it was voluntary, and it was presumed to cover the full costs of education. The voluntary feature meant that students from affluent families would not have participated, and that those who fared particularly well in postcollege years could "buy out." The result would have tended to leave the bank with the poorer income risks and thus would partially have failed to pool the individual returns on investment in education. The assumption in the Zacharias proposal of full-cost pricing and primary reliance on contingent repayment financing also implied that the total amount of outstanding loans would rise at a staggering rate.

I would propose that participation in the contingent loan arrangement be voluntary, but that the one-fourth of educational costs contributed by the federal government be withheld if a student did not avail himself of the loan feature. Thus, in a representative public institution, if the total cost of education were $2,400 per year, the student who did not wish to participate in the loan pool would have to pay at that time (or have paid for him, probably by parents) three-quarters of the cost of his education (the parents' quarter, the student's quarter, plus the forgone federal portion). The affluent student who chose not to pool future income uncertainties would

5. For a brief description, see Jerrold R. Zacharias, "Educational Opportunity through Student Loans: An Approach to Higher Education Financing," in *The Economics and Financing of Higher Education in the United States: A Compendium of Papers Submitted to the Joint Economic Committee, Congress of the United States* (Washington: Government Printing Office, 1969), pp. 656-58.

not be eligible for the federal funds designed to maximize equality of opportunity.

Some persons will object to the pressure placed on the individual to participate in the contingent loan program. I believe, however, that nearly complete participation is the best way of making the program successful, and that the program itself is a good incentive system for making educational decisions more rational. Insisting that most students bear part of the burden is, in my view, a highly desirable feature; the present system only forces this burden on the disadvantaged, imposing even heavier inequities. I am also convinced that a workable contingent loan program must be federally sponsored. The follow-up and collection problem is monumental for a single institution or even for a single state; for the federal government, it is a simple annual entry on the individual income tax form. The negative dowry arguments raised against contingent loans ignore current borrowing experience. It seems unlikely that middle and upper income female students would be more heavily penalized than the large number of low income women who are now resorting to National Defense Student Loan funds and guaranteed loans. A reasonable, simple arrangement of aggregating a husband's and wife's liability and forgiving one-half of the expected payment for a non-working wife with dependent children would seem to minimize the problem.

A TYPICAL CASE

The four-part contribution to the cost of college education may be illustrated for representative public and private institutions. In Table 2, I have assumed that the public institution spends $2,400 per year on educational costs and the private college $3,000, and that the federal formula is based on an average cost of $2,800 per student. For simplicity, it is assumed that the public college has no gifts or endowment and that the private college does not receive any state funds.

The price (nominal tuition) ratio between private and public colleges, as seen by parents, is effectively reduced from what would ordinarily be 4:1 to only 2:1. The student and federal contributions reduce the burden on state treasuries by about two-thirds. Nominal tuition levels would rise modestly at public colleges, but adequate scholarship funds would be provided as partial tuition waivers. At private colleges, the nominal tuition level would decline significantly (from something close to $3,000 to only $1,800), and additional scholarship funds would be generated. The major shifts are the input of federal funds, and the redistribution of the burden among families according to their ability to pay.

TABLE 2: *Illustration of Shared Burden of College Costs*

Source of Financing Higher Education of an Average Student	Public College	Private College
1. Federal grant..	$ 600	$ 700
2. State subsidy...	600	—
3. Gifts and endowment income...........................	—	400
4. Average parents' contribution........................	600	1,200
5. Student's contingent repayment loan...................	600	700
6. Cost of education....................................	$2,400	$3,000
7. Nominal charge to parents (average contribution of parents has been inflated by 50 percent to permit funding of tuition waivers for students from low income families)..........	$ 900	$1,800
8. Total burden on family and student (5 plus 7)..........	1,500	2,500
9. Cost to family and student if student does not take contingent repayment loan (8 plus 1).....................	2,100	3,200

This sketchy outline of a possibly more effective and equitable scheme of funding the costs of education illustrates a way in which real equality of opportunity might be supported with little, if any, additional input of public monies. Federal direct aid largely displaces current state aid, so that public funds are not increased significantly but only used more efficiently. Today's heavy reliance on state subsidies for public institutions and tuition charges for private institutions aggravates rather than alleviates the problem of attaining equality of opportunity. I believe that the suggested support program, or some variant of it, would retain all the advantages of institutional diversity without the concomitant penalty of continuing both educational and economic inequalities. Of equal importance, it would be a major step toward a system where public and private institutions could live together in a complementary fashion. Without such a step it seems increasingly likely that the private college and university will gradually disappear from the scene, with the whole burden being shifted to the states.

CONCLUDING THOUGHTS

Present-day provision of opportunity to higher education is a significant improvement over that of fifteen or twenty years ago, though still a long way from providing *equality* of opportunity. The likely financial constraints on both the public and private sectors in the years ahead suggest that the present attainment may lose ground unless there is some dramatic revision of the entire system of financial support.

It is particularly discouraging that sufficient resources are being devoted to higher education to provide equal opportunity for the proportion of the age group now in college, but the confused pricing structure of our dual system makes inefficient use of these resources. Many students from affluent families are highly subsidized, while many students with substantial financial need are either penalized or eliminated. Today's budgetary pressures are making the situation worse, for institutions of all types are being forced to make decisions that protect their own welfare at the expense of the broader societal goal of achieving equal opportunity. Studies undertaken for the College Scholarship Service panel reviewing systems for analyzing financial need showed that public institutions, almost as frequently as private institutions, were forced to depart from their proclaimed objectives in allocating financial aid. In general, the greater the financial need of the individual, the smaller his chance of being admitted to college and the smaller the fraction of his need being met by financial aid. In many institutions, both public and private, we also found that the greater the individual's need, the smaller the percentage of grant funds in the financial aid package. These findings, based on a detailed study of an eighty-six institution sample,[6] leave us little room for complacency about the accomplishments of the present system. On the other hand, universal higher education within the present dual system, and without a change in pricing philosophy, is likely to be a terribly expensive way of assuring greater equity.

The record of post-World War II higher education is commendable in broadening educational opportunities for half or more of college-age youth, but much remains to be done. One great obstacle to further progress toward the goal of equal opportunity is the failure to view all educational institutions as essentially public resources, and to have a coordinated plan for their support. Such an overview requires a sophistication of the body politic which it may not possess. Yet the cost of not adopting a more rational approach to the funding of educational opportunity may be exorbitant both in terms of real resources and in sacrifice of educational quality.

6. Robert P. Huff, *Report on a Study of College Admissions and Financial Aid Policies as Revealed by Institutional Practices* [Cartter Panel] (New York: College Entrance Examination Board, December 1970) .

On Closer Examination . . .

EDWARD SANDERS

MR. CARTTER HAS PROPOSED A PLAN FOR FINANCING STUDENTS IN A WORLD of universal higher education which he believes will lead to: (1) comparable enrollment in all income segments; (2) the maintenance of strength in the private institutions; and (3) satisfaction of Mr. Cartter's philosophical judgments about the "way it's s'pposed to be." The proposal has simplicity and boldness. Unfortunately, it must be taken on faith, for the factual material given is insufficient to make a technical judgment on the effectiveness of the proposals, and Mr. Cartter presumably wants the idea considered on its general merits rather than on the details.

Under the plan, (*a*) the federal government would make grants to institutions to cover 25 percent of their costs. The grant formula would apply to both public and private institutions. (*b*) States and communities would supply 25 percent of the cost to public institutions. Private institutions would be expected to secure something less than a quarter of their costs from philanthropic and endowment sources. (*c*) Parents would provide 25 percent of the cost, with charges being set at a level that families who were able to do so would pay their share of the 25 percent plus the share for parents who were not able to pay. He suggests that the adjustment be achieved by needs analysis procedures similar to those used elsewhere. (*d*) Students would provide one-fourth of the cost through long-term contingent loans.

Unfortunately, the cost figures given—$2,400 for public colleges and $3,000 for private colleges—are different from any in common use, and there is no definition of what they include. More important, earlier in the paper the statement is made that the cost being considered does not include cost of maintenance, personal expenses, and the like. If parents and students must meet these costs in addition to the one-half of the institutional cost stipulated, parents and students would assume a heavier burden than they now bear.

No justification is offered why the federal government, state governments, and parents should each contribute 25 percent of the cost. There appears to be no relationship between the proposal and the first of the goals Cartter states—to promote comparable initial enrollments among income groups—and for low income students, the proposal may well be less attractive than present programs. Further it should provide some assistance to private colleges but at a cost they may well consider to be too high a price: a sharp limitation on the luxury of the existing pluralism in educational systems, which is to say, far more unified central control over private institutions. Should such a bill be passed, it seems prudent to predict a long-lasting field day for lawyers. One provision is that if a student chooses to pay immediately instead of accepting the long-term contingent loan for one-quarter of the cost, then he or his parents are required to replace the federal contribution. A law which states that a student in a private college who refuses to take a contingent loan for part of his cost may be required to pay not only the 25 percent he would normally pay but also the 25 percent the federal government pays—such a law in my judgment would have a stormy and brief legal history! In fact, the argument advanced that the public would be quite content to see students from poor families take large loans if they could be assured that students from more affluent families were also required to do so is, to say the least, questionable.

Mr. Cartter provides a rationalization for contingent loans for all students: it is essential that students pay part of the cost of their education if they are to work hard and appreciate their education. This statement has a history of service to politicians but I can think of no social issue on which the evidence is more plentiful, compelling, and universally ignored. For a hundred years private colleges have charged substantial tuition and public colleges have had free or very low tuition. I know of no study which shows that students in private colleges study harder and value their education more than those who attend public institutions. Or to look only at public institutions: the University of Vermont charges $1,000 tuition and the University of California has been free. I know of no argument that students in the University of Vermont work harder and value their education more than do students at California.

One reason perhaps that the differences are not apparent is that, regardless of the amount of tuition, the student and his parents pay the major portion of the cost of college attendance. Hansen and Weisbrod, in a widely quoted study of the distribution of cost and benefits in California, show that the annual amount borne by students and parents was $2,700, or 68 percent, of the total cost. The taxpayers paid $1,248, or 32 percent, of the total. Whether or not these figures are precisely correct, all students and parents, if not all economists, know that it is expensive to pursue higher education, regardless of the amount of tuition. It may well be that getting enough money to operate postsecondary education will require that students borrow against their future income. If this is true, then it is the justification for contingent loans.

A question should be raised about the meaning of the term *equity* as used in Mr. Cartter's paper. In the analysis made by Joseph Pechman of the data collected by Hansen and Weisbrod, he found that California families from the upper half of the income distribution paid most of the taxes which support higher education and their children received most of the benefits. On balance, however, he concluded that the upper income groups were slightly subsidizing the lower income groups. Insofar as the term *equity* means impartiality, this represents an equitable distribution of costs and benefits of higher education. If we think of equity in a broader sense as meaning social justice, there is a real obligation on the part of the more affluent to pay for more educational services than the poorer families are able to pay for their own children. The ambiguity in the definition of *equity* seems to retard the discussion.

The appropriate judgment about Mr. Cartter's clearly fresh approach is that it is not possible to balance the various trade-offs which would follow until the proposal is fleshed out in considerably greater detail.

Post scriptum. There is an alternative plan under which enrollment has increased steadily whenever it is tried, and from among low income students. It is simple to administer and presents no legal complications. Extend low or free tuition through grade fourteen. If it seems desirable to push more genuine responsibility for his education onto the student, then leave to him the responsibility for his own support. Extend the Work-Study program sufficiently to make jobs truly available for those who need them and provide nonsubsidized loans to be open to students without a means test. Students who wish to live simply can do so with minimum work and loans; those who wish to live expensively have the chance to earn it or borrow it. If private education requires assistance, provide it through vouchers to be used in private institutions.

Financing Students

VALERIE A. RIDDICK

IN AN AFFLUENT SOCIETY LIKE OURS, THE NEED FOR UNIVERSAL HIGHER education is "clear and present." If we are to have a progressive and affluent nation, we must certainly have persons who are capable of asserting themselves in it in all capacities. If we are to fulfill the need for universal higher education, then we must derive channels by which it may be financed.

Before I comment on the possible workable channels of financing universal higher education, I will comment on the three definitions offered by Mr. Cartter.

First, *equal opportunity with merit constraints*—this version of "universal" higher education would in all probability be the least difficult to finance. "Education for the talented tenth." Although it would be financially feasible to finance the talented tenth on a short-run perspective, in a long run only a few would benefit; besides, if we consider only the talented tenth as educable, that would be retrogression on our part—on the part of the affluent society.

The second—*universal access to postsecondary education*—would be the most practical in our affluent society because of the tremendous value we place on education. As soon as we say "access," we give the individual the right to make his own decision and to some extent to determine his destiny. Postsecondary education is by far the most inclusive of all types of matriculation—from technical to professional.

The third alternative—*universal college education*—would by far be the most expensive. Making college education compulsory could possibly be unconstitutional inasmuch as it could deprive the individual of his liberty and pursuit of happiness. If universal higher education were compulsory, it would be similar to the public schools in being tuition-free. Compulsory universal college education would probably prove disastrous for us from the view that eventually our society would be composed solely of professional persons and few, if any, persons would possess skills.

With this analysis of the possible types of universal higher education, we can better understand what we are trying to finance. Since we believe that the effects of universal education can be felt by the masses, then it may be suggested that the financing of universal education be shared by the federal government, the state government, the student, and the parents of the student—with each paying one-quarter of the total cost of the education. This would alleviate some of the financial difficulties for all concerned parties.

The current system of financing students' education at the Community College of Baltimore can be compared and contrasted with the financing of universal higher education if the 25 percent plan were to be utilized. The percentage formula now being used by the Community College of Baltimore is 50-30-20: the state government finances 50 percent, the city finances 30 percent, and the student finances 20 percent. When tuition for the year is $1,200, the state pays $600, the city pays $360, and the student pays $240. This formula has proved beneficial to those desiring postsecondary education—especially to persons in the middle and low income brackets. Although the student is to pay 20 percent of his tuition, he or she may apply for various types of financial aid, depending on the qualifications to be met.

The Community College of Baltimore, under the leadership of Dr. Harry Bard, presented the 50-30-20 plan before the Maryland legislature and the Baltimore City Council. The Community College of Baltimore believes that the entire community can reap the benefits of this small investment in the very near future.

The Community College of Baltimore plan demonstrates on a minute scale how universal higher education, if financed through a sharing plan—the 25 percent plan—can be of great value to this affluent society of ours. An excellent point that Mr. Cartter makes about the 25 percent plan is that it can be planned so that private as well as public institutions of higher learning can receive the highest benefits, since both federal and state governments would be giving them money. In the past, private colleges seldom were financially assisted by the state.

The 25 percent plan would, for the first time in many instances, give students the responsibility of financing their way through school—to a limited degree. I do not feel that each student should have to get a loan to finance his 25 percent, although I can see some advantages.

As a whole, I think that the 25 percent plan of financing universal higher education is definitely workable and would give great and numerous benefits, first, to the student but especially to this affluent society of ours. Realizing that it is the society—the affluent society—that shapes the destiny of men, it is only fitting and proper that this same society offer help in a very tangible way to all those who desire to realize their destiny in this, the affluent society.

S. P. MARLAND, JR.

A Strengthening Alliance

SINCE MY APPOINTMENT TO THE POST OF U.S. COMMISSIONER OF Education is still relatively recent, it was natural in preparing this paper that I should search for insights into the academic community's views of the state of relationships between higher education and government. Not unsurprisingly, I discovered that the thoughts, as expressed in various Council publications, mirror my own. Though our points of view are necessarily different, we recognize in common that the alliance between the federal government and our institutions of higher education is strong, productive, and necessary, and, I hope, mutually trusting, though with ample room for change and improvement on all counts. I found, in sum, neither overwhelming approval nor disapproval but a lively concern that the federal partner choose the wisest and most effective means of supporting and influencing the course of higher education in America. I share that concern.

Although I have met with many individuals and groups in higher education informally, I am formally joining the debate on higher education for the first time in this on-the-record, prepared paper. To begin, I shall make two points: I claim no credit for the splendid success of recent and current federal undertakings in higher education; and I regard myself as free as those in higher education to criticize the things that clearly are not working. The policies to which we are reacting—whether positively or adversely—were ratified while I was engaged elsewhere.

Now, ten months of in-service study have familiarized me with the various policies and have persuaded me that federal plans and programs to stimulate reform of higher education are in substantial need of reform themselves. That process—with the assistance of the academic community—is well along. Our deliberations during these months have been immeasurably enriched by the contributions of an ad hoc committee of representatives from higher education, an entirely unexpected but welcome byproduct of the annual meeting of

210

the Council last year in St. Louis. At that time, Patrick Moynihan, then a counselor to President Nixon, described the tepid support the higher education community was giving the President's programs. Council Chairman Arthur S. Flemming countered with the assertion that the higher education profession was anxious to become deeply involved in the legislative process, if only the administration would ask.

We in government asked—and received—higher education's help, particularly in reshaping the National Foundation for Higher Education concept and in designing a way to provide federal aid directly to colleges and universities, an add-on to the original proposal. In my estimation, as a result of our collaboration, not only do we have a far better legislative package before the Congress than would otherwise have been produced, but also we have achieved a deeper mutual understanding and hence better prospects for a productive relationship in the future. We seem finally to appreciate the extent to which our fortunes are interlocked. We seem finally to know that the question is not whether the federal government will be involved in shaping a new order of higher education, but what form its contribution will take. Today, I believe, that form is clearer and sharper and more logical than ever before.

ADMINISTRATION POLICIES

The administration's legislative designs are self-evidently calculated to produce a bond of growing strength between government and higher education in order to come much closer than we now do to *matching opportunity for intellectual and professional advancement with our individual and national needs.* The President has left no doubt of his intense conviction that we must build now a national policy of long-term effective support for our colleges and universities, which are, after all, the instruments through which any higher education policy must be carried out—one by one, pluralistically, campus by campus, with no Washington high priest pretending to direct the action. And this goal will be accomplished cooperatively (there is no other way) as well as in a manner that recognizes and expresses sympathy for the legitimate aspirations of the individual institutions and their specific goals. The nation does not need standardized higher education; it does need a system that, though diverse, is broadly committed to public needs, to adaptability, and to large social goals illuminated by federal support.

The President's intentions toward higher education were made clear in his budget request for fiscal year 1972, where he asked for a record total of more than $6 billion for all federal higher education programs. Of this amount, some $1.8 billion—the largest component—was established for Office of Education programs, an amount $800 million more than the 1971 appropriations. The President sought this authority in order to redeem his 1970 pledge to provide more federal aid to those students least able to pay the costs of college.

Since Washington is the place where purposes, policies, pledges, and politics come finally to the mixing bowl, the 1972 higher education budget came in at less than had been requested—some half-billion dollars less. But it still is some $370 million more than last year, and the extra money has provided the opportunity to boost substantially the Work-Study, Educational Opportunity Grants, and Student Loan Programs, as well as to expand such enterprises as Upward Bound, Strengthening Developing Institutions, and Language and Area Centers. All of these efforts are directed at enhancing individual opportunity in compatibility with social needs and federal priorities. It is of special satisfaction to me that we have been able administratively to direct more of the student aid funds toward the underprivileged, with the result that thousands of youth who would otherwise have been excluded are now enrolled in classes, many of them in institutions represented among the American Council's membership.

Particularly gratifying are the latest figures for the Guaranteed Student Loan Program, the workability of which had been in deep question because of its fixed interest rate in a rising interest market. In fiscal year 1971, students received more than $1 billion through the program, the first time it has crossed that psychic barrier. And the growth goes on: during the first two months of this fiscal year nearly 385,000 loans, totaling more than $430 million, were made—nearly 35 percent *more* dollars than the year before.

LEGISLATIVE PROPOSALS

The success of this effort and nearly all of the federal aid programs to higher education is encouraging, but our real hope lies with the legislative proposals now pending before the Congress. It is, I believe, extremely fortuitous that I have the privilege of addressing you at this moment in the Congressional calendar—rather than, say, two weeks ago, or two weeks from now.

I am referring, of course, to the four fundamental concepts of aid to higher education which the administration has advanced—first, equality of opportunity; second, institutional aid compatible with a national purpose; third, support for research; fourth, encouragement of innovation and reform. These four initiatives are included in S. 659, which was passed by the Senate unanimously in August, and three of them in markedly different forms are in H.R. 7248, the bill which is moving toward floor action in the House. Undoubtedly the legislation will be modified as it moves to conference, but with the strong support of the higher education community, I believe the law that goes to the President for his signature—perhaps in November—can include the concepts embodied in the administration's original proposals. I would be less than forthright to imply that the House versions are as satisfactory as the Senate's. Indeed, I cannot help but wonder at the cautious conservatism from members of Congress ordinarily known for their liberal stance. Administration policy asks that federal laws and corresponding funds—both for students and institutions—respond to the desperate problems of the poor, the suppressed, the minorities, the have-nots. It also asks for new authority and funds for institutional reform and renewal by those institutions which wish to undertake change. On both counts the Senate says aye. The House, at least at this stage, is saying, The disadvantaged and institutional reform are not priorities here; we wish to continue the status quo in higher education.

Enactment and funding of the measures contained in the Pell bill would enable government in partnership with the higher education community to undertake really significant new efforts with strongly beneficial implications for both students and institutions, efforts that would promote realization of the new order of higher education that we are seeking in America.

The first of the proposals is for still further expanded student grants and loans including establishment of a secondary market—the National Student Loan Association—which can make possible a vastly expanded NDEA type of loan program for students. This proposal would give important added leverage in the struggle to close the gap between privilege and poverty because the principal beneficiaries would be low income students; federal funds would go first, and in largest amounts, to the neediest, with pro rata differences in resources reaching those more economically favored but still of limited income.

The Senate bill, while accepting the idea of a secondary market, has made major changes in the loan provisions, though the measure is still consistent with the President's intention that no student be barred financially. The present student aid programs are benefiting a million and a half students this year; the new program would add still another million from the most deprived economic group, those whom society has routinely bypassed through almost conscious exclusion from opportunity through higher education. It is proposed to save them now—and, with higher education's help, to redress this historic inequity. And in evidence of the commitment, the administration is proposing appropriations to match the scale of our rhetoric.

Beyond student aid looms the unanswered question of institutional aid. An expanded program of student aid and other forms of assistance *without* a parallel program of operational support for the colleges suggests a tactic widely practiced at one time in minor league baseball— selling more tickets to the opening game than there were seats in the stadium. Waves of students, many of them federally aided, have swamped our colleges and universities, which must find seats for them, and dormitories, and lab equipment, and fill the thousand and one domestic needs that the presence of a student creates, particularly the disadvantaged student who brings with him more than ordinary unfilled needs which institutions find costly. Yet the normal financial strain, which is severe enough, has become well nigh unbearable under the impact of recession, inflation, and slashed research funds.

The Association of American Colleges predicted in September 1971 that two hundred colleges and universities will run out of cash within a year and that, if the trend continues, 365 institutions will go under financially within ten years. Hundreds have reported operating losses, in some instances running into the millions, and many have been forced not only to curtail basic operations but also, sadly, to cancel entirely the creative, innovative thrusts their students need, almost above all else. I don't know how accurate the AAC figures are, but we are all aware that the situation is gravely serious and even dangerous. There is, indeed, as the Carnegie Commission has pointed out, a new depression in higher education.

The American Council, representing the colleges and universities, has long maintained the necessity of federal operational support and, within certain restrictions, this view has now become that of the administration as well. I would call attention to the effective leadership of Secretary Richardson in this important policy development. We have proposed to the Congress carefully qualified cost-of-education allowance funds that would be tied to the institution's total federal student aid funds in recognition of the burden imposed on colleges and universities that seek to educate large numbers of economically, socially, and educationally disadvantaged.

Under this plan, unlike the Senate version, the allowance *as proposed* would match the dollars of federal student aid going to the college or university, not the numbers of students aided. The intention is to avoid creating incentives in institutions to spread aid thinly over the maximum number of students to get more cost-of-education allowance. We hope that a provision more closely resembling the original proposal will emerge out of the House deliberations and the conference.

Finally, both the level of funding for the allowances and the structure of the student aid program on which it is based should effectively present the creation of artificial inducements and incentives for state and local governments and, for that matter, private givers to shift major financial burdens to the federal government.

EDUCATION RESEARCH

The third administration priority for higher education is encouragement and support of basic and applied research. It now appears that the higher education measure will include an administration initiative of major significance to colleges and universities—the National Institute of Education. NIE, as we hope it will emerge from the legislative process, would be a new HEW agency reporting to the Commissioner of Education but separated from the Office of Education. It would be concerned with how to restructure our educational system for greater effectiveness. We want to find ways to increase access to education, to broaden the age range of learning, to increase the reality of the learning place, to design learning programs for individuals, to increase the range of resources for learning. NIE will examine education not as rigidly divided into elementary schools, high schools, colleges, and so forth, but rather treat it as a system of continual renewal that begins with the very young and never stops.

In laying the groundwork for NIE, we are examining all levels of education from three very broad viewpoints: improvement of the quality of education, improvement of education of the disadvantaged, and effective use of resources in education. Higher education will be an important part of all three problem areas. We will want to examine the notion of a university not located in a single spot but permeating the city, the suburbs, and the country. We will want to look at experiment-minded institutions (Friends World College in New York and our University Without Walls are examples, as is the TV system in Nebraska, and Yale's student loan experiment) and learn from their successes and their problems.

NIE would, in sum, be the focal point in educational research, tying together a vast assortment of scattered theories and experiments into a coherent whole, and in the process would move the art of education to a new level of competence and respectability. We estimate that about 90 percent of the NIE funds will be distributed to contract sites such as colleges and universities, with 10 percent devoted to in-house research and development.

Closely complementing NIE is the last of the administration's higher education proposals, the National Foundation for Higher Education. The foundation is cast in the spirit of encouraging innovation and supporting institutions to meet additional costs of exemplary programs. As such, it is a direct and highly imaginative response to a need for renewal that education associations and individual administrators have long recognized and in many instances are now struggling to meet. This enterprise could help break the deplorable lockstep in postsecondary schooling and open it up to new ideas and to new people as well—individuals who are now excluded as too old or disqualified by reason of circumstance. The foundation could significantly enhance the capabilities of the institutions themselves to fulfill their distinctive role as teachers of men and women and as infinitely useful resources in the building of America, a task both demanding and complex. Certainly there is a growing body of evidence that such institutional self-scrutiny is long overdue and in many instances well under way. The problem has been exhaustively documented—in such works as the Newman Report, the various Carnegie Commission studies, and the investigations of Riesman and Jencks. This matter, of course, is the responsibility and the trust of the institution. The federal government has no power and, I would say, neither the desire nor the competence to impose its will in matters of organization, curriculum, and instructional practice. The Congress has written some instructions into the legislation authorizing programs that prohibit any sallies in that direction. I accept these caveats, and indeed applaud them.

The National Foundation would provide the means to seek and effect useful and necessary change, on the terms of the individual institution. It would be up to the institution to make use of foundation grants to examine its purposes and to appraise how effectively these purposes are being carried out. Again, the information—on dropouts, on surplus degrees, on student disenchantment, on economic solvency —suggests a pressing need for this kind of basic investigation.

In a few months, if the pattern of recent years reasserts itself (there is no reason to believe it will not), many of the young men and women now in college will begin dropping like autumn leaves, and for reasons not necessarily related to finance. If the pattern holds, no more than 30 percent of the 1971 freshmen at the University of Texas will hang on to graduate in four years. In the California State College System only 13 percent of this year's freshmen will graduate in four years from the college they enter. For the nation as a whole, the percentage of students graduating within four years from the first college they attend varies from 80 percent to 85 percent at the fifteen most selective private universities to only 20–25 percent at those institutions with the poorest retention, the public junior colleges.

This is the obverse, tarnished, and in some measure predictable side of the growth phenomenon of recent years. I personally see little gain to the institutions of higher education, the dropouts, or society at large for the federal government to help finance it. Certainly there is small satisfaction to any institution—university, college, two-year or four-year, public or private—in failing to give its students what they are led to expect, that is, a useful and personally significant and satisfying educational experience.

The National Foundation embodies the notion that higher education needs a center where it may begin devising ways to cope with the terrible pressures of steadily expanding enrollments, increasing student disenchantment, and profoundly altered expectations of higher education on the part of practically everybody—parents, students, educators, the community, government, business. The foundation should be a substantial help to institutions in resolving their problems, whatever they may be, through the purposeful engagement of minds and wills and talents. The foundation would be a source of money—$100 million in the first year of operation—which could be used by institutions to probe both their own potential and that of students and to develop new and imaginative answers for each.

CAREER EDUCATION

At this point I will reveal my personal bias toward the specific concept of career education and express the hope that those in the higher education enterprise will devote energies and funds, whether from the National Foundation or elsewhere, toward integrating it into the curriculum, or perhaps integrating the curriculum into it. For career education as it is being viewed at the national policy level is a very large idea indeed, and one that we in the Office of Education are working to spread throughout elementary, secondary, and at least community college circles.

Dropouts are not created in the freshman year of college. Their aimlessness is usually the product of twelve prior years of aimless education. Many of their classmates from those years, lacking funds or college-minded parents, drop out of the system without attempting college. The colleges have the dubious honor of receiving the fully developed product—restless, dissatisfied, unmotivated, unguided in any realistic sense toward mature recognition of the responsibilities and opportunities of adult life—and wondering, I'm certain, just what it is one should get out of college, apart from a taste for Herbert Marcuse, ski weekends, and liberation from parents.

Although corrective action is needed at the higher education level, the preventive medication must be applied very much earlier, perhaps beginning at age eight or ten. In my judgment we need a thorough overhaul of both elementary and secondary curriculum and procedures. OE researchers are working toward this end; they are producing a model career education program for use in the schools, one to encourage and expand cooperative educational ventures with business and industry, and one to reach adults and dropouts through the use of television, tape cassettes, and other technology in their homes and through community organizations. Career education is a developing notion in the Office of Education and we are not attempting at all to limit its potential scope or even to nail down its formal definition. We believe it can eventually affect the education of virtually everyone at one time or another: guiding youngsters to occupational awareness and desire, leading adults to a reexamination of opportunities missed in their earlier lives, touching and enhancing the life prospects of everyone from a mechanic to a surgeon, always holding open the option for all students to enter higher education—with a purpose—or to enter the world of work with readiness and pride. We hold there is no longer a place for the in-betweens. We also hold that given the option to enter the world of work following high school, the young person should retain his option to enter higher education later—not unlike beneficiaries under the GI bill.

Degree fixation, the misguided notion that the only road to respectability leads at least to a bachelor's degree, is at the heart of the career dilemma in America. Students and their parents, as well as our society at large, must come to understand that many worthwhile, decent, and fulfilling occupations do not necessarily require a degree and will not in the foreseeable future, and that human excellence and fulfillment have more than one configuration. The Bureau of Labor Statistics has forecast on the basis of some rather extensive investigation and analysis that no more than 20 percent of all the jobs in the United States during the decade of the 1970s will require as much as a bachelor's degree. The remaining 80 percent will be within reach of a high school diploma or—and this, I believe, will be an increasingly relevant component—nondegree postsecondary schooling.

I hope that the explorations by institutions and others associated with higher education will linger on the possibility of offering this type of program in the colleges and universities—two-year occupational training of the sort now offered by more than a hundred and thirty state colleges—with increasing sophistication and articulation with our economy and our social needs.

I have sometimes been charged with anti-intellectualism as I have advanced the career education theory. I hope the reverse is true. I believe that elementary and secondary education will become far more realistic, with the implicit motivation for academic learning undergirding the career mode. I also believe that those young people choosing higher education following high school will do so with reason and purposefulness as distinct from a folklore of snobbery, and that will be better for higher education, and higher education will be better for them. The real hidden agenda under career education is the expectation for greater academic success for many thousands of young people in high school.

I wish to conclude on the note with which I began: we in the Office of Education will continue to look to the American Council and to its colleagues in all of higher education for guidance and for support in our continuing and, I hope, increasingly fruitful efforts to stimulate and help achieve the reform and development of all postsecondary education. I shall continue to read the Council's publications faithfully and seek out and listen carefully to the counsel from that organization and its constituencies. The understanding and wisdom available from these sources are essential to building an alliance between higher education and the people of this country that will be ever more cordial, ever more cooperative, and ever more productive for the individuals engaged and the society served.

PART FOUR

Optional Approaches to Higher Education

A. J. JAFFE and WALTER ADAMS

Two Models of Open Enrollment

THERE IS NOTHING NEW OR ORIGINAL ABOUT THE OPEN ENROLL-
ment movement in American higher education. In 1862, midway
through the Civil War, the First Morrill Act provided for the establishment of a national complex of land-grant colleges. In a sense, the
land-grant movement initiated open enrollment, challenging the vir-
tual monopoly of higher education enjoyed by the elitist institutions.
The land-grant movement, like today's drive toward open enrollment,
sought extension of the college franchise to a new student population
largely from the lower socioeconomic segments; transformation of the
traditional curriculum, in that instance with major emphasis on the
agricultural and technical problems relevant at that time; relaxation
of traditional academic requirements for students; and provision for
empirical services to the outside community.

Late in the century the Second Morrill Act added the final major
ingredient we find in today's open enrollment movement: the extension
of higher educational opportunity to racial minority students, at that
time through provisions for "separate but equal" and, therefore,
primarily Negro public colleges in the South. The form and features
of the open enrollment models, then and now, differ widely, but the
dominant egalitarian and liberal themes remain the same. Today, as
then, the proposed innovations are heatedly debated.

Beyond extending the college franchise to youth formerly excluded,
the stated educational orientation of the land-grant institutions has
a strikingly familiar and modern ring. It is suggestive of the demands
of many students today who enter under liberal access policies and
programs and whose caveats are expressed in attempts at college and
university "reform." We quote from "Features of the University" in
Cornell's 1867 First General Announcement:

> The idea of doing a student's mind some general good by studies
> which do not interest him will not control. . . . There is to be . . . liberty

of choice. Several courses . . . will be presented . . . and the student can make his choice among them. . . . All good studies will be allowed their due worth. . . . There will be no petty daily marking system, a pedantic device which has eaten out from so many colleges all capacity among students to seek knowledge for knowledge's sake. . . . Those professors will be sought who can stir enthusiasm. . . . It enters into the plan adopted to bring about a closer and more manly intercourse and sympathy between faculty and students than is usual in most of the colleges. . . . By the terms of the charter, no trustee, professor, or student can be accepted or rejected on account of any religious or political opinion he may or may not hold.

There is yet another historical parallel. The form that the land-grant colleges ultimately assumed was only dimly perceived at the time of the First Morrill Act. Initially, there was no consensus on precisely who should be taught what, for how long, and toward what ends. It was late in the century before the land-grant model became clearly defined, and it was early in the present century before these innovative institutions began to have a real impact on the largely rural society they served.

OPEN ENROLLMENT TODAY AND YESTERDAY

Today, there is a similar lack of consensus on open enrollment. During the immediate post-World War II years, and until the latter 1960s, the open enrollment model in California, officially labeled "differential access," was widely acclaimed and much imitated elsewhere. By the late 1960s, however, the California system, which had received the official seal of approval in the State Master Plan of 1960, was under vigorous attack at home.

In 1970, the City University of New York (CUNY) announced adoption of its own model of open enrollment, which proposed that differential access not be abandoned, but be made far less prominent. Under the CUNY program, the colleges explicitly assume a large measure of responsibility for the academic success of the less-qualified entrants, offering them extensive remedial assistance. In California, in contrast, educational researchers have documented the unofficial, but apparently real, process through which less-qualified entrants to junior colleges are effectively "cooled out" of these institutions.[1]

Even before the day of differential access in the California public colleges, many Midwestern state universities were obliged by law to

1. Burton R. Clark, *The Open-Door College: A Case Study* (New York: McGraw-Hill Book Co., 1960).

admit all high school graduate applicants from the state, but at the point of admission the student became responsible for his own academic fate. In many instances half or more freshmen were flunked out within a term or two. California somewhat eased the academic burden on the student by creating a network of less rigorous lower division colleges. The newest model of open enrollment—CUNY—however, implicitly assumes that it is the function of the college system not only to admit all applicants to college, but also to admit many with unimpressive academic credentials to the senior and more prestigious schools, and to graduate them if humanly possible without irrevocable subversion of academic standards.

As the proportion of the relevant age cohort attending college has risen, the stream of students has been directed increasingly to the public colleges, in recent years principally to the two-year institutions. Around 1890 just under one-third of all collegians were attending public colleges; by 1968 the proportion was about three-fourths.[2]

The proportion of collegians attending public institutions differs greatly among the states. In 1968, for example, in Massachusetts, one-third of all collegians were attending public institutions (the proportion nationally in 1890); in New York, just over a half; in Florida, with its extensive complex of two-year colleges, nearly eight students in ten; and in California, with its relatively mature public higher educational system, about nine in ten.[3] In fall 1970, 94 percent of first-time entrants in California entered public colleges.[4]

The basic question raised by these statistics is whether the proportions of students entering college and the proportions receiving baccalaureates are especially high in states where a high proportion attend public institutions. Since the public institutions have chief responsibility for open enrollment programs, does a state such as California, with both a high proportion entering public colleges and a mature open enrollment program, enroll an unusually large proportion of the relevant age cohort? If so, does it graduate an unusually large proportion of entrants? Presumably, an egalitarian program should result in a larger number of college graduates.

Finally, since the target students for open enrollment programs are

2. James H. Blodgett, *Report on Education in the United States at the Eleventh Census: 1890* (Washington: Government Printing Office, 1893), pp. 123, 125; U.S. Bureau of the Census, *Statistical Abstract of the United States, 1970* (Washington: Government Printing Office, 1970), p. 129.

3. *Statistical Abstract, 1970*, p. 129.

4. National Center for Educational Statistics, U.S. Office of Education, *Advance Report on Opening Fall Enrollment in Higher Education, 1970* (Washington: Government Printing Office, 1970), pp. 5–8.

in large part the less able, the socioeconomically disadvantaged, and the racial minority students, to what extent do such programs enroll and graduate these groups as compared with more advantaged entrants? Our data, though less than definitive, afford some insights.

THE DIFFERENTIAL ACCESS MODEL IN CALIFORNIA

The date of origin of differential access in California is essentially arbitrary. One could specify 1910, the year the first public junior college was opened in Fresno. Or one could specify 1948, the year of the "Strayer Report,"[5] when the model had become clear enough to permit projections of its future in some detail.

By 1950, only 25 percent of all full-time collegians in California were attending private colleges. By 1960, the year of the California Master Plan, the proportion had dropped to 17 percent, by 1967 to 14 percent, and further reductions have occurred since that time.[6] The fall 1970 figure of 94 percent of first-time entrants in public colleges, noted above, simply indicates that today higher education in California implies "differential access" public higher education. If we consider full-time undergraduates attending the three rungs of the California public education ladder in 1968, one in five was attending a state university; one in four, a state college; and one in two, a public junior college. In the decade beginning late 1950s, there was a slight increase in the proportion of students in the lower two of the three public institutional levels and in the graduate schools of the university, but the principal change was the loss of students suffered by private institutions.[7]

Ratifying the Status Quo

By 1959, when the Liaison Committee of the State Board of Education and the Regents of the University of California were asked by the legislature to frame a state higher educational master plan,[8]

5. Monroe E. Deutsch, Aubrey A. Douglass, and George D. Strayer, *A Report of a Survey of the Needs of California in Higher Education* (Berkeley: University of California Press, 1948).

6. Joint Committee on Higher Education, California Legislature, *The Academic State* (n.p., 1968), p. 13. Proportions attending private institutions are based on enrollments in member institutions of the Association of Independent California Colleges and Universities (AICCU), for whom reliable enrollment data are available, and who account for about 90 percent of private enrollments. The proportion might be several percentage points higher if non-AICCU schools were included, but the trends and the overall predominance of the public sector would maintain.

7. Joint Committee on Higher Education, California Legislature, *The Challenge of Achievement* (n.p., 1969), p. 31.

8. Master Plan Survey Team, *A Master Plan for Higher Education in California, 1960–1975* (Sacramento: State Department of Education, 1960).

the three-level university-college network approached a monopoly of student enrollments. Three possibilities were open for the Master Plan: (1) Abandon the existing structure entirely. Politically, and in light of the social and economic investment, this step was unthinkable. (2) Maintain the external features of the three-level system, but recommend considerable change in such matters as access to the institutions at the various levels, the relative prominence of each level, their respective academic roles, and the extent of autonomy enjoyed by each level and by the individual institutions.

In fact, those who framed the 1960 Master Plan chose a third alternative: overall acceptance of existing structure with only minor, and chiefly administrative, alterations. Their deliberations took place during a time of economic prosperity, so that their chief concern was to plan sufficient expansion through the differential access model to provide college places for the massive increase in applicants expected during the 1960s. As the Joint Committee on Higher Education of the California Legislature observed in 1969: "fundamentally, the 1960 Master Plan represented a ratification of the *status quo*."[9]

Let us examine that status quo in more detail. First, though all high school graduates should have access to some kind of college, immediate entrance into the state university system would be limited to the academic upper eighth of high school graduates. The state colleges would accept upper third graduates, and the commuter two-year colleges would be open to all applicants with a high school diploma, plus a few lacking this credential. Second, the two-year colleges would offer terminal vocational courses, as well as transfer programs for students hoping to continue in college at a four-year institution; the state colleges would offer four-year undergraduate study plus a master's program; and the institutions of the state university would offer undergraduate programs and programs leading to the master's and doctoral degrees. Third, overall development of the system would, in large part, be centrally planned. New institutions would be created, and existing facilities expanded, chiefly to meet the current and projected demographic requirements of particular locales, rather than to enhance the academic self-image of a community already possessing adequate higher educational facilities.

The Master Plan was also notable for what it *failed* to recommend; that is, it did not offer significant support to the private higher educational sector. Certainly it provided no measures to curtail or reverse the attrition experienced by these institutions. The Master Plan enjoyed an extremely favorable reception both at home and nationally,

9. *Challenge of Achievement,* p. 4.

and in large part the state accepted and implemented its recommendations throughout most of the 1960s.

The Master Plan broke no new ground as such. Its widespread publicity can probably be attributed to its clear and explicit codification of a commitment to liberal opportunity to higher education and to the codification of specific features of the system designed to implement that commitment. In 1960, the basic premise—equality of higher educational opportunity through universal access to college, but careful maintenance of elite versus nonelite institutions by academic sorting of all applicants—seemed to accord with two basic characteristics of American ideology—the democratic impulse and the pursuit of excellence. Because of the relative economic prosperity prevailing at the time the Master Plan was formulated, it was generally felt that the recommended broad expansion of public higher education could be financed without undue strain on the economy.

Criticism of the Master Plan

In recent years the California Master Plan and California higher education in general have been under heavy attack by a variety of critics. In part, the attacks have centered on the ideological desirability of differential access, in part on the empirically measured educational output of the system, and in part on the cost to the taxpayers. A ramified and expensive public higher educational system like California's is particularly vulnerable during an economic downturn. Student unrest and violence, since their initial appearance in 1964, have simply served to secure for the critics a broader and more emotionally involved audience. As early as 1968, Arthur G. Coons observed: "It is by now no news that California has been and is in a great crisis in higher education . . . it is only in the last year or two that its meaning in finance and control have come directly home to the general public."[10]

The essential problem is that of having all one's eggs in one basket, in this instance, an all-encompassing public higher educational establishment under unified central control, according to the blueprint of a single development Master Plan. If this single model works well—economically, ideologically, and academically—then all is well. But if the economic climate deteriorates or major flaws become apparent in the model as it develops in practice, then all is in jeopardy, for the possibility of alternatives has been largely eliminated.

10. Coons, *Crises in California Higher Education* (Los Angeles: Ward Ritchie Press, 1968), p. 210.

The crisis in California higher education is clearly not over. Two major developments have emerged. First, criticism of the system plus actual lack of state money have caused curtailed funding of the institutions, which in turn threatens the orderly operation and development envisioned in the Master Plan. Second, the crisis has stimulated a number of government-sponsored studies in which past, present, and projected data for California higher education form the base for new evaluations and recommendations.[11]

Student Attrition

From the evidence presented in these studies and in other recent sources of data, we can estimate what differential access public higher education in California has accomplished and what it has failed to accomplish. Since it has virtually supplanted the private sector (for good or for ill), we will focus on the public sector, where the input-output (cost-benefit) relationships are being questioned today.

We will begin with basic educational statistics for California for the late 1960s: "Of 1,000 students who enter high school in California, about 800 will be graduated. Of these graduates, some 540 will enroll in a college somewhere. Of this group, fewer than 250 will complete more than their freshman year. Between 100 and 150 will eventually be graduated from some college somewhere."[12] The authors express great satisfaction with the high school graduation rate (80 percent) and with the college entrance rate (68 percent), but they express considerable dismay over the proportion of entrants continuing in college beyond one year (46 percent) and with the proportion of entrants finally obtaining baccalaureates (19–28 percent).

Attrition rates for all students and for full-time students, alike, appear to have increased considerably over the decade from the late 1950s at all three of the types of public institutions. The increased attrition has been particularly marked at the junior colleges, which attract the large majority of all entering freshmen: "The junior colleges have experienced larger declines in already low persistence rates. The sophomore-freshman ratios have declined 37 percent from .570 to .360 for full-time students."[13] Here indeed is an accelerating revolv-

11. A one-year $150,000 restudy of the Master Plan, ordered by the state legislature, is in process. Earlier studies, though less closely addressed to a review of the Master Plan, were ordered by the legislature in 1966 and 1967, and produced two major documents, *The Academic State* and *Challenge of Achievement*, already cited. Both present abundant statistics on what has and has not been achieved under the Master Plan, and both suggest major departures from the 1960 model.
12. *The Academic State*, p. x.
13. Ibid., p. 23.

ing door phenomenon. The question that concerned the authors of the report is the value of the circuit, to the student and to the taxpayer.

A better perspective for evaluating the entrance and attrition rates in California may be obtained by comparing them with those for other parts of the country, especially areas that have not moved significantly toward open enrollment. Using Bureau of the Census data from the Current Population Survey for the 1960s, it is possible to compare entrance and attrition rates of younger age cohorts for the nine census divisions.[14]

California accounts for about 75 percent of the recent younger population in the Pacific division, and if the state of Washington is added to California (Washington has a similarly large public higher educational establishment, including numerous junior colleges), the proportion rises to almost 90 percent of the division. Data for the division principally reflect the situations in California and Washington. There are insufficient numbers of cases for comparisons of non-whites, but, for whites, who constitute the great majority of the prospective college entrants in the Pacific division, the divisional comparisons are clear.

The divisional comparisons yield the following overall findings:

1. For the four Western divisions, including Pacific, proportions of younger *age cohorts* in the late 1960s completing high school are a few percentage points higher than those for the Eastern and East Central divisions of the country.

2. The West South Central and Pacific divisions have the highest proportions of *high school graduates* entering college.

3. The West South Central, Mountain, and Pacific divisions have the lowest proportions of *college entrants* completing four years of college.

4. Of all divisions, Mountain and Pacific, in that order, have the lowest proportions of the *age cohort* completing four years of college.

5. Of all divisions, Pacific and Mountain, in that order, have by far the lowest proportions both of *college entrants* who complete the *first* year, and *college entrants* who complete the *second* year of college.

14. Special tapes of selected data from the October 1967, 1968, and 1969 Current Population Surveys were obtained by the present authors from the U.S. Bureau of the Census and were analyzed at the Bureau of Applied Social Research, Columbia University. Data for the three survey years were combined to afford sufficient numbers for divisional analyses. The nine divisions are: New England, Middle Atlantic, East North Central, South Atlantic, East South Central, West North Central, West South Central, Mountain, and Pacific.

The Pacific division, which largely is the California experience, may be summarized as follows: Although particularly large proportions of younger age cohorts in the late 1960s reached college (compared with East Central and Eastern divisions), exceptionally large proportions dropped out within the first two years. The net effect is that the proportion of the total age group receiving the baccalaureate is the second lowest of all nine census divisions. In short, other parts of the nation, in which open enrollment was far less prevalent, provided four or more years of college to a larger proportion of the total college age group than did California.

A Question of Priorities

It is not clear whether the California Master Plan, and other related state literature, gave priority to college entrance or to completing the full four years. Both goals are cited as desirable, but the Master Plan did not anticipate that proportions of the college-going age cohort completing college under differential access would be next to lowest in the country. It seems equally clear that it did not expect that about half of college entrants in the latter 1960s would fail to complete two years of college, that is, fail to complete an associate of arts program or its equivalent. Nearly half of such dropouts failed to complete the initial year of college.

Just why attrition is so high in the California system is not certain. In recent years, the sharp curtailment in higher education funds has, to be sure, caused a sharp decrease in space available in the upper division of the California system for lower division transfer students. Yet attrition is very high prior to completion of lower division study, and in earlier years was not attributable to lack of space in senior colleges. Also, attrition was on the rise even before the present economic drought. All of this suggests that attrition is in the main related either to the nature of the California system itself or to the nature of the students or, more probably, to both elements. Hard data on the reasons for attrition are conspicuous by their absence, but the simple fact of paramount importance remains: differential access in California is associated with considerably higher rates of attrition than the more traditional and academically selective access systems that prevail in many other parts of the country.

Matriculating Minority Students

A primary objective of liberal access programs is to enable relatively disadvantaged racial minority students to enter college and, presumably, to progress through college in proportions commensurate with those of their white classmates. Table 1 presents the best available summary of minority participation in higher education in California.

TABLE 1: *Racial and Ethnic Distribution for California Public Schools and Public Higher Education, Fall 1967*

Level of Enrollment	Spanish Surname	Negro	Chinese, Japanese, Korean	American Indian	All Other	Total
Elementary (K–8)......	14.4	8.6	2.1	0.3	74.6	100.0
High school (9–12).....	11.6	7.0	2.1	0.2	79.1	100.0
Junior colleges.........	7.5	6.1	2.9	0.1	83.4	100.0
State colleges..........	2.9	2.9	1.9	0.7	91.6	100.0
University of California.	0.7	0.8	4.6	0.2	93.7	100.0

Source: Joint Committee on Higher Education, California Legislature, *The Challenge of Achievement* (n.p., 1969), p. 66.

Clearly, differential access in California has not led to minority group representation in higher education commensurate with their share of the school age population—if one excepts Oriental Americans, who are actually overrepresented. The more academically rigorous the type of college, the greater the underrepresentation. Obviously, a number of causal factors must be at work. Inasmuch as Oriental Americans are overrepresented and are not a particularly affluent group, one must assume that cultural values in large part are responsible for this overrepresentation. For the underrepresented minorities, cultural values must negate college entrance, since junior colleges are open to all, irrespective of academic background.

But one must qualify this last statement. Apart from the cultural values, other forces must inhibit many Negroes and Spanish Americans from entering college. In the first place, relatively many ethnic minority students (with the exception of Oriental Americans) appear to be high school dropouts and thus are not in a position to enter college. In the second place, even though the cost of college may be nominal, it still represents forgone earnings. In addition, two-year commuter colleges in many parts of California are not located within convenient commuting distance on public transportation for large aggregates of minority groups who would tend to lack private vehicles. Thus, the Master Plan, which hoped to assure minority groups at least some college experience, has failed to accomplish this goal in proportion to its success with the white majority. This discrepancy, glaringly obvious, was noticed early at the state university level, and elicited modifications of the differential access formula to permit more minority students to enter the university. Early in the 1960s academic criteria were relaxed at the university for 2 percent of all entrants;

the exception was later raised to 4 percent. Even with this favorable action, Negroes and Spanish Americans were notable by their absence on the university campuses. One of the chief demands advanced by recent critics of the present system is further dilution of the differential access formula, as well as creation of new colleges in, or adjacent to, centers of minority group populations.

We do not wish to convey the impression that differential access has failed to achieve a number of its major objectives. As we have pointed out, a high proportion of high school graduates in California (about 68 percent in the latter 1960s) do enter college. Also, the elite institutions in the system, the branches of the state university, are distinguished institutions academically, however measured—by quality of the student bodies and faculties, available academic hardware and software, or scope and quality of the graduate programs. It is, however, precisely the success of differential access in its elite sector that highlights the failure of the system to achieve stated goals in the academically less selective institutions. Curtailment of higher educational funding simply has brought into the open the latent conflict of whether priority should be given to educational quality or educational equality.

A Conflict of Goals

The conflict has many facets. At the university branches, should undergraduate or graduate education receive priority for the limited funds available? Should limited funds be supplemented through the imposition of substantial tuition and other charges, and thereby decrease access to college for less affluent population groups? Should the state college system be considerably expanded to assure places to all junior college transfer students? Should the sharp academic distinctions between the three types of institutions in the system be minimized by permitting less qualified students, particularly racial minority students, to enter the elite colleges in far greater numbers? Should or should not the individual colleges have the right to determine their own destiny in terms of length and type of program, academic standards, commuter or resident status, and so forth? Should the less affluent students receive not only free tuition, but also additional funds amounting to a subsidy for forgone earnings? These are but a few aspects of the great debate, which in sum questions the basic viability and desirability of the differential access formula.

At the heart of the debate, we believe, is the basic question of what is the goal—or are the goals—of higher education. What is mass higher education supposed to impart to the average student, and what is the student supposed to return to the society? The 1960 Master Plan was quite explicit with respect to the role of the university-level institutions, especially the graduate schools: to supply rigorous training for an academic elite which, in turn, was supposed to enter high-level professions and contribute to the economic, technological, and scientific progress of the state. Apart from the minority of two-year college terminal vocational students, the Master Plan and other related literature never concretely defined the purpose of college study for the majority of students (particularly those with less academic ability) who enter the middle and lower levels of the three-level system. Given high dropout rates for such students, in combination with severe financial problems, the original assumption implicit in the Master Plan—that the democratic principle of open access to college is its own sufficient justification—appears less convincing today than ten years ago, particularly to the California taxpayer.

Perhaps the most significant attempt to find a new and meaningful role for the California higher educational complex is presented in the 1969 *Challenge of Achievement,* where an "urban focus," both in academic programs of study and in related programs of community service, is suggested for the future, based upon the "rural precedent" of the land-grant colleges.[15] The emphasis here would be on practical training in empirical techniques designed to resolve specific and pressing urban problems, analogous to the technical and agricultural approach to rural problems developed by the land-grant colleges.

The Moral of the Story

The major moral of the California story is clear, we feel. As the system has matured, its shortcomings as well as its achievements have become evident, especially so when money is in short supply. The model is then called upon to justify itself on a cost-benefit basis, rather than principally on the basis of ideological desirability. Since the California model has served as a precedent for many other egalitarian efforts in higher education down the years, what emerges from the present crisis in that state is of national significance. It seems that open enrollment programs, sooner or later, must face the difficult question of just what the college is supposed to impart to "Everyman," and just what "Everyman," so educated, is supposed to return to society. The further question is whether or not college is a "meaningful experience"—however that term may be defined—for the nearly

15. Pp. 127–33.

half of California open enrollment entrants who drop out prior to completion of two years. We assume here that open enrollment in other locales would yield dropout rates roughly similar to those on the West Coast, in the absence of massive tutorial and other support on the part of the colleges.

Finally, we should observe that differential access minimizes the actual dollar costs of open enrollment, both to the students and the taxpayer. If high dropout rates can be interpreted as indicating considerable waste of time and effort, the dollar cost is kept as low as possible. Most California dropouts attend the commuter junior colleges, where state expenditures per lower division student and direct costs to the student in the latter 1960s were appreciably less than at the state colleges and universities.

If students with characteristics associated with high dropout rates were permitted to enroll in formerly elite residential senior institutions, the cost to the student and the taxpayer would be much greater. Nevertheless, current critics of the California differential access system single out the low cost of two-year college study as direct evidence of the inferior academic offerings of these schools, and, they argue, represents nonegalitarian discrimination against the students enrolled. Regardless of the merits of the argument, the pressures for elimination of the differential element of the California model are strong, and similar pressures are clearly present in the open enrollment model of the City University of New York.

THE CUNY OPEN ENROLLMENT MODEL

In the spring of 1971, some eight months after its inception, the City University of New York's new experiment in open enrollment faced the possibility of considerable belt-tightening, or even of premature burial, as a result of the city's financial crisis. In September 1971, CUNY managed to enter its second year of open enrollment without eliminating any of the official provisions of the program, but its fiscal problems remain extremely serious. Though the 1971–72 CUNY budget is substantially higher than that for 1970–71, normal expansion in enrollments, inflation, and additional entrants produced by open enrollment mean that per student educational dollars are even scarcer this year than last. The total university budget and the funds available for the open enrollment program were in short supply last year and remain so today. Though the official provisions of the program remain intact, it is not clear whether this year's open enrollment student will receive the same quantity and quality of academic services as last year's. The longer future is even less predictable.

Nevertheless, whether or not CUNY open enrollment survives intact beyond its initial year, its significance remains. Even if the program were to be severely curtailed, sooner or later strong pressures would be exerted to reinstate it in full. In addition, we strongly suspect that the massive interest the CUNY program has aroused throughout the country simply means that it will serve as the model for similar approaches elsewhere, just as the California Master Plan served as the model for differential access programs in other states.

The chief difficulty in discussing CUNY open enrollment is its infancy and the consequent lacunae in hard data during its first year in operation. The problem is compounded because City University has not as yet analyzed or released much data. When we wrote to CUNY requesting access to data on 1970 freshman entrants, we received the following reply from the director of Open Admissions Research:

> Concerning the basic data on characteristics of entering freshmen, I am sorry to say that we cannot release this information at this time. The University is committed to a five year program of research aimed at addressing several aspects of the open admissions policy. We plan to collect various pre- and post-measures on items such as test scores. The analyses are complex, and we have not really begun to carry these out. As is standard practice, when our analyses have been completed, we would then make the data available to other interested researchers.

Within five years, then, we may know the answers. We are not suggesting that CUNY release unverified data. We also recognize that the CUNY institutional research budget is limited and that the task of gathering comparable data from its many relatively autonomous institutions is formidable. We do feel, however, that every effort should be made to assess the strengths and weaknesses of CUNY open enrollment as soon as possible. The California experience indicates that once a basic higher educational innovation is institutionalized with the passage of time, it becomes very difficult to modify that plan, however desirable modification might be.

Actually, a great deal is known about CUNY open enrollment even without definitive and official data on the students newly enrolled. One can speak of its impact on non-CUNY colleges in the area: describe the kinds and proportions of students being lost to CUNY because of open enrollment. One can summarize the statistics on entrants, racial mixes, and student academic preparation under CUNY —statistics that CUNY has released to the newspapers. Moreover, one can trace the course of events that led to the CUNY experiment. It is also possible to specify the actual provisions of CUNY open enrollment, and compare the model with others such as the California model.

The CUNY program is of particular interest because it is the first large-scale open enrollment program in which virtually all of the potential entrants live within commuting distance of both two-year and four-year participating colleges. There is no problem of physical access, as in parts of California, and the CUNY program should fully test the true response to open enrollment. If the three relatively liberal-access State University of New York branches located in Nassau and Westchester counties are included as resources, a population of perhaps ten million persons, urban and suburban, is living within reach of an open-door college.

It should be noted that the principal targets for open enrollment—high school graduates disadvantaged academically or socioeconomically, and racial minority graduates—have not been altogether neglected in the past by CUNY. For some years, relatively small groups of poverty area students have been enrolled in such collegiate programs as SEEK and College Discovery. Open enrollment simply extends the college franchise to the total age cohort of high school graduates, whether advantaged or disadvantaged.

CUNY officials have been moving in the direction of open enrollment for some years. On the first page of its 1968 Master Plan, the Board of Higher Education of the City of New York had committed itself to a timetable for open enrollment: "The Board reaffirms its determination to offer admission to every high school graduate and proposes the expansion of facilities and programs to meet its 100% goal by 1975." The decision to implement the program in full in fall 1970 simply accelerated an earlier schedule to respond to increasing pressures from students and other groups.

Provisions of CUNY Program

To begin, a few words of explanation about CUNY and SUNY are in order. CUNY is the New York City system of public colleges, and SUNY (State University of New York) is the state system. A New York City resident may apply for admission to either system. In recent years SUNY has expanded considerably in the immediate area around New York City. Although SUNY does not have all the open enrollment features of CUNY, it is sufficiently "open" so that large numbers of New York City students can take their choice of either system, and many do attend SUNY.

First, at CUNY, as in California, a college place is guaranteed to every area-resident high school graduate who applies. Second, access to the formerly selective four-year colleges in the system is substantially liberalized. Prior to open enrollment, a high school grade average of around 82 was required for admission to a four-year college, but under the new plan a grade average of 80 or placement in the top half of the high school class suffices for acceptance.

The open enrollment provisions resulted in fall 1970 four-year college acceptances in which about 40 percent of the students had grade averages under 80 and about 20 percent had grade averages under 75. The point is that *either* a grade average of 80 *or* placement in the top half of the class qualifies a student for admission to a senior college. A mediocre student with low grades in a class of even poorer students might well rank above average in the class. About 69 percent of the two-year college acceptances had grade averages under 75.[16] Quite clearly, under open enrollment, the senior institutions remain far more academically selective than the two-year colleges, but over 40 percent of the September 1970 acceptances to senior colleges would not have qualified in former years.

Need for Remedial Work

Under open enrollment, CUNY has assumed considerable responsibility for the academic fate of entrants. The extent of this burden, as measured by proportions requiring remedial reading or mathematics courses, has been estimated on the basis of tests administered in May 1970 to students accepted by CUNY for fall entrance.[17] Approximately half of all acceptances needed remedial work in math or reading or both; of this half, about half were in need of *intensive* remedial math and about a fifth were in need of *intensive* remedial reading. A CUNY official estimates that, as a result of open enrollment, the proportion in need of remedial work has about doubled. At the senior colleges, with higher entrance requirements, the proportion in need of remedial work is lower than at the two-year schools. About one in three of senior college acceptances was in need of remedial math and/or reading; of this third about one in three was in need of *intensive* remedial math and one in ten in need of *intensive* remedial reading. The need for remedial work is based on test scores indicating inability to handle the verbal or numerical components of college level study.

In the past, dropout prior to graduation for degree-credit students

16. " 'Open Admissions' Begins at City University Today," *New York Times,* Sept. 14, 1970, pp. 1, 34.
17. Ibid.

at all CUNY colleges combined was estimated at 20–25 percent of entrants. The data on the need for remedial work simply measures the size of the remedial task the CUNY system has accepted under open enrollment, if the dropout rate remains at its historical level.

Composition of Student Body

The figures in Table 2 on past and present ethnic composition of the CUNY colleges and of the New York City schools reveal another aspect of the impact of open enrollment. The statistics lead to a number of conclusions.

1. Since 1967, the proportions of matriculated black and Puerto Rican first-time freshmen at CUNY have been steadily rising, but open enrollment in 1970 does not seem to have accelerated the rate of increase.

2. Both black and Puerto Rican *accepted* applicants, especially Puerto Rican, seem far more likely to fail to matriculate than accepted applicants from the racial majority. (We have no information that might explain this finding.)

3. In fall 1970 CUNY matriculations, blacks were slightly over-represented and Puerto Ricans moderately underrepresented relative to their proportions among 1970 *public and private* New York City high school graduates. In combination, however, they were nearly fully represented.

4. Relatively few minority youth progressed far enough in public secondary school to apply for college entrance, as revealed by the last column of Table 2.

TABLE 2: *Ethnic Minority Representation in CUNY Freshman Classes and in New York City Public and Private Schools*

Ethnic Group	CUNY-Matriculated First-Time Freshmen				Early Estimate of 1970 CUNY First-Time Freshmen	New York City	
						Graduates, Public and Private High Schools, 1970	Public Junior High School Enrollment, 1964–65
	1967	1968	1969	1970			
Black..........	6.5	9.3	13.7	17.1	21.7	16.0	28.0
Puerto Rican....	4.0	5.0	5.9	7.7	11.7	10.1	18.7
Black *and* Puerto Rican..	10.5	14.3	19.6	24.8	33.4	26.1	46.7
Other..........	89.5	85.7	80.4	75.2	66.6	73.9	53.3
Total..........	100.0	100.0	100.0	100.0	100.0	100.0	100.0

Source: Data on matriculated first-time freshmen and 1970 graduates of public and private high schools provided by Lester Brailey, dean, CUNY Office of Admissions Services.
Early estimate of 1970 first-time freshmen is based on CUNY applications accepted for fall 1970 " 'Open Admissions' Begins at City University Today," *New York Times*, Sept. 14, 1970, p. 34.
New York City public junior high school enrollment, 1964–65 reported in Eleanor Bernert Sheldon and Raymond A. Glazier, *Pupils and Schools in New York City: A Fact Book* (New York: Russell Sage Foundation, 1965), pp. 116–17.

5. The statistics on ethnic representation in California public colleges and CUNY colleges are not strictly comparable, and comparisons are difficult to make. Oriental Americans seem to be well represented in both systems (see Table 1). A recent CUNY study indicates prominence of Oriental Americans among CUNY full-time open enrollment entrants.[18]

6. It seems that about five in ten black and Puerto Rican CUNY day freshmen in 1970 entered senior colleges,[19] whereas in California under differential access the overwhelming majority of black and Spanish-surname students enroll in two-year schools.

Overall, CUNY enrollment of first-time students approximately doubled between 1967 and 1970, rising from about 17,000 to roughly 35,000.[20] About five-sixths of this rise, however, occurred between 1969 and 1970, and CUNY officials estimate that most of it is directly attributable to open enrollment rather than normal expansion of the system: "Seventy six percent of last year's (1970) city high school graduates went on to some form of full-time higher education . . . [compared] with 57 percent the previous year and 55 to 60 percent on a national level. The substantial differences were attributable to the City University's new open-admissions policy. . . ."[21]

These then are the basic data available on the impact of open enrollment at CUNY. It is too early to estimate final dropout rates and, consequently, to determine the effectiveness of remedial efforts. CUNY data on freshman dropout for the 1970–71 academic year, released to the *New York Times*, are shown in Table 3. At the more rigorous senior colleges, the dropout rate for students newly eligible for admission under the provisions of open enrollment was more than twice the rate for students who would have been eligible in former years. At the less rigorous community colleges, the newly eligible students were about one-sixth again as likely to drop as those who would have been eligible formerly. For both types of colleges combined, the "open admissions students" were about four-fifths again as likely to drop as the "regular" ones.

18. "City Finds a Jump in College Bound," *New York Times*, May 11, 1971.
19. This proportion is the best approximation possible from the data available to us. It was reached by applying CUNY figures for black and Puerto Rican representation at two- and four-year colleges in the system ("City U. Is Adjusting to the Sharp Increase in Number of Freshmen," *New York Times*, March 26, 1971, p. 21) to the 1970 first-time enrollment figures at the two types of institutions (USOE, *Advance Report on Opening Fall Enrollment, 1970*, pp. 31, 34).
20. *Advance Report on Opening Fall Enrollment, 1970*, pp. 31, 34; National Center for Educational Statistics, U.S. Office of Education, *Opening Fall Enrollment in Higher Education, 1967* (Washington: Government Printing Office, 1967), pp. 98–99.
21. "City Finds a Jump in College Bound."

TABLE 3: *Comparison of CUNY Attrition Rates in 1970–71
for Regular and Open Admissions Day Freshmen*

Level of College	Regular Admissions		Open Admissions*	
	Number Admitted	Attrition (Percentage)	Number Admitted	Attrition (Percentage)
Senior.................	10,362	13.6	6,749	29.6
Community............	4,251	34.4	8,447	40.1
Total................	14,613	19.9	15,196	35.8

Source: "Open-Entry Dropouts Double Others at City U.," *New York Times*, Nov. 18, 1971, p. 61.
Note: Figures do not encompass special admissions programs, students for whom high school averages were unavailable, and one college for which data are not yet available.
* Students with high school averages below 80 admitted to senior colleges and below 75 admitted to community colleges.

The overall freshman attrition rate at the CUNY senior colleges rose from 16 percent in 1969–70 to 20 percent in 1970–71, and from 35 percent to 39 percent at the community colleges. At the senior colleges attrition rates for "regular students" actually dropped several points between 1969–70 and 1970–71, possibly a reflection of a policy under which, in the latter academic year, under open admissions, no students were flunked out for academic reasons. In brief, all 1970–71 dropout was voluntary.

Whether or not these early attrition rates for "open enrollment students," relative to those for "regular" ones, represent cause for alarm or jubilation remains unclear. It is the final dropout rate for the openly enrolled students that will be the critical one. Furthermore, it is a moot point just how many of the generally less able "open enrollment students" will survive, if and when those who perform poorly become subject to dismissal for academic reasons.

Overall Effects on Private Institutions

In California, as already noted, about 94 percent of the fall 1970 entering freshmen enrolled in public colleges and universities, continuing a steady trend away from private higher education down the years. The same trend appears to have been occurring in the five New York boroughs, as well as in adjacent suburban Westchester and Long Island, where SUNY colleges are increasingly available. Table 4 documents the trend, 1967–70, for the New York City metropolitan area.

The private colleges lost well over a thousand entrants over the three years, and their share of all entrants in the area declined from over half to just over a third, whereas CUNY and SUNY combined gained more than twenty-two thousand entrants and increased their

TABLE 4: *Fall First-Time College Students, Five New York City Boroughs and Nassau and Westchester Counties, 1967–70, by Control of College*

Institutions	Number of Students		Change, 1967–70		Percentage Distribution of Students	
	1967	1970	Absolute	Percentage	1967	1970
All private colleges.....	25,328	23,937	− 1,391	− 5	53	35
All public colleges......	22,094	44,375	+22,281	+101	47	65
SUNY colleges.......	4,730	9,605	+ 4,875	+103	10	14
CUNY colleges......	17,364	34,770	+17,406	+100	37	51
CUNY four-year...	9,817	20,180	+10,363	+106	21	30
CUNY two-year...	7,547	14,590	+ 7,043	+ 93	16	21
All colleges...........	47,422	68,312	+20,890	+ 44	100	100

Source: National Center for Educational Statistics, U.S. Office of Education, *Opening Fall Enrollment in Higher Education, 1967* (Washington: Government Printing Office, 1967), pp. 98–99; *Advance Report on Opening Fall Enrollment in Higher Education, 1970* (Washington: Government Printing Office, 1970), pp. 31, 34.

share of all entrants from under half to just under two-thirds. In sum, the private sector rapidly lost ground.

We are not suggesting that student attrition in the private sector is due exclusively to implementation of the CUNY open enrollment program in fall 1970, but rather that this program compounded the difficulties of private colleges, as inexpensive public higher education became more readily available in the New York area. It appears that educators and officials concerned with liberal access to public colleges and universities, whether in California, New York, or elsewhere, believe that a healthy private higher education sector is highly desirable. But these same officials have not presented effective measures for maintaining the health of the private sector, relative to the public.[22] It may well be that direct federal aid to colleges and universities, such as is pending in the Congress at the time of writing, could represent the most effective approach to preservation of the beleaguered private institutions.

Attrition in the private sector is, of course, of paramount significance to the colleges themselves. It could also have profound effects on large numbers of students expecting to enter public colleges under open enrollment, should the present financial crisis facing the area result in suspension or curtailment of the open enrollment program, or cause a slower-than-normal rate of expansion of facilities in the public sector. The private sector, curtailing programs in response to attrition to CUNY and SUNY, might find itself hard put to reabsorb

22. Total enrollments in private colleges, including religious institutions, rose fairly rapidly to the mid-1960s, after which growth virtually stopped. Enrollment in public colleges, on the other hand, increased rapidly all through the 1960s.

the students no longer served by the public sector. The bind would closely resemble that in California, where curtailed budgets have led to insufficient numbers of public college places to handle applicants. The above observations are, of course, speculative. Nevertheless, the possibilities would be better understood if more were known about the effects of CUNY open enrollment on freshman enrollments at private colleges in the area, both specific institutions and particular kinds. The data are anything but definitive, but the scattered information does permit a few general conclusions and a few examples.[23]

Effects on Various Types of Private Institutions

CUNY open enrollment seems not to have made inroads on freshman enrollments at the most prestigious schools, such as Columbia College, which tend to enroll large proportions of students from outside the CUNY area. Nor does open enrollment seem to have affected highly specialized private colleges, such as schools of music and art, whose programs are not duplicated within CUNY.

The severe student losses to CUNY experienced by many private colleges in the area apparently were not anticipated by the New York City Board of Higher Education: "it does not appear that open admissions at City University of New York will markedly affect admissions patterns at other New York City institutions."[24] The board somehow failed to foresee that many able students would enter CUNY, rather than the private colleges, to take advantage of the financial savings.

The private colleges that have lost freshmen to CUNY seem to be middle-level general-purpose colleges and the technical institutions —those with medium admission standards and largely local enrollments. In one instance, a mid-Manhattan technical college has considered closing its new central city campus as a direct result of loss of students to CUNY, in which case it would operate only its branch campus on Long Island, located beyond the range of strong effects from CUNY.

In another instance, a mid-Manhattan private business and liberal arts college suffered about a 17 percent decline between 1969 and

23. Our data on individual colleges and universities in the New York area derive in part from their institutional research and in part from our tabulations of records to which we were permitted access. The confidential nature of the information precludes identifying institutions. An excellent summary of the impact of open enrollment on New York area private colleges in 1970 is: "Open Admissions: Unfair Competition," *Change*, September-October, 1970, pp. 17, 20.

24. *1969 First Revision, 1968 Master Plan, Section II* (New York: Board of Higher Education in the City of New York, 1969), pp. 4–5.

1970 freshman entrants to its regular academic program, and a massive 75 percent decline in entrants to its somewhat academically less demanding continuing program. Here, again, an expensive new campus is involved. The losses cited are specific losses to the CUNY and SUNY two- and four-year colleges. For this college, the only two categories of 1970 entrants that maintained or increased over 1969 levels were transfer and out-of-area, chiefly New Jersey, students. Perforce, intensive recruitment is expected for these two groups.

In this mid-Manhattan college, roughly seven in ten of the lost accepted applicants for the less ambitious two-year continuing program were lost to CUNY senior colleges, and about nineteen in twenty of the lost acceptances for the regular four-year program were lost to CUNY four-year colleges. For the accepted applicants lost to this college, Scholastic Aptitude Test scores are available, and largely explain why such large proportions of the applicants, even of those accepted for two-year study, managed to qualify for CUNY senior colleges. For those lost to the two-year program, average SAT scores are appreciably above the national mean. In brief, if the evidence at this one college is typical, CUNY open enrollment seems to be attracting large numbers of reasonably able students accepted by private institutions.

The experience just cited is supplemented by that of a very large Roman Catholic university with branches in two of the boroughs. For this institution, accepted freshman applicants who failed to enroll in fall 1970 ranged from about 46 percent in the less ambitious and chiefly two-year general studies program to about 73 percent in the more ambitious four-year liberal arts college, with losses in the education, business, and technical programs standing between these extremes. About half of all losses were to CUNY or SUNY, depending on which of the two systems served the area in which the prospective student lived. If one excepts losses to other Roman Catholic schools, about two-thirds of all losses were to CUNY-SUNY. In terms of SAT scores, the lost students appear to be an academic cross section of the acceptances, with SAT mean scores at a level that would assure their acceptance, by and large, at CUNY-SUNY senior branches. The threat posed by CUNY-SUNY to this large university appears to be particularly severe, for less than 2 percent of its acceptances lived outside the CUNY-SUNY area.

Statistics from a number of other private institutions in the CUNY-SUNY area indicate parallel severe losses in fall 1970. In sum, CUNY-SUNY seem to be enrolling a large number of reasonably able students accepted by area private colleges, representing an academic cross section of acceptances plus large proportions of less able (but far from hopeless) students who formerly entered less rigorous programs at the private colleges. The test scores indicate that the large majority of the lost students would qualify for entrance to CUNY-SUNY senior colleges, and should not present too formidable a remedial problem once enrolled.

Probably many of the students who shifted from private colleges to CUNY branches come from middle-class, or even upper-middle-class, backgrounds. Richard Waldron of Fordham University's admissions office is quoted as remarking: "What kid is going to pay two thousand dollars a year for an uncertain education when he can get the same uncertainty at City for almost nothing?"[25]

We do not know from the data now available what proportion of the 15,000 increase in CUNY-SUNY entering freshmen, 1969–70, is not accounted for by these above-average students rerouted from private institutions. This unknown proportion would represent the best measure of the size and depth of the remedial problem under CUNY open enrollment. In brief, we simply do not as yet know how much of the 15,000 freshman increase represents high school graduates who would not normally have applied to, or qualified for, any college, public or private, in earlier years.

Impact on Taxpayers

If CUNY open enrollment has the effect of inducing reasonably able students who would otherwise enter private colleges to enter CUNY instead (presumably because costs are lower), then the following questions apply: Should taxpayers be asked to finance students who, by the past record, are able to finance themselves in college? Is open enrollment achieving its objective if it fails to enroll large proportions of high school graduates who otherwise could not attend college? Is a major shift from private to public higher education desirable, given the vulnerability of the entire public system in a time of financial crisis?

These are but a few of the policy questions raised by the scattered data we have presented.

Furthermore, according to the 1970 experience of one private college in the New York area, the large increase in funding requested from the federal government to budget for open enrollment at CUNY simply curtailed funding available to the private colleges and their students. This private college actually received only 36 percent of

25. "Open Admissions: Unfair Competition," p. 20.

1970 Student Loan, Work-Study, and Educational Opportunity Grant funds requested. Per student instructional costs at this private college are estimated to be nearly $300 less per year than at CUNY. For the taxpayer, we can indicate roughly the additional burden represented by expansion of CUNY enrollments. The CUNY 1968 Master Plan estimated instructional costs per full-time equivalent student in the academic year 1966–67 at $1,320. The equivalent projected figure for 1970–71 was $2,355.[26] The Master Plan also gives trend data from 1948 through 1967 for sources of funds in support of university expenditures. In 1948, 18 percent of funds came from state sources, 63 percent from city sources, and 19 percent from student fees plus federal tuition aid. In 1967, the equivalent percentages were 41 percent, 45 percent, and 14 percent.[27] Quite clearly, as the total university budget rose from $18 million in 1948 to $172 million in 1967, decreasing proportions of the funding derived from student sources, and increasing proportions from tax sources, especially from New York state. The budget projected in the latter 1960s for 1971–72 was $421 million and for 1975–76, $712 million.[28] The budget projection for 1975–76 assumed considerable growth of CUNY colleges. It did not, however, assume implementation of open enrollment in fall 1970, with consequent acceleration in the rate of growth, and increased budget requirements to meet this growth and to institute remedial services.[29]

The above figures indicate the enormous burden placed on the city and state tax bases by expansion of CUNY, and in large measure explain why city officials today are pleading, with something close to desperation, for increased state revenue.

In California, differential access has meant that in 1970 about 86 percent of first-time entrants in public colleges entered junior colleges,[30] where instructional and other expenses are much less than at the senior institutions. Also in 1970, at CUNY, only about 41 percent of freshmen entered the less costly two-year colleges. Since fall 1967

26. *Master Plan of the Board of Higher Education for the City University of New York* (New York: The Board, 1968), p. 177.
27. Ibid., p. 172.
28. Ibid., p. 174.
29. Later 1969 budget projections made by CUNY, which include the presumed incremental costs of open enrollment, indicate that the new program would entail just under a 10 percent budget increase at its outset and about 15 percent increase by the mid-1970s. This increment would be added to the increment attributable to basic expansion of the system, so that by mid-1970s total costs would be roughly 2.5 times the 1970–71 figure. Continuing inflation is assumed. *1969 First Revision, 1968 Master Plan, Section II.*
30. USOE, *Advance Report on Opening Fall Enrollment, 1970.*

the proportion entering two-year colleges has decreased 1.5 percent (see Table 4).

Data are not available to carry the financial analysis further, given the uncertain outcome of the current financial bind. The few figures from recent years, plus the comparisons with California, seem to indicate that New York open enrollment is facing a financial crisis similar to that in California, but exacerbated by the nature of the CUNY system. We simply conclude that such programs as California and CUNY, and SUNY also, with or without the added ingredient of extended open enrollment in the future, must face the acid test of fiscal viability, regardless of their ideological justification.

SOME GENERALIZATIONS ON TWO SYSTEMS

1. Both the California and the CUNY programs face uncertain futures for largely financial reasons. In both states, and elsewhere in the country as well, dollars for higher education are scarce in relation to need if liberal access is to be assured to all segments of the population.

2. For both the California and CUNY models, open enrollment is a relative term. The financially poorer whites, as well as the minority groups, are still underrepresented in college. In California, for example, according to data for the late 1960s, only about 66 percent of Mexican Americans, 60 percent of whites, and 48 percent of blacks live within commuting distance of a free access college.[31] Furthermore, if student aid were to cover the college student's forgone earnings, in addition to direct educational costs, then access to college would certainly be increased for lower socioeconomic groups. The Carnegie Commission on Higher Education estimates forgone earnings for community college students at about $3,000 per year.[32]

3. Both the California and New York systems are experiencing pressures to become even more "open." In California, finances permitting, the differential aspect of "differential access" may be relaxed in response to recent demands. In New York, the less stringent requirements for admission to senior colleges may be further reduced—once again, if finances permit.

4. Further "openness" can be achieved by still further lowering of admissions requirements—indeed, they could be abolished altogether—reducing the requirements for a degree, and introducing a "fail-

31. Warren W. Willingham, *Free-Access Higher Education* (New York: College Entrance Examination Board, 1970), p. 56.
32. *The Open-Door Colleges* (New York: McGraw-Hill Book Co., 1970), p. 46.

safe" curriculum. With such modifications, together with massive financial support from the federal government, virtually everyone could be brought into college and kept there long enough to receive a degree.

5. Private colleges, except for specialized institutions, are hard-pressed by the present degree of openness. With increased openness and increased tax monies going to public institutions, private colleges with but few exceptions will be virtually phased out. Already free (or almost free) tuition is siphoning off relatively more able as well as less able students who used to attend private colleges. The taxpayer is subsidizing more and more students whose families can afford to send them to private colleges.[33]

6. For the nation as a whole, and for men and women alike, proportions of the relevant age cohort attending college *for a year or more* nearly doubled between the immediate post-World War II years and the latter 1960s. For example, for white males the proportion rose from 30 percent to 52 percent, for white females the rise was from 20 percent to 36 percent. By the latter 1960s, in the Pacific division 56 percent of white males in the relevant age cohort enjoyed a year or more of college, a percentage slightly higher than the national average.[34] The point is that enrollment has become increasingly open throughout the country down the years, not simply in locales where formally codified programs foster "openness."

7. On the other hand, over this time span the proportion of entrants completing college appears to have decreased as access to college was liberalized. For example, in the Pacific division the proportion of white males completing a year of college who subsequently obtain baccalaureates has declined from 59 percent to 45 percent since the immediate post-World War II period.[35] For the Pacific division, increasing access to college is associated with decreasing graduation rates for entrants.

8. Considering the trends described in points 6 and 7 above, we may well ask: What is the purpose and the payoff of less than four years of college—often less than a year—both for the student and

33. For a highly critical discussion of this turn of events, see Milton Friedman, "The Higher Schooling in America," *Public Interest,* Spring 1968, pp. 108–12. Friedman's article is part of a symposium, "Financing Higher Education."

34. See footnote 14 above.

35. It should be emphasized that the Bureau of the Census data referred to here are for highest grade completed and so do not include freshman dropouts in the college-going population. If freshman dropouts were included, the college completion rates would be even lower, as indicated by the 19–25 percent completion rate of California college entrants, cited in *The Academic State* (p. x).

for society? What should the dropouts study? Is a thin veneer of traditional liberal arts experience particularly "relevant" or rewarding? The payoffs of baccalaureate and graduate degrees in occupational and economic terms are large, as has been amply documented. Save for the minority of terminal vocational students in brief college programs, the payoffs and purposes of part-college, as compared with full-college or more, are largely undetermined and undefined—at least as far as tangible benefits are concerned. The limited data available suggest that the tangible payoff for part-college is relatively slight (see Tables 5 and 6). Substantially the same conclusions apply to lifetime earnings (age twenty-five to death), both in the latter 1950s and the latter 1960s.[36]

It is not clear just what leads to this pattern of financial and occupational advantage associated with rising levels of educational attainment. But it is clear that the major advantage is associated with com-

TABLE 5: *Yearly Income of U.S. Younger Employed Males,*
by Level of Educational Attainment, Late 1960s

(Base: High school graduation income = 100)

Level of Educational Attainment	Income	Percentage of All College Dropouts
High school graduation..........	100	—
One or two terms of college	110	40
Three or four terms of college...	119	37
Five to seven terms of college....	121	23
Eight or more terms of college....	150	—

Source: Unpublished tabulations of the October 1967, 1968, and 1969 Current Population Surveys of the Bureau of the Census, in which the occupations of younger persons, and the imputed earnings for the various occupations were related to levels of educational attainment.

TABLE 6: *Percentage of U.S. Younger Employed Males*
in Professional and Managerial Occupations, by Level
of Educational Attainment, Latter 1960s

Level of Educational Attainment	Percentage, Professional and Managerial
High school graduation only...................	7
One or two terms of college....................	13
Three or four terms of college.................	28
Five to seven terms of college.................	32
Eight or more terms of college.................	82

Source: Same as Table 5.

36. See also Walter Adams and A. J. Jaffe, "Economic Returns on the College Investment," *Change*, November 1971, pp. 8–9, 60.

pleting college. Probably the market value of the diploma is largely responsible, rather than some sudden flash of expertise and knowledge on graduation day. On the other hand, those with the motivation to finish college also possess characteristics conducive to success in the labor market—characteristics largely unattributable to the college experience. Uncertainties like these reflect our fragmentary understanding of the impact of the college experience per se and, consequently, its impact on the types of students to whom open enrollment programs are chiefly addressed—those in the lower socioeconomic and racial minority groups.

A recent study of college students receiving Federal Educational Opportunity grants (typically, the kind that open admissions are concerned with) yields a very significant cluster of findings: (1) Well over half of these students feel that the "most important function of college is to develop job or career skills." About eight in ten of these students feel that this function is "very important," and virtually all of the rest feel that it is "somewhat important." The lower the socioeconomic status of the student, the more likely he or she is to emphasize this vocational function of college. (2) Over half of the students expect to go to graduate or professional school, irrespective of socioeconomic background. (3) About nineteen in twenty of these students expect to obtain baccalaureate or higher degrees.[37] Quite clearly most "target" students for open enrollment programs are vocationally oriented, concerned with upward socioeconomic mobility, and at least as ambitious traditional college entrants from more favorable socioeconomic backgrounds. The high attrition rates for such entrants and the relatively slight objective returns on the part-college experience suggest that large proportions will fail to realize their expectations.

The intangible benefits would be even more difficult to estimate. We believe, however, that these are the questions that must be faced and answered as the nation moves toward ever more open enrollment, and as proportions of entrants failing to graduate from college steadily increase. For locales with formal open enrollment programs, the questions are only somewhat more critical than elsewhere.

9. If we are to justify the expenditure of time, money, and energy involved in experiencing some college, but less than the full four years, then we must determine just what this rising tide of dropouts is supposed to learn, and just what specific programs of study (if any) benefit both the dropout and his society.

37. Nathalie Friedman, "The Federal Educational Opportunity Grant Program," mimeographed (New York: Bureau of Applied Social Research, Columbia University, 1971).

The literature on open enrollment, whether in California, New York, or other parts of the country, seems to have shied away from confronting these questions directly. We feel that direct confrontation is long overdue.

Open Enrollments: Quo Vadis?

WERNER Z. HIRSCH

THE WELL-DOCUMENTED TREATMENT OF HOW OPEN ENROLLMENT IN California and New York evolved and the evaluations offers many insights. I shall make it my task to take issue with a few select, yet crucial concepts, analyses, and interpretations of the data; then I shall offer some extensions, mainly in the policy area.

How is the efficacy of open enrollment to be evaluated? The authors recognize the "two basic characteristics of American ideology—the democratic impulse and the pursuit of excellence." Yet most of their evaluation concentrates on the effects of open enrollment on the proportion of high school students entering college and receiving baccalaureates, with special attention given to socioeconomically disadvantaged students. They are also concerned about the side effect of open enrollment on attendance in private colleges.

I see here a great need for carefully defining goals and criteria to evaluate open enrollment. As an economist, I like to separate this issue into efficiency and distribution, and I shall also examine briefly the factor of the public's willingness to finance higher education.

In general, the efficiency criterion says that as a nation we would want to offer higher education up to a point where the social costs of additional schooling equal the social gains derived from it. The distribution criterion is less clear inasmuch as it depends on society's value judgments of how much education should be provided for whom, and who should pay for it. The level of financial support depends on what efficiency and distribution criteria prevail and therefore on what each of us expects to get from the higher education system and at what cost.

The efficiency and distribution criteria can be inconsistent with each other, but they clearly affect the level of support that the public can be expected to make available for higher education. Reconciliation is called for, and the process might be facilitated by making explicit many of the assumptions. Maximizing the number of age cohorts who complete four years of college, however, is clearly only one of many strategies, though it seems to loom large in the analysis of Jaffe and Adams.

Let us focus, for a moment, on the completion rate criterion. It raises questions about the dominating importance of obtaining a baccalaureate. On the surface, the emphasis on completion is consistent with economists' empirical research, which shows that marginal expected lifetime earnings increase disproportionately in the fourth year of college, compared to one, two, or three years. Earnings are private benefits, not social benefits, however, and it is not at all clear that social benefits will behave in the same manner. Furthermore, there is one area in which completion is perhaps unimportant. A predominant proportion of girls who enter college do not make major use of their education to increase their own lifetime earnings. But most college women who obtain some liberal education will, as a direct result, provide a distinctly more cultured home for their families and for the next generation. Most likely, for the purpose of providing a cultured home, the greatest marginal benefit occurs during the first year of college education, and thereafter returns diminish rapidly.

Let me now turn to the interpretation of certain data. I am little surprised that the Census' Pacific Division, overwhelmingly dominated by California, is among those with the lowest proportion of college entrants completing four years: it is among the divisions with the highest proportion of high school graduates entering college; with proportionately so many high school students going on to college, many entrants have neither the ability nor the desire to complete four years of college. California probably also has a high rate of high school dropouts, for it has a disproportionately high percentage of blacks and Mexican-Americans who, through no fault of their own, have been poorly prepared for high school and college by both their homes and schools. This large percentage of blacks and Mexican-Americans probably explains the Pacific Division's low proportion of those age cohorts completing four years of college.

A second issue is related to the fall 1967 enrollment figures, which show a substantially smaller proportion of blacks and Mexican-Americans among enrollments in public colleges and universities in California in comparison with their proportion in the public high schools.[1] This fact, however, cannot be used to decide whether or not open enrollment in California in the 1960s made college attendance easier for blacks and Mexican-Americans. We do not know whether

1. See Jaffe and Adams paper, Table 1.

this proportion has been increasing under open enrollment. Under both open and nonopen enrollment, we could expect lower college and university attendance by blacks and Mexican-Americans in 1967 because they are usually relatively poorly prepared in high school, tend to be uncertain about jobs once graduated (and perhaps also about slots in the University of California in case they entered a junior college or state college), are handicapped by location of junior colleges, and held back by the financial status of their families. However, open enrollment might modify these factors by affecting their desire to enter college.

Finally, the New York data do not bear out the contention that open enrollment did not accelerate the rate of increase in the proportion of blacks and Puerto Ricans entering college. We must recognize that huge increases took place in the years just preceding the initiation of open enrollment. Thus the proportion of blacks entering college in New York increased from 6.5 percent in 1967 to 9.3 percent in 1968, to 13.7 percent in 1969, and 17.1 percent in 1970.[2] Further, by 1970, when open enrollment was initiated, their proportion among CUNY freshmen exceeded their proportion of high school graduates. It becomes increasingly difficult to augment the entrance percentage, particularly for a community that in the past had been educationally and culturally deprived. But more important, one of the two minority communities, Puerto Rico, experienced in the first year of open enrollment a rate of increase of college enrollment that exceeded in the previous four years for which data were given.

Where do we go from here? As I stated earlier, open enrollment must be examined for its contribution to efficient as well as equitable provision of higher education, and also the community's willingness to foot the bill. The examination must take cognizance of the status of private higher education in light of the paramount importance of fostering a variety of institutions of higher learning. Yet resources are scarce, and under these collective circumstances we may consider modifying the notion of "universal" higher education. At the outset, I suggest that open enrollment is altogether a mystical concept: all enrollments are encumbered by some constraints. Nobody can argue that all California and New York City high school students with an IQ of 80 consider colleges effectively open to them. Moreover, the children of many blacks, Mexican-Americans, Puerto Ricans, and certain whites —particularly itinerant workers—frequently do not have the necessary information even to apply for admission, and many do not live suffi-

2. Ibid., Table 2.

ciently close to a college to afford becoming a student. Thus "open enrollment" does not now amount to real access for all. Many Californians and New Yorkers, taking the concept literally, have been outraged by the notion that everyone, including those with less than a minimum aptitude for college, can and should become a college student. They resent paying for such extreme and costly measures; many have decided to use political means to end what they consider abuses by reducing funds for higher education.

Under these circumstances, would it not be more efficient and equitable to establish a threshold band below which students are not admitted to college? This level must be low and yet reflect a realistic view of minimum innate ability to benefit from higher education combined with learning potential, as well as the public's willingness to fund education. The level should not be based on IQ because of the great difficulty of interpreting such tests across cultural lines, but rather on grades and potential. From time to time the level could be changed. Moreover, and this is most important, students on the margin—particularly those with high potential—would get special attention and tutoring to increase their probability of getting a good education. Thus there would be heavy investment in students at the two ends of the spectrum, that is, students with relatively low grades but high potential, and students with exceptional intellectual ability. Also provisions for ready transfer are needed to enable students who successfully complete their freshman year in a junior college to continue at a four-year college or university.

Furthermore, I suggest the development of a system that would make available some indirect financial contribution, consistent with the parents' ability to pay. For example, the assistance could take the form of a deduction of tuition from federal income taxes. The deduction would be inversely related to parents' income. Without such a step, not only will the higher education system become increasingly inefficient, but also private higher education will be driven out of existence, a development I consider detrimental to the national interest.

To the extent that public institutions of higher learning levy tuition fees, I suggest that, in order to provide maximum access for all high school graduates, regardless of financial ability, the freshman year be made virtually tuition free. Especially the socioeconomically deprived youth would then find it easier to get into college. Once there, students could apply for scholarships, and if they attended the summer quarter (which usually suffers from great excess capacity), they could automatically get a remission of tuition during regular quarters. For students who want to attend private institutions of higher learning, the state could make available more and larger scholarships.

The present division of labor within the three-tier system is efficient. If anything, the blurring of the lines between the three types of institutions should be reduced. Thus, junior colleges should not duplicate the first two years of state college education except for those students for whom junior colleges provide geographic convenience. Instead, junior colleges should make greater efforts to provide vocational education, which is likely to prepare students for the kinds of occupations they will seek. And junior colleges should be located within the state to maximize ease of access to students of small or moderate means. State colleges should, primarily, provide excellent four-year education and, secondarily, join the state university in selected areas in graduate education.

Such a modified open enrollment policy involves a broad view of all three tiers of higher education and their financing. At the moment, with state university and state colleges forced to limit enrollment because of financial considerations, an increasingly heavy burden is placed on junior colleges and indirectly on the local property tax base. Forceful coordination of all three tiers is needed, with the state government having major financial responsibility for all higher education.

The suggestions offered would, I believe, counteract possible trends toward inefficiency and further prolonged taxpayer revolt. They amount to modifying open entry, or—to be more precise—explicitly and realistically imposing minimum constraints to replace the now-hidden constraints. I believe that such a system, particularly if supplemented by careful attention to high potential students, could serve the entire nation well, and also open the door of education wider to socioeconomically deprived groups.

A Further Look into CUNY's Open Enrollment

T. EDWARD HOLLANDER

THERE IS NOTHING NEW ABOUT THE OPEN ENROLLMENT MOVEMENT IN America; as Jaffe and Adams indicate, open enrollment schemes are at least one hundred years old. But there is a lot that is original about the open admissions program at the City University of New York.

The unifying element in all former open enrollment schemes is their largely political orientation. They developed in their present form to maintain public financial support, but they fell short of providing universal higher education. Acceptance of all students (usually only graduates from accredited high schools) gave the Midwestern public colleges a democratic aura. In reality, remote geographic location and prohibitively high room and board costs screened out the poor, and an insurmountable gate in the form of rigorous freshman-year courses limited success for students with poor high school preparation.[1] By permitting all comers a "chance to succeed," the university was able to pin responsibility for failure on the student. But by failing a predetermined number of freshmen, the university was also able to operate free from attacks as being "elitist oriented" while permitting the faculty to educate a well-screened student body.

The University of California model advances beyond the Midwestern model in providing differential access and by offering students admission to college in the communities in which they live. Differential access gives students a chance to study with students with like preparation, supposedly increasing their chances of success. As Jaffe and Adams point out, however, the gate-keeping function is still present, evidenced by the difficulty that even successful students have in transferring upward from community colleges to the state colleges and universities. Under a more benevolent governor, the California system could be transformed into a system of universal higher education by (1) putting greater resources into remedial programs, (2) providing more generous financial aid for poverty level students so they might afford to delay entry into the job market, and (3) giving community college graduates freer access to a four-year college of their choice in the California system.

As now constituted, the Midwestern and California systems may more properly be classified as "cooling out" systems and not as "open enrollment" systems.[2] They are based on the premise that everyone has the right to flunk out of college.

The CUNY model is the first realistic attempt to provide equal higher education opportunity for high school graduates. It is based on the premise that every high school graduate has a right to a reasonable

1. The importance of proximity in the accessibility of higher education is discussed by Warren W. Willingham, *Free Access Higher Education* (New York: College Entrance Examination Board, 1970), pp. 9–10.
2. Burton R. Clark, *The Open Door College: A Case Study* (New York: McGraw-Hill Book Co., 1960), documents this process for San Jose Junior College. Midwestern public colleges with high attrition rates perform a similar function.

chance for success in college and that the college's responsibility is to adapt its program to compensate for educational disabilities attributable to socioeconomic causes that limit the student's ability to compete.[3] Several factors peculiar to the New York City and perhaps other urban environments demand this approach.

An increasing proportion of job opportunities in the city require college level skills, but increasing numbers of city residents lack the requisite education to fill them. The number of factory jobs is still declining in the city, and the closed shop craft unions offer job entry opportunities to only limited numbers from selected groups.[4] Open admissions is a realistic attempt to match skills with job opportunities.

The city's problems also are complicated by a long-range change in the ethnic composition of the city. Although the absolute number of city residents has remained constant during the last decade at 8 million, the number of black and Puerto Rican citizens has increased by more than 700,000.[5] Prior to 1965, only a handful of minority group students were admitted to City University under an admissions system tied directly to high school performance. Because the high-risk students were screened out, CUNY appeared to be one of the most productive systems nationally, with 70 percent of its entering freshman class receiving a baccalaureate degree. Under normal circumstances such a selective admissions system seems to be successful, but in light of the lack of equal opportunity to obtain a high school education in New York City, the system is highly discriminatory. The Board of Higher Education, in 1965, established a number of special programs aimed directly at poverty level students, and this latter group at CUNY is 85 percent black and Puerto Rican. By 1967, the university's freshman class of 17,000 included 1,800 black and Puerto Rican students, a threefold increase since 1965.[6]

In the spring of 1968, the black and Puerto Rican communities

3. University Commission on Admissions, *Report and Recommendations to the Board of Higher Education of the City of New York* (New York: City University of New York, 1969), p. 4.

4. *Master Plan of the Board of Higher Education for the City University of New York* (New York: City University of New York, 1968), p. 6. It is projected that by 1975, 58.4 percent of expected job openings will be for professionals and technicians, managers, officials and proprietors, and clerks; only 34.1 percent will be for craftsmen, foremen, operators, service, and laborers; 7.2 percent of the openings will be for salesmen.

5. In 1960, 1,141,322 residents were classified as nonwhite by the Census Bureau; in 1970, the figure was 1,844,225 (U.S. Bureau of the Census, *1970 Census of Population: Advance Report, New York General Population Characteristics* [Washington: Government Printing Office, 1971], PC (V2)-34, p. 13).

6. "Report of the Fall 1970 Undergraduate Ethnic Census" (MS; Office of Data Collection and Evaluation, City University of New York, December 1970), p. 3.

pressed for still greater expansion of the university's commitment to the city's minority communities, and that was what the seizure of the south campus at City College was all about.[7] However, a backlash in the white community, especially from the labor movement, precluded any expansion of special admissions for poverty area residents without also ending the university's discrimination against lower middle-income sons and daughters of the working class of New York City.[8] So viewed, open admissions was a solution to a social and political problem upon which the university's survival depended.

Thus, like its predecessor models, open admissions at CUNY is also a political response, a response that was essential both to retain public support for the university's expansion and to protect the university from becoming a focal point for racial conflict in the city. As one city official put it, "the program offered the only real 'shot at the top' for the city's poverty populations." A less enthusiastic supporter grudgingly approved the program as a "bad idea whose time has come."

The Jaffe-Adams paper raises questions about the value of expanding enrollments to the extent that dropout rates rise. It questions the value of college work short of the baccalaureate degree. The tone of the paper suggests that perhaps we have reached the point where the marginal value of further enrollment expansion is not warranted by the cost.

I question the value of such economic calculus because it is impossible to measure the full value of education except in narrow "certification and accreditation" terms. The real value of education is always indeterminate in the short run because it relates to the social structure of society. The appropriate level of education for John Doe is a political judgment that the taxpayer will ultimately make, based on a wide variety of factors, including national income level, attitudes toward education, manpower needs, and levels of unemployment, not the least of which will be the number of unemployed university administrators and professors.

7. A main demand issued to the CCNY administration was for "a racial composition in the future freshman classes that reflects the black and Puerto Rican population in the city's high schools—about 50 percent" ("CCNY to Close Again: Negroes Agree to Talks," *New York Times*, April 24, 1969, p. 34).

8. At a special meeting of the Board of Higher Education just after the City College rebellion, Donna Menna, attorney for the New York Central Labor Council, testified, "We notice . . . that what seems to be the popular thing to do these days is to pay attention to the people who make a lot of noise . . . but we don't think that attention should be given to those people to the exclusion of other people who are just a bit more fortunate . . . who also need a lot of help and . . . also are crying out for the aid which you are responsible to give them." At the same meeting Harry Van Arsdale and Morris Ishuwitz, president and secretary-treasurer respectively of the Central Labor Council, and Mathew Guinan, president of the Transport Workers Union, also supported open admissions.

Besides, we have yet to identify a measure for predicting success in college for students who suffer the disabling effects of poverty. A system based on high school performance or tests that correlate with high school performance is absurd if the performance of the high school itself is suspect.[9] Any predictive mechanism that minimizes student attrition maximizes the possibility of screening out students who could have succeeded. The social cost is especially high if we screen out specific ethnic or racial minorities, as is now the prevailing practice.

CUNY's open admissions policy should be judged not in terms of how many or what proportion of its students earn baccalaureates. The program should be judged in terms of who is now coming to college at CUNY and by CUNY's ability to prepare students for useful lives, recognizing that, for many, this goal will involve only one, two, or three years of college.

Open admissions at CUNY was the sole factor responsible for increasing the college-going rate of New York City high school graduates from 57 percent in 1969 to 76 percent in 1970. Who were these new students? They were almost exclusively students whose grades fell in the bottom half of their high school graduating class. In New York City, this group is drawn primarily from poverty level families, and a high proportion are black and Puerto Rican. After open admissions, 65 percent of all New York City high school graduates with incomes of less than $3,700 were enrolled in college. In New York City, now, 67 percent of all black and Puerto Rican high school graduates are enrolled in college. Of course, the percentages for white and higher income families are higher, but the most radical improvements are among those two minority groups. Marked improvements in college-going rates occurred, between 1963 and 1970, among high school graduates with general diplomas (20 percent to 50 percent) and among vocational high school graduates (13 percent to 67 percent). During this same period, the college-going rate of high school graduates with academic diplomas remained relatively stable.[10]

The evidence clearly indicates that CUNY's enrollment expansion

9. The "Report on Special Admissions Policy" approved by the City University Faculty Senate stated, "To a significant degree, the deficits of the black and Puerto Rican students are the result of inadequate preparation in the public and high schools. . . . The inadequacies . . . are not peculiar to New York. . . . But a private university is largely free to select students from the population of all American high schools and the most prestigious colleges do just that. The City University, however, is tied to one set of high schools; it is not free to sample the secondary school universe. . . ." (New York: City University Senate, Feb. 12, 1969, pp. 1.6, 1.7).

10. This paragraph draws on Robert Birnbaum and Joseph Goldman, *The Graduates: A Follow-up Study of New York City High School Graduates of 1970* (New York: City University of New York, 1971), pp. 3, 5, 8, 9, 70–71.

since 1963, culminating in open admission in the fall of 1970, has served primarily the poor, the city's racial minorities, and students whose high school achievement was poor. These are not the students sought after by private institutions.

What is the evidence with respect to the first semester performance of CUNY's open admissions class?[11] Jaffe and Adams point out that the attrition rate remained relatively stable at CUNY between 1969 and 1970. At the very least, we may conclude that enough students benefited sufficiently from their first semester's work to continue a second semester. Analysis of attrition rates in relation to high school performance, by college, shows that the group of students who would have been admitted under pre-open admissions standards have a lower attrition rate (9.2 percent) than open admissions students (14.2 percent for "below standard" students, and 23.0 percent for students whose average high school grades were below 70 percent). This latter group did surprisingly well (three out of four students survived) when one considers that this group comprised students who passed through high school taking vocational and watered-down, "modified" courses. Data from individual college programs suggest that one of every two students entering college with reading and mathematics skills below the tenth-grade level were able to attain at least tenth-grade level skills, and 25 percent of the original group showed sufficient progress to reregister for additional compensatory work.[12] All such students registered in their second semester for some college level work. Four years' experience with the SEEK program is beginning to bear fruit. Attrition rates of SEEK students, all of whom are drawn from poverty areas, stood at 11 percent for the fall 1970 semester compared to 9 percent for students admitted under pre-open admissions standards. All of the SEEK students are drawn from among high school graduates who could not meet regular pre-open admission standards. Of course, the data at this early stage are crude and inconclusive, but clearly the debacle that detractors of open admissions predicted has not yet occurred.

11. The Jaffe-Adams paper criticizes CUNY for its failure to make data available concerning characteristics of the freshman class. These data are available in the university-sponsored Birnbaum-Goldman paper cited above. The university is now sponsoring a comprehensive study of the performance of the freshman class which, of course, will become available only as the students progress or fail to progress through college.

12. Analysis of individual reports of CUNY college presidents to the vice-chancellor of academic affairs of the City University of New York, March and April 1971 (Data on file with the vice-chancellor for academic affairs, City University of New York).

Finally, I should like to comment on the Jaffe-Adams concern for the future of private institutions, a concern we all share. All institutions of higher education have fallen upon hard times, and the plight of New York City's institutions reflect the national problem. The declines in graduate and engineering enrollments in the city are especially severe, even at tuition-free institutions.[13] In addition, private institutions in urban areas face unique urban problems which are more related to the cities' overall malaise than to open admissions. The less rigorous institutions, which draw upon a commuter group of students, have been suffering a long-term erosion in student applications[14] because the relative attractiveness of their institutions has been declining and the pool of middle income students that has been their market is also contracting. Their situation is indeed precarious, but expanded public higher education opportunity in the city is not the villain.

The number of high achievement freshmen students at City University in 1970 shows little change from the 1962 figure. In 1962, when all students needed the equivalent of about an 85 percent average for admission to the four senior colleges, 6,990 freshmen registered. In 1970, according to estimates made by Birnbaum and Goldman, 6,603 freshmen with averages of 85 percent and higher registered at all units.[15]

The university's major expansion has been among students who could not afford to attend private colleges or would have been excluded as high-risk students. However, the great increase in the 1970 open admissions class, by 16,000, at CUNY did take about 1,400 students from several New York City private institutions previously in special programs at private institutions. But, as Jaffe and Adams seem to suggest, should CUNY have prevented 14,600 students from going

13. Data for engineering schools in New York City compiled by the Commission on Independent Colleges and Universities show a decline in applications between 1970 and 1971 of 14 percent for the Cooper Union and 17 percent for the Polytechnic Institute of Brooklyn (Report No. 12, June 12, 1971). Similar declines have been reported at City College and New York University.

14. Application rates for fall 1971 fell appreciably: at Long Island University, 5.3 percent; Yeshiva University, 17 percent; Finch College, 50 percent; Wagner College, 22 percent; Academy of Aeronautics, 38 percent. On the other hand, increases of 1.2 percent were noted by both Columbia and Fordham Universities. New York University showed a decline of 9.4 percent between 1970 and 1971.

The 1971 data reflect a longer term trend indicating declining rates of increase in applications or increasing rates of decrease in applications.

15. For 1962 figures, see *Proceedings of the Board of Higher Education of the City of New York, 1962* (Secretary, Board of Higher Education, New York City), p. 663. For 1970 figures, see Birnbaum and Goldman, *The Graduates*, Table 4–13. p. 94, pp. 70–71.

to college in order to maintain enrollment at private institutions by 1,400 students?

Private higher education should be maintained and strengthened in New York State as an alternative to mass public higher education. To achieve this goal by limiting the expansion of public higher education is too high a price to pay. Rather public funds should be made available to private institutions, in ways that will permit them to flourish in their separate and distinctive identities, will encourage consolidation and restructuring of their programs where appropriate, and will support their efforts to play a meaningful role in educating students from racial minorities; but all within the context of a rational plan. The height of folly, in my judgment, would be to force private institutions to play a major role in providing mass public higher education with public support. If we take that route, they may as well join the public sector.

The Education Component in Job Requirements

JAMES M. MITCHELL

JAFFE AND ADAMS HAVE PRESENTED AN ABLE DESCRIPTION OF THE California and New York City experiments with open enrollment, and I hope they will follow it up as more data become available. The points are convincingly made that the value of open enrollment is questionable, both from the standpoint of the student and of the taxpayer.

The authors refer to fiscal viability as a major consideration. I shall make the assumption that fiscal viability is of only temporary importance, suggest that a more vital issue is being raised, and to propose a research program to help deal with that issue. As the authors point out, "At the heart of the debate . . . is the basic question of what is the goal—or are the goals—of higher education."

According to a recent article in the *London Economist*, the gross national product of the United States will double in the next twenty years, and in 1990 will be $2 trillion. Whether this estimate is correct or not, I am assuming that our expanding economy, even correcting for inflation, will make open enrollment fiscally viable in the foreseeable future. If more than four out of five parents continue to want their children to attend college, and if the economy can support such an expenditure out of the GNP, the need for a great increase in personnel research is clearly indicated.

As a personnel psychologist, I suggest that, if open enrollment is economically possible in the future, we need to know much more than we now do about the maximum and minimum education requirements for all major occupations in this country. Equally important, both for society and the individual, we should know much more about certain other factors that have received some attention in the past but still remain largely unknown: the early identification of artistic and scientific talent, successful occupational guidance, the best teaching methods, the causes of mental illness and health, the prevention of criminal behavior, and—of greatest relevance here—the most desirable kind of higher education for a society that allows its citizens an increasing amount of leisure time.

I shall attempt here only a brief exploration of one of the "optimum qualifications" for employment. Observation and possibly experience have taught that the university graduate who is placed in a job requiring no more than an eighth-grade education will not enjoy his work. Ivar Berg's *Education and Jobs: The Great Training Robbery* cites many examples of personnel policies that have caused such misplacements of the products of our higher educational machinery.[1]

One small and inexpensive research undertaking with which I am familiar can serve as an example. Some years ago, during an economic recession, an organization that had recently installed "a machine accounting system" was hiring a large number of punch-card operators. The number of applicants, many of them university graduates, far exceeded the supply. Selections were made primarily on the basis of interviews.

It soon became apparent that some of the employees were much more productive in their card-punching than others. Productivity was compared with scores on a widely used clerical aptitude test (a thinly disguised test of general intelligence) and with scores on a simple reaction time test. It was clearly demonstrated that those who scored high on the clerical test and low on the reaction test were not as productive as those who did poorly on the clerical test but scored high on the reaction test. As a result, selection standards for future use were set at a maximum score on the clerical test, above which no one would be hired. According to a report by the supervisor to the personnel office, productivity gradually increased, and so did morale. (A practical question arises in setting a maximum test score: if applicants are aware of the cut-off point, they may do less than their best. This is another issue, however, and it is manageable.)

1. New York: Praeger, 1970.

Even though this small piece of research was easy to conduct and today could be done with far greater precision for many occupations, too little research of this kind is being carried on. Human resources are harder to manage than physical resources, and poor management of people is enormously costly to society as well as to the individual. A national research program, committing the necessary resources to give us badly needed facts about employment and guidance policies, should be undertaken now. Among other things, such research could determine which occupations that now call for college graduation do not really require it for satisfactory performance, and the information would help inform the shaping of policy for higher education. A program or programs could be sponsored by major employers—both public and private, by employer associations, by unions, by associations of personnel officers. University psychologists should be asked to cooperate.

Much more scientific study is needed also of the psychic income requirements of all employees, for pay is only one reward derived from work. An affluent society can make it possible for many persons who are not capable of staying in college, under an open enrollment plan, to find rewarding employment without higher education. Then the issue raised by the Jaffe-Adams paper about a choice between quantity, in open enrollment, and top quality will be easier to settle.

In the future, after optimum requirements are determined for most jobs, open enrollment may make it possible for most Americans "to reach their highest potential."

JEROME KARABEL

Perspectives on Open Admissions

*That there should one man die ignorant who
had the capacity to learn, this I call a tragedy.*
Thomas Carlyle

THE DEBATE OVER OPEN ADMISSIONS—THE PROVISION OF A PLACE
in college for all high school graduates—has been among the most
passionate in recent years. Clark Kerr, chairman of the Carnegie Commission on Higher Education, has called it the most important single
development in higher education.[1] Although the culmination of a
long-term trend, open admissions challenges some bedrock assumptions
about the nature and purpose of higher education and has, in consequence, aroused considerable opposition and hostility in some quarters. Moreover, its connection with the struggles for minority rights
and for an end to poverty has added to its controversiality. For these
reasons, the rationale for and potential effects of open admissions
merit careful examination.

The movement toward equal opportunity in American higher education dates back to the Morrill Act of 1862, which encouraged the
establishment of land-grant colleges: institutions designed to emphasize
vocational training and community service. From a tiny number of
colonial colleges modeled after elitist European institutions, American
higher education has evolved into the largest and most accessible system in the world. It expanded at a rapid rate; between 1900 and 1970,
the proportion of 18–21-year-olds attending college rose from 4 percent
to 40 percent.[2] Yet, for all its massiveness, the present system of higher
education virtually excludes some major groups in American society.
Prominent among these are racial and ethnic minorities: blacks,

1. Kerr, "Should Everybody Be Able to Go to College?" Address at the First
Interim Session, University of Hawaii, January 1970, p. 5.
2. Carnegie Commission on Higher Education, *A Chance to Learn* (New York:
McGraw-Hill Book Co., 1970), p. 2.

Puerto Ricans, Chicanos, and American Indians. But though public attention has focused on minority groups, disadvantaged whites have always constituted the majority of those excluded.

Some recent studies indicate the extent to which socioeconomic status (SES) is correlated with access to college. According to 1969 census figures, families with incomes of over $15,000 were almost four times more likely to send their children to college than families with incomes of under $3,000. Similarly, Etzioni and Milner report that, even among young people who graduated from high school, children of college graduates were about four times as likely to enter college as children whose fathers' education was limited to grade school or less.[3]

The effects of SES on access to college are particularly striking if one looks at groups of young people whose measured talent is similar. Using Project Talent data, Jencks and Riesman found that, when ability was taken into account, a child of the highest socioeconomic quintile was much more likely to attend college than a child of the lowest socioeconomic quintile (Table 1). A study of Wisconsin high school graduates revealed differences of equal or greater magnitude: Among boys in the highest ability quartile, for example, only 52 percent of low SES graduates, as compared with 90 percent of high SES

TABLE 1: *Percentage of High School Graduates Entering College Immediately, by Academic Aptitude, Socioeconomic Status, and Sex, 1960*

Academic Aptitude	Socioeconomic Status					
	Low	Lower-Middle	Middle	Upper-Middle	High	All
Men						
Low.............	10	13	15	25	40	14
Lower-middle......	14	23	30	35	57	27
Middle...........	30	35	46	54	67	46
Upper-middle......	44	51	59	69	83	63
Upper...........	69	73	81	86	91	85
All..............	24	40	53	65	81	49
Women						
Low.............	9	9	10	16	41	11
Lower-middle......	9	10	16	24	54	18
Middle...........	12	18	25	40	63	30
Upper-middle......	24	35	41	58	78	49
Upper...........	52	61	66	80	90	76
All..............	15	24	32	51	75	35

Source: Christopher Jencks and David Riesman, *The Academic Revolution* (Garden City, N.Y.: Doubleday, 1968), p. 103.

3. Amitai Etzioni and Murray Milner, *Higher Education in an Active Society: A Policy Study* (Washington: Bureau of Social Science Research, 1970), p. 15.

graduates, went to college (Table 2). For girls, the differences were even greater.

TABLE 2: *Percentage of Wisconsin High School Graduates Who Attend College, by Socioeconomic Status, Intelligence, and Sex*

Socioeconomic Status	Intelligence Levels				Total
	Low	Lower-Middle	Upper-Middle	High	
Men............(N	= 1,070) (N	= 1,100) (N	= 1,083) (N	= 1,133) (N	= 4,386)
Low..........	6.3	16.5	28.0	52.4	20.5
Lower-middle..	11.7	27.2	42.6	58.8	33.8
Upper-middle..	18.3	34.3	51.3	72.0	44.6
High..........	38.8	60.8	73.2	90.7	73.4
Total.......	15.0	33.5	51.0	73.8	43.7
Women.........(N	= 1,122) (N	= 1,205) (N	= 1,183) (N	= 1,111) (N	= 4,621)
Low..........	3.7	6.3	8.9	27.5	8.5
Lower-middle..	9.3	20.2	24.1	36.7	21.2
Upper-middle..	16.0	25.6	31.0	48.1	30.5
High..........	33.3	44.4	67.0	76.4	62.6
Total.......	11.4	22.5	34.7	54.9	30.7

Source: William H. Sewell and Vimal P. Shah, "Socioeconomic Status, Intelligence, and the Attainment of Higher Education," *Sociology of Education*, Winter 1967, p. 13.

These data indicate that the net effect of traditional admissions standards is to provide the greatest opportunity to those students who are the most economically and socially advantaged. Many poor students, to be sure, find their way to college, but the odds clearly favor the more affluent. Whatever the reasons for exclusion, their effects are obvious: the present educational system perpetuates existing differences between rich and poor.

Sensing this contradiction between democratic ideology and social reality, colleges and universities are recruiting talented members of disadvantaged groups. Some students, particularly blacks, have benefited from these efforts, but as long as the merit criteria of high school grades and aptitude test scores are applied, many low SES students, both black and white, will be shut out from the system of higher education. Thus, the harsh choice faced by the American educational community is either to continue excluding these groups or to abandon traditional admissions standards. One approach taken by institutions that follow the latter course is the adoption of open admissions.

CHALLENGES TO TRADITIONAL ASSUMPTIONS

Open admissions challenges some of the most fundamental assumptions about the role of the university. Traditionally, universities have viewed themselves as most essentially concerned with transmitting culture from generation to generation and with discovering new truths about man and the universe. According to this conception, teaching and research—carried on by devoted scholars and students sheltered from the outside world—are the core functions of the university. This model is useful as long as it is recognized as a normative preference rather than an empirical description. Not that teaching and research do not go on today in American colleges and universities; they do and, indeed, are often of the highest quality. But these activities are not to be confused with the prime *social* function of an institution which, as Bell and Kristol observe, "has gained a quasi-monopoly in determining the future stratification system of society."[4]

This function was noted by Talcott Parsons, who maintains that the educational system has become "the principal channel of selection . . . in an increasingly differentiated . . . society."[5] The university is the prime societal mechanism for determining who is to occupy the top and upper-middle levels of the stratification system. At stake, then, in who is given access to the university is nothing less than the distribution of privilege in contemporary America.

Whether the university should have assumed this allocative function is a matter of debate. Nathan Glazer, for example, argues that, in so doing, it has overstepped its proper bounds:

> Perhaps it is primarily because the colleges and universities have taken over so critical a role in the career of tens of millions of people that [our] ability to maintain the primacy of tested academic achievements as a means of distributing rewards is disintegrating. I believe that if colleges and universities remain, as they have become, the major means by which a rough status is distributed among men, they cannot maintain the primacy of tested academic ability, except in those areas where they have a strong case that tested academic talents and skills are necessary for further advancement—particularly in the sciences. Otherwise, why, in a time of social revolution, would and should they be allowed to apply *their* standards for selection? These are standards which may be suited for further school work, but are only doubtfully suited for determining the distribution of status and power in society.[6]

That academics often lose sight of the university's allocative function is indicated in a recent article by Martin Trow. Discussing the

4. Daniel Bell and Irving Kristol, *Confrontation* (New York: Basic Books, 1969), p. ix.
5. Parsons, "The School as Social System," *Socialization and Schools*, Reprint Series No. 1, compiled from the *Harvard Educational Review*, 1968, p. 90.
6. Glazer, "Are Academic Standards Obsolete?" *Change*, November-December 1970, p. 44.

role of the university in American society, he distinguishes between the autonomous and the popular functions of higher education. The former are defined by the university itself, whereas the latter are taken on in response to external needs and demands. According to this scheme, the autonomous functions of the university are the transmission of high culture, the creation of new knowledge, and the training of elite groups. In contrast, its popular functions are the provision of places in higher education for as many students as possible and the provision of useful knowledge and service.[7]

Quite apart from his peculiar inclusion of elite training in the category of autonomous university functions, Trow ignores the fact that the university has become one of the principal mechanisms for distributing rewards in American society. He focuses on the autonomous functions of the university and the alleged threats to them. Yet universities are far from autonomous: their role in perpetuating the class structure is unmistakable. The transmission and discovery of knowledge may be the essence of the university in some philosophical sense, but, in the present society, this emphasis serves to obfuscate the real issue: the distribution of privilege.

In addition to its allocative function, the university, Samuel Bowles suggests, plays a critical role in the legitimation process. Having been given the illusion that equal educational opportunity exists, the successful see themselves—and are seen—as the deserving. The other side of the coin, of course, is that the poor tend to blame themselves rather than the system for their "failure." The result of this internalization process, Bowles asserts, is that the "successful completion of higher education has come to confer a modern form of 'right to rule' at least as persuasive and politically invulnerable as any of its divine, aristocratic, or plutocratic predecessors."[8]

If one recognizes that the contemporary educational system has the dual functions of allocation and legitimation, one of higher education's cherished images is lost: that of the university as a scholarly sanctuary from the pressures and conflicts of the external world. Clearly, if the modern university conferred no benefits on anyone and consisted solely of people so interested in the discovery and transmission of knowledge that they were willing to take a vow of poverty to pursue their scholarly interests, there would be little clamor for universal access. But this is simply not the case, and higher education

7. Trow, "Reflections on the Transition from Mass to Universal Higher Education," *Daedalus*, Winter 1970, pp. 1–42.
8. Bowles, "Contradictions in U.S. Higher Education" (MS, Harvard University, 1971).

cannot return to this somewhat fanciful model. Universities are irrevocably committed to the business of conferring rewards and, once this fact is recognized, their exclusionary stance, based on an idealized image, becomes less defensible.

One assumption about higher education challenged by open admissions, then, is that the college of today is primarily engaged in the pursuit and dissemination of pure knowledge. In addition to pointing out the class function of higher education, advocates of open admissions have controverted the assumption that a college education is of greatest benefit to students who, through aptitude test scores and grades, have already demonstrated considerable academic talent. Traditionally, universities have considered it their mission to educate the academic (or social) elite of each generation. The masses, whatever their educational needs, have generally been left to look out for themselves.

Admissions officers, in their quest for meritocratic selection procedures, have developed elaborate methods of determining who is "college material." Using the twin criteria of high school grades and scores on standardized tests, they are able to predict, with some degree of accuracy, who is likely to do well at their institutions. But they are still far from knowing who is likely to get the most from a college education. Instead, they function much as handicappers do; they are more interested in predicting performance than in improving it.[9]

THE CONCEPT OF "VALUE ADDED"

The philosophy underlying open admissions emphasizes not picking winners but rather maximizing the educational growth of the student, whatever his level at entrance. The critical variable is the value added by college attendance; a truly successful institution would change a student's performance level rather than ensure its own prestige by a combination of stringent selection procedures and subsequent elimination of the lowest performers. Usually measured in terms of cognitive achievement, "value added" can also apply to the noncognitive growth that occurs among college students. Trent and Medsker, in a study of 10,000 high school graduates, found that "college seems to foster, or at least facilitate, the growth of autonomy and intellectual disposition, whereas early employment and marriage seem to retard and even suppress development of these traits."[10]

9. Alexander W. Astin, "Folklore of Selectivity," *Saturday Review*, Dec. 20, 1969, p. 69.
10. James W. Trent and Leland L. Medsker, *Beyond High School* (San Francisco: Jossey-Bass, Inc., 1968), p. 268.

A comprehensive review of the literature on college impact concludes that "declining authoritarianism, dogmatism, and prejudice, together with decreasingly conservative attitudes toward public issues and growing sensitivity to aesthetic experiences, are particularly prominent forms of change—as inferred from freshmen-senior differences."[11] Keniston and Gerzon, in a discussion of the human and social benefits of higher education, suggest that college tends to include not mere attitude changes, but "developmental changes in personality structure and functioning."[12] Higher education, and especially "critical" higher education, enables men and women to avoid foreclosing their psychological development "before they reach the levels of autonomy, complexity, differentiation, and integration of which they are capable."[13]

To summarize: Value added refers to attitude changes and to developmental changes in personality structure, as well as to cognitive growth. Selectivity works at crosscurrents with the concept of value added; indeed, it may well exclude precisely those students who would benefit most from further education. That an open admissions policy enables the institution to foster growth in the student rather than to serve as a talent scout for business and industry is considered by its advocates to be one of its main strengths.

When admissions is approached from the perspective of value added rather than viewed as a process designed to identify those who have already proved themselves able, the use of traditional meritocratic criteria becomes difficult to justify. Selectivity grows out of the root assumption—and one that may well be inimical to democratic ideals—that a prime function of the university is to cultivate an elite. Its corollaries are that societal progress depends upon the efforts of the elite and that the elite are most capable of rule. Sir Eric Ashby, former vice-chancellor of Cambridge University and member of the Carnegie Commission, makes these assumptions explicit: "All civilized countries . . . depend upon a thin clear stream of excellence to provide new ideas, new techniques, and the statesmanlike treatment of complex social and political problems. Without the renewal of this excellence, a nation can drop to mediocrity in a generation. . . . The highly gifted student . . . needs to be treated as an elite."[14]

Moreover, the elitist view assumes that contact between the elite and the masses is relatively unimportant; by its very nature, elitism precludes a social mix in higher education. Indeed, many proponents

11. Kenneth A. Feldman and Theodore M. Newcomb, *The Impact of College on Students* (San Francisco: Jossey-Bass, Inc., 1969), 1:326.
12. See p. 64 of the present volume.
13. Ibid., p. 56.
14. Ashby, *Any Person, Any Study* (New York: McGraw-Hill Book Co., 1971), p. 101.

of the elitist view think that a campus where students ranging widely in ability come together may constitute an unwholesome climate for the elite; the implication is that their progress will be impeded by the presence of the less academically adept.

The argument that institutional selectivity makes a critical contribution to the quality of education that talented students receive is one of those rare assertions in the open admissions controversy which is subject to empirical investigation. Alexander Astin, in two longitudinal studies, sought to discover how an institution's selectivity affects student achievement. In the first, a study of 265 institutions, he found that the probability of a student's obtaining a Ph.D. was unrelated to the selectivity of the undergraduate institution he had attended. Although elite private men's colleges produced a disproportionate number of graduates who went on to get the doctorate, their high output could have been predicted from the quality of their freshman classes; in fact, the relationship, where one existed, was slightly negative: students of equal ability at less selective institutions were somewhat more likely to obtain a Ph.D.[15] The second study concluded that undergraduate achievement, as measured by scores on the area tests of the Graduate Record Examination, was also unaffected by the institution's selectivity. Moreover, the bright student did not benefit more than the average student from being exposed to a "high quality" institution as indicated by such conventional measures as proportion of Ph.D.'s on the faculty, Scholastic Aptitude Test (SAT) scores of entering freshmen, and size of the library.[16]

This evidence, though by no means definitive, does indicate that a gifted student at an unselective institution does not mysteriously lose his talents. Upon reflection, the success of the academically able in almost any institutional setting should not be too surprising; the bright have a capacity for taking care of their own education. Further, gifted students tend naturally to associate with each other and with the faculty.

Finally, even if these considerations are ignored, one must conclude that open admissions—in its present form—poses little threat to the elite. As long as the bulk of open admissions students are channeled into community colleges, and highly selective admissions policies are maintained at a few prestigious four-year colleges and universities, the elite and the great majority of the population will continue to be segregated. (This point is discussed later in a different context.)

15. Astin, "'Productivity' of Undergraduate Institutions," *Science*, April 13, 1962, pp. 129–35.

16. Astin, "Undergraduate Achievement and Institutional 'Excellence,'" *Science*, Aug. 16, 1968, pp. 661–68.

TESTS AS INSTRUMENTS OF DISCRIMINATION AND PREDICTION

Another belief upon which the open admissions movement casts doubt is that tests are a fair and efficient way of determining who is to get a higher education. Paradoxically, the standardized test, now the target of so much criticism, was once the darling of liberals and egalitarians. Designed as objective measures of academic aptitude and achievement, these tests played a vital role in reducing discrimination and in opening the gates of higher education to several ethnic groups, especially Jews and Orientals. But as time went on, it became clear that these tests—whatever their contribution to "meritocracy"—resulted in blacks and the poor being shut out.

The standardized test is frequently attacked on the grounds that, being culture-bound, it discriminates against blacks by overlooking their true potential. For example, Whitney Young says, "it has been clearly demonstrated that now traditional terms of admissions predict little or nothing about what a minority student will do in college."[17] In short, he asserts that national tests predict achievement only for white and not for black students. Empirical investigations, however, suggest that these tests predict just as well for blacks as for whites.[18]

But this is not to say that tests provide equal opportunities for minorities; the issue is much more complex. In discussing the problem of bias, Robert M. O'Neill, a lawyer, makes a useful conceptual distinction between *discrimination*, the failure to apply the same standards to different groups, and *exclusion*, the process of disproportionately denying access to specific groups.[19] Whether or not one chooses to call these tests discriminatory, one cannot deny that they have the net effect of being exclusionary. In view of the magnitude of this exclusion (see Tables 1 and 2), it is not surprising that such fine conceptual distinctions are often lost on proponents of open admissions.

Although tests predict academic performance, as measured by college grade point average (GPA), as well for blacks as for whites, the simple fact is that measures such as the SAT's are subject to a considerable margin of error for individuals in all groups. Correlations between aptitude tests and freshman GPA are, at best, modest: .35 and

17. Young, "Response to Spiro T. Agnew on College Admissions," *College Board Review*, Summer 1970, p. 25.

18. Julian Stanley, "Predicting College Success of the Educationally Disadvantaged," *Science*, Feb. 19, 1971, pp. 640–47; Alexander W. Astin, "Racial Considerations in Admissions," in *The Campus and the Racial Crisis*, ed. David C. Nichols and Olive Mills (Washington: American Council on Education, 1970), pp. 113–41.

19. O'Neill, "Preferential Admissions: Equalizing the Access of Minority Groups to Higher Education," *Yale Law Review*, March 1971, pp. 699–767.

.43, respectively, for men and women.[20] High school grades predict freshman GPA with considerably more accuracy: correlations are .51 for men and .52 for women (Table 3). Even when high school grades, aptitude test scores, and college selectivity level are combined, and when errors of measurement in these predictors are corrected for, the correlation will increase to .7 at most. Another way of expressing the modest relation between standard admissions criteria and freshman GPA is through the variance; conventional predictive measures account for less than half of the variance among freshman grades.

Standard admissions measures are imperfect not only as predictive mechanisms but also as indicators of what a student *learns* in college. Although they give a rough estimate of probable freshman grades, grades themselves do not measure value added but simply indicate a student's performance relative to the performance of other students at some point in time. A recent longitudinal study carried out at the University of Georgia suggests that students who were receiving D's or failing grades might, in fact, have been learning as much or more than students with higher grades.[21] The implications are far-ranging; it seems likely that institutions are flunking out or altogether excluding many thousands of students who would profit significantly from further education.

Conventional measures are even less effective in predicting attrition than in predicting freshman GPA. One study found that high school grades correlated only −.18 and −.16 for men and women, respectively, with dropping out before the sophomore year. Aptitude test scores were no better: −.18 and −.17 for men and women, respec-

TABLE 3: *Correlations between Freshman GPA and Various Combinations of Predictors*

Predictor	Correlation with Freshman GPA	
	Men	Women
1. High school grades...........	.51	.52
2. (1) + aptitude test scores.....	.52	.55
3. (2) + college selectivity.......	.54	.58
4. (3) + 13 personal characteristics............	.59	.61

Source: Alexander W. Astin, *Predicting Academic Performance in College* (New York: Free Press, 1971).

20. Astin, "Racial Considerations in Admissions," p. 117.
21. John Harris, "Gain Scores on the CLEP—General Examinations and an Overview of Research," Paper presented at the annual meeting of the American Educational Research Association, Minneapolis, March 1970.

tively.[22] Bruce Eckland, in a longitudinal study of University of Illinois students, found that one out of three who were in the bottom half of their high school class in ability managed to graduate from college.[23] Yet many of these students are precisely the ones who would be excluded by standard admissions criteria.

Even if conventional measures were infallible predictors, the importance of GPA itself would remain questionable. That college grades may have little relevance to achievement outside the academic world is suggested by Donald Hoyt's comprehensive review of the literature on this topic, which concludes that "college grades have no more than a very modest correlation with adult success, no matter how defined."[24] Ivar Berg, after studying actual job performance in a variety of occupational settings, found that educational attainment had little to do with competence on the job.[25] Neither GPA nor educational attainment as such seems to have more than limited applicability to the occupational world.

In a sense, the attack on tests may be misdirected; perhaps critics of traditional college admissions standards should be attacking not the tests themselves but rather the criterion against which the tests are validated: college grades. The tests, after all, are only intended to predict what a student is likely to do within the narrow confines of higher education. B. Alden Thresher, former director of admissions at Massachusetts Institute of Technology, describes the consequences of this emphasis on prediction: "We get a tight, closed circle of prediction (using school marks or tests or both) followed by selection, based on prediction, followed by validation against grade-point averages, from which new prediction equations are generated, and the closed circle continues. We forget that the whole evaluation is based on a unidimensional scale of marks and test scores, which ignores the rich variety of human talent."[26]

The critical point here is that tests reinforce the present structure and values of higher education to the point of excluding alternatives. This is fine if one believes that the present system is sufficiently broad and flexible to provide options for all who might benefit from further

22. Astin, "Racial Considerations in Admissions," p. 121.
23. Eckland, "Academic Ability, Higher Education, and Occupational Mobility," *American Sociological Review*, October 1965, p. 745.
24. Hoyt, *The Relationship Between College Grades and Adult Achievement: A Review of the Literature* (Iowa City: American College Testing Program, September 1965), p. 45.
25. Berg, *Education and Jobs: The Great Training Robbery* (New York: Praeger, 1970).
26. Thresher, "Frozen Assumptions in Admissions," *College Admissions Policies for the 1970s* (New York: College Entrance Examination Board, 1968), p. 13.

education, that it is not in need of fundamental reform. But if one is of the opinion that the university, especially since it has taken upon itself the function of distributing privilege, must develop new roads to excellence and must cultivate talents outside the conventional academic mold, then one can be only disturbed by the closed circle of grades, tests, and prediction.

In short, these considerations suggest that standard measures of scholastic aptitude or academic achievement may be an inappropriate means of determining who should enter college. Test scores and high school grades are subject to a large margin of error in predicting GPA, are even less accurate in predicting dropouts, and may have almost no validity in predicting educational growth. Moreover, the pertinence of GPA to actual job performance is highly dubious. Finally, the whole circle of tests and grades ignores other critical human capacities.

Effects on Academic Standards and Value of the Diploma

"But what will happen to academic standards if we admit just anyone to college?" ask critics of open admissions. The banner of academic standards has led the main line of attack against open admissions. According to those who raise this objection, abolishing selectivity in admissions will result in debasing the level of instruction in American higher education; paradoxically, "quality" seems to reside less in factors internal to the educational process than in the selective exclusion of people from this process.

At the outset, it should be noted that open admissions is nothing new for the rich. The wealthy student has always been able to get into college somewhere. Under discussion is not the entrance into higher education of ability groups hitherto unrepresented in American colleges and universities, but rather a change in their relative proportion. Secondary school students from the bottom ability quartile have long been going to college; their admission ticket was their ability to pay the price.[27]

Part of the confusion over academic standards results from a failure to distinguish between a student's performance level at the point of entry and his level at graduation. But academic standards are more appropriately linked "to the kind of degree a university awards, not to the batting average of its dean of admissions."[28] Otherwise, the uni-

27. William W. Turnbull, "Dimensions of Quality in Higher Education," in *Higher Education for Everybody?* ed. W. Todd Furniss (Washington: American Council on Education, 1971), pp. 126–36.

28. Timothy Healy, "Will Everyman Destroy the University?" *Saturday Review,* Dec. 20, 1969, p. 55.

versity becomes a kind of funnel through which both the gifted and the average flow, often experiencing little educational growth along the way. The highly selective college ensures its own "success"—its production of distinguished graduates—if it accepts only those whose talents have already been demonstrated. But can the university take the credit when many of its students were already performing at or near graduation level when they entered?

The crucial question, then, becomes whether those institutions willing to accept students whose success is not ensured can maintain their current academic standards. Failure to raise sufficiently the performance levels of underprepared students can result in one of two outcomes: a large dropout (or flunkout) ratio or a "second-rate" degree. Critics of universal access are concerned about both possibilities, but its advocates are convinced that neither need happen.

The City University of New York (CUNY), the largest and most prestigious university so far to have adopted open admissions, is engaged in a massive effort to maintain standards while simultaneously keeping the open door from becoming a revolving door. It has adopted expanded counseling, extensive remediation, new pedagogical techniques, more time for the attainment of a degree, and increased flexibility in curricular offerings. Clearly, just to accept any student, regardless of academic preparation, is insufficient if expanded educational opportunity is to be genuine rather than token. If everyone is to be brought up to the current acceptable level of performance, increased funding and intensive effort are also required. Some students may take a considerably longer time than others to attain such a level, but there is no reason to believe that academic standards need be sacrificed.

A more likely possibility is that many students will not graduate. They will either flunk out or drop out because of insupportable academic pressures and resultant discouragement. This issue must be faced squarely. At the same time, some perspective on the question of dropping out is needed. According to the Newman Report, 30–40 percent of students at large state universities and 50–65 percent of students at state colleges never graduate.[29] Although almost all these institutions exercise at least some degree of selectivity, large numbers of students must still be considered dropouts. Open admissions, then, is by no means likely to be the only, or even a major, cause of the attrition problem.

The proportion of open admissions enrollees who graduate from CUNY will be one test of the effectiveness of the program. But it is

29. U.S. Department of Health, Education, and Welfare, *Report on Higher Education* (Washington: Government Printing Office, 1971), p. 2.

not the only test; indeed, how can one determine what proportion constitutes a success (10 percent, 25 percent, 50 percent)? The dropout issue is obviously important, but it is not susceptible to sloganeering or to neat mathematical formulas. Those who support open admissions consider that American society can ill afford to lose the talents of thousands of students capable of attaining a degree but at present shut out from the system of higher education.

Both evidence and common sense, then, indicate that nothing inherent in open admissions will bring about a lowering of academic standards. Since the admissions process need not dictate standards for graduation, anxieties about bargain-basement diplomas seem unfounded. William Birenbaum remarks that open admissions has deflected attention from the quality of those admitted to the quality of those turned out.[30] A possible result of this change in focus may be not only the maintenance of present standards but also the salvaging of untold numbers of students previously denied a chance at a college education.

Assuming that academic standards are maintained, it is still possible that open admissions will have an adverse effect on the value of a college degree. Diplomas may continue to represent the same level of educational attainment as in the past, but more of them will be in circulation. Inevitably, this will have some effect on the job market.

The standard argument about open admissions and degree devaluation is based on the assumption that universal access will lower graduation standards. As pointed out previously, such a situation is by no means a foregone conclusion. A more sophisticated version of the devaluation argument is that more degrees, even holding quality constant, will mean that a diploma is worth less. The basic idea is that the supply of degrees will outrun the demand for highly trained manpower. Some observers assert that, by 1975, there will be 3 million–4 million college graduates beyond the number that can be absorbed by the types of jobs which required a diploma in 1960.[31]

No one denies that the future economy will need people with generally higher educational attainment. Professional, technical, and kindred workers increased from 10.8 percent of the labor force in 1957 to 14.5 percent in 1969.[32] Estimates tell us, for example, that New York City, increasingly a white-collar metropolis, will lose a quarter of a

30. Birenbaum, "The More We Change the Worse We Get," *Social Policy*, May-June 1971, pp. 10–13.
31. Kerr, "Should Everybody Be Able to Go to College?" p. 43.
32. Bureau of the Census, *Statistical Abstract of the United States* (Washington: Government Printing Office, 1970), p. 226.

million manufacturing jobs by 1980.[33] What *is* in dispute, however, is whether a college diploma will still virtually guarantee a good job. Manpower expert John K. Folger thinks not and suggests that many degree-holders will have to enter clerical or white-collar service jobs.[34]

Not only is such speculation highly tentative, but also it fails to take into account that the number of available good jobs is, in part, an act of political will. As an alternative merely to filling slots in the private economy, it might be possible to create hundreds of thousands of useful and rewarding jobs requiring a high level of skill: in the health fields, social services, environmental science, and education. If it indeed comes to pass that college graduates are unable to find worthwhile jobs, the reason will be not that there is no need for highly trained people but that our economy is not geared to accommodate them. In short, the problem of an oversupply of trained manpower results, in part, from a failure to distinguish market needs from social needs.[35]

INFLUENCE ON POLITICAL VALUES AND SOCIAL STRUCTURE

Those concerned about degree devaluation are worried about far more than an excess of highly educated people. Logan Wilson, president emeritus of the American Council on Education, expresses this concern when he observes that "the mounting frustration of college and university graduates . . . causes the number of malcontents in society to multiply."[36] Edmund K. Faltermayer, referring not to graduates but to dropouts, is even more explicit: "The grave danger, of course, is that many of the marginal students will wash out, exiting from the system more embittered than if they had never entered."[37]

It is, indeed, a real possibility that an educational system unable to fulfill its promise will create vast numbers of discontented, embittered people. By a combination of eliminating some students and of failing to deliver the expected rewards to those who graduate, the system of higher education may inadvertently bring into being vast numbers of people who question the foundations of American society. Whether or not one welcomes such a possibility depends on one's political and social values.

33. Healy, "Will Everyman Destroy the University?" p. 68.
34. Folger, "Student Pressures and Manpower Needs," in *Higher Education for Everybody?* ed. W. Todd Furniss, pp. 109–11.
35. Robert Paul Wolff, *The Ideal of the University* (Boston: Beacon Press, 1969).
36. Wilson, "Alternatives to College for Everybody," in *Higher Education for Everybody?* ed. W. Todd Furniss, p. 170.
37. Faltermayer, "Let's Break the Go-To-College Lockstep," *Fortune*, November 1970, p. 101.

Even if dropouts continue to internalize their failure and graduates are able to obtain desirable jobs, open admissions is still likely to have a significant political impact. In general, college attendance has a liberalizing effect on attitudes, particularly with respect to noneconomic issues such as foreign policy, race, and civil liberties.[38] For instance, better-educated people would probably be more critical of authoritarian job environments and would demand a greater voice in management. A reversal of the tendency to shape people to jobs may also grow out of expanded educational opportunity.[39]

Although hailed as a "poverty interrupter"[40] and as a means of achieving equal educational opportunity, open admissions is likely to have no more than a light impact on the American social structure. Education has been expanding for a long time in this country, but the evidence indicates that it has not significantly increased social mobility or equality.[41] Open admissions may be the next step in the long history of raising general educational attainment while failing to narrow relative differences. There is, however, some reason to think that open admissions may modify what has until now been a relatively static structure of opportunity.

However dramatic the effort made to give disadvantaged groups a chance at a college education, open admissions is not likely to provide full equality of opportunity. Since it is generally limited to high school graduates, it denies opportunity to those who never complete high school, a sizable proportion of the population. In 1969, for example, 21.7 percent of all people between the ages of twenty and twenty-four did not have a high school diploma.[42] In addition, open admissions does not generally affect those adults who failed to enter college immediately after high school graduation or who dropped out of college before finishing. Moreover, this kind of barrier is only one of several. Richard Ferrin, in a study of access to higher education, has identified three other major barriers: financial, motivational, and geographical. Together, these obstacles make equal opportunity a still distant dream.[43]

The financial barrier consists not only of tuition (which is often low) and incidentals but also of forgone income. Many poor people simply cannot afford to be other than fully self-supporting. The mo-

38. Etzioni and Milner, *Higher Education in an Active Society.*
39. Kerr, "Should Everybody Be Able to Go to College?"
40. Healy, "Will Everyman Destroy the University?" p. 69.
41. Etzioni and Milner, *Higher Education in an Active Society.*
42. Bureau of the Census, *Statistical Abstract*, p. 111.
43. *Barriers to Universal Higher Education* (Palo Alto, Calif.: College Entrance Examination Board, 1970).

tivational barrier is more subtle, but no less real: many poor and minority youth lack the parental and peer group encouragement so critical to college aspirations. The geographical barrier is physical and psychological: the excluded are often far removed from a college campus, both literally and figuratively.

Nonetheless, it is undeniable that the poor have been making some gains, particularly with respect to access to higher education. Until recent years, the middle class was the prime beneficiary of the expanding system of higher education.[44] In view of the welfare state's tendency, noted many years ago by T. H. Marshall, to confer a disproportionate share of its benefits on the middle class,[45] this is hardly surprising. But in recent years, the trend seems to have been reversed: the bottom income quartile showed a rate of increase in college attendance of 100 percent between 1959 and 1966, compared with a 9 percent increase for the top income quartile.[46] With almost all the children of wealthy families who wish to attend college already enrolled, the bulk of the new enrollment necessarily comes from the poorer groups. In view of this fact and in view of the increasing role that education plays in allocating rewards,[47] a sudden halt to the expansion of higher education would seem designed to limit opportunities for the poor.

Even if universal access were to become a reality, however, class differences would still be perpetuated. As the system of higher education becomes larger, position *within* the pecking order of colleges and universities takes on increasing importance. In this way open admissions—generally viewed as a great egalitarian measure—reproduces the very class divisions that many had hoped it would overcome. In general, open admissions students tend to enroll in community colleges, the least expensive and least prestigious institutions of higher education. Only 15–30 percent of community college entrants eventually graduate from a four-year college.[48]

As the net result of this pattern, a stratification system has developed within higher education almost exactly parallel to the class and racial divisions of American society. Almost half of all black students attend predominantly black colleges, institutions generally near the

44. Jencks and Riesman, *The Academic Revolution.*
45. Marshall, *Class, Citizenship, and Social Development* (Garden City, N.Y.: Anchor Books, 1965).
46. K. Patricia Cross, "Alternate Paths to Excellence," Position paper prepared for the White House Conference on Youth, Washington, 1971, p. 2.
47. Peter M. Blau and Otis D. Duncan, *The American Occupational Structure* (New York: John Wiley & Sons, 1967).
48. Department of Health, Education, and Welfare, *Report on Higher Education,* p. 2.

bottom of the prestige hierarchy colleges and universities.[49] Class differences are also salient in the various tracks of higher education. Among public institutions in 1970, the proportions of entering freshmen coming from families with annual incomes of less than $10,000 were 51 percent at two-year colleges, 41 percent at four-year colleges, and 26 percent at universities.[50] These racial and class differences correspond to differences in the potential earning power of graduates from each of these types of institutions. Thus, even though poor and minority youth are beginning to benefit from the expansion of higher education, the institutional structure is such that relative differences among social classes will probably be maintained.

Perhaps this picture is too bleak, however. Despite the pecking order within higher education and the difficulty in reaching the most depressed sectors of society, there is reason to believe that open admissions may have some effect on inequality and on inequality of opportunity. The expansion of higher education will soon reach its upper limits; a situation where everyone will attend a graduate or professional school is unlikely. As the process of escalation halts and access to college becomes virtually universal, relative differences in educational attainment may diminish. Consequently, rewards may be distributed in an increasingly egalitarian manner.

Universal access may be somewhat more effective in fostering social mobility than in promoting equality. Even if the college degree becomes devalued, either through lowered academic standards or supply outstripping demand, every poor student who obtains a degree is likely to move upward through the class structure. But even here the outlook is not entirely bright; for reasons outlined earlier, it is unlikely that most deprived sectors of society will be able to take advantage of the open door.

EQUALITY VERSUS EQUALITY OF OPPORTUNITY

The central problem faced by those who would give everyone an "equal chance" is that equality of opportunity is extraordinarily difficult to achieve in a class society. Although theoretically a highly stratified society may be fully mobile—may be one in which the position of a person's parents has no effect whatsoever on his life chances—it simply does not work that way in practice. Any attempt to give the

49. Astin, "Racial Considerations in Admissions," p. 113.
50. American Council on Education, Staff of the Office of Research, *National Norms for Entering College Freshmen—Fall 1970* (Washington: American Council on Education, 1970), p. 38.

poor an equal chance necessarily founders on the rock of social class. Proponents of equality of opportunity often fail to realize that an attack on inequality itself would be the most effective means of increasing equal opportunity.

The distinction between *equality* and *equality of opportunity* is often lost on those who would reform the educational system. The Carnegie Commission, for example, in discussing its vision of the day when minority persons will be proportionately represented in the higher occupational levels, asserts that this would be an "important signal that society was meeting its commitment to equality."[51] Apparently, its conception of equality is really one of equality of opportunity; the commission is less interested in reducing gross differences of wealth, status, and power than in giving everyone a chance to get ahead of everyone else.

Advocates of equality of opportunity are hopeful that open admissions will enable large numbers of people from poor white and minority backgrounds to become upwardly mobile. Implicit in this hope is the belief that America needs increased mobility more than it needs greater social and economic equality. Yet there is little reason to believe that a meritocracy is either more just or more humane than social order based on tradition.[52] What a meritocracy does, as Arthur Stinchcombe points out, is to substitute a genetic lottery for a hereditary one.[53] A meritocracy is more competitive than an overtly class-based society, and this unrelenting competition exacts a toll both from the losers, whose self-esteem is damaged, and from the winners, who may be more self-righteous about their elite status than is a more traditional ruling group. Apart from increased efficiency, it is doubtful whether a frenetically competitive inegalitarian society is much of an improvement over an ascriptive society which, at least, does not compel its poor people to internalize their failure.[54]

Open admissions has aroused controversy precisely because it carries within it the seeds of an attack on the meritocracy. The system of higher education is a bulwark of the meritocracy in that it not only allocates people to the upper positions, but also provides simultaneous

51. *A Chance to Learn*, p. 28.
52. See Michael Young, *The Rise of the Meritocracy* (Baltimore: Penguin Books, 1970) for a critique of the liberal ideal of equality of opportunity.
53. Stinchcombe article in Review Symposium of Robert Dreeben's *On What Is Learned in School, Sociology of Education*, Spring 1970, pp. 218–22.
54. For data showing the extent to which income and wealth are unequally distributed in American society, see Gabriel Kolko, *Wealth and Power in America* (New York: Praeger, 1969), and Herman Miller, *Rich Man, Poor Man* (New York: Thomas Y. Crowell Co., 1971).

legitimation of that placement. Open admissions, based on the assumption that everyone is entitled to a fair share of the society's higher educational resources, suggests that colleges and universities exist to educate people, not to put them in their proper slots in the meritocratic structure. Moreover, by abandoning merit as a criterion for determining who receives society's educational resources, it casts doubt on the meritocracy's means of distributing resources in general. Finally, open admissions implies that, thus far, universities have served mainly to transmit from parent to child an upper-middle-class status that entitles the child to a disproportionate amount of wealth and power.

As long as open admissions remains limited to a few institutions, it poses no threat to the meritocracy. Recruitment into the elite will be based not on *whether* one went to college but on *where* one went to college. Universal open admissions, however, would destroy the close articulation between the meritocracy and the system of higher education; further, by the very act of abolishing hierarchy in admissions, it would cast doubt on hierarchy in the larger society.

Open admissions may fail to develop in this direction and, indeed, may merely serve to make the meritocracy more efficient by identifying talent that otherwise would have been overlooked and by providing just enough upward mobility to make the ideology of equal opportunity plausible. Nonetheless, there is no gainsaying the inherent tension that exists between open admissions and the meritocracy, a tension that may well develop into overt conflict.

Opponents often express concern that universal open admissions would destroy diversity and variety in higher education and lead to a dull homogeneity of institutions. Yet there is a real question about whether the present higher educational system is genuinely diverse or merely hierarchical. Does Podunk's conception of its mission really differ from Yale's, or would it be exactly the same if it had the chance? Like similar objections raised against egalitarian economic measures, the argument assumes that equality is somehow incompatible with variety. One could, however, argue forcefully, as does R. H. Tawney, that true individuality, whether among men or among institutions, is most easily achieved in a less stratified society.[55] Open admissions precludes neither excellence nor genuine diversity, but it is antithetic to invidious distinctions that derive not from educational philosophy but rather from an unholy alliance between the campus and the meritocracy.

55. Tawney, *Equality* (London: George Allen & Unwin, Unwin Books, 1964).

THE MEANING OF OPEN ADMISSIONS

The advent of open admissions raises some fundamental questions about the nature and purpose of the university. Conceiving of itself as most essentially devoted to the discovery and transmission of knowledge, the university has, in reality, become a principal mechanism for distributing privilege in American society. Avenues previously open to those who did not attend college are now closed; most middle-level jobs and all elite positions now require a college degree. The pressure for open admissions arose, in good part, as a response to this trend.

The controversy over open admissions has been impassioned. Opponents have waged battle primarily on the grounds that universal access will lower academic standards, but the evidence indicates that such an outcome is by no means inevitable. Advocates have described open admissions as a poverty interrupter and as a powerful egalitarian force, but it is quite possible that the degree of inequality and of inequality of educational opportunity in American society will remain constant, especially if the institutional pecking order within higher education is maintained. Clearly, both the promise and the menace of open admissions have been exaggerated.

What open admissions *will* do, however, is give every high school graduate a chance to pursue a college education. One possible side effect is that admissions tests will be used for diagnostic rather than exclusionary purposes. Another is that the conception of the university as an institution whose primary social responsibility is to serve as a training ground for the academic-social elite will gradually vanish. No longer will thousands of potentially educable students be excluded from the system of higher education.

The philosophical rationale for open admissions is that the educational mission of the institution is not to select winners or to serve as a talent scout for future employers but rather to foster growth in the student. Value added, not high GPA's, should be the mark of the successful institution. As one observer has noted, "There is no such thing as an unfit or unqualified seeker after education."[56] Open admissions, at long last, will end that peculiar arrogance which has led many colleges and universities to say to many aspiring entrants: "Shift for yourself if you want an education—you are not worth our time."

But open admissions is not a panacea; no educational reform is more than a limited means of attacking vast political, social, and

56. B. Alden Thresher, "Uses and Abuses of Scholastic Aptitude and Achievement Tests," *Barriers to Higher Education* (New York: College Entrance Examination Board, 1971), p. 39.

economic ills. It will bring with it a plethora of problems, and its long-term effects remain unclear. Yet, as indicated by the proliferation of state master plans for universal access and by the vast growth of free-access institutions, it is fast becoming a national reality. The question now is not whether there will be open admissions, but rather what form it will take and how it can best be made to work. These are the topics to which attention and energy must now be directed.

WALTER PERRY

Britain's Open University

FOR A NEW BABY, BRITAIN'S OPEN UNIVERSITY IS ATTRACTING
no little attention, not because it yells too loudly, but because it is a
bit of a freak. Much of the attention has come from the United States
—indeed I am tempted to believe that Pan American could run a
successful weekly package tour from New York to Milton Keynes.

STRUCTURE

First of all, the Open University is still very small. It started teaching only in January 1971, so that we do not yet have the full results
for even one year. Second (by way of an aside), the real fascination of
the "baby" is that it will grow to be an adult, and we think that the
adult is going to make such a stir that the educational world will
never be quite the same again.

In January 1971, 24,000 students began study in the Open University. They were all part-time students. They were nearly all in full-
time employment. They were all twenty-one years old or more, about
7 percent were over fifty, and one student is eighty-two! Furthermore,
none of our students ever sets foot on the campus. No school certificate
or any other qualification was required for entry. The only reason for
refusing some applicants was shortage of money. There were 43,000
applicants. The 24,000 admitted were selected on a first-come, first-
served basis, save *only* that we applied quotas for the courses of study
and for the regions of the country. It would never have done to run
one course for 24,000 students and three others for no students at all;
and we could not have survived the criticism had all our students
come from Scotland and none from England or Wales. The teaching
year runs from January to November and lasts for thirty-six teaching
weeks. The "vacations" are dictated by Wimbledon and the Open
Golf Championship, when all educational broadcasting ceases for the
benefit of sports-lovers.

287

Of the 24,000 students who began in January 1971, some 4,000 did not finally register in April, so that we now have about 20,000 left. My current expectation, based on summer school attendances and performance in assessments, is that 16,000–17,000 will continue their studies in 1972.

In January 1972, we shall admit the second freshman year. We have had another 35,000 applications, this time from people who have *seen* what the courses are like, and we shall be able to admit about 19,000 of them. Again, the number must be kept down because of lack of funds. Like all British universities, we recover less than 15 percent of the costs from fees. The rest is all direct government grant. Our total grant is related to the *total* student number. So, paradoxically, the more successful we are—the more students who stay on to second-level studies—the fewer the number of new students that can be admitted.

In its first year, only four courses are being offered. These are multidisciplinary—so-called *foundation*—courses in arts, science, mathematics, and social science. Next year we shall add twelve courses at the second level and one more foundation course, in technology. Eventually we shall offer courses at four levels corresponding roughly to four years of college. The third- and fourth-level courses will tend to be advanced, single discipline courses of the more conventional type.

Each course lasts thirty-six weeks and calls for a minimum of ten hours study per week, and for a one-week residential summer school. The summer schools are held in one of eight other universities during their long vacation. This, of course, increases the utilization of the capital tied up in their buildings.

Credit in a course is awarded on the basis of performance in continuous assessments throughout the course, in summer school, and in a final written examination. A student obtains a B.A. degree by obtaining credits in a minimum of six courses. He may take two courses concurrently if he wishes, or he may accumulate credits over a long period of time.

Each course is given an integrated multimedia format, the aim being to take education *to* the student, not to bring the student *to* education. One week's work, usually called a *unit*, consists of a half-hour television program; a half-hour radio program; a correspondence book of structured learning; reading from the *set* textbooks; written work for assessment, sent by post; and special course requirements (course experiment kits in science, for example). The radio and television programs are broadcast by the BBC on open circuit once on a weekday evening, with a repeat on Sunday morning.

Students may, in addition, attend a study center near their home, but this is not compulsory. We have set up study centers in 290 townships all over the United Kingdom. Space is hired from other educational institutions in the evenings and on weekends. In the study centers a student, who would otherwise be isolated and working independently, can meet colleagues and monitor the broadcasts (say, if his family want to watch another channel), can consult a counselor on any problem, can meet a tutor for remedial tutorial help when he is stuck, can see a film of a television show that he missed or wants to revise, and can use a computer terminal needed for the mathematics course. Some study centers are minicampuses in their own right. The study centers are manned by part-time staff who nearly all have full-time jobs in other institutions of higher education and who do one or two extra evening sessions for us. We have some three thousand such staff. They are managed from regional offices—each region has about twenty-five study centers to control.

Courses are written by the full-time academic staff—about 180—at the campus at Milton Keynes. The academic staff is of high quality—there were about 40 applicants for each job—and is backed by a large administrative and secretarial staff, so that there are already about 900 on the central staff.

Each course is the product of a "course team." This is a new idea in British university teaching, for it removes control from the department. The team consists of academics, educational technologists, and BBC production staff. It is charged by the senate with overall responsibility for *all* the components in the integrated multimedia mix. Since the producer plays a part in designing the syllabus and in determining what parts require visual presentation, we avoid the confrontation common when one creative artist (the academic) writes a program which another creative artist (the producer) is unwilling to make.

The partnership of the university and the BBC has been crucial. A university status was necessary for attracting staff and for credibility of qualifications; the BBC expertise was necessary for production and it also provided the transmission times—up to thirty hours of television and thirty hours of radio per week.

All costs are paid by the university. Thus we need not think of the public audience in designing programs, only of the students. Since the public pays for the BBC, our independence would not otherwise have been possible.

That, then, is a brief sketch of what the Open University is now and of how it came about. I shall turn now to the more difficult question, "Why is it like that?"

OBJECTIVES AND COSTS

The Open University was born of two ideas, one social, one technological. The social need was to provide higher education for anyone who wanted it—the theme of this conference. Even now less than 12 percent of the age group in Britain get any higher education. This compares with 62 percent in the United States. In 1930, less than 1 percent went to a university in Britain. We have an enormous backlog, much bigger than that in the United States, a pool of untapped resource. The Open University was to take education to them, so that even if they had to work to support a family they could still study. This we are already doing. Yet many people thought that the people who most needed the service were the working class—the lorry drivers. And we have been heavily criticized because most of our students are so-called middle class—the schoolteachers. *But* our schoolteachers were often the children of working-class parents and started off deprived. Indeed they were denied a university place by the elitist system. So the criticism is misplaced. Furthermore, we are already, in 1972, getting more applications of the lorry-driver variety.

The second idea behind the Open University was that of using modern technology to bring education *to* the people by using the mass media of communication—the "University of the Air." In the future this concept will, I believe, be even more important in the *continuing education* of people—the updating refresher courses, the postexperience courses—that the accelerating pace of progress makes a necessary feature of an efficient industrial society. We cannot spare the workers from industry for full-time refresher courses every five years. Only a system like the Open University system can possibly solve the problem.

This objective is ultimately far *more* important than giving more undergraduate training. *But* the B.A. courses had to come first, for they are the mark of a credible university, and only a credible university could provide continuing education that was acceptable.

Similiar arguments explain why we could not begin with courses that were preuniversity remedial programs for the really deprived groups—reaching out to salvage the wrecks of the system. The catching-up *can* be done, but once again only by a credible university. To start with such courses would be suicidal for a new institution very much on trial.

And now, a word on costs. The Open University in absolute terms is not cheap. No institution making use of broadcasting media and designing new software can be cheap. But it is relatively cheap provided the number of students is large, for there is great economy of scale. It is for this reason that we started with so many students, and it is why we would like to see our materials—of which we are very proud—used more extensively.

The total cost in 1973, when we will reach our plateau figure of 40,000 students, will be about $20 million, or $500 per student. At this rate we will cost as much *per graduate* as the conventional university only if the dropout rate reaches 90 percent. Any percentage of graduates of over 10 percent will be a cost benefit.

INFLUENCE OF THE OPEN UNIVERSITY

Four things, at least, about the Open University are likely to cause profound change in education. (1) The system can, with great economy of scale, provide education—conventional undergraduate, preuniversity remedial education, or postexperience refresher education—for very large numbers of students. (2) The system can bring education to the students, with the result that there are immense savings in capital, students can continue in full-time employment, and there is no national loss of productivity. (3) The teaching is done *openly:* The courses are put out on open circuit, and the written material is available in book shops, so that students in other institutions and the general public can see what university teaching really is. The "demonstration" removes some of the mystique of higher education, which, for those who really believe in it, is a good thing. Another result may be a student demand for higher standards of teaching in other institutions. (4) The possibilities offered by programs of study that make partial use of our new system and partial use of conventional systems are obvious. They will be explored, and radical reorganization of the patterns of higher education may follow.

Because the United States has similar problems, its educators are taking much interest in what we are doing. But Americans must hasten slowly, for their problems, though similar, are not identical. The U.S. population of deprived adults is drawn from the 40 percent of the age group who do not go to college. Ours is drawn from over 80 percent and will, therefore, include more people of higher innate ability. The United States has gone so far in providing opportunities that further extension encounters increasing problems of lack of ability.

In Britain, our courses are written for adults and would need to be modified for young Americans. The social sciences may require more modification than mathematics, and changes may range from those in spelling, through changes in illustrative examples, to changes in total content. We hope that by establishing some sort of an agency in the United States, we can undertake, after pilot studies, such necessary modifications.

I have tried to convey the sense of excitement, the dedication, the drive, and the mounting awareness of achievement that pervade the Open University campus and study centers in Britain. I hope that some of the experience we have gained may be of service to education in the United States.

ALEXANDER M. MOOD

Another Approach to Higher Education

THIS PAPER PROPOSES A RADICAL REARRANGEMENT OF OUR system of higher education and argues that it could go far toward solving some of the basic problems facing our system and could also meet urgent needs that are not now being met. Briefly, the main features of the rearrangement are:

1. The vast majority of students will attend college as full-time students for only one year, instead of four or two.
2. Additional higher education will be a part-time activity extending over one's lifetime.
3. Essentially every youth will attend college for one year, whether or not he or she has graduated from high school.
4. The roles of residential and community colleges will be essentially reversed: the one year of full-time attendance will be at a residential college, and the part-time lifelong learning will lie more in the domain of the community college.
5. The year of residence for those who do not now go to college will be financed by the public subsidy that now supports students who attend college for more than one year.
6. The bulk of education beyond the first year will be accomplished by learning at home, using primarily video cassettes played through the home TV set.

I need not have stated the rearrangement as education fiction (which may not finally be fictional) because there are some caveats later on. I wanted, however, to turn attention away from paths our thoughts naturally take when we consider higher education.

PATTERNS OF ATTENDANCE

Many educators agree that it does not make sense to have students concentrate their education in a single, nonstop, sixteen-year dose and then swear off for the rest of their lives. Nor does it make sense to restrict young people to learning entirely from experience with one social institution, with no provision for encounters with other social institutions. Young people need the wider experience in order to make rational plans for their further education. Of course, their decisions will likely change as they get older; philosophy of life and career goals will change; and quite frequently the changes will generate requirements for more learning. Personal initiative aside, the individual meets—at an increasing rate—changes in his environment, which alter the conditions of his life and require him to make adaptations that, again, call for additional learning.

There is no need to elaborate further the point that continuing education is becoming a necessity. With need and demand accepted, proposals have been made and practices instituted for spreading postsecondary education over a number of years and interlacing it with other activities. Work-study arrangements, such as those at Antioch and some schools of the University of Cincinnati, are familiar and of long standing. They had sound justifications in more stable times; many of the justifications make still stronger cases in changing times. In my judgment, the past slow rate of growth of work-study programs will accelerate considerably in the future.

Several proposals have been made in recent years for special work-study universities in urban areas. Substantial portions of the curricula would be built around urban affairs, and the research program would focus on urban problems and issues. Students would alternate terms of work in urban governmental or civic agencies with full-time studies on the campus: from their work experience they would bring first-hand knowledge of urban processes to the campus, and they would take back to the agencies results of research related to their work. Progress along career ladders would normally require both increasingly responsible work experience and increasingly advanced studies.

The pattern of alternating between work and study on campus may be appropriate and useful in many lines of endeavor. I suspect, however, that a more common pattern will see a student spend one year in full-time campus attendance, followed by part-time work and part-time study, with study the smaller part, amounting to a few hours per week taken from work to pursue one course. Even this degree of campus involvement may be characteristic for the minority rather than the majority of students. I suspect further that, as educational materials improve, we shall see more and more people pursue education through individual effort. Commercially produced video cassettes may well provide a sufficiently dramatic improvement to produce change from our prevailing mode of learning.

ROLES OF EXISTING INSTITUTIONS

I propose that all youths at about age seventeen spend a year in residence at a college or university or in some form of national service that would take them away from home. After the year away from home, young persons would ordinarily find jobs, near home or elsewhere, and proceed along their careers, obtaining experience and education simultaneously.

After young people complete high school—sometimes, before they complete high school—they need to get away from home for a year. Literally, the most important role that colleges and universities can play for most youths is to provide a residence where they can learn to live by their own decisions. The campus community is an especially suitable environment, for here a young person finds the company of others who are struggling with the same problems of what they believe and what principles shall govern their behavior. Interaction with their peers helps them achieve some kind of reasonable balance outside the possibly outmoded or unduly repressive constraints of home. This reasoning undergirds the argument for reversing the usual order of attendance at community colleges and residential colleges.

The year on campus would expose students to quite a different curriculum from the customary freshman studies. It would recognize that most subsequent formal learning will be pursued through individual study. Accordingly, the campus year must focus on learning that cannot be effectively undertaken through individual study—personal development and development of interpersonal skills. Much learning in this domain develops in dormitory bull sessions; yet colleges give it little attention. The institutions would attempt to coordinate the new curriculum with this kind of learning, to allow students opportunities to present a wide range of personal philosophies and value systems together with their pros and cons, to help youths analyze their special talents and inclinations and modes of personal satisfaction so that they may choose philosophies and careers compatible with their natures. Thus the curriculum would revolve largely around counseling, interpersonal psychology, psychiatry, philosophy, sociology, anthropology. For those interested, extensive opportunity for encounter group experiences and sensitivity training would be available. Much more attention may be paid to living arrangements, with opportunities provided for a variety of experiments in group living.

Another important curriculum element would deal with models of social organization of the future. Universities, as a natural consequence of their researches, are primary inventors of such models, and it is the campuses that transmit the models to the next generation. This activity, which does not lend itself to dissemination through the one-way communication of cassettes, may provide society with its most effective means for adapting to changing times and conditions. New models of society, being unfamiliar, are likely to be rejected as outrageous or unnatural; a certain amount of give and take may be necessary to make them believable and to obtain a fair hearing for the advantages and disadvantages over the current models of social organization.

The relatively small number of students who have decided to become lawyers, physicists, doctors, engineers, and the like will pursue the traditional curricula. Yet here again, the traditional path, involving several years of full-time study, may become unusual. All careers might better be pursued by mixing study and experience; thus, medical doctors might ordinarily begin their careers as nurses.

Alternatives to Formal Higher Education

Many young persons just out of high school will have no interest in further formal education. They should have the option of devoting a year to national service before embarking on a career and intermittent postsecondary education. In addition to military service, a variety of opportunities would be offered for service in education, health, welfare, environmental improvement, international understanding, and the like. The Peace Corps, Teacher Corps, and Vista are good examples.

The concept of national service has several arguments to recommend it in addition to the education considerations I shall discuss. The twelve years of concentrated schooling leave most youth quite ignorant of other social institutions; they pick up in school smatterings of second- and third-hand information, but the little knowledge acquired is no substitute for getting into other institutions and observing how they operate. There is the further consideration that many youths are bored, bored, bored with book learning and badly need a quite different kind of experience to recharge their batteries before they embark on still more book learning. Youths in national service activities will also profit tremendously from learning to cope with living and working conditions altogether different from the authoritarian supervision of behavior that many of them endure at home and in school.

Of course, youths who have devoted a year to national service should have the option of also spending a year in residence at a college if they later desire to do so. Others may choose instead some of the learning opportunities for personal development described above, and the community colleges may serve an important function by providing them. The community colleges would be the logical place for development of interpersonal skills that require practice and coaching—skills that cannot be effectively learned in isolation.

Institutional Services

Colleges and universities would have a role in providing laboratories for science courses. Some external degree programs in other nations require students to come to the campus for a week or so in the summer for the purpose of running through the whole sequence of laboratory exercises associated with a given course by working at it eight to ten hours a day. This tactic would be useful for advanced courses but perhaps not for others.

Undergraduate laboratory work today uses elaborate and expensive equipment that is rarely necessary. Students have easy access to a wide range of equipment around which excellent laboratory exercises could be developed. Bathrooms and kitchens can serve quite well as biology and chemistry labs, especially if they are augmented from time to time by simple, imaginatively designed, mailable kits. A wide range of physics laboratory exercises can be assigned using refrigerators, freezers, automobiles, radios, TV sets, record players, tape recorders, telephones, musical instruments, clocks, cameras, binoculars, bathroom scales, thermos bottles, small electric appliances, and the like. Thus students could go quite far along a scientific course of study without having to do laboratory work on a campus. On the other hand, everyday gadgets have their limits; advanced students in some lines of study will have to do laboratory work on a campus or other location possessing the required equipment.

Similar difficulties are encountered with some kinds of vocational education. One cannot, by viewing cassettes at home, become adept at operating or maintaining computers or construction equipment or airplanes or electron microscopes. The role of postsecondary educational institutions as trainers of students in the use and maintenance of all the complicated technological gadgetry of our civilization will doubtless increase along with the increase in mechanization of the dull, unrewarding tasks that fill much of the typical day for many working people.

Institutions may well assume roles in assisting students pursuing individual study. Diagnosis of learning difficulties and tutoring will probably constitute significant responsibilities for existing institutions, although the teaching process may be very differently organized in the future. Institutions, instead of putting faculty in classroom contact with students to deal with their difficulties in a continuous and fairly casual way, will hear from individual learners who have found themselves unable to solve substantial difficulties by searches through books and cassettes. In this function, the campus may take on a semblance of the counseling activity in which the counselor must develop background knowledge of the difficulty before he can arrive at an appraisal and a potential remedy.

Communities that have no postsecondary campus will almost surely have at least a library or a school or a church that can serve as a minicampus for those pursuing interpersonal learning programs. Their activities might be guided by local persons or by college faculty members serving in an extension role. Often such arrangements would require few physical and human resources; young people might carry out the activity almost unaided by arguing matters among themselves, as they do now in dormitory sessions. Perhaps more advanced students in the community can sometimes join less advanced ones in activities that will benefit both; that is, the more advanced interpersonal studies might require that the more advanced students assist the less advanced.

Because I confine my attention here to the educating role of institutions, I shall pass over the research role of universities, which would likely be larger than ever. At the research level, universities would, of course, continue the considerable educating function of training research apprentices.

Costs

The extension of opportunity for one year of higher education in residence to all young people would cost society approximately the same amount that it now devotes to higher education. If the present subsidy were used in this way, little would remain to subsidize additional years, which would have to be financed by the student or his family from their own or borrowed resources. In 1969–70, the public subsidy to higher education was about $13.0 billion, in 1969–70 dollars, contributed as follows:

Source	Billions of Dollars
Federal government	5.0
State governments	6.0
Local governments	0.8
Endowment income and gifts	1.2

as given by the U.S. Office of Education in *Projections of Educational Statistics to 1979–80,* except for the endowment and gifts component which I have estimated independently from data developed by the Rivlin Committee in its 1969 report to the President, *A Long-Range Plan for Federal Financial Support for Higher Education.* Inasmuch as about half of the federal component is directed to research, I shall count the subsidy to education to have been about $10.5 billion.

The *Projections* (page 155) shows the total number of eighteen-year-olds in the fall of 1969 as 3,682,000; the average cost of educating a student (page 85) as $2,025; and the average cost of room and board (page 107) at about $910. Rounding the sum of these last two figures up to $3,000, we find that a grant of that size to every youth age eighteen would require about $11.0 billion—very little more than the actual subsidy. If the grant were somewhat diminished for those youth able to pay a part of their expenses, the subsidy would easily cover the basic needs of all youths for one year of higher education with money to spare to cover incidentals and travel expenses for those who need additional assistance to cover expenses.

THE VIDEO UNIVERSITY

Now we turn to lifelong learning acquired by whatever means but primarily through individual learning by means of video cassettes. Assisting this form of learning would be some kind of institutional structure which I call the Video University. Video University would (1) clarify possible learning opportunities for students, (2) make such opportunities available, (3) verify and record what is learned by students for various purposes of the students themselves and of society at large.

The Video University is expected to achieve several desiderata that are quite outside the realm of possibility with our present system. The foremost is equality of educational opportunity with respect to age. Related to that kind of equality of opportunity are several other considerations: the need for schedules to fit the individual's free time; minimal personal expense; freedom from institutional barriers to learning such as requirement of high school diplomas, course prerequisites, entrance exams, and transcripts; and freedom from psychological barriers. These desiderata point to individual learning in the home as the primary mode of education. In the past the medium for individual learning has been correspondence courses, but they have failed to cultivate motivation.

Now we must reconsider the medium for individual learning because it is about to be revolutionized by the arrival of video cassettes. Textbooks are, indeed, poor motivators of students; even on campus, though students are hounded by the steady exhortation of professors, they mostly find textbooks too utterly boring to open. Professionally produced films can be fascinating, and, considering the huge potential market, entrepreneurs will make them to be fascinating. I am willing to estimate that 99 percent of video cassettes will be more stimulating than 99 percent of campus lectures. Students will make this discovery pretty fast, and we may as well prepare ourselves for the consequences. In fact, surely the proper attitude is: we are all delighted that learning is about to become a captivating preoccupation of a large number of people.

Producers of films will not be adamant about prerequisites: they will gladly produce versions appropriate to various levels of preparation and various vocabularies; they will gladly produce versions in various languages and dialects. Nor will they be adamant about order: if some students want to learn about atomic fission before learning about specific gravity or learn about Freud before learning about ganglia, producers will not be even slightly troubled. There will also be a tremendous range of depth available so that the learner can sweep through the high spots of English literature in a couple of hours or spend several hours on a single sonnet.

Traditional courses will often be fragmented into a number of one- or two-hour segments so that a person can assemble his own courses and design his own curriculum to suit himself. Some inefficiency will be involved because each segment will have to stand alone and hence will have to repeat certain orientation from other segments. Perhaps there will be both segmented and unsegmented versions of some courses.

CASSETTE CATALOGUE

What with all these courses, segmentations, levels of depth, and levels of student preparation, there will soon be thousands of video cassettes to choose from and eventually tens of thousands, with subjects ranging from *how to stuff a duck* to *the unified field theory of general relativity*. The catalogue of cassettes may be somewhat fatter than catalogues of long-playing records and audio cassettes, which now list some 50,000 items that give only title of the composition, composer, performer, manufacturer, number and type of records or cassettes, price. A video cassette for educational purposes will require more extensive specification, including not only the data mentioned but also a paragraph describing content, somewhat as course descriptions in college catalogues also give designations of depth, prerequisites, language, and so on. Some of the data will be highly codified as in the record catalogue; if cleverly designed, the codes become valuable learning tools.

A New Organization of Knowledge

The cassette catalogue cannot escape being a spectacular learning tool even if it is poorly designed, and with good design, it could become nothing less than an organization of knowledge. A little speculation here about some of its features will give a view of this form of postsecondary education.

The content description of a cassette will be constructed to reflect accurately the prerequisites for good understanding of the material: the description of a study of Greek literature in the original might be written in Greek; the description of an advanced course in quantum mechanics will mention basic concepts such as Schrödinger theory, invariance principles, many particle formations, creation and destruction operators, boson fields, Brillouin zones, Fermi surfaces, and the like. Commercial producers of cassettes will likely have their own content descriptions designed to stimulate sales and hence may sometimes exaggerate scope or learning level. The catalogue we have in mind must, therefore, have an origin other than commercial, and its items must be subject to approval of an objective source of information.

The catalogue will not rely solely on the vocabulary of the content descriptions to cover prerequisites: the annotation for a given cassette will list one or more cassettes that reasonably immediately precede it. The user of the catalogue can then start tracking back and discover a minimum chain of cassettes leading from his present state of knowledge to the given cassette. This process of finding chains with desired constraints will be computerized.

Role of the Computer

By the same token, the user of the cassette catalogue will often want to know the forward potential of a given cassette, and hence the annotation must list a set of cassettes that logically follow it. One annotation in combination with another will have still greater potential for individual curriculum building, and for this reason the chaining process must be computerized. A printed cassette specification cannot take the space to list all other cassettes with which it might be paired to increase its potential and then for each pair, list the set of cassettes to which the pair leads. Then there are triples, quadruples, and so on.

Obviously, the student cannot explore curriculum design without the aid of a computer, even if he is looking only a year ahead. Thus there will be two versions of the catalogue—a printed one containing all information about a cassette except higher order chaining information (but including first order chaining connections) and a computer version which will probably not include the complete content descriptions but will give elaborate chaining information. The computer version for each cassette should include, not the complete description, but rather two keyword lists: (1) a list of concepts essential for understanding the cassette—the "prerequisite list," and (2) a list of concepts that the cassette is intended to present to the student—the "content list."

Of course, the catalogue will not get computerized by simply waving a wand. All the interactions and connections between cassettes will have to be individually determined by experts familiar with the whole array of cassettes that a given one might touch. In programing, each new cassette will have to be assigned its place in a variety of hierarchies and in a variety of cassette specifications as a prerequisite or a follow-on. The two keyword lists, however, will offer mechanical aid to forward chaining: the content keywords for one cassette can be the code for searching the computerized catalogue for other cassettes having those keywords in their prerequisite lists; the computer will then produce a maximum list of forward cassettes. An expert, using his own judgment, can select the list to be put in the chaining file for the original cassette. The reverse process could discover a maximum list of cassettes to precede a given cassette. Of course, students, by using keyword lists and chaining information, can design their own curricula.

Vocabulary will be a critical factor in the individual's design of his curriculum. In general, except for advanced work, the range of cassettes should offer an option between technical and nontechnical language (perhaps more than one level of nontechnical language should be available so that even persons with limited vocabularies can have access to learning about a subject). For both student and curriculum specialist, the exploration of chains will reveal that level of depth beyond which it will pay off in student time for him to learn the technical vocabulary. It will also be clear that, in survey or overview studies, learning the technical language is a waste of time—something today's students may realize but can do little about (another barrier to learning).

The cassettes that employ very limited vocabularies will doubtless lean heavily on diagrams, illustrations, microdramas, demonstrations, experiments, and the like. These devices may in time become symbolized and could become powerful adjuncts to ordinary language, especially if there is some international coordination of the symbolization process. Marshall McLuhan would enjoy that outcome on two counts—the global village coming together in a threat to print.

With regard to quality, should Video University catalogue include cassettes entitled *Astrological Selection of Planting and Harvesting Dates* or *Curing the Common Cold by Chiropractic?* The answer is doubtless *yes* on grounds of freedom of speech and freedom of the press. People should be free to put baloney on films, and others should be free to label it baloney. That does not quite get to the heart of the issue because when labelers have official status, their labels have the effect of curtailing the freedom of baloney peddlers—but perhaps we have no need to worry about this matter. Educated people will not be long misled by either baloney or erroneous labeling. We think of our nation as educated but we ain't seen nothin' yet; when learning becomes a joy unfettered by constraints of institutions, teachers, time, and money, we may, indeed, see a learning explosion.

The Computer Network for Testing and Curriculum Design

Let's hypothesize further. There will be several large regional computers in the nation accessible by remote consoles located at local libraries, high schools, and colleges. The computers will be interconnected and also connected to a large central control computer. This network will handle the catalogue and have other functions; it will not be a device students will use frequently—perhaps a few times per year; its primary function will be to help students identify cassettes and chains of cassettes appropriate to their objectives.

One disadvantage of home learning without teacher or tutor is the dead stop the student encounters when he meets a concept or an explanation he simply does not understand. The computer network may help by giving the student a tool for searching for related cassettes at a more elementary level. The student either goes to a nearby console to conduct the search, or he telephones a console operator who will conduct the search for him. The search will be based on the keyword lists of clues to cassette content.

The computer will also handle the testing program. A student should be able to go to a console at any time and test himself on a limited area of knowledge or a larger subject area of a complete field or a combination of fields or even in all fields of knowledge combined. Besides giving him a test score, the computer will give him a list of cassettes that provide reasonable next steps in the domain in which he has been tested.

The testing mechanism will consist of a huge file of questions, most of which can be answered by unique short answers readily transmitted by the student over the console. There will be literally hundreds of thousands of questions coded by subject area. When a student specifies the domain of knowledge in which he wants to be tested, the computer will randomly select a small set of questions from the large central file (twenty or thirty, perhaps, for a small domain; more for larger domains—enough to get a reasonably reliable appraisal of competence). The purpose of the large central file is to enable the student to retest himself from time to time without encountering the same questions.

The computer will then construct (1) a forward chain of cassettes for the student's next study by matching keywords in correct answers with *prerequisite* keywords in the chained cassettes, and (2) a list of cassettes having *content* keywords that match keywords in the incorrect answers to identify cassettes that will illuminate the missed concepts. These two cassette lists will be separately identified to give the student data for selecting his next set or chains of sets of cassettes. Of course, he may decide to limit himself to a narrower domain of study than he specified to the testing program.

A student will always have the option of instructing the computer to transmit test results to any agencies or persons he specifies. The certified test scores will play the role of today's transcript but with substantial improvement: continually updated scores would reflect the student's growing knowledge, experience, and enlarged scope of learning.

OPERATION OF VIDEO UNIVERSITY

The Video University responsible for the individual learning mode of postsecondary education might be a new national university chartered by the federal government, or it might be a consortium of existing institutions. The former would likely operate more energetically in the crucial early years. In the long run the higher education establishment will benefit tremendously from these developments, but considerable rocking of the boat will be necessary during the transition period (it would probably be expecting too much to suppose higher education would do that very vigorously). In any case, the great bulk of the work would doubtless be carried out by existing institutions under contractual or cooperative arrangements.

The primary functions of Video University would be:

1. Ownership and operation of the cassette library. It would be stored at numerous points over the nation so that cassettes would be available to students within one day by mail service; those in great demand might be stored in every community library and every high school.
2. Operation of the computer network
3. Maintenance of the two catalogues
4. Operation of the testing program
5. Maintenance of student records of accomplishment
6. Operation of a TV network for dissemination of information about learning opportunities and career opportunities
7. Design of various external degree programs and the awarding of degrees

I shall not speculate here about Video University's organization to carry out these functions or the form of participation of existing institutions.

My view of financing is that the institution would be essentially self-supporting after a sizable initial infusion of capital to get it under way. Students would rent cassettes; a small part of the rent would pay royalties to the cassette producers, but the net proceeds would be a major source of income for the institution. Students would pay fees to use the computer network to consult the catalogue, use the testing program, order a transcript mailed to someone, and so on; the fees might be set high enough to cover costs and provide additional income.

I intend no implication that Video University would have any kind of monopoly. Producers of cassettes and others would likely rent them out in competition with the university, but the university itself would probably have to produce and distribute a great many cassettes whose demand would be insufficient to be profitable to commercial producers. Existing universities could offer external degrees using their present structures for correspondence courses; perhaps some institutions would maintain their own catalogues and testing programs although it would probably be more efficient for them to purchase such services from Video University.

TV NETWORK

This huge, continuing enterprise will require large quantities of information to be continuously available to the general public which, in our present view, is simply one great body of students. Obviously, the means should be television. Perhaps initially a few hours per day will be sufficient, but as the enterprise grows a full-time channel may be required.

One primary function of the TV network will be to keep the public apprised of the state of the catalogue, that is, of the whole spectrum of learning opportunities available. The catalogue will be revised continuously as new material is added and old material is revised and improved. The TV network might exhibit short portions of new cassettes and inform viewers about their implications for current curricula and for creating new curricula. Advertising revenue from commercial producers of cassettes might help support this function.

A second extremely important function of the TV network will be news about careers—both vocational and avocational. One of the greatest defects of our present postsecondary educational system is its reliance on past momentum, with little concern about careers of the future. As a result, students are allowed to prepare for careers that offer only the slimmest chances of proving satisfactory; equally, other careers will come into great demand but are overlooked entirely because no one has prepared formal training programs for them. This unfortunate state of affairs exists at least in part because no single institution can afford the resources necessary to arrive at a reasonably competent appraisal of career patterns in the United States. A central institution will definitely have to undertake this responsibility to help avoid horrendous blunders being made by large segments of the student population. That is, a nationwide blunder is an altogether different matter from a random concatenation of many small blunders which may in part cancel each other out.

Using nationwide data on the utilization of cassettes, estimates will be made of the numbers of persons preparing for various kinds of careers. The estimates will be continually updated and broadcast so that a student can judge whether a field that currently appears attractive might be overcrowded by the time he is ready to enter it.

Too, great effort will have to be given to developing and publicizing learning programs. For example, if a given career is judged to have a substantial potential, what curriculum offers the best preparation, and how may a student best prepare himself to undertake the curriculum?

The TV network will be equally involved with avocational activities across the nation. News about intellectual and artistic matters and about crafts would inform individuals how they may enrich their lives by developing the knowledge and skills to participate in these activities with others of like mind. Much educational endeavor could be stimulated by news about public service activities of civic-minded persons who are effectively working for better government, tax reform, stricter zoning, pollution control, population stabilization, integrated schools, open housing, fair trade practices, fair employment practices, mental health centers, mass transit systems, housing for low income families, beautification of our cities, universal health care, universal access to higher education, and so on and on. An avocation can bring tremendous satisfaction to a person who has equipped himself educationally to bring it off successfully.

MISCELLANEOUS PROS AND CONS

I see the main advantage of Video University as the removal of numerous critical barriers that now exist to postsecondary learning for large segments of the population—barriers of age, convenience, cost, scheduling, level of education, institutional rules and regulations, fear of inadequacy, fear of humiliation, and boring courses.

The chief disadvantages are lack of community and interpersonal learning experiences—including tutoring and counseling of individual students—and lack of access to special facilities and equipment.

I have attempted no cost estimates of Video University. I suspect that the cost to taxpayers would be zero and the cost to the student would consist mainly of unburdensome rental fees for cassettes and the cost of cassette viewing attachments for home TV sets (mass production should keep the price reasonable).

In light of the auspicious beginning of the British University of the Air and its external degree programs, why have I chosen video cassettes over a TV network? Cassettes offer overriding scheduling convenience:[1] many a person interested in pursuing a regularly scheduled TV course would find the time conflicted with something else equally important. In addition, there are economic advantages to cassette courses: they are easily and cheaply repeatable; they do not use a sizable segment of the extremely limited electromagnetic spectrum (a complete TV curriculum might require twenty full-time channels). A cable system, with some advantages, involves the extremely costly installation of coaxial cable to individual residences. Mailing cassettes is much cheaper.

The rigid forty-hour week is probably a serious deterrent to lifelong learning. Learning requires effort, and the full-time worker

---

1. Robert Bickner first brought this advantage to my attention.

often finds the effort beyond him; he needs time for personal chores, leisure activities, relaxation. So if we believe in continuing education, we must arrange work so that the worker-student may work thirty-five hours a week or even twenty-five in case of a larger educational undertaking.

The flexible work week is also pertinent in the matter of jobs for college-age youth versus lifetime postsecondary education. One argument runs: there is not enough work available for young people; the campuses provide a valuable warehousing service until the economy is ready to absorb youth into the work force. Nonsense. Obviously, there is endless work to be done in rebuilding our dilapidated cities and repairing our butchered environment but it is fair to say that our political and economic organization is not very effective at finding ways of getting that kind of work done. In any case, a general policy of permitting people to work less than forty hours a week would likely uncover a number of persons who would prefer to do so and would therefore make available a certain amount of work for others. When postsecondary education becomes cheap and convenient, quite a sizable amount of work might be relinquished by full-time workers who would like to get more education but now find it too costly in time and money.

We must not overlook the gross discrimination of society against non-degree-holders. Jobs are generally upper status or lower status depending on whether or not entry requires a college degree. The amount of learning and experience makes no difference; only possession of the degree matters. No one need look far from wherever he happens to be sitting to find horrible examples of degree-holding nincompoops supervising able persons who do not hold a degree. It is one of the devices of the privileged segments of society to hold on to their privileges; those who have the leisure and the money to get a degree enter the upper status career ladders. Automatically, then, we have serious barriers to continuing education. Those who can afford a college degree will not spread out their education because they would spend years in lower status jobs. Those who cannot proceed directly to a degree know they will gain little advantage to their careers in plodding toward degree because, even after they get it, they will have become identified with lower status career ladders. There is little crossing-over by older persons from lower status ladders into beginning jobs in higher status ladders because those jobs are designed for and deemed suitable only for *young* college graduates.

If we are to have continuing education, we must end the discrimination in employment based on amount of education and age. Especially we must make war against unnecessary educational requirements for jobs.

BIBLIOGRAPHY

Astin, A. W. *The College Environment.* Washington: American Council on Education, 1968.

Astin, A. W. "A Researcher's Proposal for Changes in Higher Education," *Educational Record,* Summer 1970, pp. 225–31.

Bell, D., and Kristol, I. *Confrontation: Student Rebellion and the Universities.* New York: Basic Books, 1969.

Berg, I. *Education and Jobs.* New York: Praeger, 1970.

Bickner, R. E., et al. *More Scholars per Dollar.* Irvine: University of California at Irvine, Public Policy Research Organization, 1971.

Califano, J. A., Jr. The Student Revolution. New York: W. W. Norton & Co., 1970.

Carnegie Commission on Higher Education. *Less Time, More Options.* New York: McGraw-Hill Book Co., 1971.

———. *The Open Door Colleges.* New York: McGraw-Hill Book Co., 1970.

Dressel, P., et al. *The Confidence Crisis.* San Francisco: Jossey-Bass, Inc., 1970.

Dunham, E. A. *Colleges of the Forgotten Americans.* New York: McGraw-Hill Book Co., 1969.

Eurich, A. C., ed. *Campus 1980.* New York: Delacorte Press. 1968.

Furniss, W. T., ed. *Higher Education for Everybody?* Washington: American Council on Education, 1971.

Jencks, C., and Riesman, D. *The Academic Revolution.* Garden City, N.Y.: Doubleday & Co., 1969.

Mayhew, L. B. *Colleges Today and Tomorrow.* San Francisco: Jossey-Bass, Inc., 1969.

Medsker, L., and Tillery, D. *Breaking the Access Barriers.* New York: McGraw-Hill Book Co., 1971.

National Center for Educational Statistics, U.S. Office of Education. *Digest of Educational Statistics: 1970 Edition.* Washington: Government Printing Office, 1970.

———. *Projections of Educational Statistics to 1979–80.* Washington: Government Printing Office, 1971.

Panos, R. J., and Astin, A. W. "Attrition among College Students," *American Educational Research Journal,* 5 (1968), 57–72.

Sanford, N. *Where Colleges Fail.* San Francisco: Jossey-Bass, Inc., 1967.

Smith, G. K., ed. *Agony and Promise.* San Francisco: Jossey-Bass, Inc., 1969.

Spurr, S. *Academic Degree Structures.* New York: McGraw-Hill Book Co., 1970.

Taylor, H. *Students Without Teachers.* New York: McGraw-Hill Book Co., 1969.

Trent, J. W., and Medsker, L. *Beyond High School.* San Francisco: Jossey-Bass, Inc., 1968.

U.S. Department of Health, Education, and Welfare, Office of the Assistant Secretary for Planning and Evaluation. *Toward a Long-Range Plan for Federal Financial Support for Higher Education: A Report to the President.* [The Rivlin Report.] Washington: The Department, 1969.

Venn, G. *Man, Education, and Work.* Washington: American Council on Education, 1964.

More Options for What?

DAVID MATHEWS

PROFESSOR MOOD'S PAPER SEEMS TO ME ESSENTIALLY AN ADVOCACY OF the advantages of the TV cassette in postsecondary education, with some additional comments on an assortment of current proposals for more community experience, less time for the undergraduate years, and greater emphasis on lifetime learning.

It is fairly easy to find educational arguments for and against any of these prescriptions, and they are so well known that elaborating on them might be a waste of time. What caught my attention was Professor Mood's lack of discussion of the philosophical imperatives and the social objectives of his proposed reforms, although there were unstated philosophical and social assumptions throughout his essay. The same lack of attention was evident in not assessing the economic implications of his reforms.

The question is not so much whether video cassettes, or any of the other schemes for that matter, will work; they all will to some degree. Neither is the question whether they will reduce the humanness of learning; the new technology may well do that. Nor is the question whether these devices are practical and will be adopted; the cassettes probably will be used. The question is what kind of education and what kind of person the new technology will produce. More serious than the issue of whether the new university will be less human is the issue of whether it will be less humane.

The proposals in the paper can be characterized, if taken as a whole, as one part Benjamin Franklin (education can be had outside the classroom), one part Thomas Jefferson (education is a lifetime activity), and one part Thomas Alva Edison (a brave new world is possible through technology). The first two gentlemen have been around for a long time, and it's good to see them again, even though some of their new clothes are a little out of character. Mr. Edison is a fine man, too, but a bit harder to believe. The last technological revolution in education was mass printing, and the classroom today looks amazingly similar to the way it did before that revolution. Students have not given up taking copious notes, nor have their professors stopped delivering elaborate lectures—even though the texts can be bought two blocks away in paperback for $2.75.

The main questions are: What aims does a university, such as Professor Mood's, assume, and what would it produce? What would we gain by making education once again an informal and tribal responsibility rather than a formal and priestly function? Such informality really seems to be at the heart of proposed deemphasis on four undergraduate years and the emphasis on on-the-job training. Who could work and who could not work as a result of putting eight million young people in the labor market, and would we agree socially or politically with the resulting division of labor? What would be the result of making the aim of the curriculum more personal adjustment and interpersonal skills, and less intellectual advancement? How would the people educated by video cassettes and computers think and feel and act? What could we predict to be the poems produced per person in the future, what skills for inner city living, what kinds of spaceships, and what destinations for them? Or is there evidence that Man will frustrate the systems and gadgets? Will the delivery system make any difference at all? Is Homer on the screen not significantly different from Homer on the page? Is all that Professor Mood is talking about "packaging," which will influence quantity without affecting quality?

What do we want? Do we want more poems, do we want different people, do we want a different social order? All visions of education have begun with a vision of Man and Society, never the reverse. The cold war rationale for education that brought us federal aid and large enrollments and research institutes has been rejected, but not replaced.

But, of course, to rest with the "keen" observation that purpose has to precede procedure is "no big thing."

Some efforts at stating a new purpose for education are evident, but they are characterized by a revitalization of the old democratic belief (Jacksonian) that privilege ought to be shared. College is status; therefore, everybody—not just high school graduates—should have one year of college. That solution is economically sound (one year for everybody would cost about the same as four years for a few), and the academic problems posed can be solved by replacing the curriculum with counseling. Such a replacement may or may not be academically sound, but the important thing to note is that it is totally an unconscious political response. In the absence of a recognized new political slogan for education, we seem to have returned to a tried and true one. We have further elaborated on the Jacksonian theme by striking at the elitism of formal education delivered by a select group (professors) through the counterproposals for experiential education, over a lifetime—delivered by cassettes.

It is worth speculating that we are on the verge of forsaking "excellence" and "national prominence" as goals for an educational rationale more consistent with our new, less nationalistic foreign policy and the new domestic politics of neopopulism. The fate of these emerging national policies may, in the final analysis, determine more than educational considerations, the use of the video cassettes, and the length of the undergraduate program. What we want economically and socially will influence the political decisions that, as Mr. Jefferson proved, are the bases for what we do educationally.

For that reason, the question should be, not "another approach to higher education?" but rather "another approach to higher education for what ends?"

Possible Economic Advantages

LEONARD A. LECHT

ALEXANDER MOOD'S PROVOCATIVE PAPER CONTENDS THAT COLLEGES AND universities, like passenger trains, are becoming obsolete in the United States. Moreover, according to Mood, the technical means are at hand, in the form of systems of video cassette instruction, to devise a more democratic and effective alternative to the present system.

Mood focuses on issues that extend considerably beyond the pros and cons of educational television or the proposal to establish a national video university. Basically, his paper is concerned with priorities and objectives in higher education, about which he raises three issues.

The first issue concerns education and access to opportunity. In a society in which almost half of the high school graduates go on to some form of higher education, colleges and universities are widely regarded as institutions that promote equality of opportunity. Yet, for the majority who do not pursue higher education, lack of a degree or other appropriate credential perpetuates inequalities in employment and earnings, in socioeconomic status, and in prospects for compulsory military service in Vietnam or elsewhere. Nonwhites, older persons who missed receiving a good education when they were young, and individuals from low-status families are heavily overrepresented in this majority.

Second, although the formal objectives of colleges and universities are concerned with teaching, learning, and research, for both parents and the community, the informal objective of channeling young people into the better paid and higher status occupations looms at least equally large. Teaching and learning have a way of getting lost beneath institutional forms involved with the credentialing and certifying functions of education. Hence, the emphasis seems frequently to get shifted to the accountancy of course credits and to less-than-inspiring lectures and textbooks geared to the accumulation of the 120 or 180 credits required for graduation. The chief educational value of the present college campuses, again according to Mood, is not so much their programs of instruction as the opportunity they offer young people to exchange ideas and better define themselves.

The third germinal idea in Mood's paper is that the present organization of higher education is no longer necessary. Video cassettes make it possible for "students" to learn at home or in local cassette libraries, and to learn more effectively than from reading textbooks or attending lectures. People can learn in their off-work hours—especially with a reduced work week—and at any age or stage in their life. The new electronic technology makes it possible to view the general public as one great body of students. If everybody were encouraged to gain an education in his own way, the gate-keeping and social channeling functions of colleges and universities would lose much of their economic significance.

I propose to leave the analysis of costs and feasibility of the video technology to others who are more familiar with the subject. It is apparent, however, that the problems in Mood's proposal are not those of greater costs, for his estimates fall within reasonable orders of magnitude. Here he appears to be paying his respects to the widespread concern with rising costs and pressing financial needs in higher education. Over the long term, present arrangements in higher education are probably considerably more costly than Mood's alternative. From the viewpoint of society, the primary cost of enabling eight to nine million young people to attend college on something like a full-time basis is the output these students do *not* produce and the incomes they do *not* earn while they are on campus. Some rough orders of magnitude will illustrate. If five million of the students now on campus full time were instead employed for thirty hours a week while participating in one or more of Mood's courses, the effects on the economy would considerably outweigh such recent developments as devaluing the dollar abroad or imposing a 10 percent tax on manufactured imports. If these young people were to produce an average output of $6,000 a year—about half the average output per labor force member in 1970—they would add a total of some $30 billion to the gross national product.

Present labor market arrangements make it difficult, perhaps even impossible, to absorb most of these young people into employment. Within five or ten years ahead, however, the decay of many of the inner cities, the absence of adequate alternatives, and the deterioration of much of the natural environment—to cite instances—argue for much challenging work to be done which could employ many more Americans in and out of college, young and old. A by-product of releasing many youth from college attendance to employment would transform another economic function of higher education, that of involving young adults in socially approved activities which minimize or eliminate their participation in the labor market for a number of years.

From my perspective as a manpower economist, there are some straws in the wind that indicate that the economic value of the credential-granting activities of colleges and universities can be expected to diminish. In many fields, such as teaching, engineering, or science, the supply of college-educated persons is increasing more rapidly than the demand. These imbalances are, of course, partially the result of the current recession. But they also grow out of longer term developments: examples are the decrease in the younger school-age population and the slackening of public support for federal expenditures for the SST and the space program. Should these trends continue, the dollar differential favoring the recipient of the college degree will become less in 1975 and 1980 than it was in 1965 and 1970. A narrowing of this differential, or perhaps its disappearance in many instances, will weaken the attachments to the present system of higher education which stem from its role as the admissions credential for a secure middle-class status.

I agree with much of Mood's thesis, yet I see many questions about home-based electronic instruction as an alternative to the present colleges and universities. Mood's proposal is far-reaching in an area in which institutional arrangements change slowly. If video universities and campus institutions attempt to coexist, will the social status of the two differ substantially? If so, one will come to be designated as "lower class" and the other as "higher class," and will draw their students accordingly. As another consideration, is the printed word in the form of books as outmoded as the advocates of electronic instruction would have us believe? If textbooks are frequently dull, is this because they are books, or because the rituals of the academic disciplines and of course credits make them so? And finally, if we produce a generation of tube-instructed leaders, who will be left who is able to write?

Challenges in a New Approach

JOHN W. MACY, JR.

As AN ADVOCATE OF OPTIMUM APPLICATION OF TECHNOLOGY IN THE service of education and as a promoter of educational reform to match the changing times, I am heartened by the radical proposals advanced by Dr. Mood. His basic restructuring of higher education, his emphasis on lifetime learning, his extensive employment of electronic means, his broadened range of options for students—all should receive the penetrating evaluation not only of educators but also of representatives from all segments of the American society.

Within the space available to me, I shall focus on several features in order to stimulate discussion of Mood's proposal.

1. *One year of residential college for everyone.* Although the educational values of the residential experience can be accepted, is this feature of educational experience sufficiently essential to warrant educators' shouldering the management and financial burdens inherent in such a plan? Recently, doubts have been arising about the justification for dormitories, dining halls, and other logistical plant to support residential students. Even if the financial load of the educational experience were removed from the student and his parents, would the student prefer the cloistered life over the greater freedom of the urban or community college? The residential year may provide an introduction to higher learning and offer stimulus for continued work on a more independent, nonresidential basis. Yet to accommodate to the high mobility of this age group, flexible patterns of institutional attendance must be devised. Further, the emphasis on universality and equal opportunity which motivate this plan may well make it too limited a residential experience for the student who wishes to engage in the rigor of a regular educational curriculum and fuller colleagueship with other students and faculty. In the professions, of course, greater

flexibility is certainly desired but a longer period of residential instruction would be necessary.

2. *Heavy reliance on video cassettes.* In my judgment, the degree of reliance on this medium is excessive. The video cassette is in an early stage of development, with several noncompatible systems vying for public attention. To date, virtually no educational program has been successfully recorded and distributed through this technological route. The prospect of converting even radically changed curricular material from existing media to video cassettes is a task of staggering proportions. The economics of the production and distribution systems are uncertain. Even if the cassettes were provided at little cost to the student—as Mood suggests—the expense of the reproduction mechanism would be considerable.

A more important problem is the development of curricular materials that, in this television-oriented age, will engage the student's attention to effect a significant learning experience. This critical element in the plan calls for highly sophisticated, profoundly imaginative, vastly expensive program production efforts. The production of 130 hours of "Sesame Street" cost $8 million to research, test, produce, and evaluate, and the reading program ("The Electric Company") currently under production by the Children's Television Workshop will cost still more for only one-half the hours of programs. Cassettes which merely reproduce the classroom or carry traditional educational material will be notably unsuccessful even in the congenial setting of a student's home.

Reliance on the video device must be supplemented by other media materials. The early experience with the Open University in Great Britain, where only 10 percent of the curriculum appears on television and radio, has demonstrated the need for printed material and—more important—the essential involvement of counselors and fellow students. Even with quality cassette material, there is the fundamental problem of learning in isolation, particularly in cases where essential parts of the learning process require the student to perform laboratory exercises or work demonstrations.

3. *The concept of the Video University.* With the reservation cited above, I am strongly attracted to the concept of a national institution responsible for "the individual learning mode of postsecondary education." The tradition of locally based educational institutions has precluded the formation of a national university. But only a national institution with federal support could offer individual students the full range of services—cassette library, computer network, testing, and degree programs. Once again, my concern is the actual production of

the programs recorded on the cassettes: Where will the responsibility for course content and presentation technique be decided? Can there be multiple offerings in certain curricular fields so that no one producer will provide a single national course on a particular subject?

As a political scientist, I wish the author would develop more thoroughly the pattern of government for Video University. Would it have a board of governors? By whom selected? Would it be attached to the federal government, or have a separate corporate perch of its own in the private sector? How would the pattern of governance provide access to this educational system to all groups and all points of view?

4. *The purpose of the TV network.* The critical information function could be effectively performed by a television network. During the transition stage, information could be distributed at least in part by the existing public television network (Public Broadcasting Service). Especially appropriate to this medium would be information on career opportunities and the relationship of acquired learning to employment opportunities nationally and locally.

And then there is the ubiquitous radio. Arrangements could be made with public radio or commercial outlets to air information supplied on relatively inexpensive audio tapes.

With the advent of broad-band telecommunications in most American communities, through CATV systems, large numbers of video channels will become available. Conceivably, one of these channels could be reserved part or full time to televise information to students within its reach. Now that national policies are being formulated, some of this additional capacity should be reserved for educational purposes.

5. *The granting of degrees.* Ours is a credential society in which there will always be pressure on the part of both students and institutions to reward academic achievement with degrees or diplomas. It is to be hoped, however, that the degree, with its associated requirements, will not become so all-important that it supersedes the opportunity for innovative curricula and a broad range of curricular choice, suggested by the Mood paper. This caveat applies particularly if the new system is to serve students of all ages, all economic levels, and in a broad variety of professions and vocations. If the testing function is properly and equitably administered, performance measurement and standards of attainment can be maintained, and perhaps the student can receive recognition in the form most satisfying to his particular pattern of motivation.

This proposal, in all its ramifications, constitutes a challenge of major proportions. It also points the way to new and promising approaches to postsecondary education in this country. The concepts outlined should be subjected to critical discussion and further development with the thought that they might be tested on a limited scale—in a single city, state, or region. One or more consortia of existing institutions might be formed to constitute a proving ground for the construction and testing of these patterns and processes.

LOGAN WILSON

The New Orthodoxies in Higher Education

ALTHOUGH CAMPUS VIOLENCE APPEARS TO HAVE SUBSIDED, harassment of the higher learning unfortunately continues and is now being led by those who would fetter institutional independence with some new orthodoxies to which educators are expected to give obeisance. I strongly protest some of these specious doctrines and urge more common sense in melding the best of the old and the new in a ceaseless effort to improve American higher education.

DEFERENCE TO YOUTH

The first of these new orthodoxies—it might be called the hobble-dehoy orthodoxy—is the notion that only the young can truly perceive the imperfections of this era and clearly foresee things as they ought to be. Reversing the deference traditionally paid by youth to age, Americans fall over themselves catering to the young and trying to accommodate to their impulses. In the field of higher education many of the far-out thinkers firmly believe that pubescent insights are indeed the wisest guidelines for the reformation of policy and practice.

"Relevance" is the current shibboleth of academic reform, and often only the young and unresponsible are accorded the privilege of defining what it means. Even though no one has yet devised an educational equivalent for television's Nielsen system of popularity ratings, an innovator somewhere probably has a gimmick almost ready for adoption.

One obvious aim of the new movement is to repeal discipline and effort as a law of growth. Some critics assert that teaching standard English grammar, spelling, and punctuation is nothing more than a WASPish conspiracy to forestall cultural pluralism and social egalitarianism. Other liberators of youth emphasize that "the torment of having to learn reading, writing, and arithmetic" can be reduced by permitting each child to follow his own bent and set his own pace. One

319

widely quoted prophet of the new era goes a step further to propose the abolition of schools as authoritarian and inhumane institutions.[1]

On higher levels, too, established beliefs in the importance of cultural continuity and institutional stability are derided as being antediluvian. Academics who watched passively while classrooms were barricaded and buildings burned are now stirring themselves to get on the bandwagons of reform. Under the banner of progress, they expedite open admissions, relax course requirements, ease grading standards, and tailor the curriculum to suit everybody's wishes. Some of the avant-garde proclaim that campuses, libraries, laboratories, and even faculties are unnecessary paraphernalia for the further extension of higher learning. Disavowing any added personal responsibilities, they would simply turn the enlarged job of diffusing knowledge over to the U.S. Postal Service.

No wonder that public confidence in higher education is at low ebb. Despite lessons from disasters at San Francisco State and Old Westbury, and from the abandonment by students of nearly all their "free universities," adherents continue to increase for the dubious doctrine that the mature should follow rather than lead the immature.

INNOVATION AS A CULT

The reformist orthodoxy, the second new doctrine, is the fetish of educational change for its own sake. Although I favor some drastic changes in American higher education and am pleased by the needed responses already effected, I object to innovation as a cult. According to its dogma, the sooner educators forget what experience has taught about the conduct of educational affairs, the better. It never seems to get through to the cultists that at times malformed individuals rather than established institutions may need to undergo adjustments.

One professor of education has gone so far as to assert, "It is the primary purpose of education and knowledge not to conserve but to unsettle, to foment discord, to stir up conflict as an essential precursor to growth and new knowledge."[2] Other radicals urge us to disregard the past and present, and turn our undivided attention to experimental ventures, such as some of those at Antioch, the College for Human Services, and universities without walls, where allegedly the most significant undertakings may be observed. The innovators are joined at times, strangely enough, by the economizers who push for new

---

1. See Ivan Illich, De-Schooling Society (New York: Harper & Row, 1971).
2. Edmund W. Gordon, "Relevance and Revolt," Perspectives on Education, 3, No. 31 (1968): 10–16.

nostrums that promise quicker and cheaper cures for the ills of higher education. In the mad rush to bring about changes, the desperate need of many colleges and universities for more funds to support ongoing programs of demonstrated worth is conveniently overlooked.

INSTANT AUTHORITY

Because I came up during an era when trained competence was arduously acquired, the occupational ladder climbed rung by rung, and authority usually earned, a third emergent orthodoxy that raises my hackles is the instant authority of the politicos, dabsters, and arrivistes. Frequently uninformed or misinformed, they set forth in no uncertain terms much of the latter-day gospel about what is wrong with higher education and what must be done to set it right. A short while ago educators were expected to keep their ears tuned to the revelations of student revolutionaries, some of whom have since gone back to nature or on to bar tending. More recently, those educators who resist politicalization and outside meddling into institutional business are being preached at and even dictated to by superboards, commissions, task forces, and other bodies often arbitrarily designated as harbingers of the new enlightenment.

During the past year, for example, the Department of Health, Education, and Welfare named a task force, largely from its own employees, for the assignment: "How the federal government can encourage change and reform in higher education." Perhaps educators should be grateful for this solicitude, but why, in a pluralistic and decentralized system of higher education, should an agency of central government be ordained for such a mission? Also, five of the nine task force members have almost no academic experience beyond their student days. Most confounding, however, is the fact that the composition of the group violates a principle, discussed below, which HEW is insisting that all colleges and universities implement. In light of this principle it is indeed unseemly that a task force of this general import should include no Chicanos, no women, no blacks, and nobody past age fifty-one.

PARTICIPATORY DEMOCRACY

Turning from these ad hominem outcries about the arrivistes as arbiters of new orthodoxies being foisted on educators, I acknowledge a pragmatic bias behind my objections to another tenet to which our adherence is being demanded. It is the "Noah's ark principle" of participatory democracy. According to the principle, *who* participates in decisions and actions is more important than *what* is decided and accomplished. The frequency with which I am reminded of this doctrine, together with my growing misgivings about disguised and unacknowledged quota systems, may be merely a sign of overripe experience.

In the past, persuading the able and often reluctant to undertake the difficult and sometimes impossible was one of the main jobs of educational administration. Now, as historian Daniel Boorstin has mentioned, the average I.Q. of a committee, commission, or other group chosen for what may be primarily a task for experts is deemed less pertinent than its E.Q., or ethnic quotient. To update this observation, we must now add the S.Q. factor, or sex quotient, a mandate which is further complicated on some campuses by the problem of the gay lib.

As we draw nearer to the egalitarian ideal of a completely homogenized society, the representational problem will undoubtedly solve itself. Eventually, perhaps, we shall merely draw lots—as is already being done in some institutions to resolve admissions issues—to determine who goes where and does what. Until that day, disproportional representation in any educational entity will be, I suppose, prima facie evidence of shenanigans on the part of somebody.

Social Homogenization

Somewhat related to the "Noah's ark principle" is the egalitarian orthodoxy which makes a fetish of equality at the expense of merit. Educators, in their commendable zeal to eliminate snobbism in higher education, may be inadvertently institutionalizing slobbism in its place. As John Ciardi has commented, there is danger that the place of the authoritarian elite will be taken over by the authoritarian ignoramus as higher education moves toward the kind of social homogenization that "keeps the cream from rising to the top."

Equality of opportunity and quality of educational endeavor are by no means antithetical. Indeed, many egalitarians seem to forget that historically it was the rise of meritocracy which enabled democracy to supplant elitism. By a strange inversion of logic, however, the merit principle of assessing human competence and worth is being denigrated and even displaced by credos that will result only in the enthronement of mediocrity. Individual competition is frowned on; the sifting and sorting functions that institutions have traditionally performed are increasingly disavowed. Even Phi Beta Kappa is pushed into defensiveness about its main reason for being, the recognition and encouragement of excellence in intellectual enterprise. Within the academic ranks, growing numbers of professors stand ready to forgo the merit principle of individual advancement as they opt for collective bargaining.

To maintain an open-class society that will strike a balance between the extremes of stagnation and chaos, educators must resist all spurious dogmas that would compromise the merit principle in higher education. Let us by all means continue to give special educational attention to those who, through no fault of their own, are less capable and less qualified. In so doing, however, we must not forget that society's greatest benefit from higher education comes through the cultivation of talent, wherever it may be found. In this connection, I was heartened by U.S. Commissioner of Education Marland's heterodoxy when he directed attention to gifted youth as "one of our most neglected and potentially productive groups of students." To move ahead as a nation, we must not let educational standards be determined by the lowest common denominators of achievement.

UNENDING CATHARSIS

A sixth protest is not against other new orthodoxies but against the self-flagellation syndrome they elicit among academics. Virtually all other groups try unabashedly to strong-arm the rest of society for more pay or profit, and often with no improvement whatever in services or products. But guilt-ridden educators scourge themselves instead of denouncing the absurdities stemming from increased public demand accompanied by reduced public support.

Continuous institutional self-examination and criticism are undoubtedly beneficial, but unending catharsis on the campus can sap energies needed for ongoing purposes. While systematic institutional research and development programs with adequate professional staffing continue to receive meager attention and funding, ad hoc studies and reports multiply. The more negative the reports the greater the press coverage, and the more breast-beating the daily laborers in academe are expected to display.

Although higher education has plenty of faults and shortcomings, colleges and universities are on the whole better institutions than their detractors would have everyone believe. As I have stated elsewhere,

> They are models of economy, for example, as compared with hospitals; of efficiency, compared with courts of law; and of effectiveness, alongside most political agencies. Unlike many other productive enterprises, private as well as public institutions of higher education do not charge

all the traffic will bear for their services. Their campuses, like businesses and industries, are sometimes shut down, but rarely because the faculty and staff are striking for shorter hours and higher pay. Although urban universities are accused of inattention to the problems of their immediate physical environment, I have heard of none charged with polluting it. In brief, a good deal can be said in behalf of the university as a place and as an institution.[3]

Even so, within the last few years enough students have behaved destructively, enough professors complacently, and enough administrators indecisively to make it high time for a "movement of affirmation." A call for such a movement has come, not only from the old guard, but also from one of the most sympathetic and insightful analysts of the youth culture, Kenneth Keniston: "In addition to the celebration of life and the expansion of consciousness, . . . the respect for hard work, persistence, and dedication which have characterized the old culture must be preserved. This will require an alliance not only of the young, the privileged, or the educated, but also of those who are not young, privileged, or educated. . . ."[4]

Despite these protests against some current tendencies, I am confident that outmoded dogmas of higher education will give way, not to false new dogmas, but to a fusion of the best of the old and the new. The behavior of some members of the academic community continues to dismay me from time to time, but I am confident that good sense will ultimately prevail and that valiant leadership will uphold our colleges and universities against mindless onslaughts.

3. Logan Wilson, "Defending the Universities," *Educational Record*, Fall 1970, pp. 351–52.
4. Keniston, "The Agony of the Counterculture," *Educational Record*, Summer 1971, p. 210.

PART FIVE

Considerations for the Seventies

THEODORE M. HESBURGH, C.S.C.

Resurrection for Higher Education

DURING THE PAST FEW YEARS, HIGHER EDUCATION IN THIS country—and throughout the world—has undergone a baptism of fire. Many books have been and will be written to assess why it happened. The more thoughtful persons will ask what may be learned from all that happened. Those perennially endowed with hope (as indeed college and university administrators must be) will now inquire, Where do we go from here?

Looking to the future implies, of course, that internal revolution, violence, vulgarity, and disintegration within the institutions of higher education have peaked out, that the high-water mark has been reached, and that the waters of contradiction are subsiding. No one can be certain that this assumption is correct. One can only surmise that a phenomenon that came upon us unsuspectedly, with the speed of summer lightning, and all of a sudden engulfed the whole world of higher learning may leave in the same rapid way. Whether or not it will is still surmise and assumption and hope.

The only certainty at this point in time is that the onslaught of the past several years has left a lot of wreckage. Most of the past distinguished presidents are no longer in their posts. Certainly many of them, after long years of service during which they presided over unprecedented growth in their institutions, must now experience some bitter memories of their final days, when everything seemed to come apart all at once, when a life of reason was suddenly smothered by blind emotion, when a place of calm civility was engulfed by violence, bombings, burnings, vandalism, and vulgarity.

I believe that what went wrong went wrong globally. The universities of Tokyo, London, Paris, Berlin, and Rome were as disturbed and disrupted as Berkeley, Harvard, Columbia, Cornell, and Wisconsin. The disorder was due in part to a wave of history, still not well understood; part could be charged to serious mistakes on the part of the total enterprise of higher education. Overall, it soon reached a crisis of credibility, of legitimacy, of authority, of frustrated expecta-

327

tions. In large measure, it was the kind of abnormal convolution of heightened tensions and conflicting convictions that characterize every revolution, when the traditional consensus is eroded and the supportive pillars that depend upon free consensus become suddenly unstable, and total collapse ensues.

Certainly there were no standard solutions. During one brief period, one president lost out because he called in the police, and another fell because he did not. I asked one great president how he had survived a difficult crisis, and he answered, "Each morning when I dragged myself from bed, I asked myself, 'What is the worst thing I could do today?' and I didn't do it."

However one explains the worldwide revolution in higher education, in the American institutions all the usual problems were exacerbated by the Vietnam war, racial conflict, sudden realization of the plight of the poor in the midst of plenty, wastage and pillage of our national resources, the horrible state of national priorities as reflected in the federal budget, and, in general, by the increasingly dismal quality of our national life. Having made little progress in their assault on racial injustice and the inanity of the Vietnam war, the young—an unprecedented proportion of whom were now college and university students for a variety of right and wrong reasons—turned their frustrations on the institution closest to hand, their college or university. The other problems continued in their grinding way, so that the new revolution fed upon itself as frustration here was heightened by impatience there, and impatience there by frustration here.

There was enough wrong within the colleges and universities, too, so that we soon had an ever more explosive mixture awaiting simple ignition. There were plenty of volunteers to light the match. Every succeeding explosion on one campus ignited others elsewhere. And so it went across the country from West to East, and back again. Few institutions escaped unscarred, some were profoundly changed, and all were affected in one way or another. Some looked in the face of death, and that more than anything else may have accounted for the *détente*.

GROWTH VERSUS DEVELOPMENT

The question is: What, really, was wrong within the colleges and universities that fueled the fires of revolution? Strangely enough, we were the victims of our own success. Higher education in its earlier American version grew slowly, from the beginning at Harvard in 1636 to a national total of 52,000 students in 1870. For the last century, this student body doubled roughly every fifteen years. This was hardly a herculian task when the doubling meant going from 12,500 to 25,000 students, or from 25,000 to 50,000, or even from 50,000 to 100,000.

But by 1950, we had a base of 2.7 million which, in doubling to 5.5 million by 1965 (and now moving toward 11 million by the end of this decade), meant doing educationally in fifteen years more than had been done in the last three hundred and thirty years. We were all so busy growing and expanding, reaching toward the enrollment of half the age group in higher education, that we did not have time to ask whether what was good for 50,000, or 2 percent, of the college-age group in 1900 was equally good for 6.6 million, or 46 percent, of the college-age group in 1970.

Moreover, change during these latter decades has meant simply and mostly external expansion and growth, but not necessarily internal development—more of the same for ever greater numbers of students, more of the same kind of faculty teaching, the same kinds of courses. Such growth may make sense in the production of more hot dogs, but in higher education it certainly must mean more than simple reduplication of what is and has been.

Suddenly, the students asked the question we had all been too busy to ask, Does this whole enterprise, as now constituted, really provide a good education for everyone? Granted that their suggestions for internal change were not always an obvious move toward certain educational improvement, but they did start us looking more seriously at what we were doing. It is no secret that we were not always greatly pleased by what we saw.

Some of our most distinguished and highly compensated faculty were teaching less and less and seeing students only when unavoidable, while graduate students carried on the bulk of teaching for slave wages. New faculty, by the tens of thousands, were trained annually for research, engaged to teach, and most rewarded when they could negotiate lucrative contracts from government, industry, or foundations that took them away from both campus teaching and on-campus, course-related research that would involve them with their students. At one time four distinguished Midwestern universities boasted that almost four hundred of their faculty were overseas.

Administrators were getting their share of the bounty too: they were not only balancing their budgets with the ever-enlarging overhead funds from research contracts, but also traveling to see how overseas and other off-campus enterprises were coming along, and finding additional time to lend their distinguished presence to all manner of industrial, governmental, military, and other activities. Meanwhile, at home, liberal education, the core of the whole endeavor, became fragmented and devitalized, as subspecialty was heaped on subspecialty, and students learned more and more about less and less, and next to nothing about the great humanistic questions such as the meaning of life and death, war and peace, justice and injustice, love and hatred, art and culture.

Few educators even mentioned that the enormous growth in their student bodies did not include those who needed higher education most. To minority youth and children in the lower socioeconomic quartile of the population, a college degree was the essential ingredient to upward mobility; yet whatever their talent or promise, they had only a one-seventh chance of entering higher education in comparison with youngsters from the upper socioeconomic quartile.

The structure of higher education remained largely the same during the doubling and quadrupling of enrollments. Student questioning about governance caught most colleges and universities flat-footed. In their eagerness to reform, many institutions over-compensated so that, from being badly governed, they now emerged as largely ungovernable. Every decision now has to run the gauntlet of many potential vetoes both within and outside the university. This, too, compounds the internal problems, for even a wise man with some plausible solutions to assist the ailing institution might die of old age before seeing them realized.

DISINTEGRATION OF COMMUNITY

This account of internal problems is far from complete. In any consideration of *why* the revolution of the past few years, however, one more potent factor of failure must be cited. Most colleges and universities during, and possibly because of, their rapid growth simply ceased to be communities. Almost everyone was culpable. Trustees were often unrepresentative of the total endeavor they ultimately sought to govern. One distinguished Western university had a board of trustees that was consistently wealthy, male, white, aged, Western, Republican, and Protestant. The obverse then reads that there were generally no middle- or lower-class trustees, no blacks or Chicanos or Orientals, no women or younger people, no Catholics or Jews, no Midwestern, Southern, or Eastern members, and generally, no Democrats. One might ask how such trustees can provide wisdom for a community that contained reasonably large numbers of all the elements not represented on the board.

One might also wonder why presidents and top administrators in higher education did not see the storm coming and strengthen their communities to meet it effectively. Obvious answers are that the storm burst suddenly and that the community had already been badly eroded. In actuality, the community had to be recreated, not simply strengthened, and the task was made the more difficult because part of the crisis was a lack of community and, often, the presence of an external quasi-community that lacked credibility, legitimacy, or even the will to govern itself.

If one must fault presidents and chancellors among others—and we must—it would have to be for a lack of moral leadership, not just in time of crisis, but more consistently in earlier and peaceful times. We too often were blind to the moral implications of unbridled growth that was certainly spectacular but of questionable educational value. We did not use our influence to move for more representative boards of trustees; greater rewards for those faculty concerned with students, teaching, and true educational reform and growth; more minority students; and stronger words at times for those students who clamored for responsible freedom but without behaving responsibly once they were granted greater freedom. We might also have labored more aggressively in the continuing education of our alumni, who also were having their own new problems in understanding each new age and change.

Once we washed our hands of any moral concern for all that was happening in our academic communities, we reaped the harvest of a disintegrating community. I grant that the great wisdom and courage required for moral leadership are not common qualities among men and women, but then neither are college or university presidencies common tasks. I grant as well that, in its early stages, disintegration of a community is almost imperceptible to all but the very wisest, and as disintegration brings on a crisis of legitimacy and credibility, superhuman courage and charisma are needed to recreate what has been largely lost.

In any case, most presidents paid their individual price for a situation created by many, not least of all by the wild men among the student body, most of whom have successfully graduated, and by some irresponsible faculty members who are still around now that the scapegoat has been driven into the desert. No need to lament further, only need to learn from all that happened. There is a gospel story of the man from whom a devil was driven, only to have him later repossessed by seven worse devils.

PRESIDENTIAL LEADERSHIP

What then can we learn from all that has happened? First, I think moral leadership is as vital to a community as the participation of all its members in its healthy life and growth. *Participation* has been a most popular word since the crisis, but too little has been said about the moral imperatives of this participation. I have a strong belief that the central person in exercising moral leadership in the life and prosperity of any academic institution must be its president. He must, first and foremost, speak for the priorities that really count in academia. Presidential leadership demands that, for his speaking to be effective, he must somehow enlist the support of the various segments of the community. Otherwise he speaks only for himself and to himself—a combination that makes for bad leadership.

There is no charmed formula for presidential leadership. Each president must establish his own credibility. He will do this best by the goals which shine through his own life and activities. The day of Olympian detachment for presidents is over. If justice needs a voice, on campus or off, the president must have the wisdom and courage to say what must be said, and he must not be the last one to say it. If faculty or students need defense, he should be the first to defend them. If either or both need criticism, the president cannot avoid saying honestly and plainly what is wrong. If the learning process is lagging because of glacial progress in reforming curricula, structures, teaching, and inflexible, outmoded requirements, the president must remind the community of what is needed for educational growth and survival in today's world of unprecedented change. In all of these things his response must be firm and clear, because the times demand it. There was a time when a president was expected to be a lion abroad and a mouse at home. No longer.

The president, above all other members in the community, must portray respect for the mind and its special values, for true learning and culture, for humanity and humane concerns, for academic freedom, for justice and equality, in all that the university or college touches, especially the lives of its students, faculty, and alumni. Of course, the name of the game is good communications on every level, at every opportunity, but I must insist that the president communicates best by what he is and what he does with his own life. If he has credibility, then the goals he proposes will be the extension of that credibility and the means of drawing the community into cohesion.

The Moral Dimension of Higher Education

Although the community is primarily academic, I submit once more that its basis of unity must be of the heart, as well as of the head. It was not merely intellectual problems that recently unraveled great institutions of learning across the world, but rather the dissipation of moral consensus, community, and concern. When members of a college or university stop caring about each other or their institution, or become unclear about personal or institutional goals, then community ceases to be and chaos results.

The mystique of leadership—be it educational, political, religious, commercial, or whatever—is next to impossible to describe, but wherever it exists, morale flourishes, people pull together toward common goals, spirits soar, and order is maintained, not as an end in itself, but as a means to move forward together. Such leadership always has a moral as well as an intellectual dimension; it requires courage as well as wisdom; it does not simply know, it cares. When a faculty and a student body know that their president really cares about them, they will follow him to the heights, even out of the depths.

Moreover, good leadership at the top inspires correlative leadership all down the line. "Participatory democracy" cannot mean simply endless discussion. Rather, if it is to work at all, it means that every member of the community, especially within his or her own segment of the community, exercises moral responsibility, especially when it hurts and when it demands the courage to say and do what may be unpopular. Student judicial courts will not survive if they never find anyone guilty or never impose adequate sanctions for obvious wrongdoing. Student government will soon enough lose all its credibility and acceptance, even from students, if its only concerns are freer sex, more parking, education without effort, and attainment of the heights of utopia without climbing. Faculty senates will be only debating societies if they never recognize the central faculty abuses and more effectively to correct them. Vice-presidents, deans, and department chairmen do not exist to pass the buck upward and to avoid the difficult decisions. Leadership may be most important at the presidential level, but it is absolutely essential at every level—trustees, faculty, administrators, students, and alumni—if the community is to be equal to the tasks that lie ahead for each college and university and for the total enterprise of higher education in America.

Where do we go from here? First, we should clearly understand the climate that results from the events of the past five years in academia. For the first time in more than a century, the end of quantitative growth in higher education is in sight. Having doubled in size every fifteen years during the last century, higher education will be leveling off by 1980, possibly slipping downward a bit. This latter movement is already perceptible in graduate education.

However, there is a more serious aspect to the climate in which we in higher education now live. After a century when the society at large could not do enough for universities and colleges, when these institutions represented the epitome of just about everyone's hopes, a degree being the closest earthly replica of the badge of salvation, suddenly the American public, our patron and faithful supporter, is rather completely disillusioned about the whole enterprise. They are, as they say, let down by the weak, vacillating, spineless presidents, their former darlings; they are disgusted by the ultraliberal, permissive faculties who were going to solve all of the world's problems but could not solve their own. And, needless to say, they find the students revolting in more ways than one, despite the fact that these are their own sons and daughters, the products of the most primordial education of all that does or does not take place in the family.

It is paradoxical that at a time when the universities are being asked to solve more problems than ever before—urban blight, racial tensions, minority opportunity, generation gap, overseas development, environmental pollution, political participation by the young, forward motion in atomic energy and space, and a host of other concerns—at this same time our colleges and universities are misunderstood, abused, and abandoned as never before by government and foundations, by benefactors, parents, and alumni, and generally by the public at large.

Obviously, the institutions—collectively, the members of the academic enterprise—are not blameless at this moment in time. I will not repeat the faults. Most dramatically, in the eyes of the public, the institutions that were supposed to have answers for everyone and everything had few answers for themselves and their own troubles; the citadels of reason fell to the assaults of mindless emotion; the centers of taste and civility spouted obscenities; the havens of halcyon peace and pranks saw within them violence, destruction, and even death.

Institutions in trouble were given extravagant coverage indeed in the media when they were at their worst. And although the worst, in terms of delinquent persons and horrible events, represented a small bit of the total scene, the stereotypes stood out and tended to be universalized. The centuries-old love affair of American society with higher education suddenly turned cold. And now, at the time of greatest opportunity and direst financial crisis in institutions of higher education, all are spurned by the very people who created them, confided their children to them, supported them, and looked at them for a solution to everything difficult.

Perhaps one central problem is that the public was encouraged and allowed to place too much hope in these less than magical institutions, to expect too much of the endeavor, to be too confident of apparent omnipotence when, in fact, there are simply many important tasks that they cannot do without perverting what they were established to do. The collective educational enterprise is not the state or the church, the Red Cross, or the Peace Corps, not the Overseas Development Council, or the Legal Aid Society. Its members may be active in any or all of these bodies, but they are not these bodies and institutionally they cannot do their work. No wonder that hopes were frustrated when myth was allowed to transcend the reality of what higher education is and what it should be doing.

Not only the supporters in government and the private sector but also students expected something far beyond higher education and, of course, received less. A Harvard professor has stated it well: "The dissolution of family and community life and the decline of secondary education have produced a generation of college students, many of whom no longer seek at the university learning and social pleasures, but also and above all affection, attention, moral guidance, and an opportunity to become personally involved in adult affairs. The universities are not equipped to provide these things."[1]

We have come out of the crisis, I believe, more disposed to provide for our students affection, attention, moral guidance, and an opportunity to become personally involved in adult affairs. Over time, the vote for eighteen-year-olds looms more important than military service. We have been listening harder to our students, which means we have been paying attention to them. We have learned that it is difficult to educate those we do not really love, and I trust I have already said enough about the moral dimension of higher education.

AGENDA FOR TOMORROW

Perhaps during that period of rapid growth, the institutions—the academic community—grew beyond its potential to be personal and human. High on the list of our agenda now must be how to correct this failing. The mea culpas should be many. The faculty, the heart of the whole endeavor, were often seduced by the possibility of being rewarded more and more for teaching less and less. Tenure too often became a safe opportunity for somnolence rather than a call to be different, to dare, and to excel. Trustees and presidents were too often too busy with the wrong things. Students were generally on target, but not always on the right one, especially when autocriticism was required. We were all less than we could and should have been. We were all caught up in unusual historical currents in a very troubled,

1. Richard Pipes, in *New York Times*, April 25, 1969, p. 28.

unjust, and unpeaceful world, yes, but we still must answer for ourselves and our personal responsibility to remake our own world of higher education in a better image.

I began by expressing the hope that the worst may be over. Ours is a resilient enterprise—its very growth is testimony—and in the days to come, we may well be better off for the many tragedies we have experienced during the past five years. Clark Kerr recently said that American higher education has entered its second climacteric in the more than a third of a millennium of its existence. That may be fearsome, but it is also exciting. According to Kerr, the last climacteric lasted fifty years, roughly from 1820 to 1870. Those fifty years were difficult; they saw many changes, but they were the prelude to the century of extraordinary growth that we have just experienced. May our second climacteric also be the prelude to better days ahead.

It would be consonant with the rapidity of change in our times, as compared to the last century, that this climacteric might be compressed from fifty into five years. Apart from hope, at least we must believe that we are in large measure, the masters of our own destiny. If we have unwittingly disestablished our credibility, we can also consciously reestablish it. If we have tarnished our integrity of purpose, we can learn from our frustrated and impossible hopes, and move to refurbish our central purpose. If we grew slack in moral leadership, spoiled by affluence and prosperity, we will surely have some lean years ahead in which to rededicate ourselves to what is right and just. We cannot undo the past five years, but we can learn from them.

There is little profit in licking our wounds or feeling sorry for ourselves. We still represent the best hope for America's future provided we learn from our own mistakes and reestablish in the days ahead what has so often testified to the nobility of our endeavors in times past. All is not lost. We are simply beginning again, as man always must, in a world filled with ambiguities, the greatest of which is man himself.

FRANK STANTON

Freedom for the Press and Academic Freedom

THE AMERICAN COUNCIL ON EDUCATION HAS LONG PLAYED AN impressive role in strengthening higher education in this country, in all respects. Concerned as it must be with the financial woes that harass the academic community and the thousand-and-one other practical problems with which it must contend, the Council has nevertheless refused to let such pressing considerations supersede its devotion to high standards of scholarship and, above all, to the climate of intellectual freedom so vital to the nourishment of our institutions of learning.

At the risk of sounding like one bent upon telling all about my recent operation, I would like to offer some reflections on CBS's recent ordeal with the Congress. I refer to the confrontation which developed in the spring of 1971 when we refused to comply with congressional subpoenas which we believed to be wholly improper and unconstitutional. My purpose is not to show my scars. Rather, it is to make the point that there is, in the circumstances of that traumatic experience, a lesson to be gleaned by all those responsible for the robustness of our democratic institutions, and perhaps particularly for those charged with higher education.

In fall 1971, during hearings before the Senate Subcommittee on Constitutional Rights, Senator Sam Ervin recalled Thomas Jefferson's advice to a college student in 1799.

> To preserve the freedom of the human mind and the freedom of the press every spirit should be ready to devote itself to martyrdom; for as long as we may think as we will, and speak as we think, the condition of man will proceed in improvement. . . ."

This is the common ground of the press and the university: preservation of the people's right to know, that the condition of man may proceed in improvement. And it is my belief that if this common ground is invaded or threatened with respect to one—whether the initial target is academic freedom or freedom of the press—it is only a question of time before the other will feel the same pressures.

Democracy is the most difficult form of government on earth. It is not for the passive, the faint of heart, or the despairing. It can stay alive only if there is concern—if enough people care. But concern is not enough. The day comes, not once but over and over again, when concern must be backed with the willingness to fight every kind of opposition, whether it is fired by fear and suspicion or inspired by misguided hopes for a never-never world of perfection.

The hour of reckoning for CBS came at nine o'clock on the morning of April 8, when two agents of the House Special Subcommittee on Investigations served me with a subpoena which contained far-reaching and very sobering demands. It called for the transcript and the film of the CBS News documentary "The Selling of the Pentagon." So far so good. We were perfectly willing to furnish these since they were in the public domain. But it also demanded that we surrender unused materials and information gathered in the preparation of the broadcast: "all film, workprints, outtakes and sound-tape recordings, written scripts and/or transcripts utilized in whole or in part by CBS in connection with its documentary." These were materials that had been developed during the course of an investigative reporting project which had consumed almost a year. They were not part of the broadcast.

CBS refused to comply with this demand. We believed that it violated the First Amendment.

Refusal to accede to the demands of a congressional committee is no slight matter. Only a principle of the utmost importance could possibly justify the risks involved. We were determined to hold our stand on the principle of press freedom, whatever the risks. Bowing to the subcommittee's demands would have meant acknowledging that broadcast news organizations could no longer report and analyze the news in light of their own best judgment, but would be subject to constant surveillance by the Congress. Broadcast journalism, we felt, soon would find itself not the servant of the public, but the creature of government.

The subpoena was not an isolated attack. It was the culmination of First Amendment attacks that had been steadily increasing in number and intensity. Investigative bodies of Congress had been sniping at us for months, indeed years. A hard-hitting investigative report, "Hunger in America," a factual illumination of the state of malnutrition in this country, was attacked by members of Congress and by government officials. An exposé on the use, and abuse, of narcotics on the campus of Northwestern University brought angry demands for a congressional inquiry, not of the distressing situation reported, but of CBS as the bearer of such disturbing facts.

With the serving of the subpoena, there began for us an arduous ordeal which lasted more than three months. But from the outset the stand we took drew vigorous and widespread public support. Telegrams and letters arrived in a flood. They came from leaders in the nation's civic organizations, from church groups, from organized labor. They came from press organizations the country over. They came from educators and leaders in the nation's academic institutions—all protesting the inescapable implications of the subpoena.

Fortunately, as has happened so often before when rights have been staunchly defended, reason ultimately prevailed. The House, by a clear majority of both major parties, returned to committee a recommendation that CBS and its president be held in contempt of Congress for refusing to yield to the subpoena.

From the searing experience through which we passed, the lessons to be drawn may be age-old, but I believe need constant reiteration. They are that no freedom, however sacrosanct we may think it, is immune from threat; and that each threat must be stoutly and vigorously resisted. For the American Council on Education—for academic institutions everywhere—the lessons have special relevancy. We can be sure that challenges to press freedom, if successful, will set a climate that is favorable to the subversion of academic freedom.

In a way, perhaps, journalists are more fortunate than members of an academic institution: freedom of the press is explicitly guaranteed in the First Amendment of the Bill of Rights, though it is often forgotten that this is not a special privilege bestowed on a publisher, an author, or a broadcaster. Rather, it is a privilege guaranteed to the people of the United States so that they may have free and uncontrolled access to the information they need to make wise and just decisions.

The Bill of Rights is mute on the subject of education except for its prohibitions against restrictions of peaceable assembly and the abridgment of speech. But the latter concept has become recognized today as applying quite as much to the classroom as to the newsroom.

The journalist has learned over and over again that the First Amendment guarantee of press freedom sometimes turns out to mean very little unless it is fought for. He has seen repeatedly that such rights are not automatically preserved. And if those whose rights are specifically protected in the First Amendment have to fight, then it is obvious how important it must be for educators to take their stand whenever, and wherever, academic independence is challenged. Freedom is the common working requirement that binds together the journalist and the teacher—freedom to inquire, freedom to report, even freedom to be wrong.

To state the obvious, education is vital to any modern society; but to a democratic society it has a very special importance. Democracy rests on two premises. One is that any system created by men is imperfect. The other is that we can improve the systems we create if people are given the facts and the opportunity to weigh things as they are against their concept of things as they ought to be. Implicit therefore to democracy is a commitment to an open society. No institution —political, social, or economic—can be immune to criticism no matter how high or powerful it may be. But fulfilling the responsibility to inform and to criticize does not come without pain, either for the institution of education or the institution of broadcast journalism.

A university is not a place designed to make people feel comfortable. On the contrary, as Dr. David Goddard, recently retired provost of the University of Pennsylvania, has pointed out, it should be a place where one hears what he doesn't expect to hear. "A university," Dr. Goddard said, "should not only be attentive to where students are, it should challenge them to go where they have never been." Obviously that kind of intellectual pursuit can flourish only when those who believe in it are prepared to combat intolerance, repression, censorship, or political attack. Journalism, by the same token, has a duty to take people "where they have never been." The profession of reporting—like the profession of teaching—carries with it the obligation to present facts as they are, no matter how controversial, how unpalatable, how unpopular, and no matter how much the analyses may offend our fellow citizens or our government officials.

Unless a society has the vision to uphold and protect the freedom of its press—and the vision to demand free criticism and inquiry in its colleges—it cannot be strong and free. Yet it is surprising how often enlightenment has to fight for its life. Time and again it must confront the censor, the silencer, the suppressor.

In fact, confrontation began within the very first decade of our constitutional history. Only seven years after adoption of the Bill of Rights, Congress passed the notorious Sedition Act of 1798 which, by banning public criticism of government officials, made a mockery of the First Amendment. Newspaper editors opposing President John Adams were jailed. One needs little imagination to recognize that they might just as well have been educators. Fortunately, when Jefferson became President in 1801, he pardoned those who had been imprisoned under the act, rescuing the First Amendment from its momentary eclipse. The moral is as plain now as it was then. Those who hold the power of government in their hands can be all too quick to attempt to silence their critics. The Sedition Act was eliminated only after the outrage it inspired in a people to whom freedom of the press was a conviction of vital importance.

Academic freedom, by contrast, grew more slowly. Early American colleges were for the most part founded by religious groups not given to tolerating the views of controversial free-thinkers. Cotton Mather, for example, charged toward the close of the seventeenth century that Harvard students were privately reading "plays, novels, empty and vicious pieces of poetry, and even Ovid's Epistles, which have a vile tendency to corrupt good manners." The Puritan ethic could tolerate no such evil habits.

In fact, for many years the choice of the dissenting teacher was to find some institution whose concepts and philosophy he could accept or to forsake teaching. Throughout the first half of the nineteenth century, when scientific thought began to spread, the advocate of science literally had no place to go. And even when this prejudice subsided after the Civil War, there was a successor—a distaste for the social scientist who increasingly was inclined to offer disturbing judgments about the condition of man and his society.

One of the classic cases, all but forgotten, was that of Richard Ely, the economist who later became the founder of the American Economic Association. In 1894, while he was director of the University of Wisconsin's School of Economics, Politics, and History, Ely was charged by a member of the Board of Regents and subsequently tried by a committee for believing in strikes and boycotts, "justifying and encouraging the one while practicing the other." Ely, however, had strong supporters. He himself proved an eloquent defender of his right to express his opinions openly. To the surprise of many, his defense not only prevailed, but brought forth from the Regents an opinion that since has become known as the Wisconsin Magna Carta. Some things that this Magna Carta said are memorable:

> As Regents of a university, . . . we could not for a moment think of recommending the dismissal, or even the criticism, of a teacher even if some of his opinions should in some quarters be regarded as visionary. In all lines of academic investigation, it is of the utmost importance that the investigator should be absolutely free to follow the indications of truth wherever they may lead. Whatever may be the limitations which trammel inquiry elsewhere, we believe the great State University of Wisconsin should ever encourage that continual and fearless sifting and winnowing by which alone the truth can be found.

But still today there is hardly a time when the intellectual freedom of a state university is not being attacked by the state legislature or state administration somewhere. One notes with concern that California is apparently attempting to dictate the work schedule of university teachers, so as to force more time to be devoted to teaching, as against scholarship and other work. President Hitch, of the University of California, has warned that this is like asking how many hours a surgeon spends in the operating room or a minister spends delivering a sermon. If politicians dictate the work schedules of university faculties, where is the line to be drawn?

Other pressures have arisen from the turmoil of recent years. In private universities, which depend so much on the financial backing of individual citizens, much support has been withheld. Some of the withdrawal has been in reaction to the views and actions of activist students and the faculty members who aided them, a form of financial pressure which could restrict the scope of the university. The principle of tenure, long regarded as a bulwark of academic freedom, also has been called into question as a kind of backlash from the recent drive for teaching quality.

In their classic study of academic freedom in the United States, Metzger and Hofstadter proudly concluded that the academic freedom we enjoy is "one of the most remarkable achievements of man." I, for one, agree. But they continue with the solemn warning, "At the same time one cannot but be appalled by the slender thread by which it hangs. . . ."

Just because no threat as obvious as a subpoena currently hangs over the head of an academic institution, we must not conclude that academic freedom is safe from encroachment by official bodies. The long history of struggle to protect freedom tells us otherwise, and vigilance must not be relaxed because we who find it necessary to take firm positions in defense of freedom are sometimes accused of being oversensitive.

A mutual difficulty of education and broadcasting is that freedom is a subjective matter. We all favor freedom for ourselves; sometimes it is difficult to concede the same degree of freedom for others. Indeed, in the name of justice the most unjust of causes are sometimes pursued.

Twenty-four years ago, on October 5, 1947, a President of the United States first used television for an address broadcast from the White House. That same President, Harry Truman, summed up the job we share:

> In the cause of freedom we have to battle for the rights of people with whom we do not agree, and whom, in many cases, we may not like. . . . If we do not defend their rights, we endanger our own.

AMERICAN COUNCIL ON EDUCATION

ROGER W. HEYNS, *President*

The American Council on Education, founded in 1918, is a *council* of educational organizations and institutions. Its purpose is to advance education and educational methods through comprehensive voluntary and cooperative action on the part of American educational associations, organizations, and institutions.